DDC®

Learning Macromedia® Dreamweaver MX

James Reidel

DDC Publishing

Pearson Education, Inc., publishing as Prentice Hall DDC, Upper Saddle River, New Jersey 07458

Acknowledgements

To Max, Travis, and Logan, my dreamweavers – James Reidel

Senior Editor
Kathy Berkemeyer

Technical Editor
Jan Snyder

Cover Design
Amy Capuano

Project Manager
Nicole Sulgit

Contributors
Catherine Skintik
Nancy Stevenson

ISBN: 0130364487

10 9 8 7 6 5 4 3 2

Printed in the United States of America.

Contents

Introduction

Learning Macromedia Dreamweaver MX works alongside you to help build the exciting, changing, and interactive Web site that today's information-driven world demands from businesses, governments, schools, and virtually every organization that needs to communicate.

In this course, you will be introduced to the latest version of Dreamweaver—with its new integrated workspace. You will learn about layout, simple and advanced Web-page design, the use of plugins, and many of the other elements available to those who want to be serious Webmasters.

What This Book Is About

- *Learning Macromedia Dreamweaver MX* is written for beginning Web page designers. The book assumes the reader has a working knowledge of the Internet, basic design elements, and common Windows navigation.

Who Should Read This Book?

- This book is for everyone who needs to know how to add solid design and interactivity to his or her Web site. You can use this book as a chapter-by-chapter tutorial on many Dreamweaver features or refer to it on an as-needed topical basis.
- You should read this book if you need to design, manage, and modify a Web site and want to learn how to add interactive and advanced elements to its pages.

What You Need

- To gain the most from this book, you will need:

  - Knowledge of fundamental Windows navigation and terminology.
  - A PC with at least a Pentium II 300Mhz processor or its equivalent; 96MB of RAM (more RAM and a faster processor will make your work go faster so that you can spend more time learning and using Dreamweaver's robust features); Windows 98, ME, NT, 2000, or XP; and 275 MB of hard disk space.
  - Dreamweaver MX. The latest update at the time this book was created is version 6.1. There are many important bug fixes that you will need for best performance. The update is free to anyone who has a licensed copy of version 6.0.
  - Macromedia ColdFusion MX testing server (optional).
  - An Internet browser version 4 or higher, such as Microsoft Internet Explorer, Netscape Navigator, or the new open-source browsers such as Mozilla, that supports multimedia, animation, and advanced interactive features.
  - For the best results, Microsoft Internet 6.0 or its latest version should be used.

How This Book Is Organized

- You begin with Web site basics and then move to advanced features.
- **Chapter 1: Dreamweaver Workspace and Menus.** This chapter introduces the program and its workspace. You will take a quick tour of Dreamweaver's menus, Insert bar, and Document toolbar. You will also learn how to start and exit the program.
- **Chapter 2: Setting Up a Site.** This chapter takes you through the process of setting up a new site in Dreamweaver MX using the Site Definition wizard. You will learn how to create and save Web pages, work with some of Dreamweaver's most useful panels, and view site files.
- **Chapter 3: Enter and Format Text.** This chapter discusses how to enter and import text to create Web site content. You will learn how to format text in many ways: change text fonts, sizes, styles, and colors; change text alignment; and create lists.
- **Chapter 4: Using Links and the Site Panel.** This chapter introduces hyperlinks (or simply links), the means by which visitors navigate a Web site. You will learn how to create relative links within a site, absolute links to other sites, links to named anchors on a page, and links to e-mail addresses. You will also learn more about the Site panel's expanded window and how to view and modify the site map.
- **Chapter 5: Code Views and Panels.** In this chapter, you will learn some code basics and explore the Dreamweaver Code view and Code panel group options for viewing and modifying HTML and other kinds of Web page code. You will insert keywords for the site and a date. You will also learn how to use the History panel to repeat or undo tasks.

- **Chapter 6: Images and Graphic Elements.** This chapter explores some of Dreamweaver's graphic capabilities. You will add horizontal rules, apply background colors and images, and insert images on Web pages. You will also learn how to modify image size and position an image so text wraps around it. Finally, you will create image maps that contain hotspots used to link to other pages.
- **Chapter 7: Templates, the Library, and Design Notes.** This chapter covers three important Dreamweaver features. You will create and use a template to give pages a consistent look. After you store items in the Library, you will insert them throughout the Web site. You will also learn how to create Design Notes for pages in the site.
- **Chapter 8: Tables and Navigation Bars.** This chapter introduces you to tables, used to organize information or an entire Web page. You will create and format a table to hold data on a page. You will also learn how to create a navigation bar to provide links to all pages in a site.
- **Chapter 9: Advanced Table Features.** In this chapter, you will structure a Web page using Dreamweaver tables and the Layout view features. You will also learn how to import tabular data into a table, sort table content, apply an automatic table format, and insert table-related tags.
- **Chapter 10: Create Forms.** This chapter walks you through the process of creating a form and inserting various types of form fields: text boxes, radio buttons, checkboxes, list-menu boxes, and buttons. You will learn how to link a form to an Access database and test it using the ColdFusion testing sever.
- **Chapter 11: Layering for Design Flexibility.** This chapter introduces Dreamweaver layers, containers that can hold any type of HTML content and be placed exactly on the page. You will learn how to create, resize, position, and format layers to add visual impact to a page.
- **Chapter 12: Frame Pages.** This chapter shows you how to create frames on a Web page to open specific Web page content. You will learn how to set up and modify frames in a frameset and how to specify target frames for links.
- **Chapter 13: Styles and Style Sheets.** Style sheets are used to apply consistent formats throughout a Web site. You will learn how to create custom styles and an external style sheet that can be applied to all pages in a site. You will also learn how to modify HTML styles to customize page formats.
- **Chapter 14: Behaviors.** Behaviors are actions that occur when visitors interact with a Web page. In this chapter, you will learn how to apply some of Dreamweaver's commonly used behaviors to specific events.
- **Chapter 15: Timelines.** A timeline is a Dreamweaver feature that allows you to create animated effects on a Web page. This chapter introduces timelines and shows you how to create animations and control behaviors using a timeline.
- **Chapter 16: Multimedia Objects.** This chapter introduces the multimedia capabilities of Dreamweaver and shows you how to insert, modify, and view Flash and Shockwave movies. You will also learn how to create Flash buttons and Flash text—in the Dreamweaver workspace.
- **Chapter 17: Managing and Publishing a Web Site.** This chapter explores some regular site maintenance operations, such as managing assets, testing a site for a target browser, checking and modifying links, and running various kinds of reports—including the new Accessibility report and Validator. You will also learn how to put files on an FTP, WebDAV, or local server and how to use the Check In/Out feature to control access to sites maintained by a team.
- **Chapter 18: Webmastering.** This set of four integrated challenge projects takes what you have learned about Dreamweaver and combines new skills with other Web-related skills used by professionals in making decisions in the design, creation, and management of Web sites.
- **Appendix A: Dreamweaver Preferences.** Dreamweaver allows you to customize the environment in a number of ways using the Preferences dialog box. This appendix explores the many user settings and provides guidance on changing them.

- **Appendix B:** This appendix provides basic information on operating systems and software.
- **Appendix C:** This appendix provides basic information on peripherals, input, storage, and output devices.
- **Appendix D:** This appendix explores use of the Internet and intranets and provides information on searching and Internet etiquette.
- **Glossary.** A comprehensive glossary lists and defines terms that appear in **boldface** throughout the book.

Conventions Used in This Book

- *Learning Macromedia Dreamweaver MX* is designed to make your learning experience easy and enjoyable. All new concepts are discussed thoroughly in the text with accompanying illustrations. Key terms are **boldfaced** to stand out from surrounding text. Step-by-step instructions for performing specific tasks appear in the Procedures section of each chapter.
- The term *tooltip* in this book refers to the descriptive context sensitive help labels that are also called *ScreenTips* in Microsoft operating systems and applications.
- The text also includes Cautions, Notes, and Tips to provide warnings or supplementary information for the topic under discussion.

  Cautions *are designed to help you avoid frustrating problems and rework and to prevent loss of data or risking the functionality and appearance of your Web files.*

  Notes *provide additional helpful or interesting information.*

  Tips *often suggest helpful information designed to provide workarounds, insightful pointers, and other ways of creating an effect or outcome.*

Data Files

- Files (such as image and sound files) that you will use in the Web you will create during this course are available on the CD-ROM that accompanies this book. You can copy and paste them to a location that will act as a Data folder on your own hard drive. You can then select all the files, right-click and choose Properties, and deselect the Read-Only attribute applied during the CD-burning process.

Personal Web Server

- If you are running the Windows 98 or Windows 2000 operating systems, you can publish you r webs to the *Personal Web Server* available on those operating systems.
  - For more information on installing the personal web server, consult Help (Start>Help). For Windows 98, search for Personal Web Server in Help and follow the instructions. For Windows 2000 Professional, search for IIS and follow the instructions. The personal web server feature is installed when the Internet Information Services 5.0 (IIS) feature is installed. You will need your Windows 98 or 2000 CD.
  - Once installed, the Personal Web Manager can be opened from the system tray in Windows 98 and from the Administrative Tools folder (Settings>Control Panel>Administrative Tools) on Windows 2000. The PWM indicates the name of the computer (which is used when publishing to the personal web server) and the location of the home directory (C:\Inetpub\wwwroot).

Chapter

1

Dreamweaver Workspace and Menus

Dreamweaver MX has many innovative features to make designing, creating, editing, managing, and publishing your new Web site easier and more intuitive.

In this chapter, you'll learn how to:

- Start Dreamweaver MX
- Identify panels and the menu bar
- Select between the Dreamweaver MX and Dreamweaver 4 workspace
- Identify the Dreamweaver MX toolbars
- Open menus and select menu commands

Start Dreamweaver

- Start Dreamweaver by clicking the start button on the Windows taskbar, clicking All Programs or Programs, and locating the Macromedia folder on the Programs menu.
- Click the Macromedia folder and then Macromedia Dreamweaver MX on the pop-out submenu to open the Dreamweaver workspace.
- If you open Dreamweaver MX for the first time on your computer, the Workplace Setup dialog box appears. It gives users of Dreamweaver 4 and earlier Dreamweaver versions the opportunity to select the “floating” palettes and panels workspace. In this course, you will use the new MX workspace. Make sure the Dreamweaver MX Workspace is selected and click OK (see illustration).

Dreamweaver MX

- The first time you start Dreamweaver MX, it launches with several panels, including the **Properties panel,** ready to use (see illustration on the following page):
    - The Insert bar contains tools for inserting and creating different Web page objects. Each panel in the group is identified with a tab.
    - The Properties panel displays the properties of an object selected in the Document window.

    Note: *Dreamweaver Help also refers to this feature as Property Inspector.*

    - The Files panel group contains one of the most important panels you will use in Dreamweaver, the Site panel, in which you can access your Web site or sites and its files and folders. This panel group is itself grouped into a collection of panel groups in the right panel group pane .
    - The Files panel group also includes the Assets tab, which allows you to track colors, images, and objects used in a site.
    - The Answers pane is a quick reference tool with several categories such as TechNotes that you can select from a drop-down list. Use it find information for using Dreamweaver MX and to check for updates from the Macromedia Web site.

    Note: *You will learn more about panels and properties in Chapter 2.*

Workspace Setup dialog box

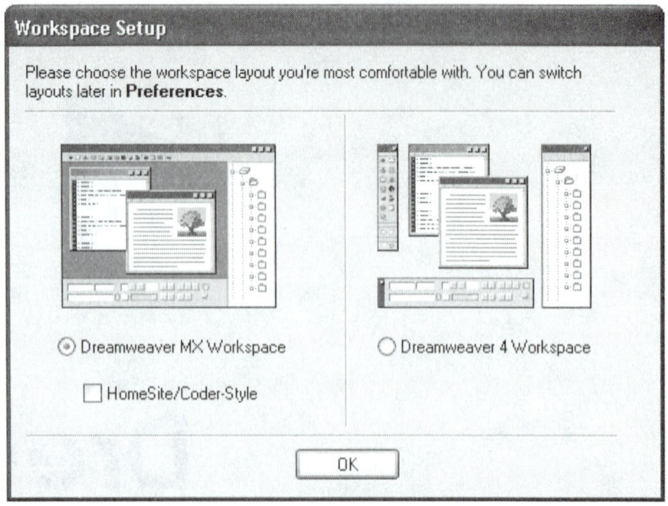

- Dreamweaver files are created and saved from the **workspace**—an area much like the document window in many of Microsoft Windows programs.
- You can keep panels open (expanded or collapsed) or close the ones you will not need immediately.
- To expand a panel group, click the expander arrow . To collapse a panel group, click the collapse arrow .
- You can also undock and drag panels to new locations to get them out of your way by clicking on the gripper in the panel group’s title bar . The mouse pointer becomes a four-pointed arrow. By holding down on the mouse button, you can drag the panel to a new location (docked) or let it float (undocked).
- A panel is docked and you can release the mouse button when a black border appears around the panel.
- Close a panel or inspector by right-clicking its title bar—or its Options menu if the group is expanded—and then clicking Close Panel Group.
- Floating panels and the Document window can also be closed by clicking the Close button .
- Dreamweaver “remembers” the workspace setup from its last session. If you close panels, they will not display when you next start Dreamweaver. To open a panel that has been closed, select the name of the panel from the Window menu.

Default Dreamweaver MX workspace

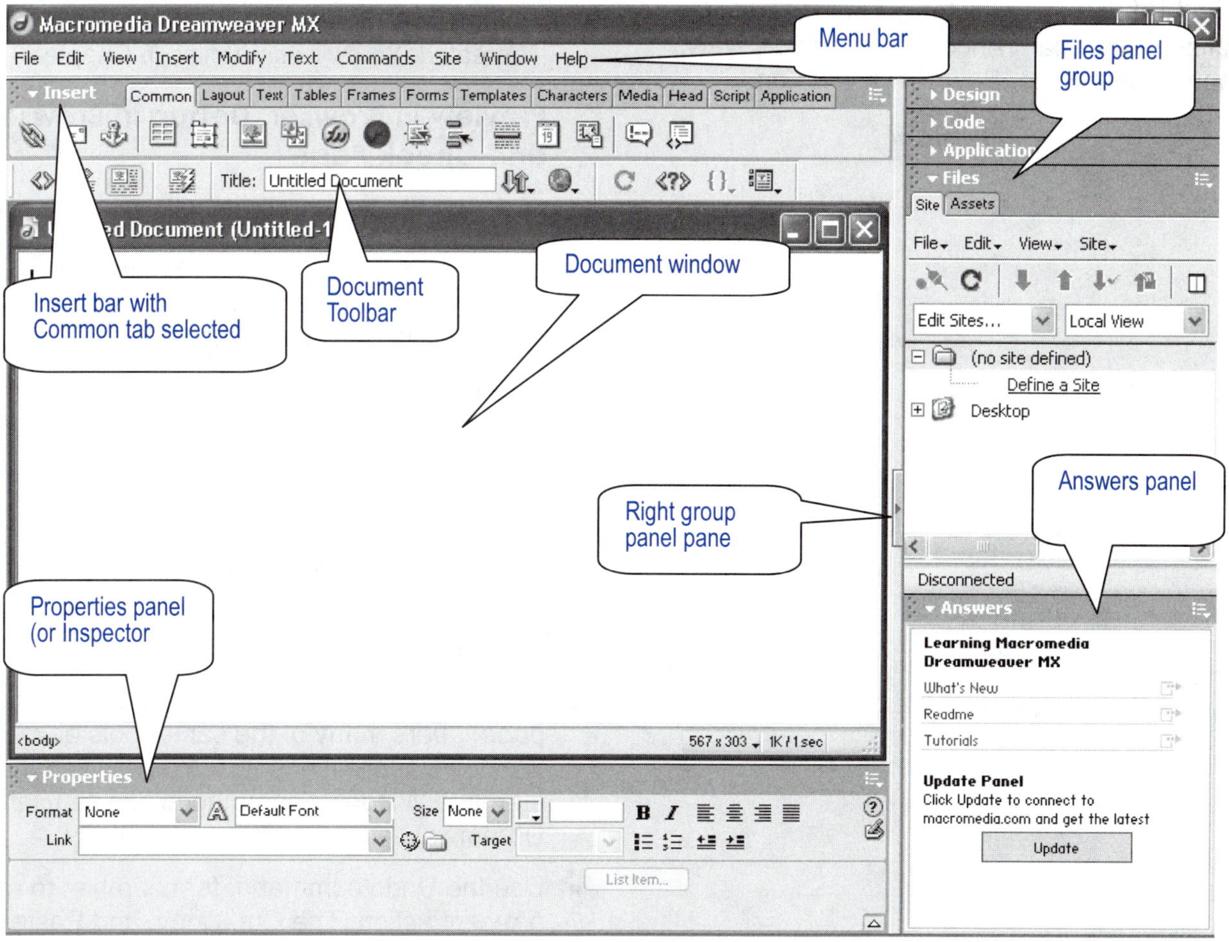

Dreamweaver Menus

- Dreamweaver makes many commands available on menus, from familiar functions such as printing and saving to more advanced features such as checking and managing a Web site.
- You will notice shortcut key combinations associated with many menu commands. Using these shortcut keystrokes can save you a great deal of time as you work with Dreamweaver features.
- Some of Dreamweaver's most important commands are available even before a site has been defined. The following sections list and discuss the most important of these commands.

File Menu

- The File menu (see illustration below) includes a number of familiar Windows commands: New, Open, Close, Save, Save As, and so on.

File menu

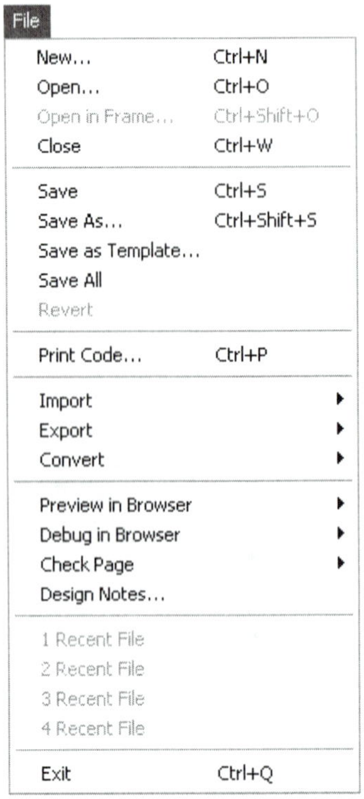

- Some menu commands are available for use only when you are working with particular features or page elements. If a command is not currently available, it is displayed in light gray text (see the Open in Frame command, for example).
- Some menu commands include right-pointing arrows at the right side of the menu. These arrows indicate that clicking the command will open a submenu with further options.
- Several commands on the File menu unique to Dreamweaver are explained in the following sections.

Design Notes

- The Design Notes feature is particularly useful if you manage a very large site or are assisted by multiple team members. You can track changes and contributions and use the information to build new sites and to train others.

Import, Export, and Convert

- These menu items are important when you are working with an existing site or files already created. You will import files in Chapter 3.

Preview in Browser, Debug in Browser, and Check Page

- Preview in Browser is important for testing your Web site. This option lets you select your primary browser—or other browsers that you can test with Dreamweaver—to see how your site will look to Web visitors.
- Another testing command, Debug in Browser is used to debug scripts in both the Dreamweaver environment and in the browser.
- Check Page contains a submenu of specialized commands for checking hyperlinks, target browsers, and special Web page coding.

Edit Menu

- The Edit menu (see illustration on the following page) offers many of the same tools as other Windows applications, too. You will find these standard Windows commands just as useful in Dreamweaver as in other applications.
- Use the Undo command, for example, to reverse a recent action. The Cut, Copy, and Paste commands help you move or duplicate text from page to page in your Web site. If you have used these commands in other Windows programs, you will find that they work the same way in Dreamweaver.

Edit menu

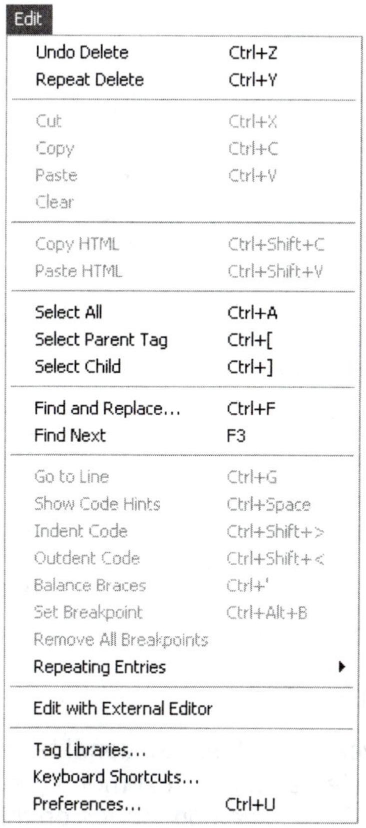

- Note that the Keyboard Shortcuts command on the Edit menu allows you to create your own keyboard shortcuts for features you use frequently. Most experienced Webmasters use a combination of keyboard shortcuts as well as the mouse to perform tasks quickly.

View Menu

- The View menu (see the following illustration) lets you control what items display in the workspace. As in many Windows applications, you can display a ruler and the status bar from this menu—and the code you and Dreamweaver use to build Web pages.

View menu

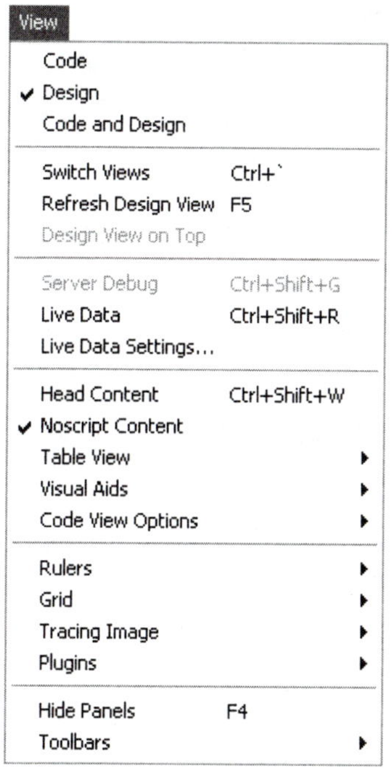

- You can also control display of items unique to Dreamweaver, such as table, layer, and frame borders—and the blue-shaded circle that shows where an image map has been added to an image. (Dreamweaver calls these items Visual Aids.)

Insert Menu

- The Insert menu (see illustration on the following page) makes the placement of Dreamweaver objects easier. You can use this menu to insert images, tables, layers, frames, data applications, and many more objects.

Insert menu

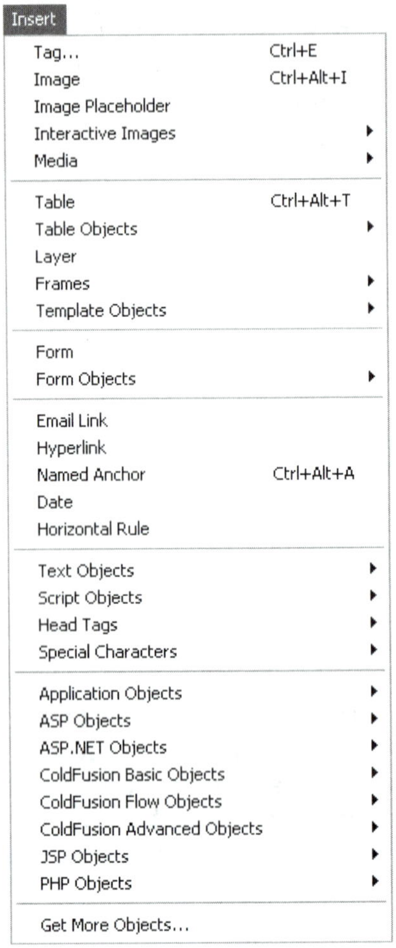

- Familiarize yourself with some of the features on this menu. In this course, you can use this menu to insert several kinds of objects into Web documents when their corresponding group panels are not open.
- Note that Dreamweaver collects some similar items, such as interactive images (rollover images and navigation bars, for example) and displays them as submenu items. This kind of organization can reduce the time you spend looking for an item on a long menu.

Modify Menu

- The Modify menu (see illustration below) offers many tools to change page properties, tags, links, library files, layers, frames, and other Web document features.
- Dreamweaver MX's Modify menu includes several new commands (Arrange, Align, and Convert) to help you control the position and layout of layers and other objects.

Modify menu

Text Menu

- Dreamweaver makes traditional text formatting tools available on the Text menu (see illustration below). Most of the commands on this menu open submenus with further formatting options. Working with this menu will make Dreamweaver as easy to use as a word processing program.

Text menu

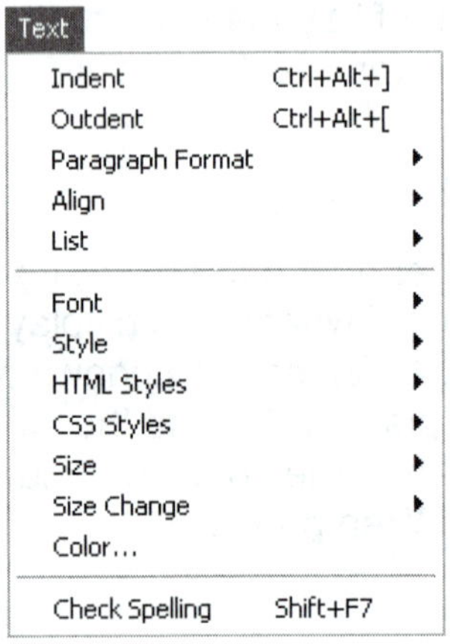

- Use the commands on this menu to apply HTML formats, fonts, font styles, font sizes, and colors. You can also edit HTML and CSS styles from this menu.

Commands Menu

- The Commands menu (see illustration below) allows macro recording and changes to the menu syntax, begins an online photo album, and more.

Commands menu

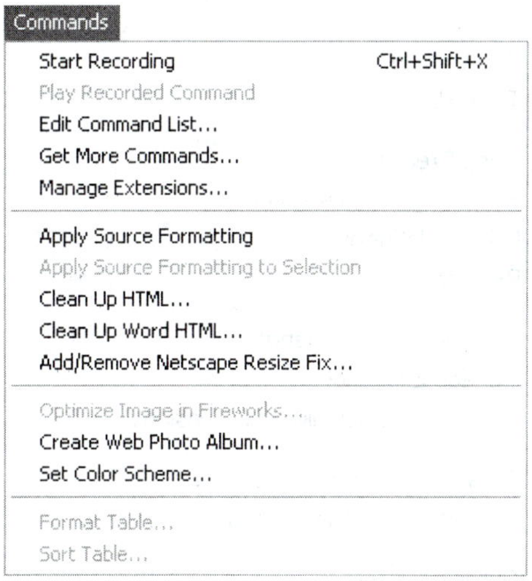

- Two features on this menu help you to ensure that your HTML code is correct and clean. Clean Up HTML and Clean Up Word HTML scan for unneeded tags, headers, and closing tags in any HTML document or, specifically, an HTML document imported from Microsoft Word.
- You will use these commands in Chapters 3 and 5.

Site Menu

- The Site menu (see illustration in the next column) offers tools to create new sites, check files in and out, control site files, view the site map—and put (publish) a Web to a remote site. You will use commands on this menu to create a new site in Chapter 2.

Site menu (v. 3)

Window Menu

- You can launch Dreamweaver's panels from the Window menu (see the following illustration). These tools are demonstrated throughout the book, and knowing how to activate them will make your experience with Dreamweaver efficient and reliable.

Window menu

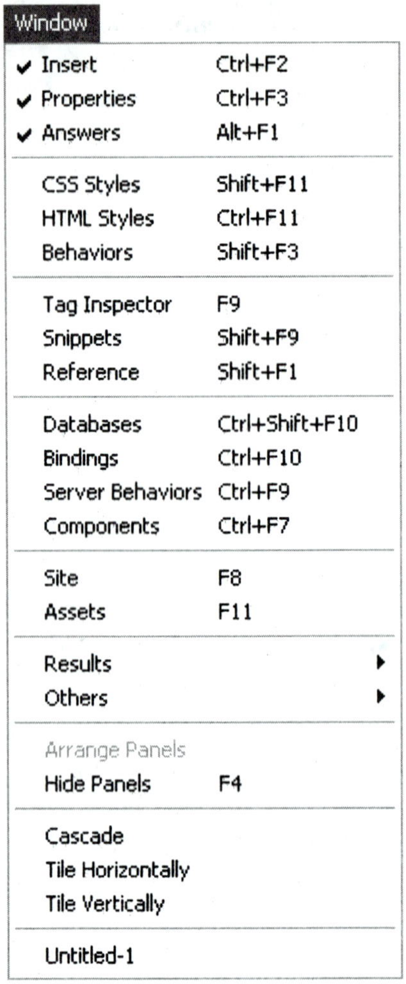

- Notice that checkmarks indicate the panels that are currently open. (The arrows next to the command indicate submenus that contain menu command "families.")
- Keyboard shortcuts are available to display or hide all of the items listed on this menu. Mastering these shortcuts can speed your work with Dreamweaver's objects.

Help Menu

- Dreamweaver provides extensive online help tools on the Help menu (see illustration at the top of the next column), including a guided tour, a tutorial, links to support, and information exchange sites. More than just the technical manual placed online, the Help menu is a tool that will serve you well as you build a solid Internet site.
- Click on the Using Dreamweaver option in the Help menu (or use the F1 shortcut key) to access Dreamweaver's Help system, a multipage HTML document that you can search for information on specific topics.

Help menu

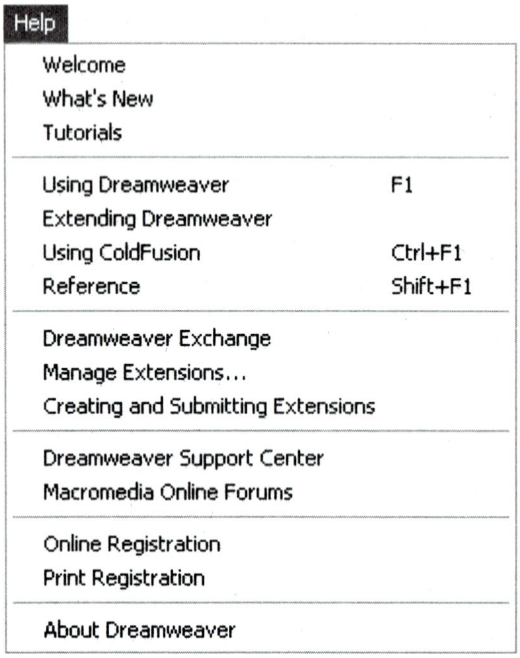

- The Help document (see Dreamweaver Help document, shown below) allows you to select topics from Contents, browse the Index, or use a Search feature. Help information for a specific topic displays in the larger frame in the window.

Dreamweaver Help document

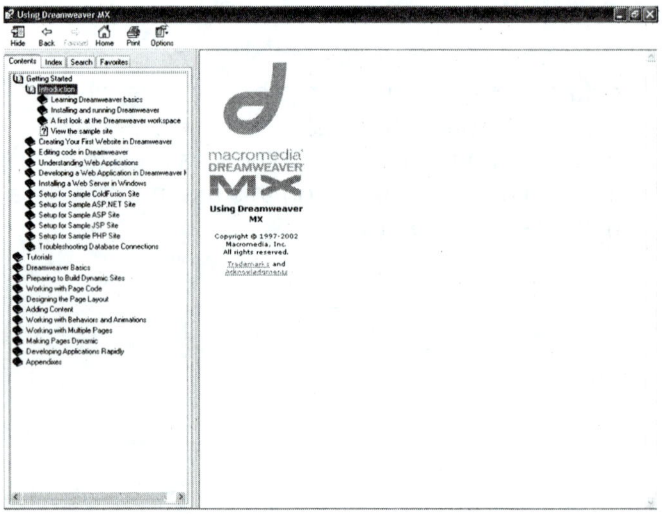

- You also access the tutorials in the Help document by clicking the link in the Answers panel.

- You can click on the Help button in a dialog box or click the ⓘ button in certain panels to access context-specific Help pages.
- If you are new to Dreamweaver, consider taking the Welcome and What's New guided tours offered on this menu and completing the Tutorials. These learning features show you how to perform a number of common Dreamweaver tasks.

Dreamweaver Document toolbar

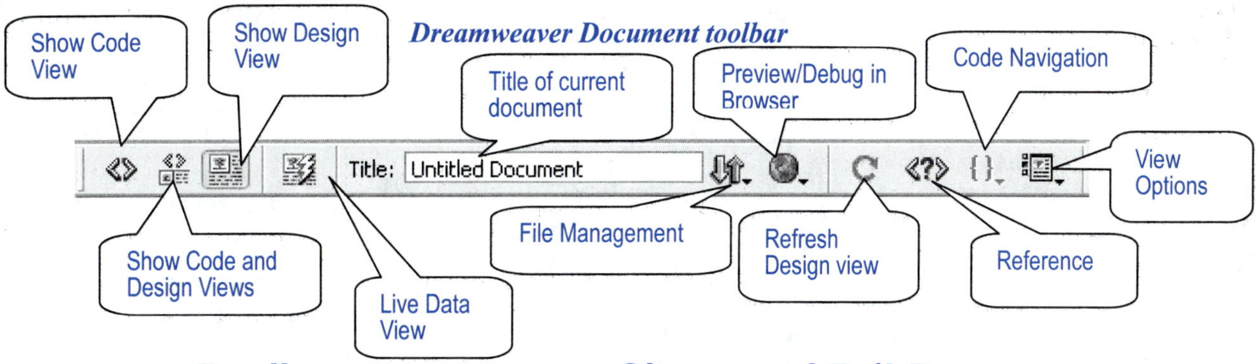

Dreamweaver Toolbars

- Dreamweaver offers a Document toolbar, positioned below the menu bar and Insert bar, that contains a number of useful tools (see illustration above).
- The Standard toolbar (not shown) provides tools for saving Web pages and cutting, copying, and pasting.
- You will find that these tools save time as you work with Dreamweaver. Use these tools to switch quickly between views of HTML code and regular text, work with HTML code, manage files, and preview documents.

Note: *To see the name of a toolbar button, rest the mouse pointer on it to display a tooltip.*

Close and Exit Dreamweaver

- After completing work on a Web page or site, close all open documents and then exit Dreamweaver. You can use File menu commands to close documents and exit the program.

Procedures

Start Dreamweaver

1. Click **start** button on Windows taskbar.
2. Click **Programs** or **All Programs** .... P
3. Click **Macromedia.**
4. Click **Macromedia Dreamweaver MX**.

Close Panels

- Right-click the panel's title bar and click Close Panel Group.

OR

- Click the panel's Options Menu if the group is expanded and click Close Panel Group.

OR

- Click the **Close** button in upper right or left corner of panel or inspector.

Hide/Show Panels

F4

1. Click **View** .... Alt + V
2. Click **Hide/Show Panels** .... P

Open Dreamweaver Menus

- Click menu name to display menu.

OR

- Press Alt and underlined letter in menu name.

Issue Command from Menu

- Click on command on menu.

OR

- Press underlined letter in command.

Open Panels

1. Click **Window** .... Alt + W
2. Click name of panel or inspector to display.

Move Panels

1. Click on the grabber in panel title bar.
2. While holding down the mouse button, drag panel (or panel group) to new location.

Access Help

F1

1. Click **Help** .... Alt + H
2. Click **Using Dreamweaver** V

OR

- Click on the **Help** button in a dialog box or the ? button in certain panels.

Close Document

Ctrl + W

1. Click **File** .... Alt + F
2. Click **Close** C

   ✓ *Click **Yes** or **No** as desired if asked to save the document.*

Exit Dreamweaver

Ctrl + Q

1. Click **File** .... Alt + F
2. Click **Exit** X

Exercise Directions

1. Start Dreamweaver.
   - Choose which workspace to use.
   - Study the Dreamweaver workspace.
2. Locate the following items:
   - Menu bar
   - Document toolbar
   - Insert bar
   - Properties panel
   - Answers panel
   - Design group panel and the three panels that it features

   ✓ *If some of these items are not displayed in the workspace, open them from the Window menu.*
3. Open each menu to see the commands that are currently active.

   ✓ *For this and other steps, use mouse and keyboard shortcut commands and determine which ones are the most productive for you.*
4. Close the Insert bar and Properties panel.
5. Use the Window menu to open the Insert bar and Properties panel.
6. Rearrange the workspace by dragging the Properties panel into the Document window and docking the Insert bar at the bottom of the workspace in the position formerly occupied by the Properties panel.
7. Drag and redock both the Properties and Insert panels in their original positions.
8. Use the Help system to read about getting started with Dreamweaver.
9. Close the current document without saving it.

   ✓ *You may need to consult with your teacher, Web administrator, or ISP to perform steps 10 through 12.*
10. Expand the Desktop icon in the Site panel by clicking the + (plus) sign. Then expand My Computer and locate the data files that you will use for this course, and the folder in which you intend to save or publish your Web site.
11. If you are using a LAN, WAN, intranet, or Internet, expand My Network Places and locate where you will access the data files you will use for this book and any other file locations suggested by your instructor such as the server(s) where you will save, test, or publish your Web site.
12. Collapse the expanded folders by clicking the Desktop icon's – (minus) sign in the Site panel.
13. Close Dreamweaver.

Next Chapter

▶▶

Chapter

2

Setting Up a Site

Correctly setting up your Web site is crucial in Dreamweaver. You might be tempted to skip this step and begin building your pages right away. But you should take time to set up a Web site folder and the Web site itself so that later in the development process you can use the site management features effectively.

In this chapter, you'll learn how to:

- Create a folder to contain a new Web site
- Create and name a new Web site
- Configure the Web site
- Create and save Web pages
- Work with panels
- View site files
- Recognize sound Web design guidelines

Set Up a New Web Site—Overview

- Setting up a new **Web site** in Dreamweaver is an automated multistep process in which you name your site and its folder, choose an application server, and a location in which to store the site folder for your Web site.
- If you know settings required to publish the Web site, you can configure the site as you create it.
- Once you have created the Web site, you are ready to add pages to the site. Pages saved to the site can be viewed using the Site window. (You will learn more about the Site window later in this chapter and in subsequent chapters.)
- You will find it helpful to plan your Web site before you begin the process of creating its pages. Take the time to prepare your site *mentally* and consider how the site will grow.

  Tip: *You can start small, with only a single page in your Web site. Dreamweaver makes it easy to expand an existing site. But anticipating growth factors, layout changes, merging company images and ideals, and so on, will result in the most efficient and professional use of the Dreamweaver tools.*

Creating a New Site

- The quickest way to define your Web site is to open Dreamweaver, use the Site>New Site command, and enter appropriate information on the Basic tab of the Site Definition wizard.
- Each screen within the Basic tab is part of a step in the process. The Editing Files screen is the first. Here you give your site a name in the What would you like to name your site? text box (see illustration). Then click Next to move to the next screen as you complete your entries.

  Note: *At any point as you work your way through the Site Definition wizard, you can click the Back button to return to a previous wizard screen.* ***Also, depending on the options you select, not all of the Site Definition wizard screens described in the following sections may appear.***

Site Definition wizard—Naming the Site

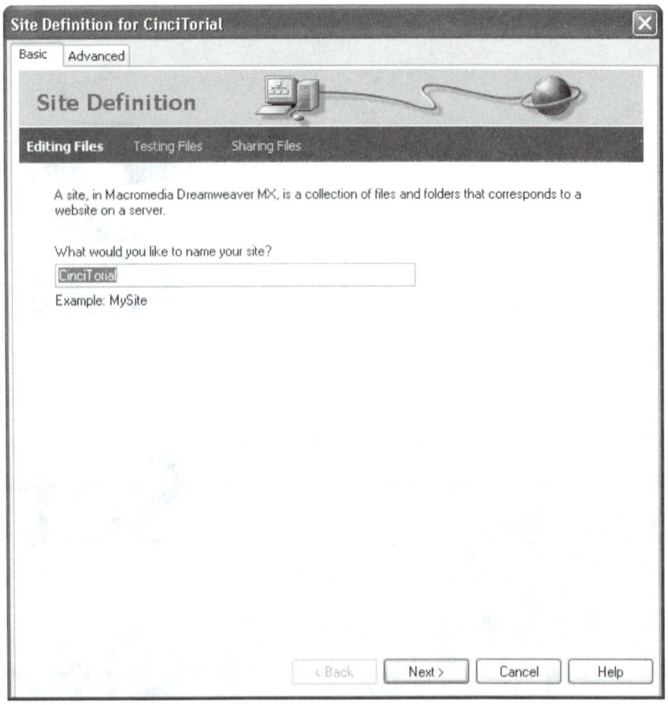

- As you choose a name for your Web site, consider where you intend to publish the Web site. Most Web servers use UNIX-based operating systems and have very specific limitations for file names.
- If you have verified that your ISP or Web server is UNIX-based, remember these file naming rules for the site names, page names, and the names used for other objects that the server stores:
  - The underscore (_) is the only special character allowed.
  - No spaces are allowed.
  - UNIX file names are case sensitive. As a general rule, use lowercase for page and other object files.
- Recognizing these rules before designing your site will save you hours of frustration that can result if you use names your server will not recognize.

Selecting a Server Technology

- In the Editing Files, part 2 screen, You have the option of selecting a **server technology**. If your site will feature a Web application, such as a form for entering data, you can select the desired server technology to support different kinds of dynamic content.
- If you are not sure, you can select No, which you can change later.
- If you know the server technology that you will use, you can select Yes and then select the desired server technology from the drop-down list (see illustration). By default, if you installed the single-user copy of ColdFusion MX during your installation of the standard Dreamweaver MX bundle, **ColdFusion** is listed first. Otherwise, None is selected first. ColdFusion MX is Macromedia's Web application server.

Selecting a Server Technology

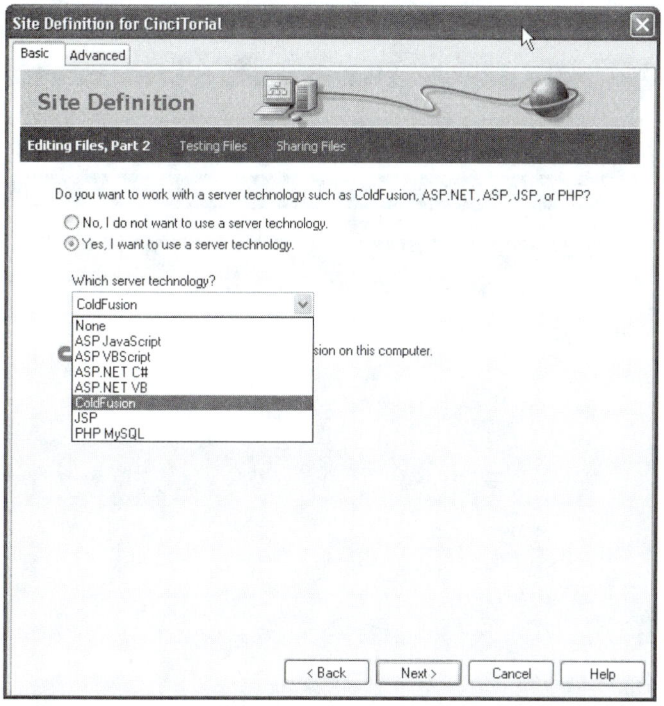

Note: *Ask your teacher, Web server administrator, or ISP if you should select ColdFusion or another server technology.*

Where to Store Your Web Site

- In the third screen, Editing Files, Part 3, you can select how you want to work with your files. You can choose to store your Web folder and files locally on your hard drive (the Local Host). This is also called the root folder.
- You can also choose to create and edit your Web site on a remote server.
- As suggested in the introduction to this book, you will probably want to create your Web site locally, taking advantage of the PWS or IIS Web server software that comes with Microsoft Windows.

  Tip: *For more information about setting up these servers on your hard drive or on another computer on your network, use the following menu command: Help>Dreamweaver Help > Using Dreamweaver > Contents > Getting Started > Installing a Web Server in Windows*

- Dreamweaver detects the presence of this software on your hard drive and will automatically select it in the Where on your computer do you want to store your files? text box (see illustration).

Selecting a Storage Location

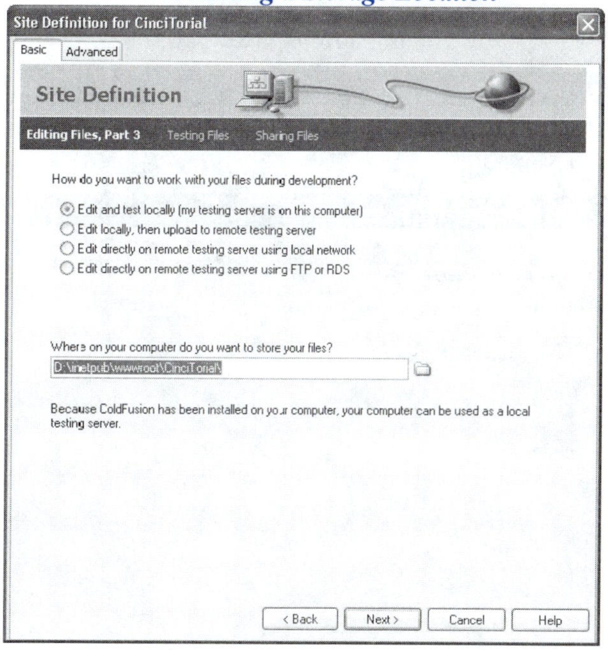

- By default, Dreamweaver will name the folder in which you store your files with the name you chose for your Web site.

- If you want to change the default location, click the Folder button and navigate to a desired location in the Choose Local [or Remote] Root Folder for Site [name of site] dialog box, and then click Select.
- If you select an FTP or RDS server, you will need additional information from your network administrator, ISP, or other site provider to set up the FTP Host, Host Directory, Login, and Password.

Note: *FTP techniques and requirements are discussed in Chapter 17.*

Testing Your Web

- If you selected a server technology, you will also see the Testing Files screen of the Site Definition wizard. You can select the URL (the Web address your browser uses) to open the Web site for testing purposes—or the URL that other users can enter in their Web browser's Address bar to open the site via a network or intranet.
- The default choice for the URL is the name of the local or remote host and the root folder in which you have stored your files (see illustration).

Setting a Root URL

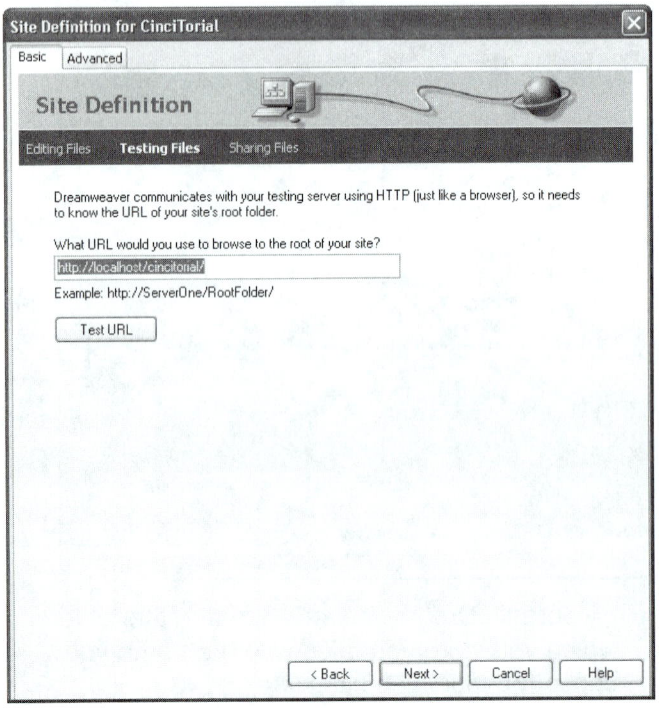

- Typically, you will want to keep the URL provided by Dreamweaver. You should also use this opportunity to test it.
- Click the Test URL button Test URL. If the test is successful, a message box will appear. Click OK. If it is unsuccessful, you will need to consult with your teacher, network administrator, or ISP, to obtain the correct URL, which you can enter in the What URL would you use to browse to the root of your site? text box.

Selecting a Remote Server

- In the Sharing Files screen of the Site Definition wizard, you can select the option for setting up your **remote server** site. This is the server where your published Web will be accessed by the production team working collaboratively on your Web—or the actual server where Internet (or intranet) users access the site with their Web browsers.

A remote server is where users will browse your site

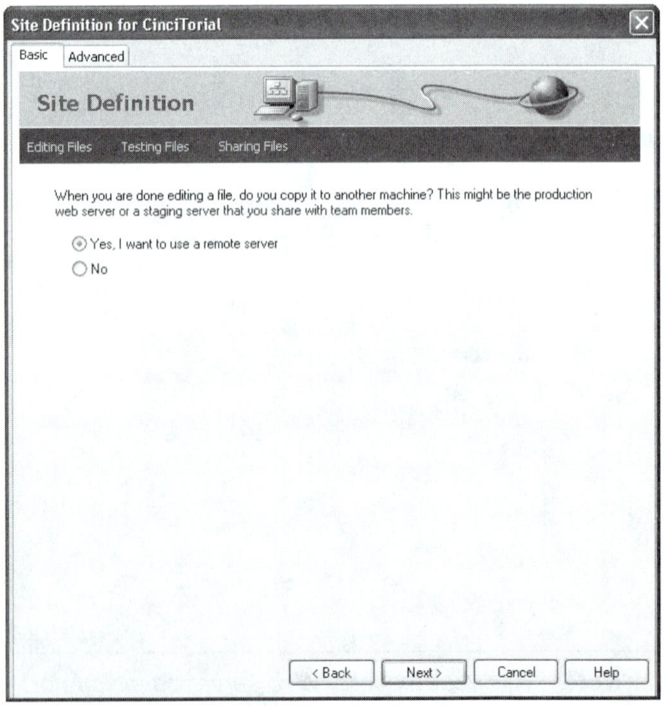

- In the Sharing Files, Part 2 screen, click the How do you connect to your remote server? list box arrow and select the type of remote server that you will use to put ("publish") your Web site (see illustration on following page).

A remote server is where users will browse your site

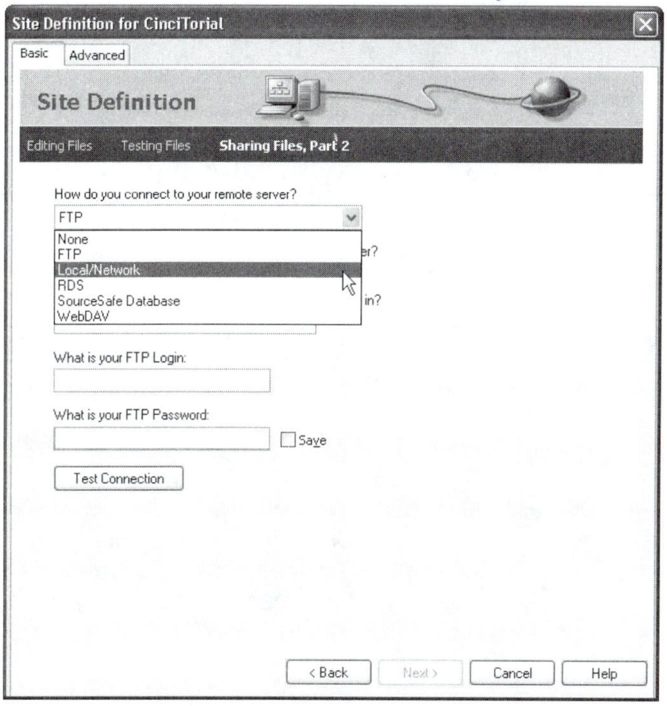

- The FTP option is selected by default, since most Internet Web sites are stored on FTP servers. An intranet site would typically be stored in a Local/Network location.
- After you enter the appropriate information for an FTP remote site—including any logon name and password—you can test the connection by clicking the Test Connection button [Test Connection]
- For a Local/Network remote site, you can enter the file path or click the Folder button and navigate to the desired location in the Choose Remote Root Folder for Site [name of site] dialog box.
- In the For a Local/Network remote site, click the checkbox next to Refresh Local File List Automatically if you want an automatic file update every time you copy files into your Web site. This feature requires only a small amount of resources and is a valuable tool for keeping your site up to date.
- These are the common remote connection types that are covered in this course. Consult Dreamweaver Help to learn about the other types of remote connections.

Note: *If you have installed ColdFusion MX and want to use it to build forms and other applications, you can set up an FTP site and/or an RDS (Remote Development Services) on your computer or network.*

Right-click the Macromedia FTP & RDS *icon in Windows Explorer or My Computer and select to install an FTP site or RDS server. Consult with your teacher, Web server administrator, or ISP about the settings you will need to configure these remote server options. You will also learn more about making a remote server connection in Chapter 17.*

Check In/Check Out Feature

- In the Sharing Files, Part 3 screen, the check in/out option allows you to set up procedures so that no member of a Web design team can edit a file at the same time. When you select the Yes, enable check in and check out option, all team members can see files that are checked out by a team member (and also see who is working on the file).
- When you open a file, you can have Dreamweaver check it out (the default option) or enter the name you want to display when the file is checked out in the What is your name? text box (see illustration on following page). You can also add your e-mail address so that other members of the team can communicate with you when a file is checked out.

Enabling the check in/out feature prevents team Web designers from editing a file at the same time

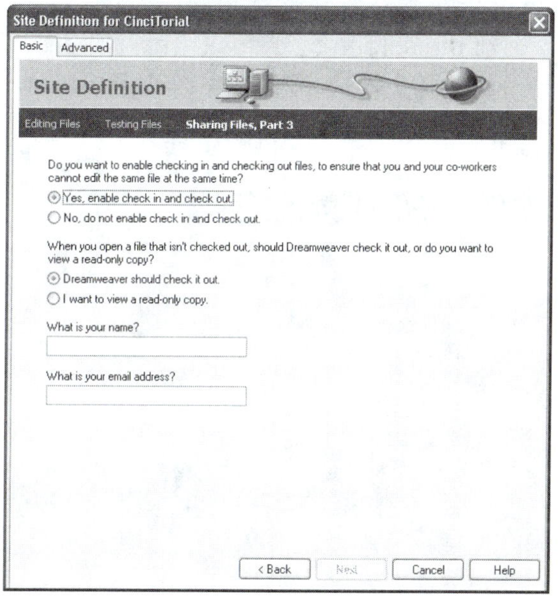

Finish the Site Setup

- The Summary screen in the Site Definition wizard lists the local and remote information about your Web site as well as other options that you have selected. Review these options and change any if necessary by clicking the Back button to return to the desired tab. If you are finished defining your site, click Done (see illustration).

Summary of a newly created Web site

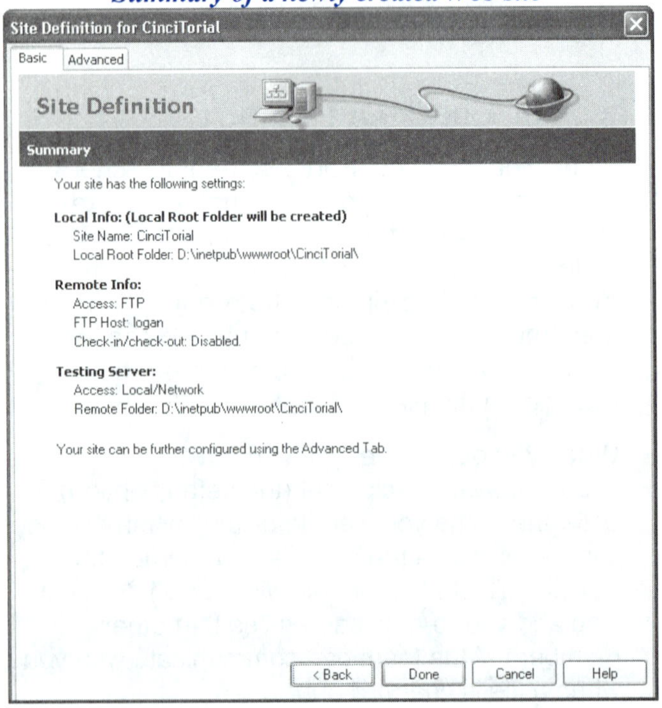

- The new site—shown as a green folder—is listed in the Site panel in the panel group on the right side of the screen by default. This panel's window is the hub of file management, and you will use it many times as you design your site (see illustration).
- You will learn about the Site panel in Chapter 4.

Site panel for new Web site

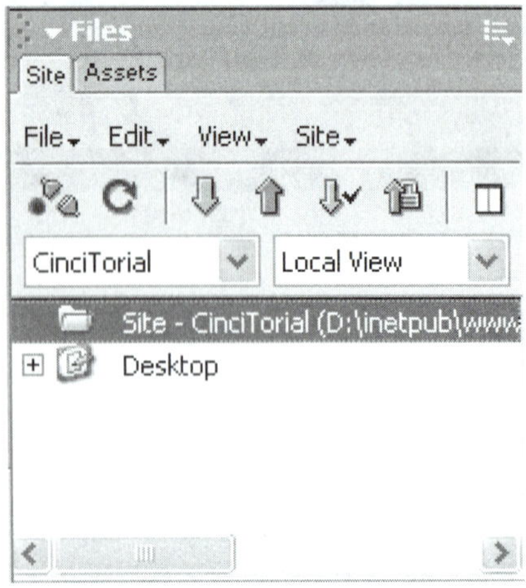

Note: *By default, the Windows Desktop is also listed in the Site panel. By expanding the Desktop, you can navigate to any folder on your computer or network much as you can do in Windows Explorer.*

Creating Web Pages

- Your Web site content appears on documents stored within the site. These documents become the **Web pages** that visitors open when the Web site is put (or published).
- Each time you start Dreamweaver, Dreamweaver displays a blank document. You can use this blank document as the first page in your Web site.

  Note: *Dreamweaver opens with the blank document by default. You can use Edit>Preferences (General category) to specify that only the Site window opens with Dreamweaver.*

- Before you begin adding content to a new page, you should save it. Use the File>Save (or Save As) command on the menu bar to save a new document.
- You can also right-click on the untitled document's tab 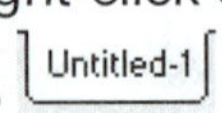

 in the lower left corner of the Document window, and select Save or Save As from the shortcut menu. If you select Close first, you will be prompted to save if any changes have been made to the current Web page.

- Each time you add a new Web page, another tab appears in the Document window for selecting and working with that page or another open page.
- The process of saving a document in Dreamweaver is very similar to saving files in any Windows program: give the new file a name and specify the location where it will be stored and the file type. If you selected an application server during your site definition, you may see that pages are saved with the file extension associated with the server. For example, ColdFusion pages are saved with .cfm (see illustration below).

Save new document in site folder

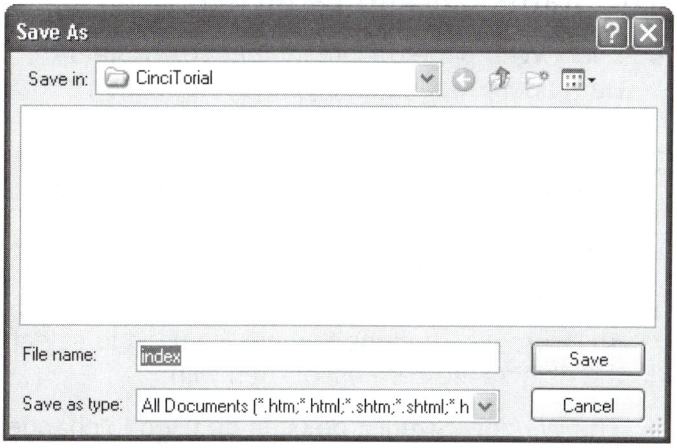

- Many servers expect the home page of a Web site to be named **index.htm** or **index.html.** The Microsoft PWS and IIS servers use *default* as the file name for the home page. To make sure your Web pages are published without error, use the appropriate name for your home pages.
- As part of the page creation process, you should also give each page a title. A page's title appears in the title bar of the **browser** when the page is opened.
- Use the Modify>Page Properties command on the menu bar to open the Page Properties dialog box. You can type the page's title in the Title text box (see illustration below). Or, type the page title right in the Document toolbar's Title box.

Add a page title to a saved document

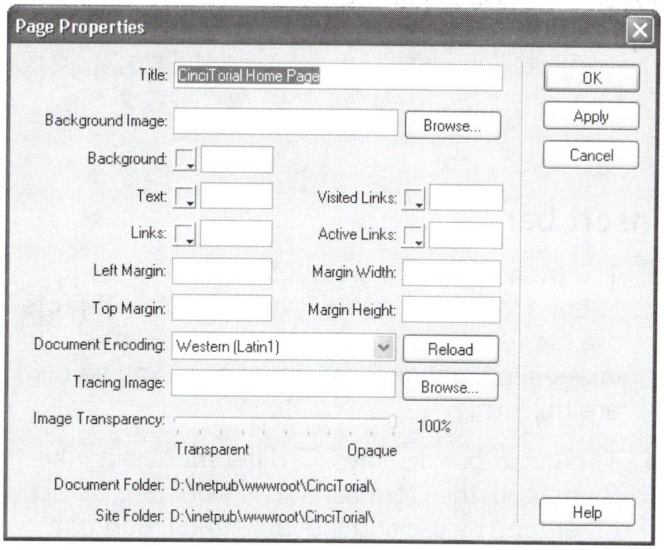

- After you specify the page title, the document window will show that title in brackets in its title bar. The title bar also shows the file folder and file name in parentheses.

  Tip: *Both page names and page titles can be changed later from the Site window or the Document window.*

- To create additional pages for a Web site, use the File>New command on the menu bar to select and create a new, blank document in the New Document dialog box.
- Remember that although most Web sites contain more than one page, it is not uncommon for a Web site to consist of only one page.

Work with Workspace Tools

- Dreamweaver opens with the panel groups you need to begin creating a Web page. (The panels that you see depend on what palettes were open during Dreamweaver's last session and any changes made to default Preference settings.)
- Panels can be opened and closed as you require. They can be floated and docked in other locations as well. They can be resized by dragging a border or combined to save room on your workspace.
- Another way to increase your workspace is to collapse the right panel group pane by clicking its Collapse/Expand button.

Common objects tab displayed

Insert bar

- The **Insert bar** is a group of tabs containing buttons for creating Web page objects. **Objects** are elements added to a Web page. Forms, images, animation files, sound files, and so on are objects.
- The Insert bar displays 12 different object tabs. By default, the Common tab is selected. Select other tabs by clicking the tab in the Insert bar (see illustration at the top of this page).
- The Document toolbar looks like it is part of the Insert bar. But it is conveniently docked below by default. The toolbar displays buttons that you can use to toggle between code view, code and design view, and design view. You will learn more about these and other view options later in the course.
- By default, the Insert bar displays above the Document window. It can be docked in another location—or floated and resized by dragging the bottom or right border of the panel.
- To identify a tool on the Insert bars, rest the mouse pointer on the tool. Dreamweaver displays the name of the tool in a tooltip.

Properties Panel

- The Properties panel is another important panel used in creating Web pages. It displays the properties of the element you select. Dreamweaver considers a **property** to be an HTML or other Web code characteristic, such as alignment or size, that you can assign to an element—such as text or pictures—in your project.
- Properties displayed in the Properties panel depend on what item is currently selected in the document. The illustration on the top of the next page shows properties for a heading.
- The most common properties are displayed in the panels fields. (If other properties are available for an item, you may need to click the **expander arrow** at the lower-right corner of the inspector to display them.)
- Use the Property inspector to select formats and position items precisely to ensure a consistent look on all pages in a Web site.

The Status Bar and Launcher

- Every Web page document features a Status Bar underneath it that displays information about the Web page, such as the type of coding it contains, the window size, and how long it takes to download on different kinds of modem and broadband connections (see illustration on the following page).
- The HTML coding symbols such as <body> and <h1> are also buttons that can be used to select the objects they are associated with.
- The Window Size list box can be used to change the window size of your Web page.
- The connection speed at which your Web pages would be downloaded by users is 28kbps by default. Since this slower modem connection is rare now, you should consider changing the connection speed shown in the status bar by clicking Edit>Preferences>Status Bar and selecting the desired connection speed in the Connection Speed list box. You will learn more about connection speed in Chapter 6.
- The Launcher is used to open and close panels that are accessed in the right panel group pane. The Launcher is shown in the Status Bar illustration below. But it is not selected by default.
- If you want to display the Launcher, you can click Edit>Preferences>Panels. Then select the Show Icons in Panels and Launcher checkbox.

Properties panel showing text properties

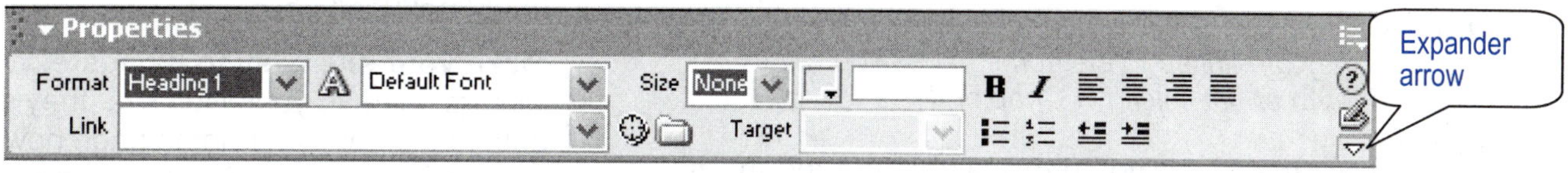

Status Bar showing Launcher

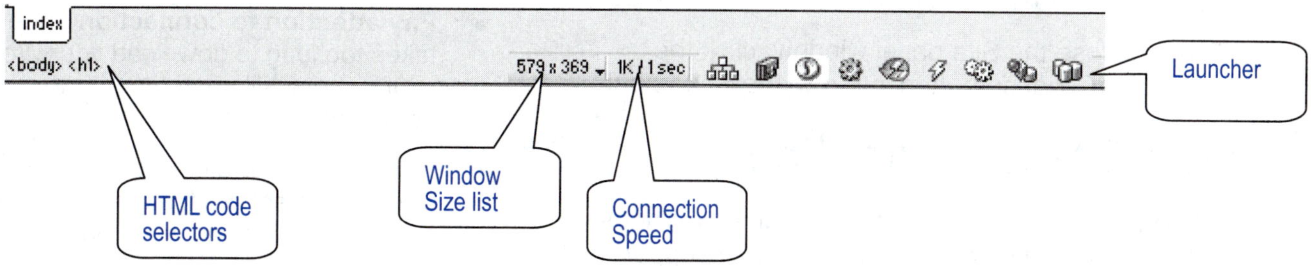

View Site Files

- As you add pages and other files to a Web site, you may need to see a more detailed and expanded view of your site than the Site panel's small window.
- Click the Expand/Collapse button in the Site panel. The expanded, window-size Site panel in Site Files view shows the Local Files in the right pane and the server information in the Remote Site pane at the left (see illustration).

Expanded Site panel window

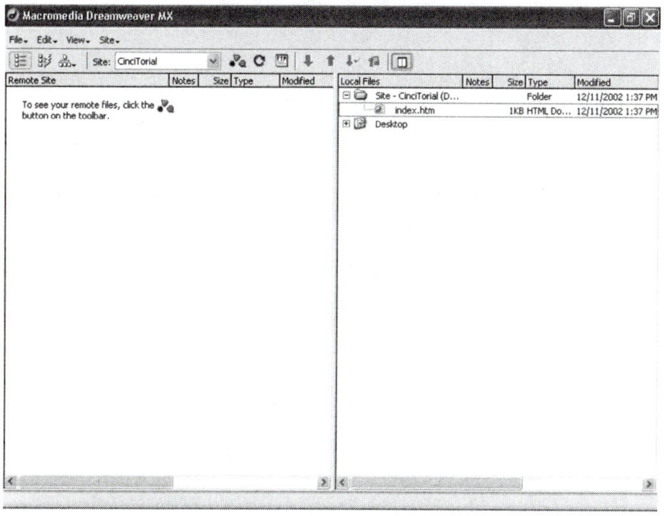

- As you begin building your site, you can designate one of its pages as the site's home page using the Site>Set as Home Page command on the Site panel menu bar either expanded or collapsed.

Note: *You can also designate the home page by right-clicking on the desired page in either the expanded or collapsed Site panel and then clicking Set as Home Page.*

- The **home page** is the first page that opens in a Web site. This page usually gives general information about the site and has links to other pages in the site.
- Click to see a drop-down menu from which you can choose to see the site map only or the site map in the left pane and the site files in the right (see illustration below). The designated home page appears at the top of the site map structure.

Site panel window showing Map and Files view

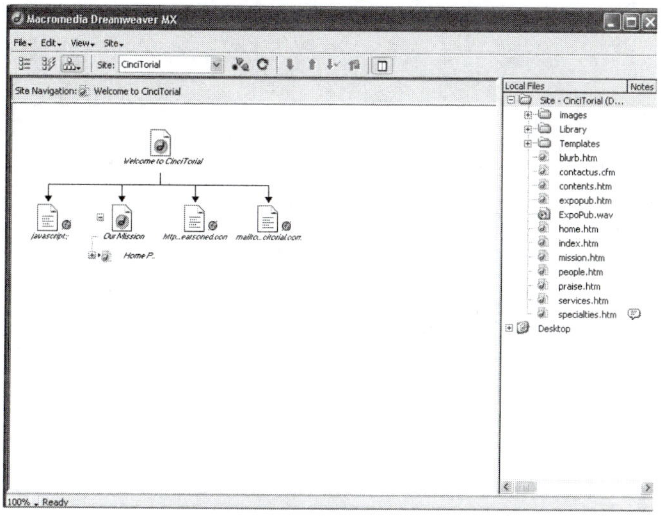

- You can toggle between the Site Map view and Site Files view in either the expanded or collapsed Site panel by pressing Alt+F8 and F8 respectively.

Note: *Other pages will appear in the site map as they are linked to the home page. You will learn about linking in Chapter 4.*

- If you click the Site Map button, a shortcut menu displays. You can choose to display only the map or the map and the files in the Local Folder.
- To collapse the Site panel window, click the Expand/Collapse button in the window's toolbar.

Web Design Guidelines

- Dreamweaver is an application that encourages creativity, and it provides considerable support and assistance in realizing a designer's ideas. Before jumping in with your site design, however, consider some design guidelines that can help you turn out professional-quality pages.

Note: *This book assumes that you are using Dreamweaver for business and informational sites, but the following design rules apply equally well to less formal content or to personal Web sites.*

- **Be consistent.** Consistency in color, graphics, and placement helps your visitor understand your site.
- **Make your site easy to navigate.** When visitors come to your Web site, they should be able to tell from your home page how to get around your site and find the features they need.
- **Pay attention to connection speed.** If it takes too long to download your Web site, your visitors will not return. Time is valuable, both theirs *and* yours.
- **Keep it simple.** Clean lines and clear, easy-to-read content are features you always should keep in mind when building your site.
- **Be unique.** Copying another's designs is not only plagiarism, but also limits your own ideas and site potential.
- **Respect your visitors.** Make sure your site looks professional from the very first moment it is online. Don't fall into the habit of posting a "construction guy" graphic or similar icon to notify your visitors that your site is under construction. If your visitors are visiting your site for information, they likely will look elsewhere.

Procedures

Create Web Site

1. Click **Site** .... Alt+S
2. Click **New Site** .... N

OR

1. Click **Site** in the Site panel menu bar.
2. Click **New Site**.
3. Click the **Basic** tab if necessary.
4. Type site name in **What would you like to name your site?** text box.
5. Click **Next** .... Alt+N
6. Select the desired server technology option:
   - **No, I do not want to use a server technology** .... Alt+O

   OR

   - **Yes, I want to use a server technology** .... Alt+Y
   - **Which server technology?** .... Alt+W
   - Select the desired server technology from the drop-down list.
7. Click **Next** .... Alt+N
8. Select the desired option for How do you want to work with your files during development?

   ✓ *Depending on the option you choose, you may, after clicking Next, skip some or all of the screens used in steps 11–15.*
9. Type path to the root folder in Where on your computer do you want to store your files? text box.

   ✓ *If you are using ColdFusion MX, then the server software on your machine may already be recognized (such as Microsoft IIS Web server software), and the path will be entered by default and the name of your Web site will be the name of its storage folder.*

   OR

   - Click browse to Web site folder, and click **Select** Alt+S.
10. Click **Next** .... Alt+N
11. Type the URL of your site in the **What URL would you use to browse to the root of your site?** text box .... Alt+W

    ✓ *If you are using Microsoft PWS or IIS Web server, the URL will be entered by default.*
12. Click the Test URL.
13. Click **Next** .... Alt+N
14. Select the desired remote server option:
    - **Yes, I want to use a remote server** ...... Alt+Y

    OR

    - **No** .... Alt+N
15. Click **Next** .... Alt+N

    ✓ *If No is selected, skip to step 19.*
16. Select, configure, and test the desired remote server type. Consult Dreamweaver Help for additional information using the remote server type as the index or search keyword(s).
17. Click **Next** .... Alt+N
18. Select the desired check in and check out option:
    - **Yes, enable check in and check out** .... Alt+Y

    OR

    - **No, do not enable check in and check out** .. Alt+N

    ✓ *If Yes is selected, click the desired option for who should check out files and type a name and e-mail address (optional).*
19. Click **Next** .... Alt+N
20. Review the information in the Summary tab and click **Done** .... Alt+D

Save Web Page
Ctrl + S

1. Click **File** .... Alt+F
2. Click **Save** .... S

   OR

   Click **Save As** .... A
3. Type file name in **File name** text box...................... Alt+N.
4. Click **Save in** drop-down arrow and navigate to Web site folder .... Alt+I.
5. Click Save.

OR

1. Right-click the Web document tab.
2. Click **Save** or **Save As**.

Set Page Title
Ctrl + J

1. Click **Modify**................ Alt+M
2. Click **Page Properties** .... P
3. Type page title in **Title** text box .... Alt+T

Add New Basic Web Page
Ctrl + N

1. Click **File** .... Alt+F
2. Click **New** .... N
3. In the Category list, click **Basic Page**.
4. In the Basic Page list, click **HTML**.
5. Click Create.

Selecting an Open Web Document

1. Click **Window**............. Alt+W
2. Select the Web document's file name.

OR

- Click the desired Web document tab in the Document window.

Close Web Document
Ctrl+W

1. Click **File**...................... Alt+F
2. Click **Close** C

OR

1. Right-click the Web document tab.
2. Click **Close**.

View Site Panel
F8

1. Click **Window**............. Alt+W
2. Click **Site** .... S

Expand Site Panel Window

1. Click ◫ in the Site panel.
2. Click ☰ if necessary to see files in site.
3. Click ☷▾ and choose Map Only or Map and Files to see site map of files in site.

Set Home Page

1. Display Site panel, if necessary.
2. Click file name in Local Folder pane.
3. In the Site panel menu bar, click **Site**.
4. Click **Set as Home Page**.

OR

- Right-click file name and select **Set as Home Page**.

Exercise Directions

1. Start Dreamweaver.
2. Create a new Web site and name it **cincitorial** using the Site Definition wizard, as follows:
   - Verify that the Web site's local root folder is also named **cincitorial**.
   - If you have installed ColdFusion as your server technology, select it. Or select the server technology that is appropriate. If you do not know what kind of server technology to use, select None for now.
   - Choose to edit locally on your computer unless otherwise instructed and select a location to store your Web files.
   - If necessary, enter an URL to browse to the root of your site and test it.
   - If you will be publishing to a remote Local/Network server, FTP site, or RDS server, specify the location and configure it in the Site Definition wizard.
   - Do not enable check in and check out.
3. Save the blank Dreamweaver document as **index.htm** in the *cincitorial* folder.

   ✓ *Make sure that your Web page is saved as an HTML document with an .htm extension—not a ColdFusion document with a .cfm extension.*
4. Give the page the title **Home Page**.
5. Create a new basic Web page document and name it **history.htm**. Give it the page title **CinciTorial History**.
6. Create another new document and name it **contactus.htm**. Give it the page title **Contact Us**.
7. Close the **history.htm** and **contactus.htm** documents and click Yes when prompted to save.
8. Undock the Insert bar and drag it into the Document window and resize it.
9. Collapse the right group panel pane to increase the Document window area.
10. Make sure that the Common tab is selected in the Insert bar and then place the mouse pointer over several of the object buttons to see their tooltips. Locate the Insert Table button.
11. Click the other tabs in the Insert bar to see the other panels available. Read the tooltips for each tool on the tab.
12. Restore the Insert bar to its original size and location.
13. View the Web site's files in the Site panel.
14. Expand the Site panel.
15. Set the **index.htm** file as the site's home page.
16. View the current site map in the Site panel window.
17. Collapse the expanded Site panel window.
18. Close the **index.htm** page.
19. Exit Dreamweaver.
20. **Optional.** Read the Web Design Guidelines again.
    - Either on your own or with other class mates, use a search engine to locate Web design criteria used by Web design firms and create a list in your Word processor to expand on the ones you have learned here.
    - Use appropriate keywords and search engine techniques such as Boolean search strategies to narrow your search.
    - Use the design criteria document that you create for creating your Web sites.
    - Share your results with others via your network or as an e-mail attachment.

Next Chapter

Chapter

3

Enter and Format Text

Text is the most important aspect of your Web page content. You rely on text—or content—to *communicate* to visitors what your site is about. Use formatting to ensure that your text is both easy to read and attractive.

In this chapter, you'll learn how to:

- Enter text on a Web page
- Import text from Microsoft Word
- Insert special characters
- Check spelling
- Modify text appearance with character and paragraph formatting
- Apply paragraph and heading tags
- Create bulleted and numbered lists
- Change text size

Enter Text on a Web Page

- After you have set up your site and created pages, you are ready to add content. Your pages should contain a balance of text and graphics to make the pages both informative and attractive.
- In this chapter, you will learn how to add text and format it in a number of ways. You will learn how to add graphics such as pictures in a later chapter.
- A newly opened Dreamweaver document displays a blinking **insertion point** at the top left of the Document window. To enter text on a page, simply begin typing at the location of the insertion point (see illustration below).

Type text at the insertion point

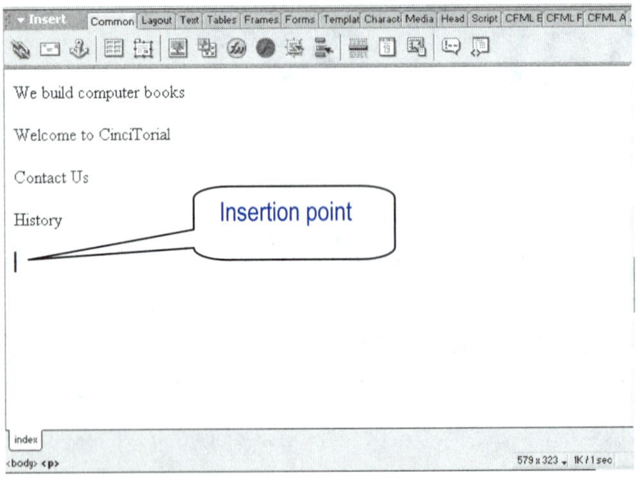

- As in a word processing document, you do not need to press the Enter key at the end of each line. Dreamweaver wraps text automatically at the right side of the page. Press the Enter key only to start a new paragraph.

  Note: *As a general rule, Web page paragraphs are not indented. Dreamweaver does not recognize tabs or spaces at the beginnings of paragraphs.*

- Dreamweaver automatically inserts space after a paragraph, so you do not have to double-space between paragraphs as you might be used to doing in a word processing document.
- If you do not want the default space after a paragraph, insert a **line break** rather than a paragraph break.
- Clicking the BR tool on the Characters tab—a tab on the Insert bar—inserts the HTML
 (Break) **tag**, which creates a new line but not a new paragraph. But as you type you should create a line break by pressing the Shift + Enter key combination.

  Note: *You will learn more about HTML tags in Chapter 5.*

Import Text

- Although you can type all the text you need for your Web site's pages, you have another option for adding text to pages: you can import the text from Microsoft Word, the popular word processing application.

  Note: *Imported text is not inserted in a current document. Rather, it becomes a new page in the site.*

- The Word file to import must be saved in Word as a Web page in HTML format. In Dreamweaver, use the File>Import> Word HTML command on the menu bar to import the page into the current Web site.
- After you issue this command and locate the file to import, click Open. Dreamweaver opens the Clean Up Word HTML dialog box (see illustration below), which allows you to discard unnecessary HTML codes and prepare the imported page for use in the current site.

Clean Up Word HTML dialog box

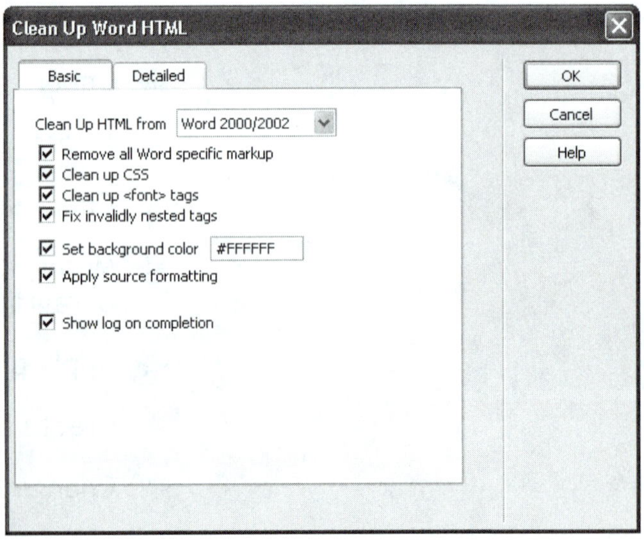

- Click OK to start the cleanup. Dreamweaver displays another dialog box to show you what cleanup operations it has undertaken (see illustration below).

Results of cleanup operations

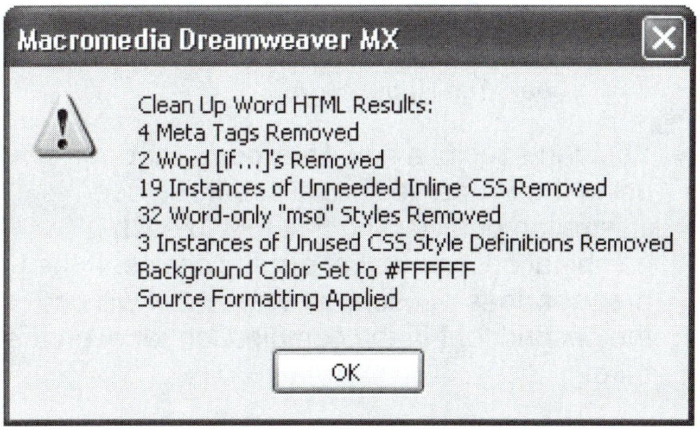

- Click OK again to complete the cleanup and import the page into the current site. The page takes its title from the original Word HTML page but must still be saved in the site.
- An alternative to importing text is to copy and paste text from a word processing document, but formatting—including paragraph breaks—is lost in this process, so this method is suitable for small amounts of text only.

Note: *You can also copy and paste text from one Dreamweaver page to another.*

Insert Special Characters

- As you create your Web page text, you may need to use special characters such as em dashes (—), copyright symbols (©), currency symbols (£), or foreign language characters (¿).
- You can find common special characters on the Characters tab (see the illustration below). Or, you can use the Insert>Special Characters command on the menu bar to display a submenu containing these characters.

Note: *The Characters tab is illustrated with the special characters and may be easier to use if you prefer a visual reference.*

- If you don't find the character you need on the Characters tab, click the Other Characters button on the Characters tab. Dreamweaver displays a dialog box containing many other special characters you can select.

Check Spelling

- Whenever you type more than a few words on a Web page, you should check your spelling. A Web site containing spelling errors is highly unprofessional.
- Use the Text>Check Spelling command on the menu bar to launch the spelling checker. If the spelling checker finds spelling errors on the page, it lists alternatives you can choose to correct spelling (see illustration below).

Check document spelling

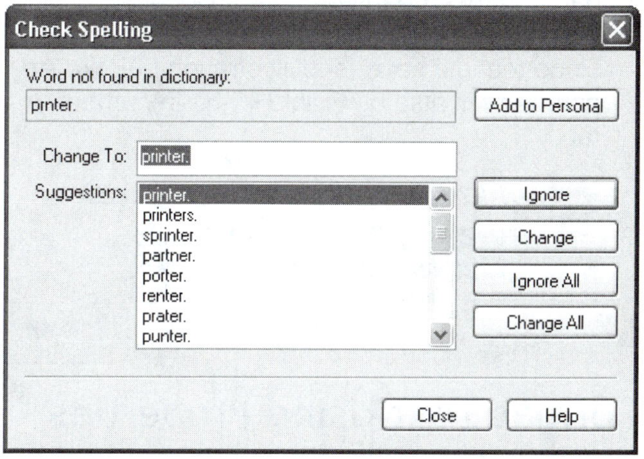

- Use the Add to Personal button to add proper names or other terms from your site to the dictionary so they will not be flagged as errors in the future. Choose Ignore or Ignore All to skip words you know are not misspelled. Use Change or Change All to replace misspelled words with correct words.

Characters tab in the Insert bar

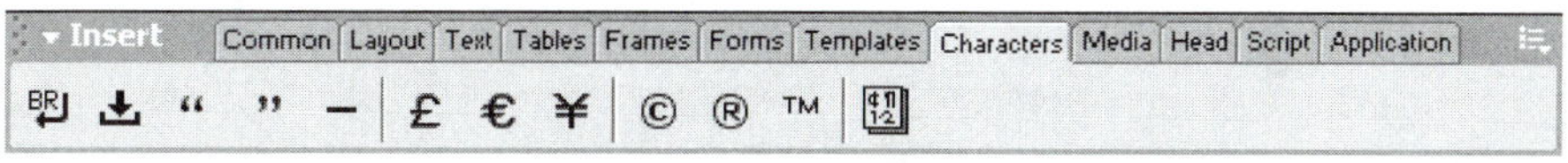

Save Edits

- As you enter and format text, you should save your work from time to time to guard against computer or power failures that can result in the immediate loss of hours of work if you don't. You can use the File>Save command on the menu bar, press the shortcut Ctrl + S, right-click the document tab in the lower left corner of the Document window and click Save, or click the Save button on the Standard toolbar. Make a habit of using one of these methods.

  Tip: *Use the Save All command—in the File menu, document tab shortcut menu, and Standard toolbar—to save all the pages open in Dreamweaver at once when you have made a series of changes to more than one Web page.*

- Dreamweaver displays an asterisk after a page name in the Dreamweaver (or Document) window title bar if changes have been made since the last save (see illustration below). An asterisk will also be visible in the document tab.

Asterisk indicates changes have been made

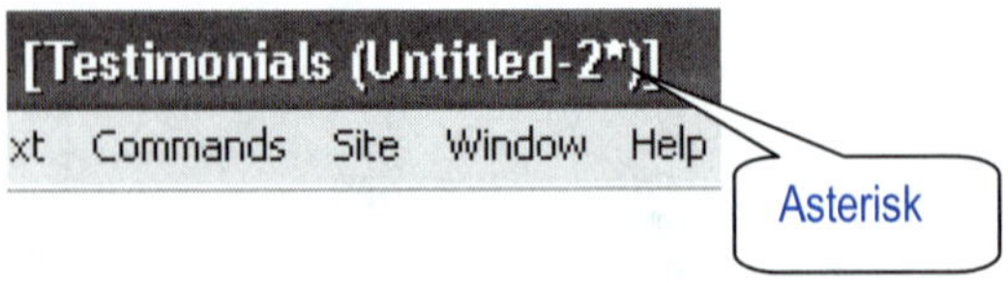

Format Text Using Properties panel

- Text entered in a Dreamweaver document is formatted with a default appearance, size, and color (black). Dreamweaver also applies a default style (Paragraph). You can change text appearance, size, style, and color using tools in the Properties panel.

  Note: *You can also use commands on the Text menu to apply the formats discussed below. Using the Properties panel can be quicker—as are available keyboard shortcuts.*

Select New Font Combination

- A **font** is a design of type. When text is first entered in a Dreamweaver document, it is formatted with the current default font, usually Times New Roman.

  Tip: *You can change the default font using the Edit>Preferences command on the menu bar. See Appendix A.*

- You can specify a new **font combination** using the Properties panel's font list (see illustration below). The first font in each combination is your first display choice. If the browser does not support that font, it will use the second font in the combination, or even the third.

Apply new font combination

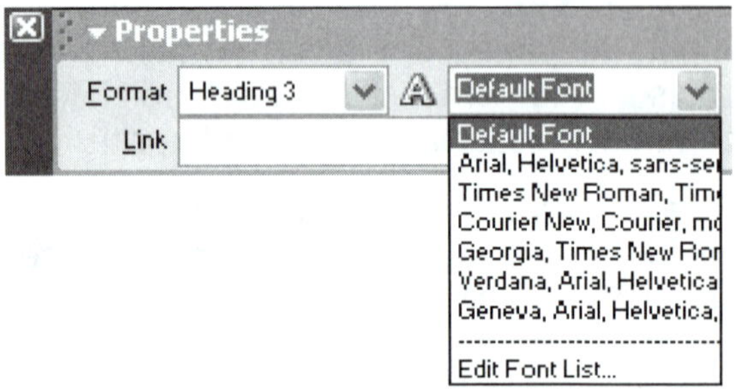

- To apply a new font combination to existing text, select the text first and then click the font list arrow on the Properties panel to display the available font combinations. Click a combination to apply it to the selected text.
- You can also apply a font combination before typing text. After the new combination is selected, all text you type will use that combination.

Add Fonts to the Font List

- By default, the Dreamweaver font list displays only a few popular fonts that display well in most browsers. You can, however, add fonts to the list using the Edit Font List option at the bottom of the Properties panel's font list (or click Text>Font>Edit Font List).

- When you issue this command, the Edit Font List dialog box opens (see illustration below), showing the current font list and the fonts available in your system's Font folder.

Edit Font List dialog box

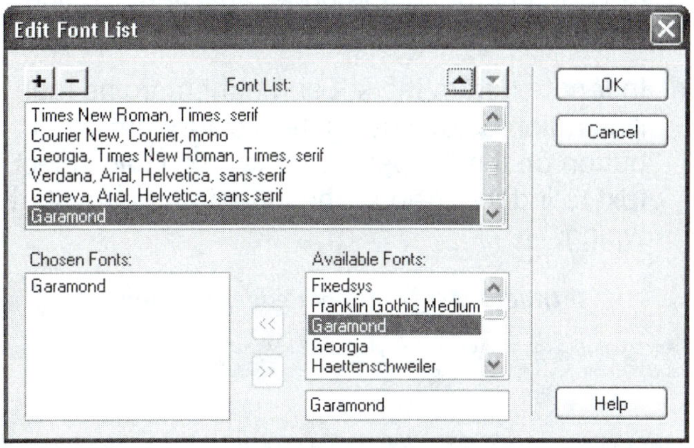

- Select a font from the Available Fonts list and click the << button to add it to the Chosen Fonts list. It will then be available in the font list of the Text menu and the Properties panel.

Apply Font Styles

- **Font styles** are changes to the appearance of a font. Font styles add emphasis to text so it stands out from surrounding text.
- Font styles used most often are **bold** and *italics*. You can easily apply bold or italic formatting (or both formats) to selected text using the Bold **B** or Italic *I* button on the Properties panel.
- These font styles can also be turned on before you type text. Click the appropriate button on the Properties panel and begin typing.

Change Font Size

- When used in a regular text document (such as a word processing document), font sizes are measured in **points**. (There are 72 points to a vertical inch.)
- Dreamweaver uses HTML font sizes rather than point sizes. HTML font sizes run from 1 to 7. The default size is 3, which equates to a regular font size of 12 points. The default font size is shown in the Properties panel as *None*.
- You can apply a different font size by selecting text and clicking the Size list arrow to display the list of HTML font sizes (see illustration below). Select a size from the list.

Choose new font size

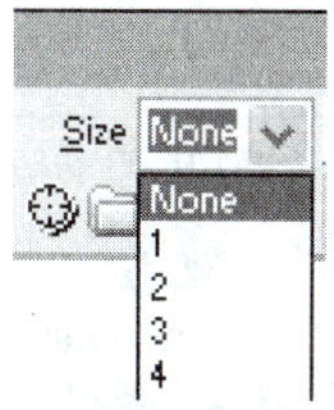

- You can also apply a new size before entering text. After you select the size, all text you type will use that size.
- The Size list on the Properties panel also includes relative font size measurements you can apply to selected text to increase or decrease the text size.
- Sizes marked with a + sign (such as +3) increase the font size by increments from the base font size (default is 3), no matter what size the text is currently. Sizes marked with a – sign (such as –2) decrease the font size by increments.
- If text is size 2, for example, applying the +2 relative font size increases the text size to 5 (not size 4), because the +2 is "added" to the default font size of 3.
- Relative font sizes can also be applied using the Text>Size Change command on the menu bar.

Note: *Many text formatting commands can also be used by selecting and right-clicking the desired text and clicking a formatting command in the shortcut menu.*

Apply Font Color

- The default text color in Dreamweaver is black. Black text provides the greatest contrast to most backgrounds and so is easiest for visitors to read.
- To add visual interest to a Web page, you can select a new color for text using the Properties panel.

- Click the Text Color button on the Properties panel to open a palette of colors that will display properly in a browser (see illustration below). Click on the desired color.

Select new font color in Dreamweaver

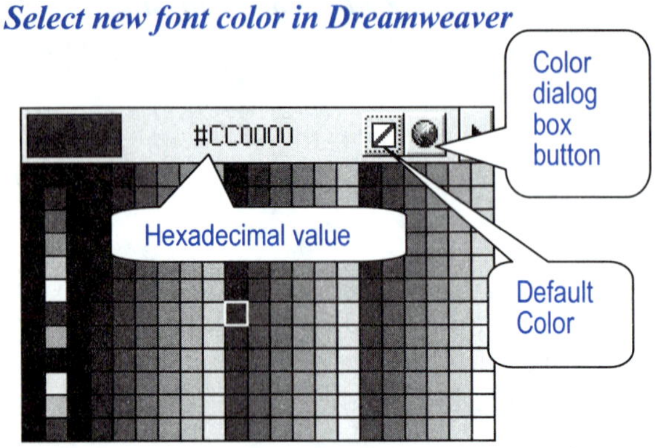

- Click the Default Color button to restore the page's default text color (usually black). You can change color palettes by clicking the right-pointing arrow in the palette and selecting a palette such as Continuous Tone.

Caution: *Only the default Color Cubes and Continuous Tone palettes are considered Web-safe; that is, colors selected from these palettes will display correctly in a browser.*

- Each color in the Text Color palette has a hexadecimal—six-digit number—value. If you know the hexadecimal value of a color, you can type it directly in the text box to the right of the Text Color button on the Properties panel.
- Custom colors can be "mixed" in the Color dialog box. However, it is best to use only Web-safe colors for creating your Web site, even though the latest browsers can support a vast array of color ranges.

Paragraph Alignment and Indention

- Text in a Dreamweaver document is left aligned by default. This means that the text lines up at the left margin of the page.
- You can change **alignment** to center text or right-align text using the Align Center or Align Right button on the Properties panel. Return text to left alignment using the Align Left button.
- Dreamweaver also supports justified text using the Justify button.
- Text that has been center aligned is spaced an equal distance from the left and right edges of the page. Right-aligned text lines up evenly at the right margin of the page. Justified text lines up evenly with both margins.
- Indent text from the left and right margins (see illustration below) using the Text Indent button on the Properties panel. You can select text to indent or apply the indent and then start typing.

Indent text from both edges of page

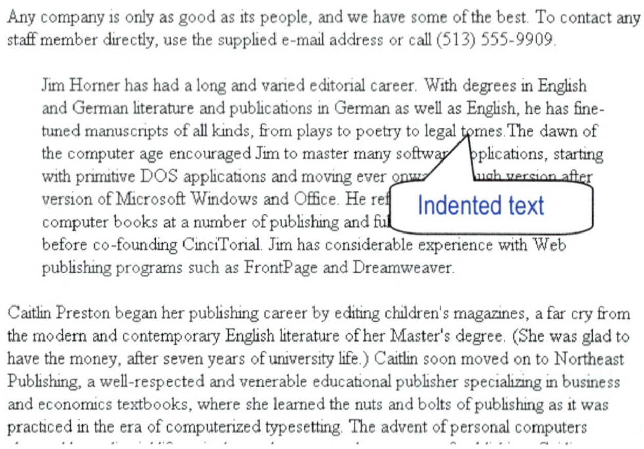
Any company is only as good as its people, and we have some of the best. To contact any staff member directly, use the supplied e-mail address or call (513) 555-9909.

Jim Horner has had a long and varied editorial career. With degrees in English and German literature and publications in German as well as English, he has fine-tuned manuscripts of all kinds, from plays to poetry to legal tomes. The dawn of the computer age encouraged Jim to master many softwa[...]pplications, starting with primitive DOS applications and moving ever onw[...]ugh version after version of Microsoft Windows and Office. He re[...] computer books at a number of publishing and fu[...] before co-founding CinciTorial. Jim has considerable experience with Web publishing programs such as FrontPage and Dreamweaver.

Caitlin Preston began her publishing career by editing children's magazines, a far cry from the modern and contemporary English literature of her Master's degree. (She was glad to have the money, after seven years of university life.) Caitlin soon moved on to Northeast Publishing, a well-respected and venerable educational publisher specializing in business and economics textbooks, where she learned the nuts and bolts of publishing as it was practiced in the era of computerized typesetting. The advent of personal computers

- Use the Text Outdent button on the Properties panel to return the insertion point or selected text to the page margins.

Use Paragraph and Heading Tags

- Text in a Dreamweaver document can be formatted with standard HTML paragraph and heading tags that control font style and size.
- By default, all new text is formatted with the Paragraph format. This format equates to the HTML <p> (Paragraph) tag. (Text that is indented is formatted with a <blockquote> tag.)
- You can use the Properties panel to apply other formats, including six levels of headings and the preformatted font that can be used to display program code (see illustration on next page).

Apply text formats with the Properties panel

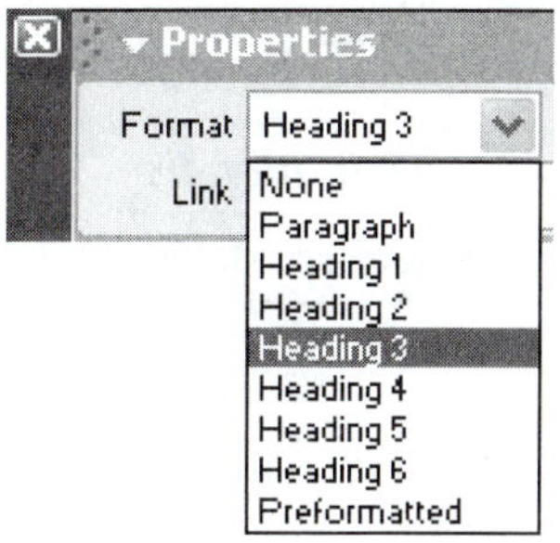

- Click anywhere in the paragraph to format and click the Format list arrow on the Properties panel to display the list of paragraph and heading formats. Or, choose the format and then begin typing to apply the format to new text.
- Heading levels are ordered from largest (Heading 1) to smallest (Heading 6). (See illustration below.)

HTML heading levels

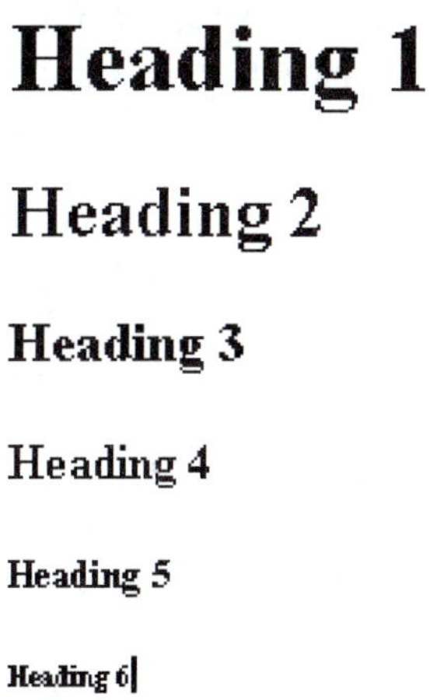

- The Properties panel will not show font sizes or styles for headings because these formats are specified by the HTML tag for that heading.

Create Lists

- Web pages often include lists to emphasize text items. You can create two types of lists using buttons on the Properties panel: **unordered lists** and **ordered lists** (see illustration at the top of the next column).

Unordered and ordered list in Web page

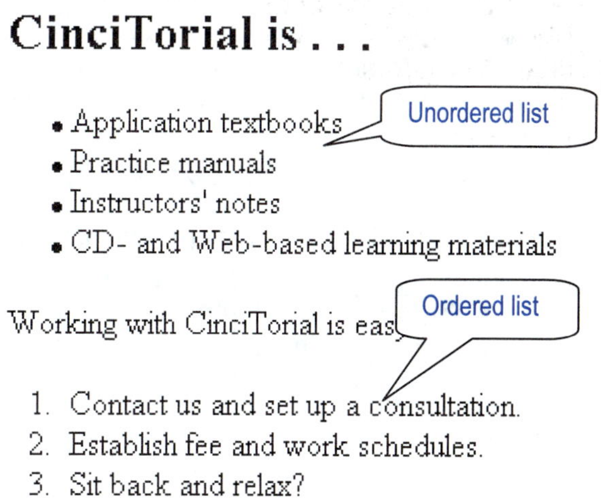

- Use the Unordered List button to create a list whose items do not have to be listed in a specific order. Each item begins with a small character called a **bullet**, so this type of list is often called a *bulleted list.*
- Use the Ordered List button to create a list whose items must be in a specific order. Each item begins with a number, so this list is sometimes called a *numbered list.*
- To apply either list format, click the appropriate button on the Properties panel. Dreamweaver automatically supplies the bullet or number.
- The unordered list is formatted using the HTML <ul> (Unordered List) tag. The ordered list is formatted using the HTML <ol> (Ordered List) tag. Each individual line is formatted using the <li> tag.

  Tip: *Remember, you can see—and select— the HTML tags for text you are working on by checking the left side of the Document window's status bar.*

- You can change the properties of ordered lists by clicking on a list item and using the Text>List>Properties command on the menu bar or clicking the List Item... button on the expanded Properties panel.

- Dreamweaver displays the List Properties dialog box (see illustration below). In this dialog box, you can change the number of the first list item (to start a list with the number 3, for example). You can also change the format of the list from the default numeric order to roman numerals or alphabetic order.

Change properties for ordered (numbered) list

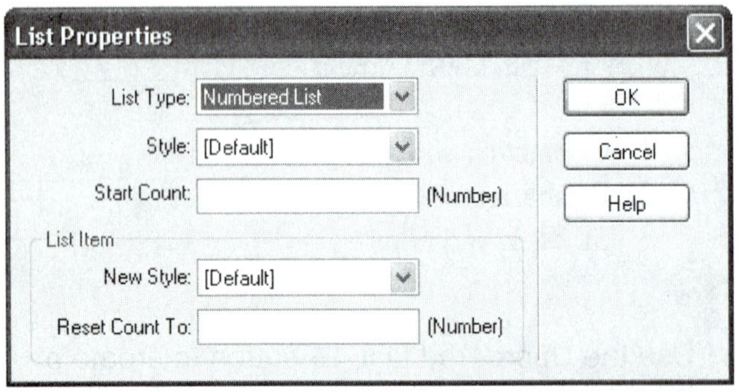

- Dreamweaver offers a third type of list called a **definition list** that you can create using the Text>List>Definition List command on the menu bar. A definition list consists of a term that is set on one line and its description, set on the next line (see illustration at the top of the next column).

- When you select the Definition List command, Dreamweaver applies the <dl> and <dt> (Definition Term) HTML tags.

Definition list

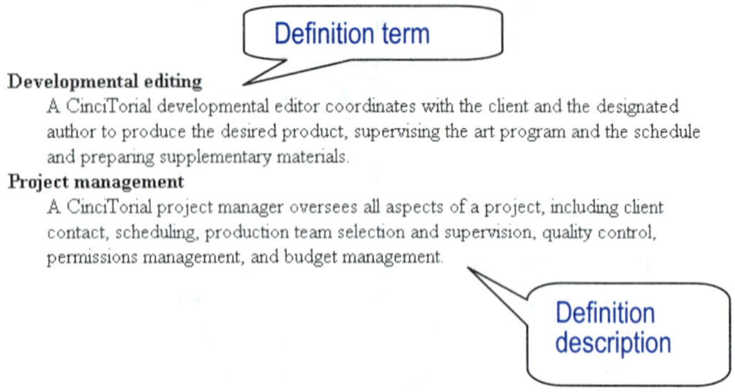

- After you have finished typing the term, press the Enter key. Dreamweaver automatically formats the next line with the <dd> (Definition Description) HTML tag, which indents the description below the term.

- Definition lists can be used for text other than strict terms and definitions. You can use this type of list to quickly create headings and indented text, a site map or table of contents, and so on.

Procedures

Insert Line Break

- Press Shift + Enter at end of line of text.

OR

- Click BR on the Characters tab in Insert bar.

Import Word HTML Text

1. Click **File** .... Alt+F
2. Click **Import** I
3. Click **Word HTML** .... W
4. Navigate in Select Word HTML File to Import dialog box to location where file is stored.
5. Click file name and click Open.
6. Click OK twice.
7. Save page in site and modify page title if necessary.

Insert Special Characters

1. Position insertion point at location where character should appear.
2. Display Characters tab in Insert bar.
3. Click or drag character to text.

✓ *A Dreamweaver message dialog box may appear, informing that certain characters may not appear in some browsers. Click **OK** to continue.*

4. Click (**Other Characters** button) to display other characters.

OR

1. Position insertion point at location where character should appear.
2. Click **Insert**................ Alt+I
3. **Special Characters**..... C, →
4. Choose desired character from submenu.................. ↓, Enter
5. Click **Other**......................... O to display other characters.

Check Spelling
Shift + F7

1. Click **Text** .... Alt+T
2. Click **Check Spelling**......... K
3. Review each flagged word:
   - Click Ignore or Ignore All to skip words.
   - Click Change or Change All to replace incorrect words with correct ones.

✓ *Click the **Add to Personal** button to add terms to your personal dictionary.*

Save Edits
Ctrl + S

1. Click **File** .... Alt+F
2. Click **Save** .... S

✓ *Asterisk following file name in title bar indicates changes have been made since last save.*

Select New Font Combination

Select text or position insertion point.

1. Click **Default Font** list arrow in Properties panel.
2. Select new font combination.

OR

1. Click **Text** .... Alt+T
2. Click **Font**.......................... N
3. Select new font combination on submenu.

Add Fonts to the Fonts List

1. Click **Text** .... Alt+T
2. Click **Font**.......................... N
3. Click **Edit Font List** .... E

OR
Click **Edit Font List** on Properties panel's font list

4. Choose font from **Available Fonts** list.
5. Click <<.

Apply Font Style

Select text or position insertion point.

- Click **B** (**Bold** button) on Properties panel to apply bold formatting.
- Click *I* (**Italic** button) on Properties panel to apply italic formatting.

OR

1. Click **Text** .... Alt+T
2. Click **Style**......................... S
   - Click **Bold** .... B
   - Click **Italic** I

✓ *Or click another font style on submenu.*

OR

- Press Ctrl+B for **bold**.
- Press Ctrl+I for *italic*.

Change Font Size

Select text or position insertion point.

1. Click **Size** list arrow in Properties panel.
2. Select new size.

OR

1. Click **Text** .... Alt+T
2. Click **Size** .... Z
3. Select size number on submenu.

OR

1. Click **Text** .... Alt+T
2. Click **Size Change** .... H
3. Select size number on submenu.

Apply Font Color

Select text or position insertion point where new font color should take effect.

1. Click (**Text Color** button) in Properties panel to display browser-safe color palette.
2. Click desired color in color palette.

OR

- Type exact hexadecimal value for color in text box to right of Text Color button.

OR

1. Click **Text** .... Alt+T
2. Click **Color** .... R
3. Select color or create color in Color dialog box.

Change Paragraph Alignment

Click in paragraph to align or position insertion point where new alignment should begin.

- Click (**Align Left** button) on Properties panel to left align text............. Ctrl+Alt+Shift+L
- Click (**Align Center** button) on Properties panel to center text............. Ctrl+Alt+Shift+C
- Click (**Align Right** button) on Properties panel to right align text............. Ctrl+Alt+Shift+R
- Click (**Justify** button) on Properties panel to justify text Ctrl+Alt+Shift+J
-

OR

1. Click **Text** .... Alt+T
2. Click **Align** .... A
   - Click **Left** L
   - Click **Center** C
   - Click **Right** .... R

Indent Paragraphs

Click in paragraph to indent or position insertion point where new indentation should begin.

- Click (**Text Indent** button) on Properties panel to indent............. Ctrl+Alt+]
- Click (**Text Outdent** button) on Properties panel to remove indent.................. Ctrl+Alt+[

OR

1. Click **Text** .... Alt+T
2. Click **Indent** I

   OR

   Click **Outdent** .... O

Apply Paragraph or Heading Tag

Click in paragraph to format or position insertion point where new format should begin.

1. Click **Format** list arrow in Properties panel.
2. Select heading level or paragraph format.

OR

1. Click **Text** .... Alt+T
2. Click **Paragraph Format** ... F
3. Select heading level or paragraph format on submenu.

Create Ordered and Unordered Lists

Select text to format or position insertion point where new format should begin.

1. Click **Text** .... Alt+T
2. Click **List** .... I, →
3. Click **Ordered List** .... O

   OR

   Unordered List .... U

OR

- Click (**Unordered List** button) on Properties panel.
- Click (**Ordered List** button) on Properties panel.

  ✓ *To remove unordered list or ordered list formatting, follow same steps.*

Change List Properties

1. Place the insertion point in the desired list.
   a. Click **Text** .... Alt+T
   b. Click **List** .... I, →
   c. Click **Properities** .... P

   OR

   - Click List Item... on the expanded Properties panel
2. Make the desired changes in the List Properties dialog box.
3. Click OK.

Create Definition List

1. Click **Text** .... Alt+T
2. Click **List** .... I, →
3. Click **Definition List** .... D
4. Type definition term.
5. Press Enter.
6. Type definition description.

Exercise Directions

1. Start Dreamweaver.
2. Open the **cincitorial** site.
3. Open **index.htm** if necessary and enter the text shown in Illustration A:
   - Create the unordered and ordered lists as shown.
   - Use the em dash special character in the *easy as 1—2—3* phrase.
4. Check your spelling and correct any errors you find.

   ✓ *You can add CinciTorial to your personal dictionary.*
5. Open **contactus.htm** and type **Contact CinciTorial** at the top of the page.
6. Apply the Heading 2 tag to the new text. Change its font combination to the one that begins with Georgia and change its color to a dark teal (such as #009999).
7. Save and close the page.
8. Activate **index.htm** if necessary and make the following formatting changes:
   - Apply the Heading 4 tag to *We build computer books*. Center the heading and change its color to a dark maroon (such as #990033).
   - Apply the Heading 1 tag to *Welcome to CinciTorial*. Change its font to the combination that begins with Georgia. Change its color to a dark blue (such as #000066).
   - Change the size of the paragraph *CinciTorial is . . .* to 4.
   - Justify the paragraph that begins *Let us put the pieces together . . .*
   - Italicize the paragraph that begins *See books we have produced* and center the paragraph.
   - Right-align the last paragraph on the page. Insert a line break after the second question mark to move the last sentence in the paragraph to a new line.
9. Import the Word HTML file **testimonials.htm** from the Data folder.
10. Clean up the Word HTML tags (accept default settings).
11. Save the imported page to your cincitorial folder as **testimonials.htm** with the page title **Client Praise**.

    ✓ *You may need to navigate back to the root folder in which your Web site files are stored.*
12. Format the **testimonials.htm** page as follows:
    - Format the *CinciTorial Clients Speak Out* heading the same way as the **contactus.htm** heading.
    - Position the insertion point just to the right of the name *Jay Fries* and press the **Delete** key to remove the paragraph return.
    - Insert a line break.
    - Repeat this procedure following the *Training Coordinator* paragraph, so that the name, title, and affiliation are grouped closely.
    - Replace paragraph returns with line breaks in the three remaining groups of names and affiliations on this page.
    - Scroll back up the page and select the three-line group that begins with *Jay Fries*.
    - Boldface the three lines and indent them.
    - Boldface and indent the remaining client names and affiliations.
13. Save and close any open pages.
14. Exit Dreamweaver.

Illustration A

We build computer books

Welcome to CinciTorial . . .

CinciTorial is

- Application textbooks
- Practice manuals
- Instructors' notes
- CD- and Web-based support materials

Working with CinciTorial is as easy as 1—2—3

1. Contact us and set up a consultation.
2. Establish fee and work schedules.
3. Sit back and relax!

Let us put the pieces together for you. Contact us today to learn how CinciTorial can help you get your computer books to market quickly, efficiently, and affordably.

Contact Us

Client Praise

History

Services

See books we have produced for Pearson Publishing at the Pearson Web site.

Questions? Comments on this site? Contact us with your queries and suggestions.

Chapter

4

Using Links and the Site Panel

Hyperlinks—or simply links—provide connections between Web pages that allow visitors to navigate your site. You can set links within a Web page, from page to page in a site, to an e-mail address, and from your site to other Web sites. Use the Site panel—collapsed and expanded—for site maintenance and to display the site map that shows how your pages are linked.

In this chapter, you'll learn how to:

- Create relative links
- Create absolute links
- Create and link to named anchors
- Create e-mail links
- Perform site maintenance tasks in the expanded Site panel
- View the site map
- Check links in a site

About Links

- Web sites rely heavily on hyperlinks or, simply, **links**. Links are the means by which visitors "jump" and "browse" from one location on a page to another, one page to another within a site, or one site to another.
- Links work by directing a browser to open a page at a specific World Wide Web address called a **URL (uniform resource locator)**. The URL www.cincitorial.com/, for example, would direct a browser to locate the site and open its home page on the cincitorial server on the World Wide Web (www)—or the server that hosts the cincitorial Web site, since one Web server can host more than one Web site.
- Links are generally formatted in such a way that they stand out from surrounding text so visitors can easily recognize them. They are usually in a different color and underlined.
- You can create four types of links in Dreamweaver:
    - Relative links—links from one page to another in the same site.
    - Absolute links—links from one site to another.
    - Named anchor links—links from one location on a page to another location on the same page.
    - E-mail links—links that open an e-mail program so a visitor can send a message to a Web site's e-mail address.

Create Links

- You can create a link using either text or a graphic. Type the text that will become the link or select existing text.

  Note: *You will learn how to use a graphic to create a link in Chapter 6.*

- Use the Properties panel's Link text box to set up a link. You can type the address of the page you want to link to directly in the Link text box or use the Browse for File button to the right of the Link text box to open the Select File dialog box for a list of your Web site pages from which to select.
- You can also use the Point to File icon on the Properties panel to point directly to a page you want to link to:
    - Select the text for the link and then click the Point to File icon on the Properties panel.
    - Drag the icon to an open page or to the file name in the Site panel (see illustration below).
- The Link box updates with the name of the page you point to. Release the mouse button to complete the operation.
- Another easy method to create a link is to select the text and right-click on it. Then click Make Link from the shortcut menu and select the desired file in the Select File dialog box.

  Tip: *Another method—like Point to File—is to select the text for the link and then hold down Shift and drag to the file name in the Site panel or to an open page that is not maximized.*

Use Point to File to point to file name to link to

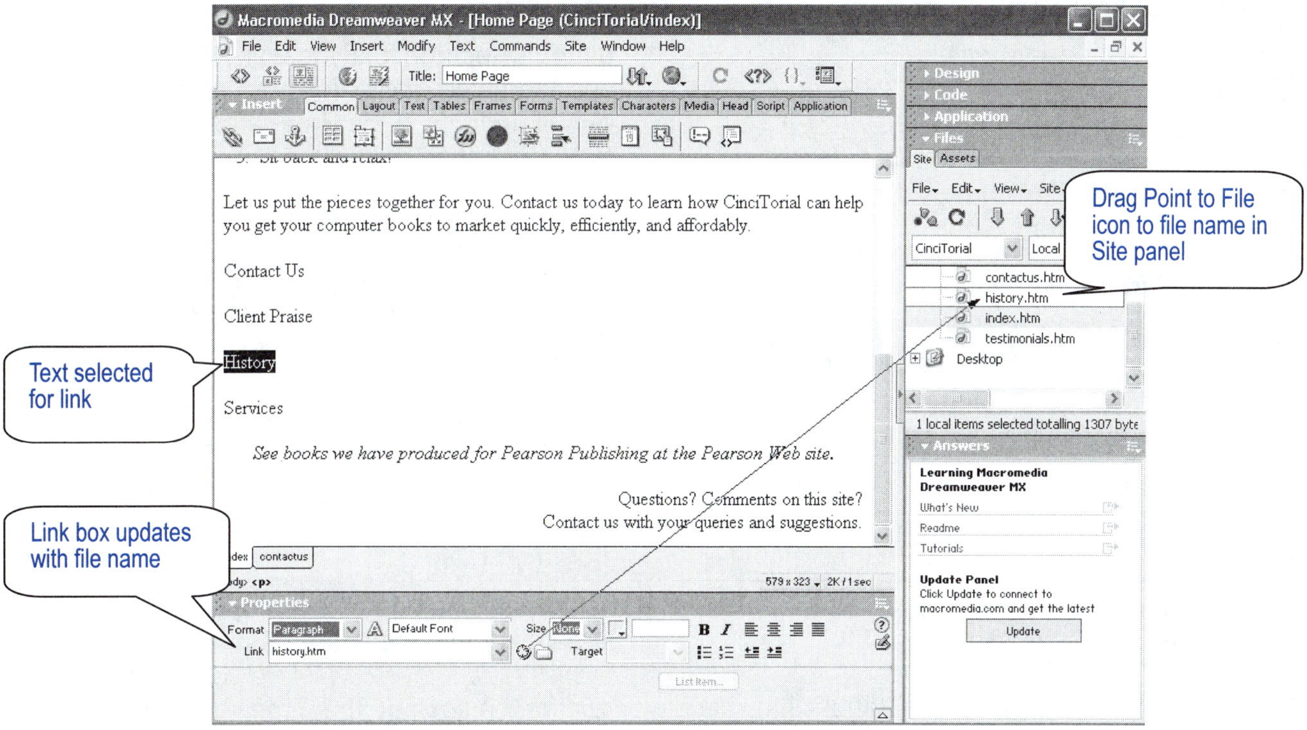

Relative Links

- A **relative link** is a link to a page within your Web site. Because pages in a Web site remain in the same locations relative to each other, you do not need to include the entire URL in the link address, only the actual page name.
- To create a relative link, select the text to be used for the link and type the name of the page to link to in the Link text box on the Properties panel (see illustration below). As soon as you complete the page name, Dreamweaver underlines and changes the color of the selected text to indicate it is a link. (You can also use the Point to File and right-click methods to make a relative link.)

Select text for link using Properties panel

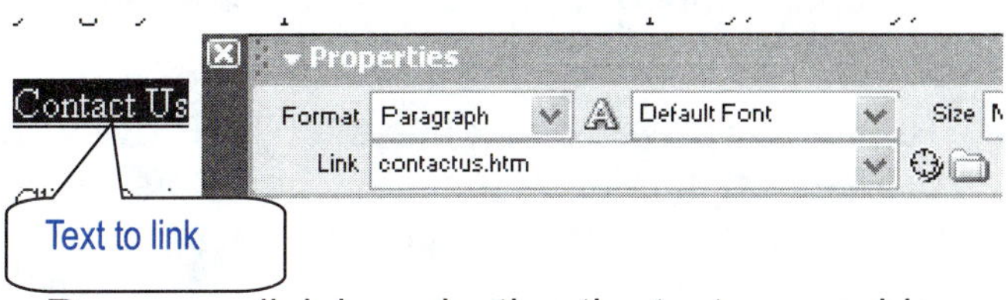

- Remove a link by selecting the text or graphic used as the link and clicking the Link list arrow on the Properties panel. On the list of links that displays, click in the blank area at the bottom of the list.
- You can also right-click a link and select Remove Link from the shortcut menu.

Absolute Links

- An **absolute link** takes a visitor from a page within your site to a different Web site. Because the browser must open a new Web site, it needs the full URL for the page it is to open.
- Create an absolute link by typing the URL in the Link text box in the Properties panel. You must include the proper protocol such as http:// or ftp://.

Link to Named Anchor

- A **named anchor**—also called a *bookmark*—is a specific location in a Web page (such as the top of the page). After you create a named anchor, you can set a link to it to help visitors navigate on a page.
- Create a named anchor by positioning the insertion point at the location for the anchor (or select text to use as the anchor). Then use the Insert>Named Anchor command on the menu bar to open the Insert Named Anchor dialog box.

- You can also insert a named anchor by clicking the Named Anchor button from the Common tab on the Insert bar.
- You can enter any name for the anchor (see illustration below). If you have selected text as the anchor, that text appears in the Anchor Name text box. You can change the displayed text if desired, however.

Insert name for anchor

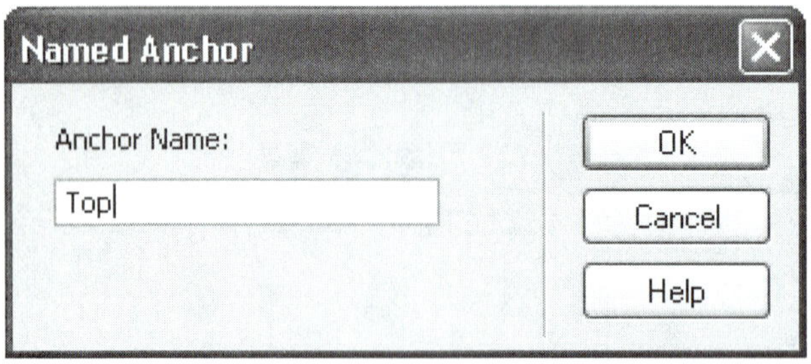

- Dreamweaver inserts an anchor marker at the location where you created the named anchor and the Properties panel changes to show the name of the anchor when it's selected.
- Create the link to the named anchor by selecting the text that will form the link and then typing a pound sign (#) followed by the anchor name in the Properties panel's Link box (see illustration below).

Note: *When you select text for the link, the Properties panel changes back to its default view.*

Named anchor link in Link box

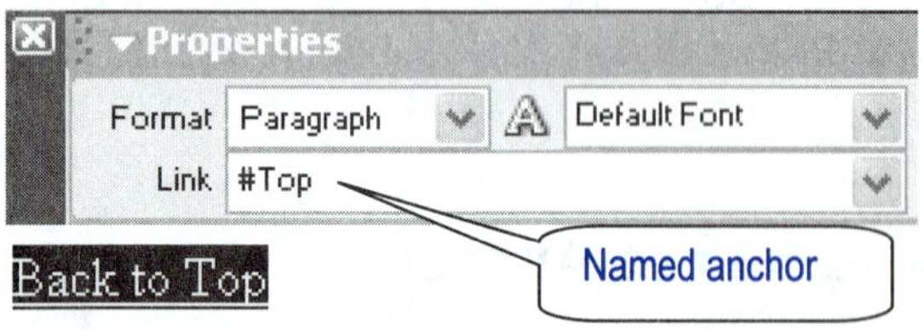

Link to E-Mail Address

- One of the most helpful items to place on your site is a link to an e-mail address where your site visitors can send you questions, feedback, suggestions—and complaints.
- When creating an e-mail link, you can type the link directly in the Link text box on the Properties panel, use a menu command, or click the E-mail Link object button on the Common tab to create the link.
- To type the e-mail link directly in the Properties panel, select the text you want to use as the link and then type mailto: followed by the designated e-mail address in the Properties panel's Link box (see illustration below).

Link to e-mail address

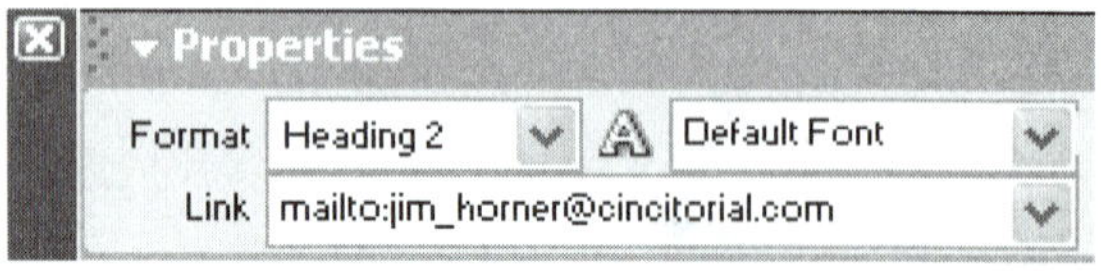

- You can also insert an e-mail link using the Insert>Email Link command on the menu bar or the Insert Email Link tool on the Insert bar's Common tab.
- When you use one of these options, Dreamweaver opens the EMail Link dialog box (see illustration below). Here you can type the text for the link and the e-mail address to link to.

Email Link dialog box

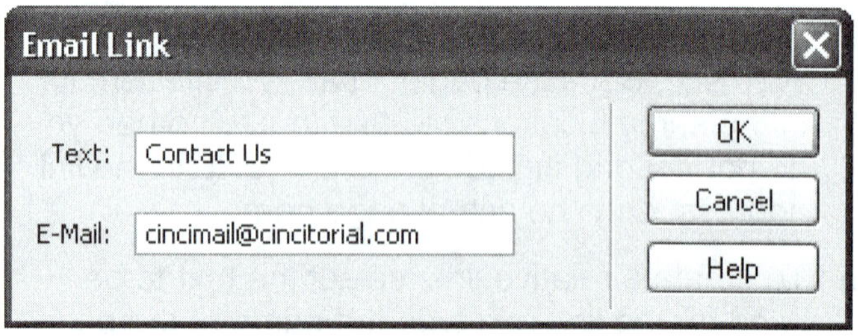

- When a visitor clicks an e-mail link in a Web page, the default e-mail program opens with the designated e-mail address already displayed in the To box.

Preview Site in Browser

- Links are not active in Dreamweaver's Document window. To test a link, you must preview a Web page in a browser.
- To preview a Web page, use the File>Preview in Browser command on the menu bar. You can select a browser from the pop-out submenu.
- You can also click the Preview/Debug in Browser button on the Document toolbar. Click the button to display a short menu of options for previewing or debugging the page in a browser.

- Each time you preview a page, Dreamweaver stores a temporary file in the testing server's folder for your Web site with a name such as TMP2lxva91m5f.htm in the URL that appears in your browser's address bar. These temporary files disappear when you close the page.

Working in the Site Panel

- The Site panel is an extremely important interface in the creation of a Dreamweaver Web site. The Site panel is one of two panels in the Files panel group in the panel group pane that is by default docked on the right side of the Dreamweaver window.

  Note: *The other panel, the Assets panel, may contain image files, URLs, Flash movies, and other "assets" you might use throughout your site. It is discussed in Chapters 7, 8, and 17.*

- The Site panel is designed to make it easy to perform maintenance operations such as creating new HTML documents, renaming files, creating folders, and deleting files. You can also view the Web site's navigation layout with a site map in the left pane.
- The Site panel is also where you set up and control the transfer of files between a local and remote site when publishing your site.
- If the Site panel does not automatically open with the Web site, you can open it from the Window menu. Choose either Site>Site Files or Site>Site Map.

Basic Site Panel Operations

- All files for the current Web site display in the Site panel's window—whether collapsed or expanded. You can work with these files in a number of ways.
  - Open a page from the list of site files by double-clicking the file name.
  - Add a new page to the site using the File>New File command on the Site panel's menu bar. Dreamweaver creates a blank page with a selected placeholder name that you can change by simply typing a new name.

    Caution: *If you are using an application server, the new page will be created with its particular file extension.*
  - Rename a file by clicking on its name twice, slowly, to select the name, or use the Site panel's File>Rename command. Once the file name is selected (see illustration below), just type the new name. You can also change the file type by typing a new file extension such as .htm in place of a ColdFusion page's .cfm.

Selected file name

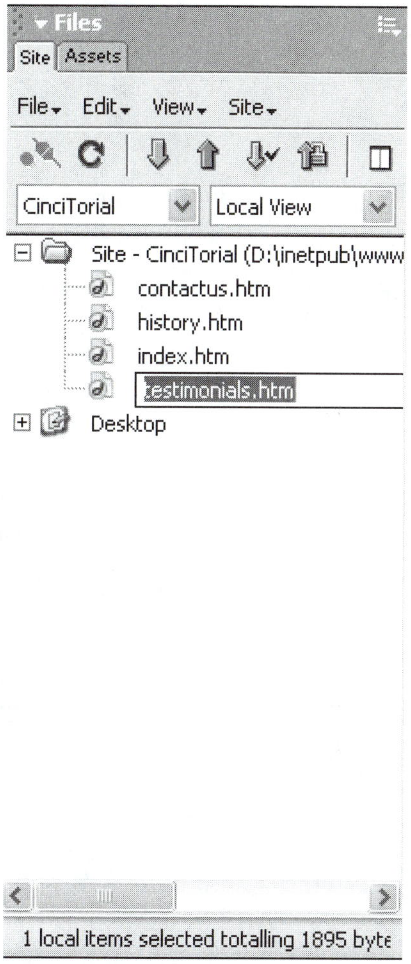

- Delete a file by clicking its icon to select all information about the file and pressing the Delete key (or use the Site panel's File>Delete command).

  Caution: *You cannot undo actions in the Site panel. But if you delete a file you didn't intend to, you can restore it from the Windows Recycle Bin.*

- If you rename a file that is linked to other pages in a Web site, Dreamweaver will ask if you want to update links with the new page name (see illustration at top of next column).

- You will generally want to click the Update button and allow Dreamweaver to update the links for you.

Update links when renaming pages

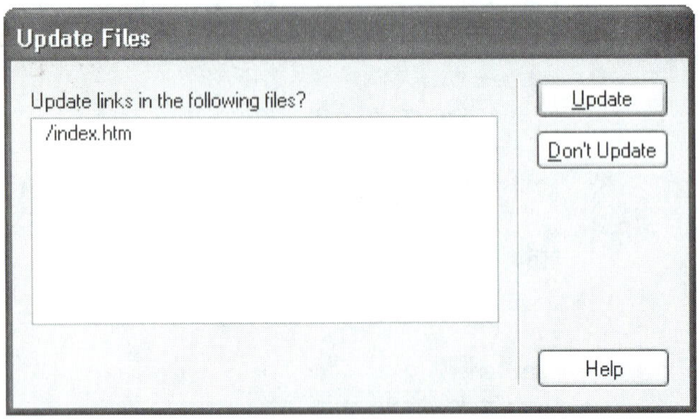

- Dreamweaver will also caution you if you delete a page that is linked to other pages in the site (see illustration in next column).

Dreamweaver warns about deleting a linked page

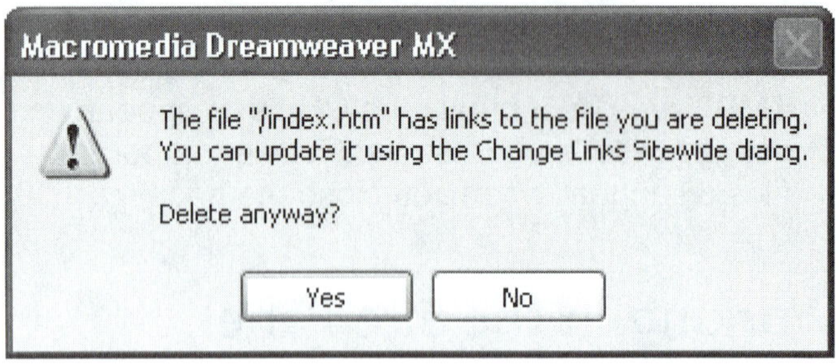

- Deleting a linked page results in a **broken link**. You will learn about ways to locate and repair broken links in Chapter 17.

View the Site Map

- The site map enables you to view your file structure as a graphic representation (see illustration at the bottom of the page).
- To view the Site Map in either the collapsed or expanded Site panel, click View>Site Map in the Site panel menu.

Site map in the expanded Site panel

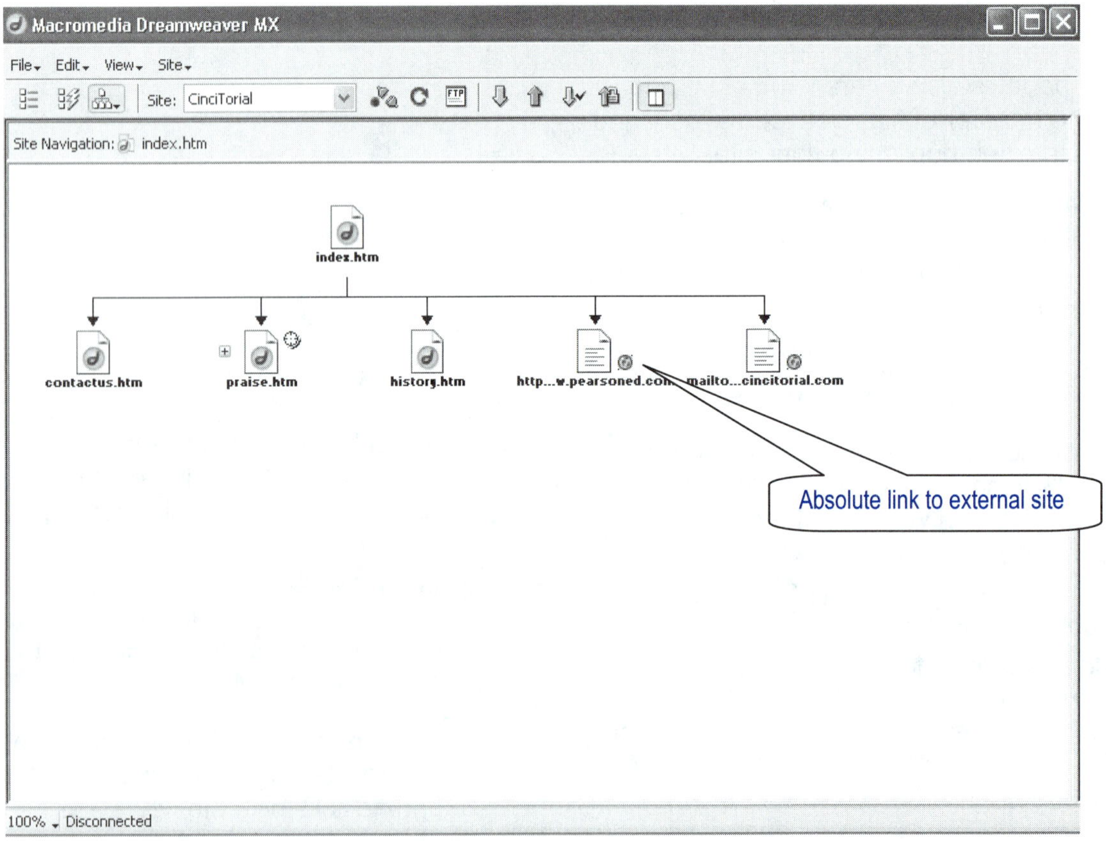

- Each page in the site is represented by a page icon with the page's name (or title) shown below the icon.
- Organization-chart type lines show the relative links between the home page and its subordinate, or *child,* pages.
- Recall from Chapter 2 that you display the site map within the expanded Site panel by clicking the Site Map button and selecting either Map Only or Map and Files.
- The page designated as the home page is at the top of the site map. Pages linked to the home page display below the home page. The site map structure also shows absolute and e-mail links on the home page.
- Child pages that contain links display a plus sign ⊞. Click this symbol to expand the site map and show links from the child page. After you click the plus sign, it becomes a minus sign ⊟ you can click to collapse the portion of the site map under the current page.
- The site map can help you eliminate problems in your Web site such as broken links. The page name or title of a page with a broken link displays in red, with a broken link symbol above the name (see illustration below).

Page with broken link

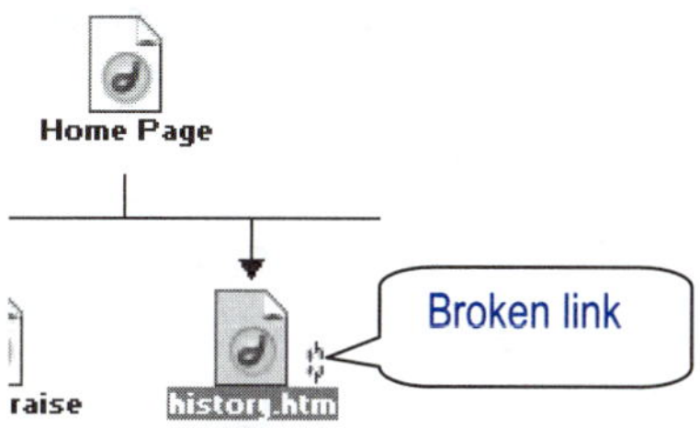

- If you delete a linked page from the Local Files pane of the Site panel, the page remains in the site map, displaying the broken link symbol until you remove it by selecting it and choosing the Site>Remove Link command on the Site panel menu bar.
- Modify the site map layout using one of the Site Definition wizard's screens on its Advanced tab. Use the Site>Edit Sites command on either the Dreamweaver menu bar or the Site panel menu bar. This opens the Edit Sites dialog box. Select the desired site to edit and click the Edit button.
- Click the Advanced tab and select the Site Map Layout category in the Site Definition dialog box (see illustration below).

Change site map layout

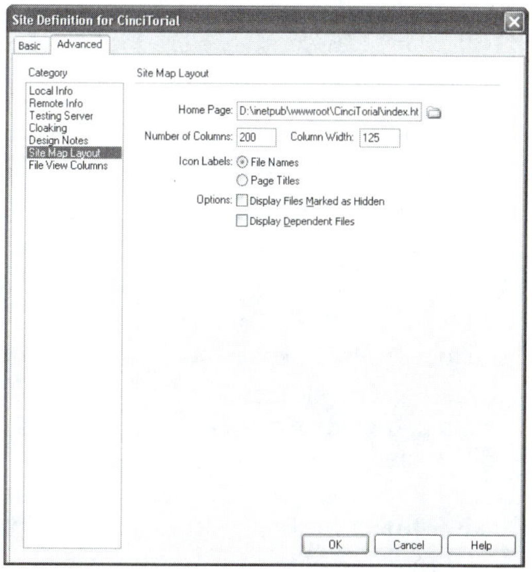

Caution: *You may get an error message if you try to click the Basic tab when you are in the edit site mode.*

- You can make the following adjustments to the layout:
  - Change the number of columns from the default value of 200. Columns equate to the number of pages displayed below the home page.
  - Change the column width from the default value of 125. Column width is the amount of space taken up by each page displayed in the site map. You must enter a value between 70 and 1000 for this option.
  - Change the label for the pages from the default of the file name to the page title. For example, you can change the label of the top-level page from index.htm to Home Page.
  - Choose to display files that are normally hidden or dependent files such as a page's images.
- You can also make these label and display changes from the View menu in the Site panel menu.

Procedures

Create Relative Link

Ctrl + L

1. Select text or graphic for link.
2. Type page address in Link text box on Properties panel.

   OR

   - Click (**Browse for File** button) on Properties panel and navigate to page.
   - Click page and click OK.

   OR

   - Click (**Point to File** button) on Properties panel.
   - Drag Point to File icon to open page or to file name in Site panel.

Create Absolute Link

1. Select text or graphic to act as link.
2. Type complete URL in Link text box on Properties panel.

   ✓ *You must include a protocol such as http:// or ftp://.*

Create Named Anchor

Ctrl + Alt + A

1. Position insertion point at location for anchor, or select text for anchor.
2. Click **Insert** .... Alt + I
3. Click **Named Anchor** .... N, N, Enter

   OR

   Click or drag (**Named Anchor** button) on Common tab of Insert bar.
4. Type name for anchor in Named Anchor dialog box.

Link to Anchor

1. Select text or graphic to act as link.
2. Type **#** followed by anchor name in Link text box on Properties panel.

Link to E-Mail Address

1. Select text or graphic to act as link.
2. Type **mailto:** followed by e-mail address in Link text box on Properties panel.

OR

1. Click **Insert** .... Alt + I
2. Click **Email Link** L

   OR

   Click or drag **Email Link** button on the Common tab of the Insert bar.
3. Type text to act as link in Text box of Email Link dialog box.
4. Type e-mail address in Email box.

Preview Site in Browser

F12

1. Click **File** .... Alt + F
2. Click **Preview in Browser** .... P, P, →
3. Select browser from submenu.

   OR

   Click (**Preview/Debug in Browser** button) on Document toolbar and select browser from menu.

Site Panel Operations

- Double-click file name to open page in Document window.
- Rename file:
  - Click file name twice, slowly in the Site Panel pane, to select and then type new name (and file type if necessary).

  OR

  a. Click **File** in the Site panel menu.

  b. Click **Rename.**

  OR

  - Right-click the file and select **Rename** from the shortcut menu.

  c. If renamed page is linked to other pages, click Update to update links.
- Delete file (***Del***):
  - Click file once to select and press Delete key.

  OR

  a. Click **File.**

  b. Click **Delete.**

  OR

  - Right-click the file and select **Delete** from the shortcut menu.

  c. If deleted page is linked to other pages, click Yes to delete.

  d. Click deleted page icon in site map.

  e. Click **Site.**

  f. Click **Remove Link.**

Modify Site Map Layout

1. Click **Site.** .... Alt + S
2. Click **Edit Sites** .... E, E, Enter
3. Select site name in Edit Sites dialog box and click Edit... .
4. Click **Site Map Layout** category.
5. Change **Number of Columns** or **Column Width** value.
6. Specify **File Names** or **Page Titles**.
7. Choose to display hidden files and/or dependent files.

Exercise Directions

1. Start Dreamweaver.
2. Open the **CinciTorial** site.
3. Open **testimonials.htm**.
4. Create an anchor named **Top** to the left of the main heading on this page.
5. Link the *Back to Top* text at the bottom of this page to the Top named anchor.
6. Save and close the page.
7. Open the **index.htm** page.
8. Create relative links from the *Contact Us* paragraph to **contactus.htm**, *Client Praise* to **testimonials.htm**, and from *History* to **history.htm**.
9. Create an absolute link to the Pearson Education Web site (http://www.pearsoned.com/) using the words *Pearson Web site* in the italicized paragraph.
10. Select the words *Contact us* in the last line on the page and use them to create an e-mail link to the e-mail address **cincimail@cincitorial.com**.
11. Save changes to this page and preview it in your default browser. The bottom of the page should look similar to Illustration A.
12. Test the links on the Home Page. Use the browser's Back button as necessary to return to the Home Page.

    ✓ *Click the e-mail link to see how it opens your e-mail program, but do not send a message.*

13. Test the link to the named anchor on the Client Praise page.
14. Close the browser.
15. Open the Site panel, if necessary.
16. Rename the **testimonials.htm** file to **praise.htm**. Update links when Dreamweaver prompts you to do so.
17. Expand the Site panel and select to display the entire site map.
18. Modify the site map layout to set 15 columns and a column width of 90. Choose to show page titles rather than file names.
19. Show both the site files and site map in the expanded Site panel.
20. You have decided you do not need a history page in the Web site. Delete the **history.htm** page in the Local Files pane and answer **Yes** when asked if you really want to delete it.
21. Remove the History page link in the site map.
22. Collapse the Site panel.
23. Open the **index.htm** page from the Site panel and remove the *History* link text from the text on this page. Notice that it is no longer underlined. (Also remove the blank line that remains after you delete the text.)
24. Save and close any open pages.
25. Exit Dreamweaver.

Illustration A

Let us put the pieces together for you. Contact us today to learn how CinciTorial can help you get your computer books to market quickly, efficiently, and affordably.

Contact Us

Client Praise

History

Services

See books we have produced for Pearson Publishing at the Pearson Web site.

Questions? Comments on this site?
Contact us with your queries and suggestions.

Chapter

5

Code Views and Panels

Dreamweaver's Web design tools make it unnecessary for users to work directly in HTML and other Web page programming code. However, you should know how to use Dreamweaver's Code View tools to modify, change, replace, or troubleshoot the tags that make up your site. As you perform tasks in Dreamweaver, the Code panel group and History panel can be used to speed up various code-related tasks.

In this chapter, you'll learn how to:

- Recognize HTML document structure
- Create HTML tags
- Use common HTML tags
- Use the Code views to enter and edit text
- Clean up HTML coding
- Add keywords to a Web site
- Insert a date
- Use the History panel

What Is HTML?

- **HTML (Hypertext Markup Language)** is the scripting language—or code—used to create text that can be viewed with a Web browser. Nearly every item on a Web page—including text, formatting, pictures, and other page elements—is controlled by HTML coding.

Note: *In addition to HTML coding, Web pages may also incorporate .XHTML (.xml), Java scripts, ColdFusion's CFML code, ActiveX, and other specialized Web page coding designed for different kinds of dynamic or interactive application and content. These codes, too, can be applied and edited in Dreamweaver.*

- The value of using a program such as Dreamweaver is that you do not have to know and apply HTML codes to create great HTML effects. Dreamweaver automatically applies the correct HTML codes as you select features from its menus and panels.
- You may find, however, as you become more proficient with Dreamweaver, that you need to "tweak" the HTML codes for a specific page element. You may also want to add tags not supplied by Dreamweaver—and, as you will find out, the natural language used by HTML is fairly easy for you to "interpret."
- Dreamweaver's various code view options make it easy for you to work directly with a page's HTML code. Before you learn how to use these tools, you will learn some basic information about HTML documents and tags.

HTML Document Structure

- HTML documents have a standard structure that consists of two sections: a Head section and a Body section.
- The **Head** section contains information that browsers need to display the Web page, such as the page title and the character set used to create the page (see illustration below; note that the right panel group pane is collapsed to maximize the Document window's view). None of the information in the Head section appears in the browser except the page title, which displays in the browser's title bar.
- The Body section contains the actual Web page content, such as the page's headings (see illustration below), paragraphs, and pictures.

Head and Body sections in source code of Web page

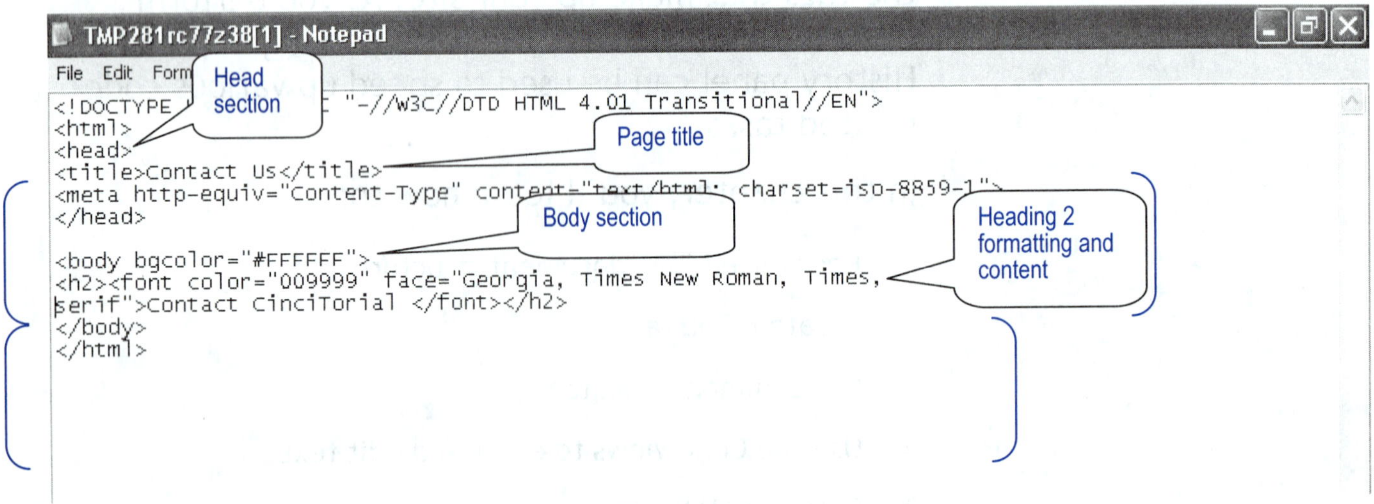

HTML Tags

- HTML coding instructions are delivered to the browser by means of **HTML tags**. As you can see in the illustration above, HTML tags have a specific structure, or **syntax**:
  - The first part of an HTML tag is the left **wicket** (<).
  - Next is the tag **element**, or name, such as title.
  - Tag **attributes** may follow the tag element. For example, the bgcolor="#FFFFFF" information that follows the body tag in the illustration above is the attribute that controls background color for the page.
  - Last is the right wicket (>).

Note: *HTML tags may be written with all capital letters or all lowercase letters. Dreamweaver's tags are all lowercase, so that convention will be used in this book.*

- Most HTML codes require both an **opening tag** and a **closing tag**. The opening tag instructs the browser to begin displaying a format or feature. For example: <title>.
- The closing tag usually has the same syntax as an opening tag, but also contains a **closing switch** (/) before the tag element. For example: </title>.
- Text that appears between an opening tag and a closing tag is affected by that tag. For example, in the following HTML code, the <h2> (Heading 2) formatting is applied to a heading:

```
<h2>Welcome to CinciTorial</h2>
```

- Tags may be **nested** to supply additional formatting to text. For example, in the following HTML code, the word *also* will appear in italics in the paragraph:

```
<p>We <i>also</i> offer three kinds of
chocolate truffles.</p>
```

Caution: *Don't forget the closing switch when nesting tags, or applied formats will not be "turned off."*

- Some HTML tags are **one-sided tags** (also called *standalone* or *empty tags*). One-sided tags do not require a closing tag. The
 (line break) tag is a one-sided tag.

Attributes and Values

- Tag attributes modify a tag element by supplying additional instructions to the browser about how to display an element.
- Attributes appear within HTML tags, usually between the tag element and the right wicket. Attributes often include **values** to supply the specific instructions to the browser. Attribute values are usually enclosed in quotation marks.
- Typically, attributes are not repeated in the closing tag.
- In the HTML code below, for example, the tag element is font. The size attribute tells the browser to display a specific size. "4" is the value, the exact size the browser should display.

```
<font size="4">
```

Common HTML Tags

- There are dozens of HTML tags and attributes that can be used to create sophisticated effects on Web pages. The table on the following page lists a few of the most common tags.

Tag(s)	Result
<html> </html>	Sets the page as an HTML document so that its code can be interpreted by the browser software.
<head> </head>	Begins and ends the section that contains information on content, language, and keywords for the page.
<title> </title>	Encloses the Web page's page title. In a browser, the page's title appears in the browser's title bar.
<meta>	Records information about the current page and supplies information such as keywords that search engines use to identify your page.
<body> </body>	Defines the section of the Web page that displays in a browser.
<p> </p>	Begins and ends a paragraph on the Web page.
 	Inserts a line break. (Does not require a closing tag.)
<h1> </h1>	Defines the first heading level (Heading 1). Use the same syntax for other heading levels, such as <h2> </h2>, <h3> </h3>, etc.
<b> </b>	Turns on and off bold formatting. Use the same syntax for font styles such as italics: <i> </i>, etc.
<font> </font>	Changes the font of text between the tags; requires an attribute to identify the new font.
<align> </align>	Changes the alignment of text between the tags; requires an attribute such as right to specify exact alignment.
<ol> </ol>	Begins and ends an ordered (numbered) list.
<ul> </ul>	Begins and ends an unordered (bulleted) list.
<li> </li>	Identifies each item in an ordered or unordered list.
<dl> </dl>	Begins and ends a definition list.
<a> </a>	Identifies a hyperlink; requires the href attribute and a value to specify target of link.
<img> </img>	Indicates location of a picture in a Web page.

Use the Code View Options

- Dreamweaver provides a number of ways to view HTML code on a page for those who prefer to write or edit HTML code. You can use Code view to display code right in the Document window, use the Code inspector to view code in a separate window, and take advantage of tools that help you understand and use HTML.

Note: *The Code inspector is discussed later in this chapter.*

Use Code View

- By default, the Document window displays page content in **Design view**. In Design view, content looks almost identical to the way it will display in a browser.
- When you switch to **Code view**, the page content's HTML coding displays (see illustration on next page). Code view allows you to write or edit HTML code in the full Document window.

Page shown in Code view

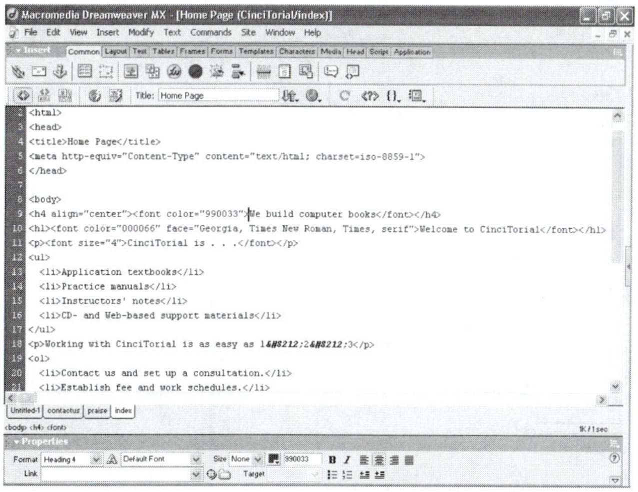

- Switch to Code view using the View>Code command on the menu bar, or simply click the Show Code View button at the far left of the Document toolbar.

Note: *Be sure to select the Show Code View button, not the Reference button, which looks similar.*

- When you have finished working in Code view, use the View>Design command or the Show Design view button to restore Design view.
- Dreamweaver also allows you to display both views in the Document window at the same time so you can see immediately the results of your coding. Use the View>Code and Design command on the menu bar or the Show Code and Design Views button to turn on a display like the one shown in the illustration.

Display both Code and Design views

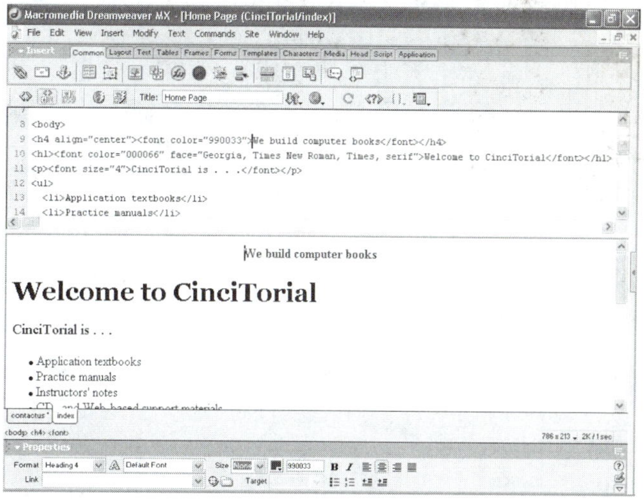

- By default, Code view appears at the top of the window. You can move Design view to the top using the View>Design View on Top command on the menu bar. Or, click the View Options button on the right side of the Document toolbar and select Design View on Top.

Use the Code Inspector

- Dreamweaver **Code inspector** is for viewing the HTML code for a page's content. It allows you to view HTML code in a floating window and is typically used with Design view.
- Use the Window>Others>Code Inspector command on the menu bar to open the Code inspector, or press F10.
- The Code inspector displays the HTML code of the current page (see illustration at the bottom of the page). To work directly in the Code inspector, click in it.
- You can drag the lower-right corner to increase the inspector's window size. Click the View Options button in the Code inspector to display a menu of options for displaying the code. Selecting the Word Wrap option from this menu causes code to wrap within the window so you do not have to scroll to the right to see line endings.

Code inspector

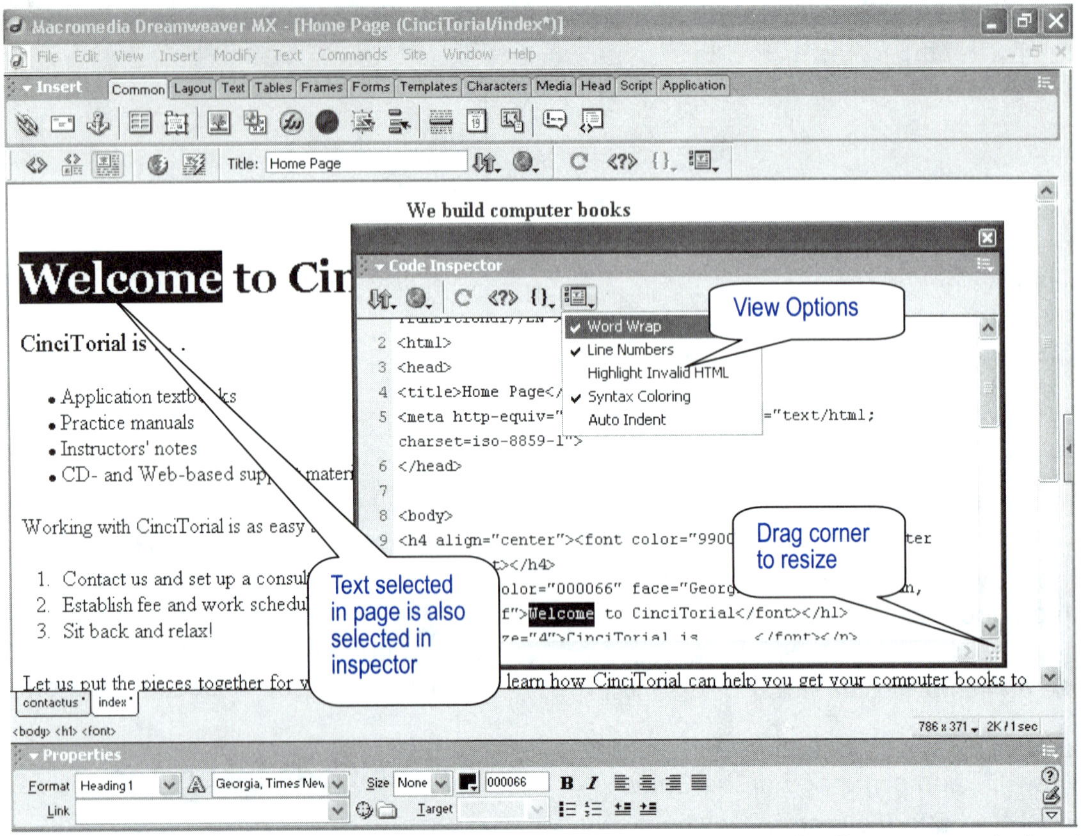

- By default, the Line Numbers view option to display a number next to each line of code is selected—as it is selected in other code view options. Line numbers assist in tracking your position in the text. Select the Auto Indent view option to automatically indent lines of code for a neat appearance.
- The Syntax Coloring view option displays HTML tags and attributes in dark blue so you can easily distinguish them from text. This option, too, is selected by default in the other code views.

  Note: *You can adjust Code inspector display settings using the Edit>Preferences command on the menu bar by selecting the Code Coloring category.*

- Enter text in the Code inspector just as you would in the Document window by typing necessary HTML codes and text. You can also edit text or codes in the inspector by inserting or deleting existing material.
- Changes made to tags in the Code inspector do not appear in the Document window until you activate the Document window by clicking in it.
- The Highlight Invalid HTML view option helps you identify mistakes in your HTML code. If you make a mistake in coding in the Code inspector, it highlights your error in the code (see illustration below). If you want errors in the code highlighted in the Document window when you are in Code view, select the Highlight Invalid HTML option in the View Options button menu on the Document toolbar. You can then easily find and fix errors in code.

Dreamweaver highlights error in code

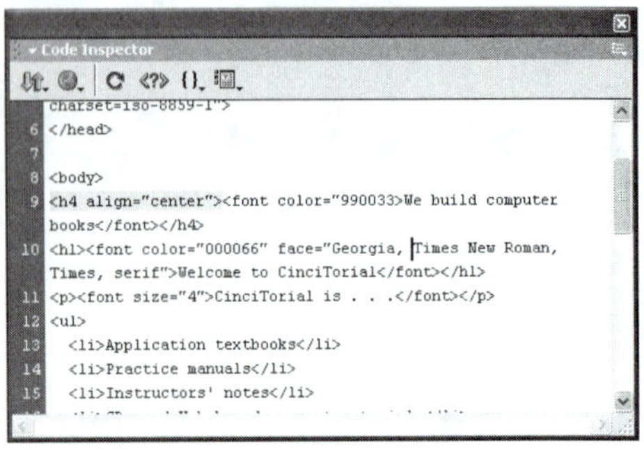

Tip: Dreamweaver provides a brief explanation of why the markup code is invalid in the Properties panel.

Code Panel Group

- The Code panel group contains three panels used to edit or write HTML code: The Tag inspector, Snippets panel, and the Reference panel.

Tag Inspector

- The **Tag inspector** contains two panes. The top one shows a map of the tags used in the Web page that is currently open in Dreamweaver. The lower pane is a property sheet. When you select a particular tag, which can be selected in the Document window or in the Tag inspector, the property sheet displays the **attributes** that it supports (see illustration). An attribute can be alignment, font color, and virtually any other kind of characteristic that can be formatted.

Tag inspector with a Font tag and its color attribute selected

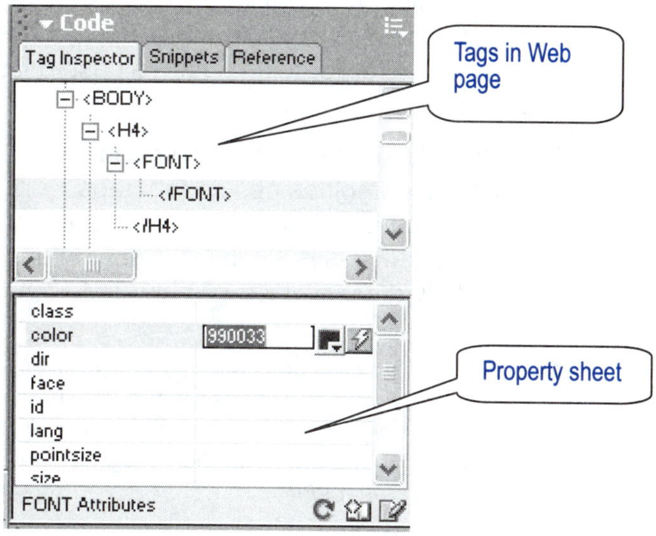

- If the tag supports an attribute, listed in the left column of the property sheet, its current value will be listed in the right column. By clicking the arrow next to the value, you can display a drop-down list and change the value directly in the property sheet.

Snippets Panel

- **Snippets** are predefined HTML forms, tables, menus for selecting month and year (handy for credit card order forms), Javascript computing the area of a circle and other shapes, headers, footers, navigation bars, and other complex and/or commonly used code objects that can be selected and inserted using the Insert button or dragged directly into your Web page (see illustration).

Snippets panel

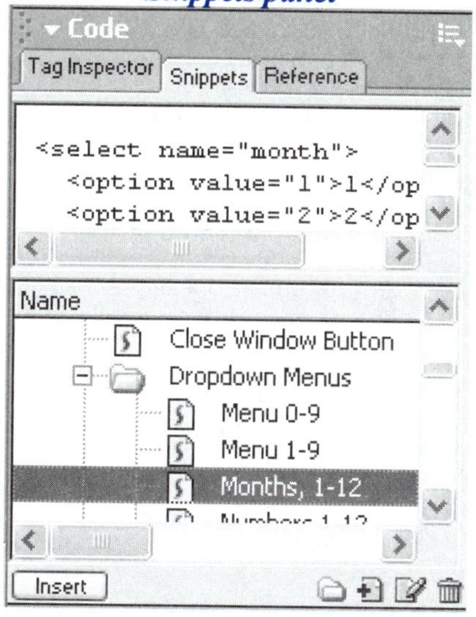

- The Snippets panel is divided into two panes. When you select a snippet in the Snippets panel file tree in the lower pane, the upper pane reveals the snippet's code.
- Dreamweaver contains many predefined snippets that you can use as a starting point to customize as you desire.

Reference Panel

- The **Reference panel** (see illustration on r page) is used to find information on HT' tags, CSS (cascading style sheets)' JavaScript objects.

Tip: To more easily read the P undock it and enlarge group panel as de

Reference panel

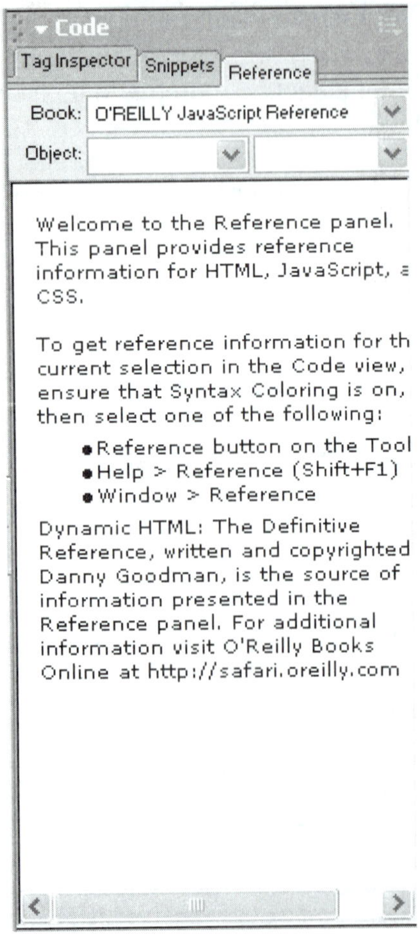

- To get help on a specific HTML tag (or other object), select the tag or object and use the Window>Reference command on the menu bar or click the Reference button on the Document toolbar or Code inspector toolbar.

  Note: *The Reference panel's content is provided by O'Reilly & Associates.*

- Use the two list boxes in the Reference panel to locate the tag or object and its properties and methods for which you want information. The Reference panel provides proper syntax and other important information about the item.

  You can also click in any HTML tag in Code view with the Reference panel open and click again to see information on that tag.

...lay Head Content

...r way to display HTML information for a ...to display the contents of its Head ...ght in the Document window.

- Use the View>Head Content command on the menu bar to open a pane at the top of the current page with icons representing each HTML tag in the Head section (see illustration below). Click an icon to see information about that tag in the Properties panel.

Display Head content in page

- You can also display head content by clicking the View Options button on the Document toolbar and selecting Head Content from the resulting menu.

Clean Up HTML Code

- One of Dreamweaver's most useful HTML tools is the Clean Up HTML command you can find on the Commands menu. Use this command on your own files, for pages created by other authors that you want to incorporate in your Web site, or for text you have pasted from another source.

- The Clean Up HTML command removes empty tags, combines nested font tags, and otherwise improves messy HTML coding on a page. This process is similar to cleaning up Word HTML codes, which you learned about in Chapter 3.

  Note: *The Commands>Clean Up Word HTML menu command is used when you insert text copied from a Word HTML page or if a Word HTML page has been copied into your Web folder.*

- When you issue the command, you can select specific items to clean up in the Clean Up HTML dialog box (see illustration at the top of the next page). Use the Specific Tag(s) box to type specific tag names you want Dreamweaver to clean up.

  Note: *Do not type wickets when entering specific codes. Type only the tag name.*

Specify codes to clean up

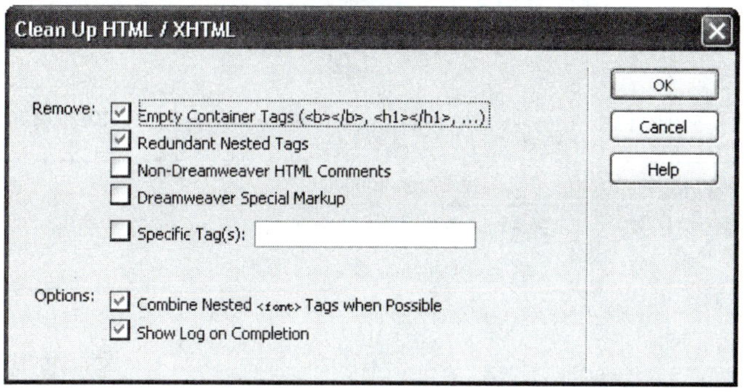

Add Keywords to a Web Site

- To make sure many visitors locate your site, you can supply **keywords** that search engines use to index a site in their databases. You add keywords to a site using the <meta> tag.
- Dreamweaver makes it very simple for you to add the <meta> tag containing keywords to your home page. Click the Head tab in the Insert bar and click the Insert Keywords  button.
- Dreamweaver opens the Insert Keywords dialog box (see illustration below). Here you can type the keywords that summarize your site's subject.

Insert keywords

- Separate groups of keywords with commas, and use care when selecting them. Some search engines accept only a specific number of keywords and ignore keywords altogether if too many are supplied.
- Clicking the OK button in the Insert Keywords dialog box inserts the keywords as a value for a new <meta> tag in the Head section of the Web page.

Inserting Code with Code Hints

- To speed typing code, Dreamweaver has two Code Hints features. When you type an opening wicket, a Code Hints list box appears in the code view that you are using. You can use the Code Hints as a visual reference or you can double-click on the desired beginning code and it will automatically be placed in your Web page (see illustration).

Code Hints

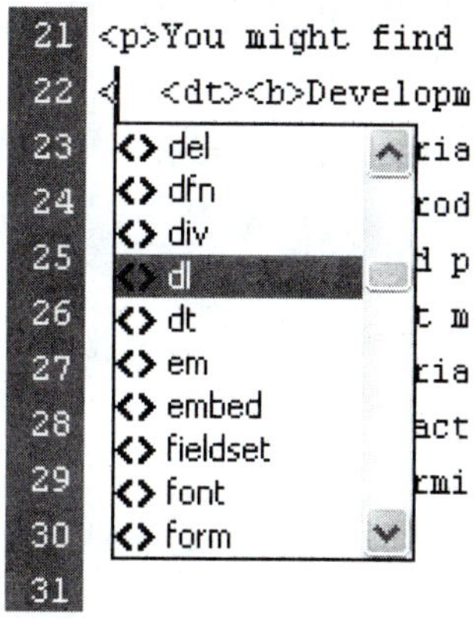

- Auto Tag Completion automatically enters the end tag. All you need to do is type the desired text between the two codes.
- Code Hints is useful for entering new codes. However, it can be a nuisance when you are editing preexisting codes. To disable the Code Hints features, click Edit>Preferences>Code Hints and deselect both Code Hints checkboxes (see illustration).

Code Hints Prefemces

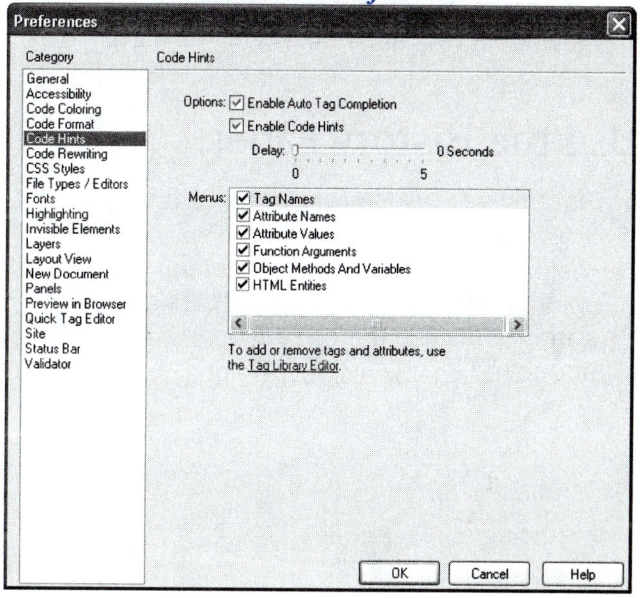

Insert a Date

- You can insert the current date on any page in your site using Dreamweaver's Date feature. If you choose, the inserted date updates each time you save the page. This is a good way to keep track of modifications made to a Web site.
- Use the Insert>Date command on the menu bar or the Insert Date button on the Common panel in the Insert bar to open the Insert Date dialog box (see illustration below).

Insert and format day, date, and/or time

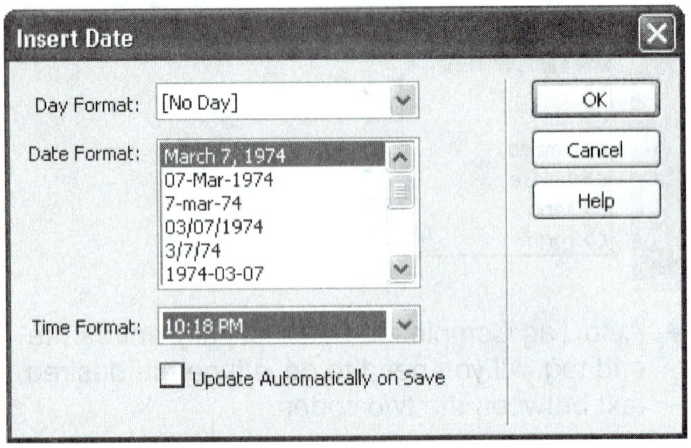

- You can insert a day, a date, and/or a time. Dreamweaver supplies a number of formats to choose among for each item.
- If you want the date/time information to update each time you save the page, select the Update Automatically on Save checkbox. Otherwise, the inserted date will stay the same as when it was inserted.

Use the History Panel

- Dreamweaver's **History panel** is a very useful tool for tracking tasks. When displayed, the History panel (see illustration at top of next column) shows a list of tasks that have been performed since the current page was created or opened.

History panel shows recent tasks

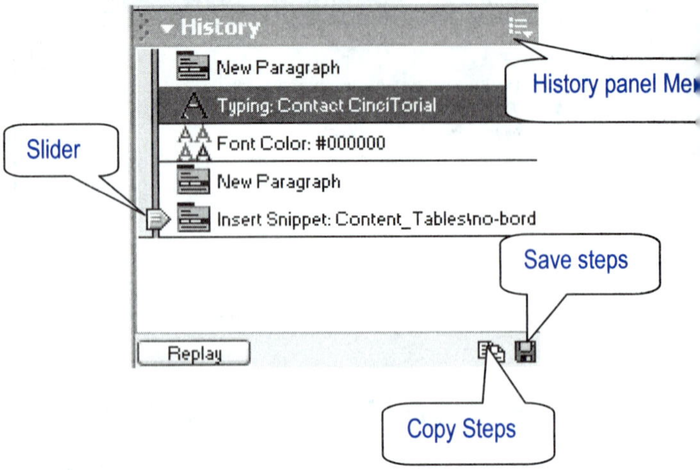

- Not only can you keep track of the tasks you have performed, you can use the History panel to repeat a series of steps or undo a number of recent tasks quickly and easily.
- Display the History panel using the Window>Others>History command on the menu bar.
- As you perform each task, the History panel displays it with an identifying icon. The icon for a text entry, for example, is a capital *A*.
- Select a step by clicking it in the panel. Select more than one step by clicking the first, holding down the Shift or Ctrl key, and clicking additional steps.
- To save time in performing repetitive tasks, you can repeat steps. Select the steps you want to repeat, position the insertion point where you want to begin the steps, and click Replay.
- To reverse a series of steps, drag the slider upward to "gray out" the steps you want to undo. You can redo those steps by dragging the slider back down to activate the steps again.
- The History panel tracks steps on the current page only. If you open another page, the History panel will be empty.
- You can, however, copy steps from one page to use on another. Select the series of steps and click the Copy Steps button on the History panel.

- Then activate the page you want to copy the steps to and use the Dreamweaver window's Edit>Paste menu command to paste the steps in the History panel. The copied steps are replayed as soon as they are pasted.
- You can also, if desired, save a series of steps as a command using the Save as Command button on the History panel.

Tip: *If you need to later delete the command, use the Commands>Edit Command List menu command, and then select the desired command, and click Delete*

- Select the steps, click the button, and supply a name for the command. Your new command displays on the Commands menu so you can issue it at any time on any page.
- When copying or saving steps, you might want to start with an empty History panel. You can clear the History panel of all entries by clicking the History panel menu and choosing Clear History from the menu.
- Dreamweaver will warn you that this step cannot be undone. Click Yes in the warning box to clear the History panel.

Procedures

Open Code Inspector
F10

1. Click **Window** .... Alt+W
2. Click **Code Inspector** .... D

Adjust Code Inspector Display

- Resize inspector window by dragging lower-right corner.
- Click (**View Options** button) in Code inspector toolbar and select options:
  - Select **Word Wrap** to force code to wrap within inspector window.
  - Select **Line Numbers** to display numbers to left of each line of code.
  - Select **Highlight Invalid HTML** to highlight coding errors.
  - Select **Syntax Coloring** to display tags and text in different colors.
  - Select **Auto Indent** to enable automatic indenting of code lines.

Enter Text and Codes Using Code Inspector

1. Click in Code inspector window to activate window.
2. Position insertion point as desired and type or edit text or codes.
3. Click in Document window to record and display changes.

Display Code and Design Views

Display Code view.

1. Click **View**.................. Alt+V
2. Click **Code**......................... C

OR

- Click (**Show Code View** button) on Document toolbar.

Display Design view.

1. Click **View** .... Alt+V
2. Click **Design**............... D, Enter

OR

- Click (**Show Design View** button) on Document toolbar.

Display both Code and Design view.

1. Click **View** .... Alt+V
2. Click **Code and Design** ..... A

OR

- Click (**Show Code and Design Views** button) on Document toolbar.

Display Reference Panel
Shift + F1

1. Select tag or object to get information on, if desired.
2. Click **Window**............ Alt+W
3. Click **Reference** .... F

OR

- Click (**Reference** button) on Document toolbar.

OR

- Click the **Reference** panel tab in the Code panel group (located in the right panel group pane).

Display Tag Inspector Panel
F9

1. Click **Window**............. Alt+W
2. Click **Tag Inspector**........... T

OR

- Click the **Tag Inspector** panel tab in the Code panel group (located in the right panel group pane).

Display Snippets Panel
Shift + F9

1. Click **Window**............. Alt+W
2. Click **Snippets** .... N

OR

- Click the **Snippets** panel tab in the Code panel group (located in the right panel group pane).

Display Head Content
Ctrl + Shift + W

1. Click **View** .... Alt+V
2. Click **Head Content** .... H
3. Click icon in head content pane to see information in Properties panel.

   ✓ *Follow same procedure to close head content pane.*

Clean Up HTML Code

1. Click **Commands**....... Alt+C
2. Click **Clean Up HTML**........ L
3. Select specific items to clean up.
4. Select **Show Log on Completion** checkbox to see a report on items fixed.

Add Keywords to a Web Site

1. Display Insert bar if necessary:
   a. Click **Window**....... Alt+W
   b. Click **Insert**.................. I
2. Click **Head** panel tab.
3. Click (**Insert Keywords** button) on Head panel.
4. Type keywords in Insert Keywords dialog box, separating keywords with commas.

Open File from Other Location
Ctrl + O

You will need this skill to complete the Exercise.

1. Click **File** .... Alt+F
2. Click **Open** .... O
3. Click the down arrow next to the **Look in** text box... Alt+I
4. Locate folder or drive that contains file to open.
5. Click file name and click Open.

Insert a Date

1. Click **Insert**................. Alt+I
2. Click **Date**........................... D

OR

- Click [calendar icon] on Common panel of Insert bar.

3. Select format for Day, Date, and/or Time.
4. Select **Update Automatically on Save** checkbox to update date/time information each time page is saved.

Disable Code Hints

1. Click **Edit**..................... Alt+E
2. Click **Preferences**............... S
3. Select Code Hints from the Category list.
4. Deselect the desired Code Hints checkboxes.
5. Click **OK**.

Use the History Panel
Shift + F10

1. Click **Window**............. Alt+W
2. Click **Other**.......................... O
3. Click **History**...................... H
4. Work with steps:
   - Click step to select it.
   - Click step, hold down Ctrl or Shift, click additional steps to select more than one step at a time.
   - Select steps and click Replay to repeat steps.
   - Drag slider up to undo steps or back down to redo steps.
   - Select steps and click [copy icon] on History panel to copy steps.
   - Select steps and click [save icon] to save steps as a command.
   - Click History panel menu arrow and select **Clear History** to empty History panel.

Exercise Directions

1. Start Dreamweaver.
2. Open the **CinciTorial** site.
3. Open **index.htm**.
4. Add the following keywords for this site: **editorial services, book production**.
5. Display the Code view or Code inspector and select the view option that will wrap text in the inspector.
6. Locate the new <meta> tag in the page's Head section. Use the Tag Inspector to find and select it quickly.
7. Display the head content pane and click the Keywords icon to see the keywords in the Properties panel.
8. Close the head content pane.
9. Open **praise.htm**. Notice that the text is different—probably a sans serif font—and not the same size as that on the **index.htm** page because this page was imported from Word and retains some of the Word default formatting as well as other unneeded coding. The text in the Code inspector may also look different.
10. Close the Code inspector and switch to the Code and Design view.
11. Edit the page in the Code inspector or in Code view as follows:
    - Select and delete all text between the <style> </style> tags and the tags themselves in the Head section of the page. Use the Tag inspector if you cannot locate it quickly.
    - Select Line Numbers in the View Options, if necessary, and delete the blank line 5 of the code.
    - Delete the lang attribute and its value following the opening body tag. (You should select and delete *class="Normal" lang=EN-US".)*

      ✓ *Do NOT delete the bgcolor="#FFFFFF" attribute and value.*
    - Scroll up to display the Head section and locate the <meta> tag.
    - Within the <meta> tag, select the character set information *charset=windows-1252"*.
    - Type **charset=iso-8859-1"**.

   ✓ *The font of the page's text will change if you click in the Document window or click the* Refresh *button in the Properties panel.*
12. Click in the Document window to record your changes. The page text should now be the same size and the paragraphs displayed in the Times New Roman default font as that on other pages in the site.
13. Switch back to Design view.
14. Save and close the page.
15. Open the **services.htm** page from the Data folder and save it in the current site.

    ✓ *See Procedures for information on how to open a page from a different location. Be sure to save the page in your cincitorial folder.*
16. The definitions at the bottom of this page could be displayed better as a definition list. Before you begin to edit your code, you must use the Edit>Preferences menu command, select the Code Hints category, and uncheck the Enable Auto Tag Completion option if necessary.
17. Make the following formatting changes in the Code inspector or any Code view option:
    - Scroll down to locate the *Developmental editing* paragraph. Click to the left of the word *Development* and press the **Backspace** key three times to remove the <p> tag.
    - Type **<dl>** to begin the definition list. If the end tag </dl> appears automatically, carefully delete it.

    ✓ *Dreamweaver will open a list box of codes and may highlight the closing </p> tag to indicate there is an error in the code.*
    - Press the **Enter** key. Type **<dt><b>** to start and boldface the first term.
    - Move the insertion point to the end of the line, just to the right of *editing*.
    - Delete the </p> tag.
    - Type **</b></dt>**.
    - Move to the beginning of the next line and delete the <p> tag. Type **<dd>**.
    - Delete the </p> tag at the end of the definition and type **</dd>**.

18. Format the next term (*Project management*) the same way you formatted *Developmental editing* and provide the proper codes for its definition.
19. Below the last definition, create a new line and type **</dl>** to end the list.
20. Click in the Document window or switch to Design view to inspect your changes. Your page should look similar to Illustration A.

   ✓ *If you did so before this step, you may have noticed that your changes did not look right. The bold text might have been in a different font. This is because the </dl> tag had not been typed yet.*

21. Use the Clean Up HTML command to check your coding.
22. Close the Code inspector, if necessary, and display Design view.
23. Look up information in the Reference panel on the <meta> tag.
24. On **index.htm**, link the *Services* paragraph to **services.htm**.
25. Display the History panel and clear the contents of the panel.

   ✓ *Dreamweaver may warn you that you will not be able to undo steps if you clear the list. Click* ***Yes***.

26. Click to the right of the last sentence on the page. Press the **Enter** key and apply left alignment.
27. Type **Last update:** and press **Spacebar**.
28. Insert the date and time using formats of your choice. Choose to update the date and time automatically.
29. Deselect the date and time you just entered on the **index.htm** page.
30. Select and replay the last four steps.
31. Use the History panel slider to undo the repeated steps.
32. Copy the last two steps (typing *Last update* and inserting the date) in the History panel.
33. Activate **services.htm** and insert a new blank paragraph below the last definition. Paste the copied steps.

   ✓ *You may need to view the HTML code in order to place the date information outside of the </dl> tag.*

34. Save and close any open pages. Note that the time updates on the pages where you inserted the date and time.
35. Exit Dreamweaver.

Illustration A

Our Services

CinciTorial can jump into a project at almost any stage, including before the first word is written. Our services include:

- Topic research
- Writing from notes or outline
- Developmental editing
- Standard copyediting
- Art and permissions management
- Project management
- Proofreading
- Indexing

You might find the following definitions helpful.

Developmental editing
: A CinciTorial developmental editor coordinates with the client and the designated author to produce the desired product, supervising the art program and the schedule and preparing supplementary materials.

Project management
: A CinciTorial project manager oversees all aspects of a project, including client contact, scheduling, production team selection and supervision, quality control, permissions management, and budget management.

Chapter

6

Images and Graphic Elements

According to the old saying, a picture "is worth a thousand words." Text content is important for every Web site, but images can be used to accomplish many things in a Web page—from illustrating it to adding a discreet but creative background. Linked graphics can be used to navigate your site and the Internet, too.

In this chapter, you'll learn how to:

- Add a horizontal rule to a Web page
- Manage graphic files
- Create a background using a color or image
- Insert an image on a Web page
- Modify and position an image
- Create an image map

Change horizontal rule formats

Insert Horizontal Rules

- You can easily insert horizontal rules on your Web pages to separate sections of text. Position the insertion point at the beginning or end of a paragraph and use the Insert>Horizontal Rule command on the menu bar or the Horizontal Rule  button on the Common tab of the Insert bar.

  Note: *If you position the insertion point at the end of a paragraph, the horizontal rule is inserted below the paragraph. If you position the insertion point at the beginning of a paragraph, the horizontal rule is inserted above the paragraph.*

- You can change horizontal rule formats by selecting the horizontal rule and changing settings in the Properties panel (see illustration above).
- By default, the rule runs the full width of the Web page. You can specify a width in the W text box using either a pixel measurement or a percent of the page width. If you specify a width less than the full page, you can choose an alignment option of left, center, or right.
- Use the H box to specify a height for the rule in pixels. Selecting the Shading checkbox adds shading to the rule that makes it look three-dimensional. Deselect this checkbox to make the rule a solid color.
- The Properties panel does not have a feature to change the horizontal rule's color. However, you can change the color of the horizontal rule by editing the HTML <hr> tag in the Tag inspector's property sheet or in code view, as shown below:

```
<hr color="009999">
```

- The rule color does not display in Dreamweaver. You must preview the page in the browser to see the color.

Note: *If you specify a color for the rule, you cannot also display shading. Regardless of whether Shading is selected, the rule will display as a solid color.*

Change Background Color

- A simple way to add graphic interest to a Web page is to change its background color. By default, Web pages have a white background. You can use any of the colors in the Dreamweaver color palette as a page background color—but Web-safe colors are recommended.
- To change page background color, use the Modify>Page Properties command on the menu bar to open the Page Properties dialog box.
- Click the Background color button to display the color palette and use the eyedropper to select a color (see illustration below).

Choose background color

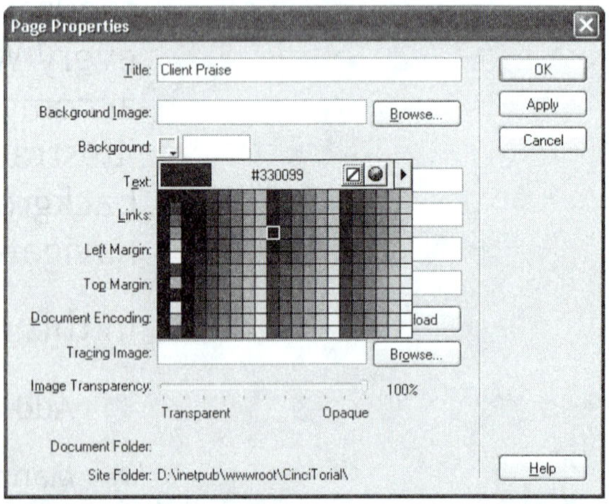

- You can use the Apply button to apply your color choice without closing the Page Properties dialog box. If you do not like the applied color, you can open the color palette and choose a different color.

Manage Graphic Files

- As you add graphic files such as pictures to your Web site, Dreamweaver will prompt you to save the graphics to your Web site's root folder so they will be available to display in the browser.
- You can store the files loose in the Web folder. However, for larger sites that may include many files, it is better site management to create a subfolder for graphic files.
- You can create a subfolder in the Local Folder pane of the Site panel. Use the File>New Folder command on the Site panel menu bar to insert a new folder in the site (see illustration below). Then type a new name for the folder, such as images.

Create a subfolder in the Site panel

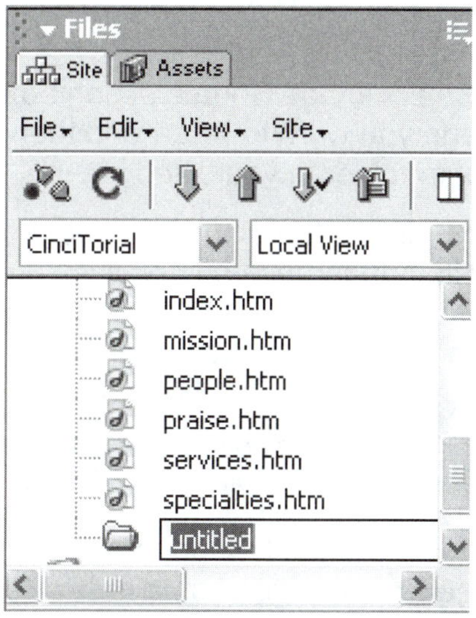

- When you are prompted to save graphic files, save them in your images folder. Be sure to include this folder when copying files for publication so the browser will be able to locate them.

Insert Background Picture

- You can also use an image, or picture, as a background. Background images can create an attractive and unobtrusive appearance that gives a Web site identity while keeping the Web file size small and download times minimal.
- Insert the background image from the Page Properties dialog box. You can use the Browse button to the right of the Background Image text box to open the Select Image Source dialog box and locate the file you want to use for the background image (see illustration below).

Locate graphic image file

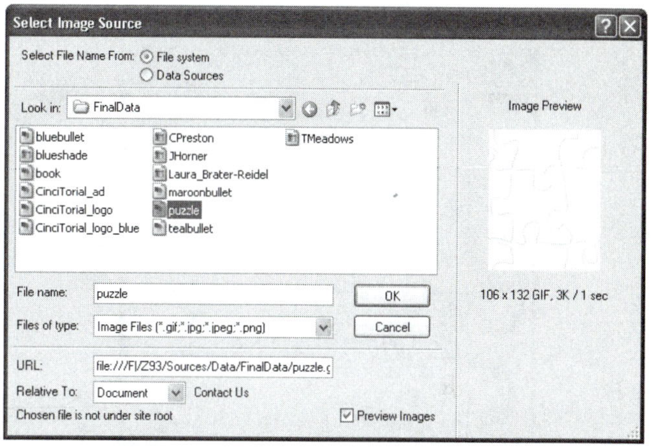

- If the Preview Images checkbox is selected in the Select Image Source dialog box, you can see a preview of the image at the right side of the dialog box when you click the image's file name.
- Click OK to choose the file. Dreamweaver then prompts you to save the image in your root folder. When you click Yes, Dreamweaver displays the Copy File As dialog box, where you can rename the file and open the images folder to store it.
- You can then apply the background image from the Page Properties dialog box or close the dialog box to see the background image in place on the page.
- If the image is not large enough to cover the entire page area, Dreamweaver *tiles* the image—repeats it across and down the page to fill the entire page area.
- The background image information appears as an attribute of the <body> opening tag in the HTML code.

Assets Panel

- The **Assets panel** is a tab in Files panel group that also includes the Site panel. It is divided into two panes. The lower pane is a list of asset files available for your site. The upper is a viewing window in which to inspect a selected asset (see illustration).

Assets panel

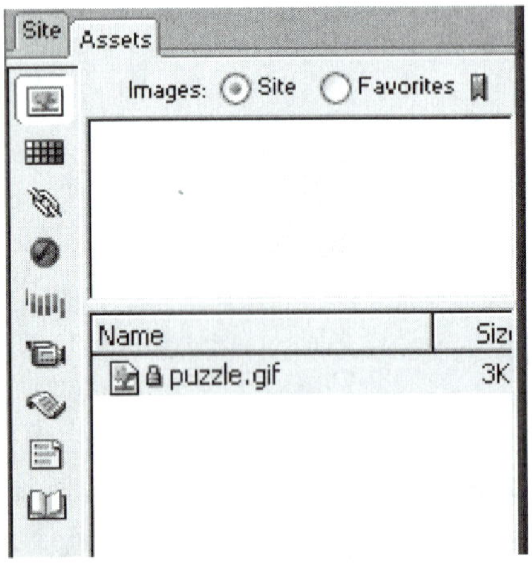

- The Assets panel also features a toolbar for choosing the different categories of objects and style elements available to your Web site.
- When you add a graphic file to your Web, it is also included as an **asset** that can be readily used in other Web pages that you create in the current defined site.
- Assets cover a wide variety of elements that you store in a site, such as a .gif or .jpeg image, movie file created in Macromedia Flash, clipart, hyperlinks, and the like.
- You can create and manage an entire library of objects such as logos, buttons, photographs and Web page templates, which—along with the Assets panel—will be discussed in more detail in the next chapter.
- If you want to use an asset in another Web site, right-click on the asset in the Site list of the Assets panel and select Add to Favorites.

  Note: *See Chapter 17 for more information about how to use this feature in the Assets panel.*

- To see your favorites in the Assets panel, click the Favorites option button to open the Favorites list.

Insert Image on Page

- Images can be used in a Web site to illustrate its text, to provide additional information, or simply to add decorative elements for visual interest.
- To display properly in a browser, images should be saved in a standard format such as **JPEG** or **GIF** format. Dreamweaver will not automatically convert image files in other formats such as BMP or TIFF to JPEG or GIF.
- You can use the Insert>Image command on the menu bar to open the Select Image Source dialog box, or you can click the Image button on the Common tab of the Insert bar to open this dialog box.

  Tip: *You can also simply drag the Image button to the desired location on the page to open the Select Image Source dialog box.*

- In the Select Image Source dialog box, select the image you want to insert and then save it in the proper folder in your Web site.
- After the picture has been inserted, you can modify its appearance and position it on the page using the Properties panel. You can also create a link from the picture or use it to create an image map using the hotspot tools.

  Note: *You will learn how to create image maps later in this chapter.*

- As you add images to a page, keep an eye on the page size/download time measurements 79K / 12 sec shown in the right side of the Status bar at the bottom of the Document window.
- Even with the rise of broadband Internet connections, images can significantly increase the size of a page and thus also increase its download time. If a page loads too slowly, it is an inconvenience to the visitors to your site, so you should try to keep download times low by eliminating large image files.
- The download time is based by default on the download speed of a 28.8 bps modem. You can set a different connection speed for this measurement if desired in the Preferences dialog box in the Status Bar category.

  Tip: *See Appendix A for more information about the Status Bar category in Preferences.*

Modify Image Properties

- An image must be selected to display its properties. Click once on the image to select it. The selected image displays a black border with square black sizing handles at the bottom, right, and bottom right corner of the image.
- The Properties panel displays a number of properties for an image (see illustration below). To see all properties, use the Expander arrow in the Properties panel.

Image properties in Properties panel

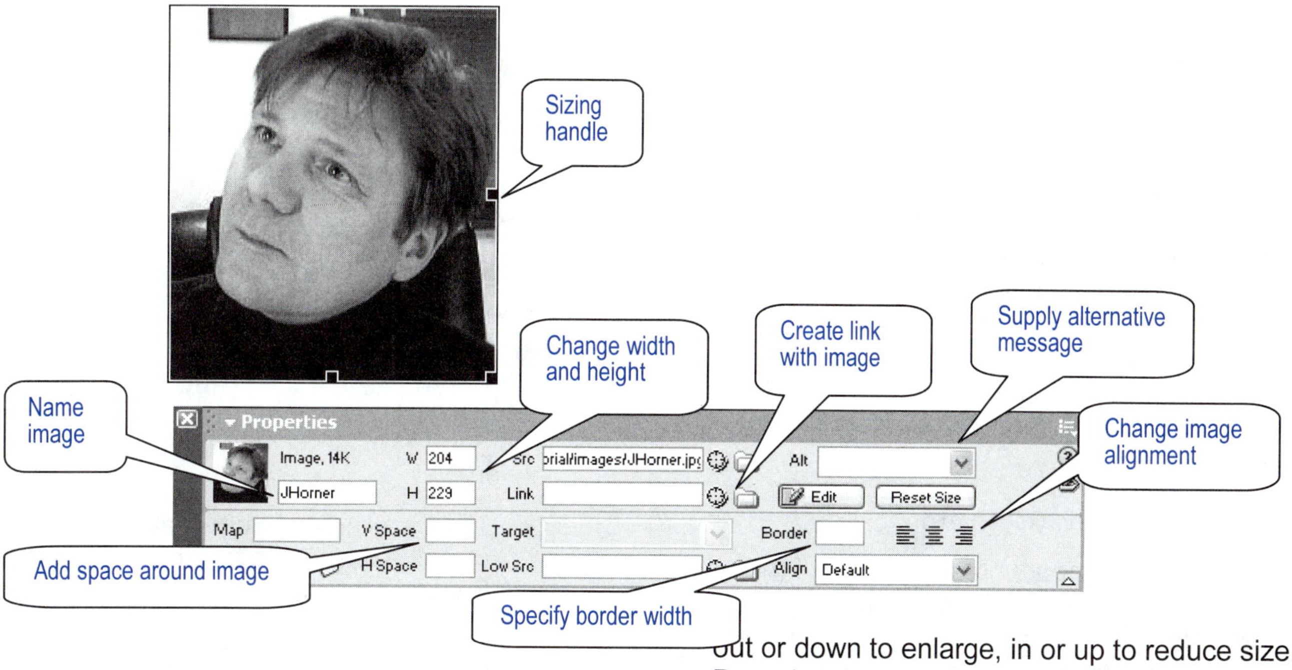

- Notice that a thumbnail-size version of the image appears at the left of the Properties panel. On pages that have more than one image or where images may be layered, this thumbnail helps you to be sure you are editing properties for the correct image.
- Next to the thumbnail is the Name text box, which is empty by default. You can supply a name for the image if you need to refer to the image in a script.
- You can use an image to link to other pages or sites in the same way you use text. Select the image and then type the link address in the Link text box, or use the Point to File icon or Browse for File button to specify the link target.
- If the image is large and may take some time loading, you can type text in the Alt box that will display during the load.

Resize Image

- You can use the sizing handles on the picture to adjust its size. Click on a handle and drag out or down to enlarge, in or up to reduce size. Dragging a corner handle adjusts both width and height at the same time.

  Tip: *If you need to resize proportionately, hold down the Shift key as you drag the corner handle.*

- To resize an image to exact measurements, use the W and H text boxes on the Properties panel. You must supply both a width and a height—Dreamweaver does not automatically resize proportionally if you supply only one dimension.
- If you need to go back to the original proportions, click the [Reset Size] button.
- Sizing measurements are supplied in pixels. Pixel measurements allow you to size very exactly. This measurement is also a Web design standard.

Add Border to Image

- By default, an image does not display a border. Use the Border text box on the expanded area of the Properties panel to specify a border width such as 1 or 2. Border measurements are in pixels.

- An image border is always black, unless the image is being used as a link. When used as a link, the image's border becomes the default link color (usually bright blue).

  Note: *If an image is moved within the HTML code, its border can pick up the color of another element, such as a heading. The border will still display black in the browser, however.*

Position Image on Page

- You have several options for positioning an image on a page. You can use alignment buttons or settings in the Align list, and you can adjust space around the image using the vertical and horizontal space text boxes on the Properties panel.

Position Standalone Image

- If the image appears on a line by itself (not on the same line with text), you can use the Align Left, Align Center, or Align Right text alignment options to position it just as if it were a text paragraph.
- Select the image and use the alignment buttons that appear in the expanded area of the Properties panel to left align, center, or right align the image.

  Tip: *You can also use keyboard shortcuts such as Ctrl + Alt + Shift + C or Ctrl + Alt + Shift + R to center or right align an image.*

Wrap Text Around Image

- When an image is inserted in the same line as text, you use the options on the Align list on the Properties panel to position the image. Options on this list allow you to wrap text around the image or position it precisely relative to the text on the same line.

- Dreamweaver selects the Default position for a new image. This setting positions the image at the left edge of the page with the bottom of the picture aligned with the baseline of text (see illustration at the top of the next page).

Default alignment

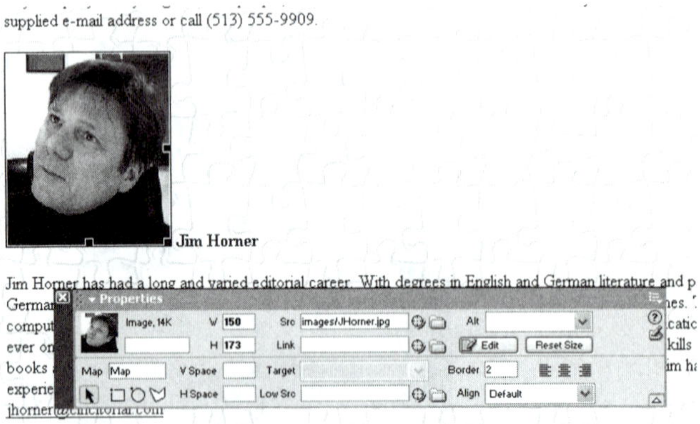

- The Align list offers nine other alignment options:
  - The Baseline and Bottom alignments both align the image and text the same way as Browser Default.
  - The Top and Text Top alignments align the top of the image with the top of the text's tall letters. If the text is a paragraph of several lines, only the first line aligns at the top; the remaining lines of the paragraph display below the image.
  - The Middle alignment aligns the middle of the image with the text baseline. Only the first line of text is aligned at the middle; remaining lines display below the image.
  - The Absolute Middle alignment aligns the middle of the image with the middle of the text line (rather than the baseline).
  - The Absolute Bottom alignment aligns the bottom of the image with the descenders (the bottom parts of letters such as *y* and *g*) of the text.
  - The Left alignment positions the image at the left margin and wraps text around it on the right side.
  - The Right alignment positions the image at the right margin and wraps text around it on the left side.

- When you apply the Left or Right alignment option, Dreamweaver places an anchor at the location where the image was inserted. Selecting this anchor is the same as selecting the image itself.
- You can drag and drop the anchor to pinpoint the graphic file's position in the text and change the way text wraps around the image. (See illustration below.)

Set Vertical and Horizontal Spacing

- You can fine-tune the position of an image by setting vertical and horizontal space measurements in the V Space and H Space text boxes on the Properties panel.
- Typing a value in the V Space box adds that amount of space in pixels above and below an image. A value in the H Space box adds space to the left and right of the image.

Drag anchor to adjust right alignment

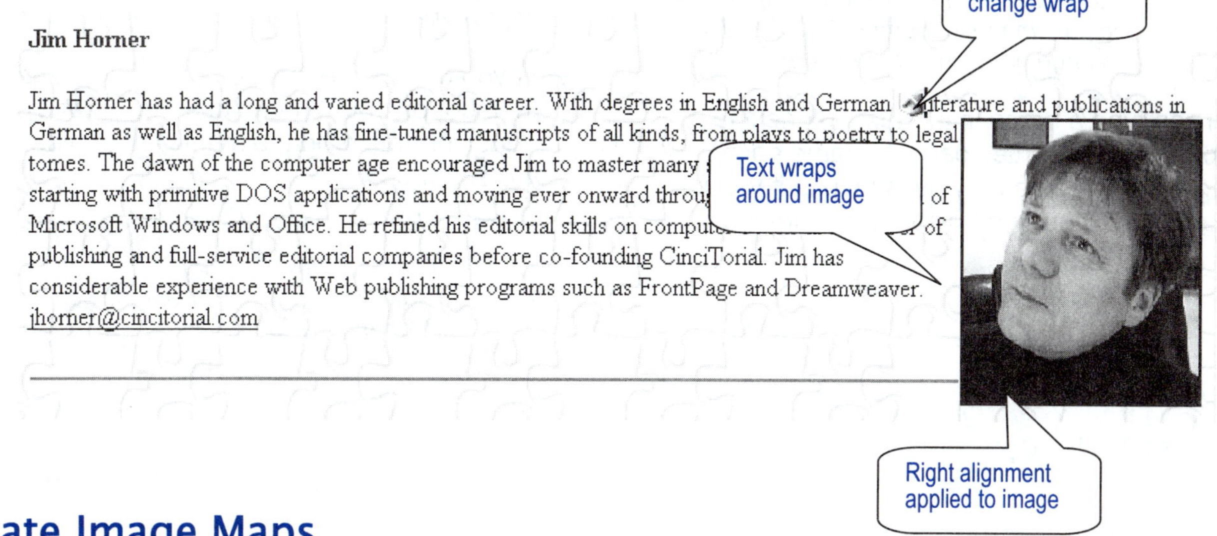

Create Image Maps

- As you have already read, you can use an entire image to create a link. You can also use an image to create an **image map,** which contains a **hotspot** that links the current page to another location. Image maps are creative ways to add both visual interest and navigability to your Web site.
- To create image maps, you use the hotspot tools on the expanded portion of the Properties panel to draw an area on the image.
  - Use the Rectangular Hotspot tool to create a square or rectangular area on the image.
  - Use the Oval Hotspot tool to create a circular area.
  - Use the Polygon Hotspot tool to create an irregular-shaped area.
- After you click the appropriate tool, the insertion point changes to a crosshair you use to draw the area on the image. Drawing a hotspot is the same as drawing an object in a program such as Paint or Word.
- The area you draw fills with a blue shading to indicate the hotspot and the Properties panel changes to display settings for the hotspot (see illustration below).

Oval hotspot

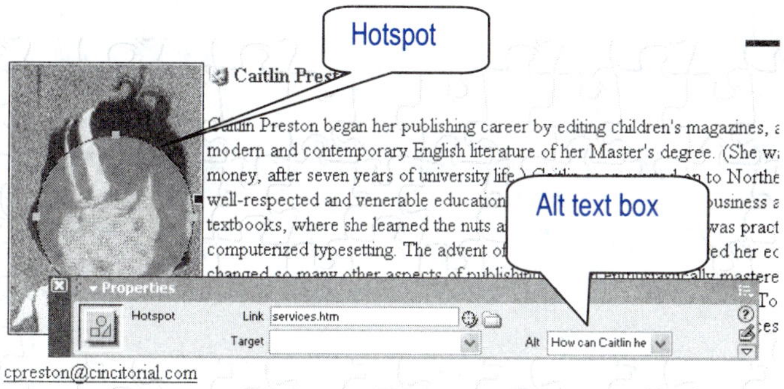

Note: *The blue shading will not appear when the image map is viewed in the browser.*

- Type the link address in the Link box, or use the Point to File icon or Browse for File button to select the page or site to which you want to link.
- Dreamweaver automatically inserts a pound sign (#) in the Link box, which indicates that the link will be a Named Anchor link. Delete the # sign in the Link box before typing a file name to create a link to another page or another Web site, or use the Browse for File button to locate the page.

  Tip: *An interesting use for an image map is to reduce an image to thumbnail size and link it to a larger version of the image.*

- You can type a name in the text box next to Map on the Properties panel to name each image map on a page. This is helpful if you create more than one hotspot on an image.
- To create a tooltip that will display when a visitor rests the mouse on the hotspot, type the desired ScreenTip text in the Alt text box.
- Adjust a hotspot's size by clicking outside the image and then clicking once on the hot spot to select it. Drag any sizing handle on the hotspot to change its size.
- Click on a hotspot and hold down the mouse button while dragging the shape to move it to another position.
- To delete a hotspot, select it and press the Delete key.
- If you do not like the look of the blue-shaded hotspot on your image, use the View>Visual Aids command on the menu bar to hide the hotspots.

  Note: *Use View>Visual Aids>Image Maps, or click the View Options button on the Dreamweaver toolbar and select Visual Aids>Image Maps.*

Procedures

Insert Horizontal Rule

Position insertion point at beginning or end of paragraph.

1. Click **Insert**................ Alt+I
2. Click **Horizontal Rule** .... Z

OR

- Click (**Horizontal Rule** button) on the Common tab of the Insert bar.

3. Modify rule properties:
   - Specify width in pixels or percent measurement.
   - Specify height in pixels.
   - Select alignment if rule is less than 100% of page width.
   - Turn shading on or off.
   - Specify color in one of the code views or in the Tag inspector using COLOR attribute and a hexadecimal value.

   ✓ *The Tag inspector uses a color palette if you prefer that method of picking a color.*
4. Copy rule to new location:
   a. Right-click rule and select **Copy**.
   b. Right-click at location to place copy and select **Paste**.

Change Background Color
Ctrl + J

1. Click **Modify**............... Alt+M
2. Click **Page Properties** .... P
3. Click **Background** color box to display color palette.
4. Use eyedropper to pick color.
5. Click Apply to apply color without closing dialog box.

Create Folder in Site Window
Ctrl + Alt + Shift + N

In Local Files pane of Site panel

1. Click **File**.
2. Click **New Folder**.
3. Type name for new folder.

Insert Background Picture

1. Click **Modify**.............. Alt+M
2. Click **Page Properties** .... P
3. Click Browse... to open Select Image Source dialog box.
4. Locate image file to use for background.
5. Click OK.
6. Click Yes to copy file to root folder.
7. Open folder in which images will be stored and rename file if necessary.
8. Click Save.
9. Click OK.

Insert Image on Page
Ctrl + Alt + I

1. Click **Insert**................. Alt+I
2. Click **Image** I

OR

- Click (**Image** button) on Common tab of Insert bar, or drag Image button to page to open Select Image Source dialog box.

3. Locate image file to use for background.
4. Click OK.
5. Click Yes to copy file to root folder.
6. Open folder in which images will be stored and rename file if necessary.
7. Click Save.

Add Image File to Asset panel Favorites
F11

1. Click **Windows**........... Alt+W
2. Click **Assets**......... A, A, Enter

OR

- Click the Assets tab in the Files panel group.

3. Click Images icon in the Assets panel's categories.
4. Right-click the desired file.
5. Click **Add to Favorites**.

OR

- Click the **Add to Favorites** button.

OR

- In the Site panel:
  a. Right-click the desired file.
  b. Click **Add to Image Favorites**.

  ✓ *To open the Favorites list, click the* ***Favorites*** *option button in the Assets panel.*

Modify Image Properties

Click image to select it and expand Properties panel.

- Click in Name box and type name for image if desired.
- Use image as link:
  - Type page or site address in Link text box on Properties panel.

  OR

  - Use (**Point to File** icon) or (**Browse for Folder**) to locate link page.
- Add alternative text for image:
  - Click in **Alt** text box and type text to display during load.
- Resize image:
  - Click sizing handle and drag to expand or reduce size.

OR

- Click in W text box on Properties panel and type pixel size for width.
- Click in H text box on Properties panel and type pixel size for height.

- To reset the original size of the image, click the Reset Size [Reset Size] button.
- Click in Border box and type value for image border.

Align Standalone Image

Click image to select it and expand Properties panel.

- Click (**Align Left** button) on Properties panel to left align.
- Click (**Align Center** button) on Properties panel to center.
- Click (**Align Right** button) on Properties panel to right align.

Wrap Text Around Image

Click image to select it.

1. Click **Align** list arrow on Properties panel.
2. Select alignment option:
   - **Default**
   - **Baseline**
   - **Top**
   - **Middle**
   - **Bottom**
   - **Text Top**
   - **Absolute Middle**
   - **Absolute Bottom**
   - **Left**
   - **Right**
3. Adjust Left and Right alignment text wrap by clicking anchor and dragging to new location in text.

Create Image Map

Click image to select it and expand Properties panel.

1. Click desired hotspot tool on Properties panel:
   - (**Rectangular Hotspot** tool)
   - (**Oval Hotspot** tool)
   - (**Polygon Hotspot** tool)
2. Draw hotspot:
   - For rectangle or circle, position pointer above and to left or right of area to map. Hold down mouse button and drag to create hotspot.
   - For polygon, click to start and click to change direction.

   ✓ *Drag a blue handle to adjust the polygon's shape.*
3. Type page or site address in Link box on Properties panel

   ✓ *Remember to delete the pound sign (#) that Dreamweaver automatically puts in the Link box if you are typing the page or site address.*

   OR

   - Use (**Point to File** icon) or (**Browse for Folder**) to locate link page.
4. Modify size or location of hotspot by clicking outside the picture and then using the pointer to drag the hotspot or one of its handles.
5. Hide hotspots:

   a. Click **View** .... Alt + V

   b. Click **Visual Aids** V

   c. Click **Image Maps** .... G

Exercise Directions

1. Start Dreamweaver.
2. Open the **CinciTorial** site.
3. Display the Site panel, if necessary.
4. Create a new subfolder in the cincitorial folder named **images**.
5. Open **index.htm**.
6. Position the insertion point to the left of the first heading on the page (*We build computer books*) and press the **Enter** key to create a new line.
7. Move the insertion point up into the new line and insert the **CinciTorial_logo.gif** from the Data folder. Save the image in the images subfolder.

   ✓ *You may need to left align the image file inserted in step 7.*

8. Apply the **puzzle.gif** image from the Data folder as a background picture on this page. Save the image in the images folder.
9. Open **services.htm** and apply the **puzzle.gif** background picture from the images folder.
10. Emphasize the **praise.htm** page by applying the lightest yellow background color to the page (#FFFFCC).
11. Activate **services.htm** and insert the **CinciTorial_logo.gif** from the images folder to the left of the first heading. Reduce its size to 257 pixels wide by 44 pixels high. Link the image to **index.htm**.

    ✓ *Refresh the files shown in the Site panel. Then drag the logo into position.*

12. Click to the right of the picture and press the **Enter** key to move the heading to a new line.
13. Select and copy the image, then save and close the page.
14. Activate **praise.htm** and paste the copied image between the named anchor and the first heading. Move the heading to the next line. Save and close the page.
15. Open the **people.htm** page from the Data folder and save it in the current Web site.
16. Apply the **puzzle.gif** background picture to the page.
17. Paste the copied image to the left of the first heading and move the heading to the next line.
18. Insert a horizontal rule above the heading *Caitlin Preston*.
19. Remove the rule's shading and change its height to **3**.
20. Modify the horizontal rule's HTML tag to read: **<hr color="990033" noshade size="3">**
21. Copy the rule and paste it above the *Tyler Meadows* heading.
22. Save the page and preview it in the browser to see the color applied to the rules. Close the browser.
23. Position the insertion point to the left of the paragraph under the *Jim Horner* heading. Insert the **JHorner.jpg** image from the Data folder. Save the image in your images folder.
24. Insert the **CPreston.jpg** to the left of the Caitlin Preston paragraph and **TMeadows.jpg** to the left of the Tyler Meadows paragraph. Save all images in the images folder.

    ✓ *In both cases, "paragraph" means the body copy under the name headings.*

25. Format the pictures as follows
    - Change the size of Jim's picture to 150 by 173 pixels. Change the size of Caitlin's illustration to 151 by 206 pixels. Change the size of Tyler's picture to 150 by 161 pixels.
    - Apply Right alignment to Jim and Tyler's pictures and Left alignment to Caitlin's.
    - Apply a 2-pixel border around each picture.
    - If necessary, drag the anchor for each picture up and to the left of the person's heading, so the anchor is just to the left of the heading.

    ✓ *The Caitlin image anchor may be "under" the image file. It is actually in the correct position.*

26. Select Jim's picture and use the Oval Hotspot tool to create a hotspot area about the size of Jim's head.

27. Link the hotspot to **services.htm** and type the following text in the Alt box: **How can Jim help you?**
28. Create similar hotspots on Caitlin's illustration and Tyler's picture.
29. If desired, hide the hotspots on the image maps.
30. Save and close the page.
31. On the **index.htm** page, insert a blank paragraph above the *Services* link and type **Our People** in the blank paragraph. Link this text to the **people.htm** page.
32. Preview the **index.htm** page in the browser and test links to and from pages using the new image links you have created in this exercise.

✓ *You have not worked on contactus.htm in this exercise, so this page will look the same as in previous exercises.*

33. The top of your CinciTorial People page should look similar to Illustration A.
34. Close the browser.
35. Open the Assets panel.

✓ *Click the Refresh button in the Assets panel toolbar if necessary to see the images that you have added to the site in the Assets list.*

36. Add the files to your Favorites.
37. Save and close any open pages.
38. Exit Dreamweaver.

Illustration A

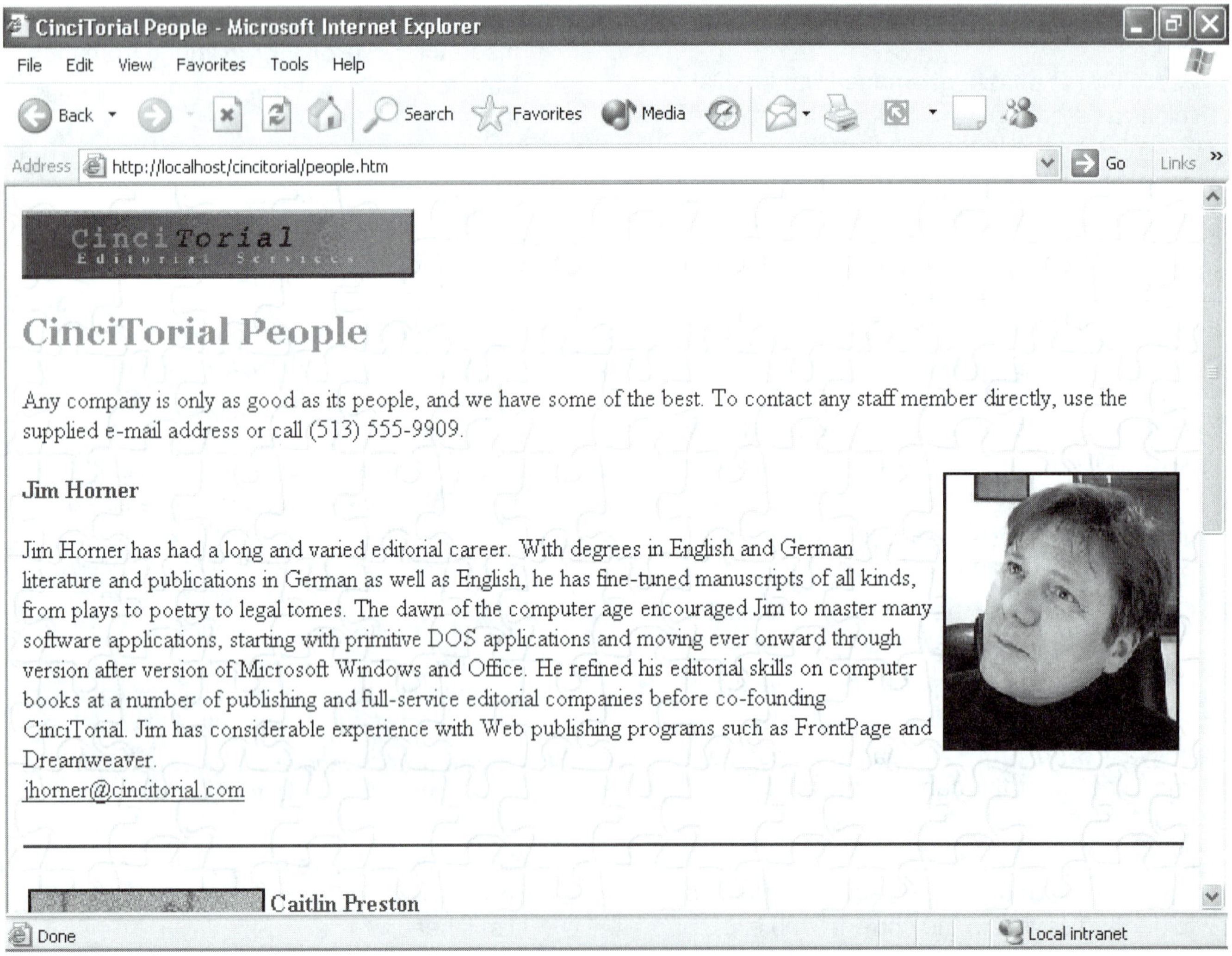

Chapter

7

Templates, the Library, and Design Notes

Templates maintain a uniform look and feel across the entire Web site. Dreamweaver provides flexible template design features. You can control individual sections of your page without affecting the basic design. The Assets panel's Library feature helps automate the insertion and changing of elements on multiple pages in your site. You can use the Design Notes feature to track your project.

In this chapter, you'll learn how to:

- Create and edit a template
- Apply a template to a new page
- Add items to the Asset panel's Library
- Insert and modify library items
- Use the Design Notes features

About Templates

- A **template** is a collection of formats and page elements that can be used to give pages in a Web site a consistent look.
- For example, a template could include a background image or color, images, and headings and text styles and formats. Using a template can save you considerable development time.
- When you create a template, you can specify **noneditable** and **editable** elements:
  - Noneditable elements are items that should remain the same on each page, such as a copyright notice or a logo.
  - Editable elements are items such as text or headings that can change on a page.
- The value of creating and using templates is that you can easily adjust formats over an entire Web site. When you modify a template, you can update all pages that use that template at the same time to show the modifications.

Create a New Template

- You can create a template from a new, blank page or an existing page that contains text and other page elements. If your pages contain complex layouts, it makes sense to use a page you have already formatted as the basis for the template.
- Create a new template in either of two ways:
  - In an open document, use the File>Save As Template command on the menu bar. Dreamweaver opens the Save As Template dialog box (see illustration in the next column) where you can name the template.
  - Or click the Make Template button on the Templates tab of the Insert bar.

Save As Template dialog box

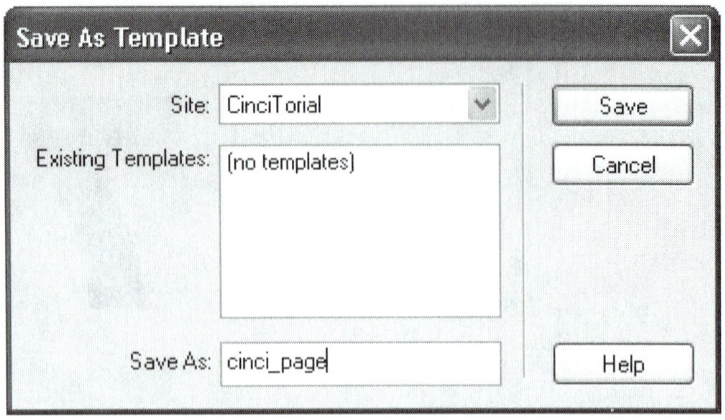

Create Templates in Assets Panel

- You have already been introduced to the Assets panel in the previous chapter. In addition to the images that were automatically added to the Assets panel, any colors used in your Web pages and URLs, including hyperlinks to Web pages and e-mail links, have been stored in the Assets panel.
- The Assets panel is divided into categories. You can access the URLs used in your site by clicking the URLs category in the Assets panel.
- You can access colors used in your Web site by clicking the Colors category.
- The same commands that you use to add images to your Favorites list in the Assets panel can be used to add URLs, colors, and other kinds of objects and style elements.
- The Assets panel's tools can also be used for creating and managing templates and library items.

Assets panel displaying template information

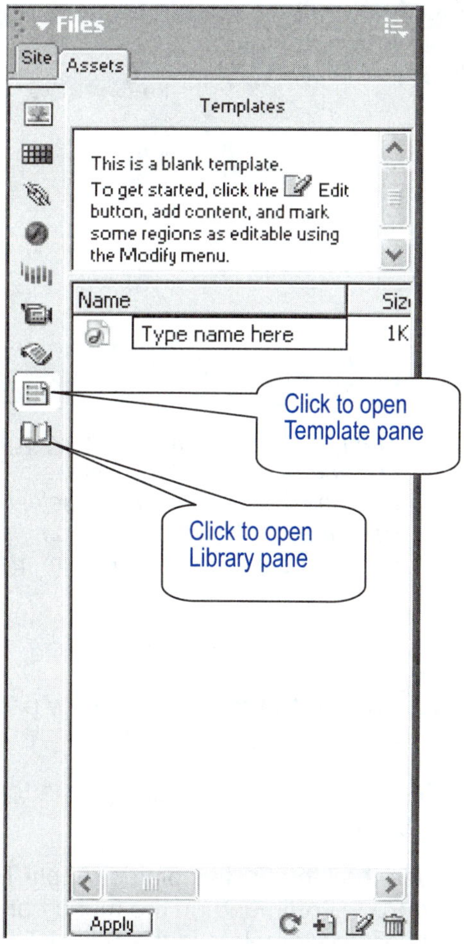

- To create a new template in the Assets panel, click the Templates category and then click the New Template button at the bottom of the panel and provide a name for the template.
- Dreamweaver stores templates automatically in the Templates folder in the current site. If no templates have been created yet, Dreamweaver will create the Templates folder as well.
- If you used the File>Save as Template method, the new template opens automatically after you save the template. If you have created the template in the Assets panel, you must click the Edit Template button to open the template.
- A Dreamweaver template looks like any other Web page. The title bar, however, shows the page title <<Template>> so you know you are working in a template page.
- If you are creating the template from scratch, add and modify page elements as you would on any Web page.
- You can use the objects and style elements in your Assets panel or insert or format new ones.
- You can specify a background color or picture, format levels of headings, format paragraph text, add a logo, and so on.

  Note: *You can also create a layout with frames or layers or attach a cascading style sheet (CSS). You will learn about frames, layers, and cascading style sheets in later chapters.*

- As you create the template, you must give some thought to editable and noneditable items. Noneditable items will be locked on any page created using the template. That is, an author will not be able to change them on the page. This helps to protect items such as logos, official photographs, and the like from being changed without authorization.
- All items on a template are noneditable unless you specify that they be editable. To create an editable item, select the item such as a heading or text paragraph. For best results, select while in Code and Design view so that you select the tags around the text as well. Not doing so may result in error messages requesting that you edit your code.
- Click the Templates tab in the Insert bar. Then click the Editable Region button. Dreamweaver opens the New Editable Region dialog box (see illustration below), where you can supply a name in place of the default name for the editable item.

Name an editable item

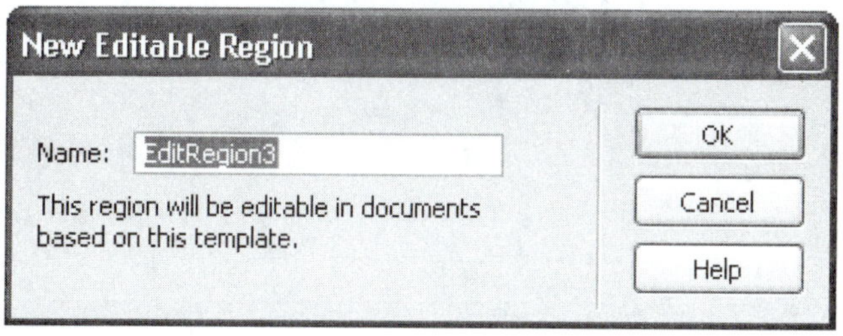

- The editable item name displays on the template page surrounded by a light blue box that has a tab containing the editable item name.
- In pages based on templates, the entire page is bordered in yellow with the template name in the top right corner (see illustration below).

Editable items in Dreamweaver

- An author can click on an editable region placeholder in a page based on the template to add new content to the page. The mouse pointer turns to a "not permitted" ⃠ symbol to inform you that the region cannot be edited (such as adding or changing text or resizing an image).

Apply a Template

- Apply a Dreamweaver template to existing pages or to new pages. Dreamweaver supplies several options for applying a template.
- To apply a template at the time you create a new page, use the File>New command on the menu bar, and click the Templates tab.
- Dreamweaver opens the New from Template dialog box, where you can select the template to use on the new page from a list of templates available for your site (see illustration at top of next column).

Apply a template to a new page

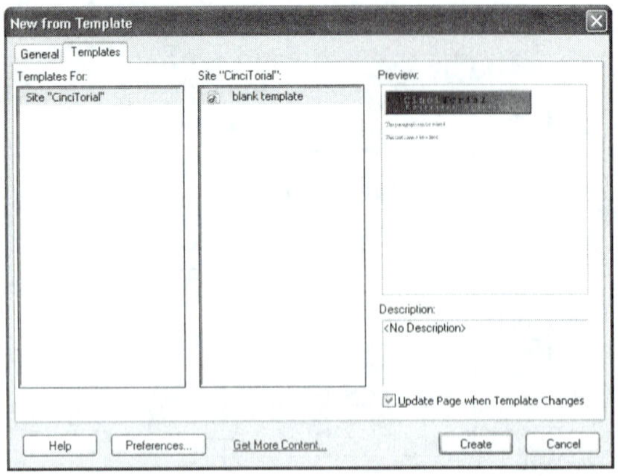

Note: *The New from Template dialog box offers the Update Page when Template Changes checkbox. This checkbox is selected by default and allows you to automatically update the page if changes are made to the template.*

- After you select the desired template, click the [Create] button to open the new page in the Document window.
- You have two options for applying a template to an existing page:
  - Use the Modify>Templates>Apply Template to Page command on the menu bar and then select the template in the Select Template dialog box (see illustration).

Select Template dialog box

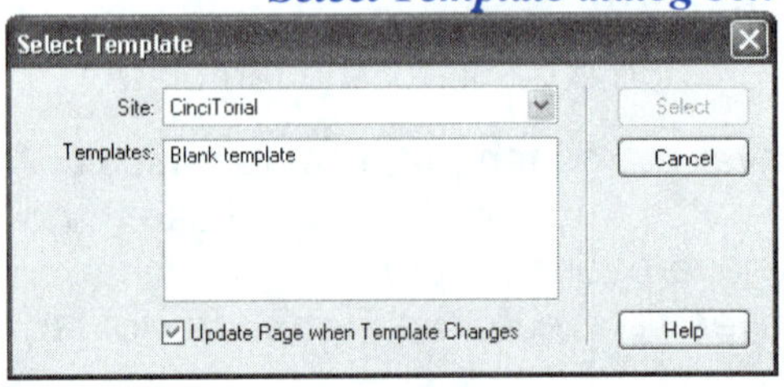

  - If the Assets panel is open, click the Templates button if necessary, select the desired template, and drag it onto the page.

- Applying a template to a page that already has text may require that you "resolve" what to do with that text. Dreamweaver analyzes the page and then displays the Inconsistent Region Names dialog box similar to the one shown below to alert you to the fact that it does not know what editable region to use for the preexisting text. You can place the text in an editable region.

Applying editable regions to existing text

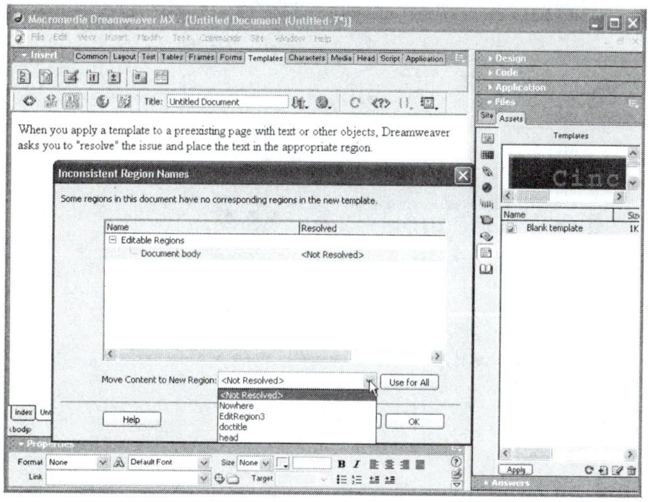

- Accepting the Nowhere option in the Move Content to New Region list throws away all content on the page and inserts the template's content. If you have only a few lines of text on the page and its format matches an editable region in the dialog box, choose that editable region.

- You can detach a page from a template using the Modify>Templates>Detach from Template command on the menu bar. All template formatting remains, but the page will not update if changes are made to the template.

Edit a Template and Update Pages

- After you have created a template, you can edit it at any point by opening it from the Assets panel. You can make changes to both editable and noneditable regions—and remove them, too.

  Note: *To open a template to edit it, double-click on the template file name in the Assets panel. Make sure the page title <<Template>> appears in the title bar.*

- When you save revisions to a template that has been applied to pages in a Web site, Dreamweaver asks if you want to update the pages that use the template (see illustration in the next column).

Dreamweaver prompts you to update pages

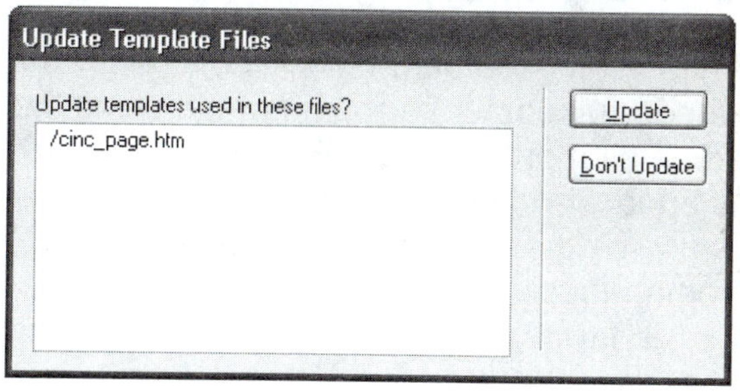

- If you click Update, Dreamweaver performs the updates for you and displays a report to tell you what pages have been updated (see illustration at the top of the next page).

- If you deselected the Update Page when Template Changes option in the New from Template—or Select Template—dialog boxes, pages attached to a template will not be changed automatically when changes to the template are saved and you will not see either dialog box prompting you to update.

Update Pages report

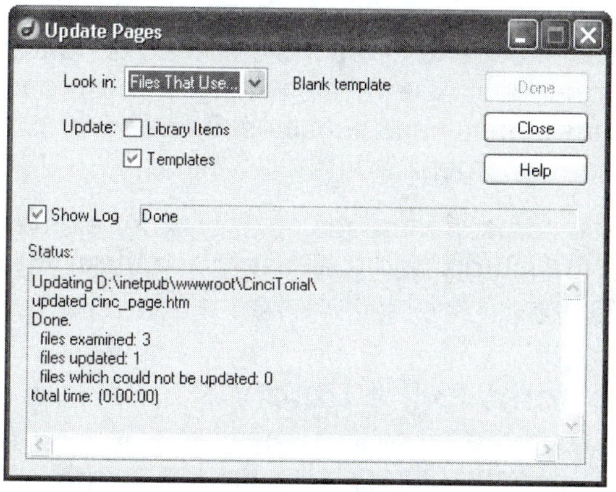

- If you choose not to update all pages, you can update pages individually using the Modify>Templates>Update Current Page command on the menu bar. This command essentially reapplies the template to the current page only.

- If you have chosen not to update pages immediately after saving changes to the template, you can at a later time update all pages using the Modify>Templates>Update Pages command on the menu bar. When you do so, Dreamweaver displays an empty Update Pages dialog box. Click the Start button to begin the update process.

Use the Library

- The **Library** feature in the Assets panel is a wonderful tool for saving time and using the same elements repeatedly—but with the ability to update and change them in every Web page that uses the element in a Web site. This tremendously reduces ramp-up time when working with a team possessing different kinds of skills.
- When you place a library item on a page, Dreamweaver inserts a copy of the HTML source code for that item into the document, and adds an HTML comment containing a reference to the original, external item—a link from the page item to the library item.
- You can modify that library item wherever it appears in the Web site by modifying the item in the Library. In this way a Library item differs from an item inserted from the other Assets panels.
- A proficient designer can create a logo and save it to the Library, for example, allowing a less experienced team member to go to the Library and use the element. This assures consistency and eliminates the need for redevelopment.
- You can store images, text, or other elements in the Library and then use these **library items** on any page in a Web site.

Add Items to the Library

- To view the Library, click the Library category in the Assets panel.
- Library items display in the upper pane of the palette. Click the library item's name in the lower pane to display it in the upper pane. You can use the scroll bars if necessary to display the entire item.
- Dreamweaver automatically creates a Library subfolder in the site's root folder to contain the library items.

Library pane in Assets panel

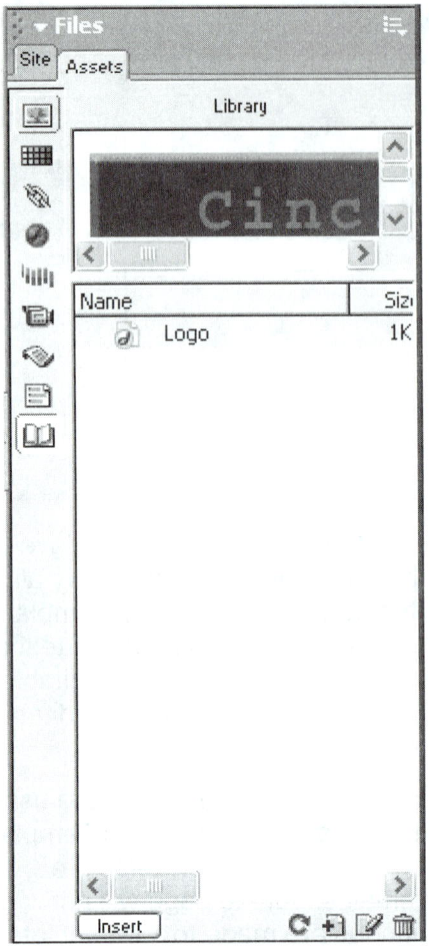

- You can create library items from existing text or images by selecting the object in the document and clicking Modify>Library>Add Object to Library.
- You can also create new library items. Click the New Library Item button and then the Edit button on the Library pane of the Assets panel to open a new <<Library Item>> in the Document window.
- Use this Document window to type text or insert images or other elements to create the library item. When you are finished, click on File>Save As to save the library item, and then close the <<Library Item>> window.
- You can remove an item from the library at any time by right-clicking its name in the Library pane and then clicking Delete—or selecting it and clicking the Delete button on the Library pane.

Insert Library Item on Page

- Inserting library items on a page is even easier than adding them to the Library. Position the insertion point where you want the library item to appear in the Document window, select its name in the Library pane of the Assets panel, and click the Insert button.
- You can also simply drag a library item or its name from the Library pane of the Assets panel to the desired position on the Web page.
- Inserted images are initially shaded but will look normal as soon as you click in the Document window. Inserted text retains a yellow shading to remind you it is a library item.
- You cannot edit a library item once it has been inserted on a page unless you break the link between the item on the page and the Library. You can detach an item from the Library by clicking it on the page and then clicking the Detach from Original button in the Properties panel.

Modify Library Item and Update Pages

- As for templates, the value of using library items is that all library items inserted throughout a Web site can be modified at once by modifying the item stored in the Library.
- Edit a library item by double-clicking either the item itself or its name in the Library pane of the Assets panel. Or, select the item name and click the Edit button.
- The library item opens in a <<Library Item>> window. You can then edit or modify it using Dreamweaver's editing tools.
- After you save the modified item, Dreamweaver will ask if you want to update all pages on which that library item appears (see illustration). You can choose to update all pages or not update.

Note: *Dreamweaver will automatically update items on open pages and ask you about updating closed pages.*

Choose to update library items

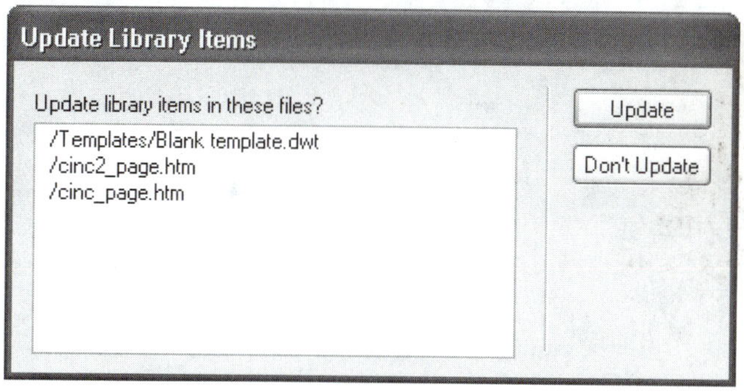

- If you choose not to update, you can use the Modify>Library>Update Current Page or Update Pages commands on the menu bar to update a single page or all pages with Library changes.
- Dreamweaver displays an Update Pages dialog box similar to that displayed when a template is updated to show you which pages have had a library item updated.

Use Design Notes

- Design Notes work much like comment tags in Word or HTML design, but you have much more control over who sees your notes.
- This is especially helpful when designing your site with sensitive data that must be shared only with your team members. Design Notes are never displayed in a browser but travel with your files.
- To use Design Notes, you must enable Design Notes in the Site Definition dialog box for the current site (see). Click Site>Edit Sites. Then select the desired site if necessary and click Edit. Click the Advanced tab, if necessary, and click Design Notes in the Category list. Make sure the Maintain Design Notes checkbox is selected. Select Upload Design Notes for Sharing if you want to send the Design Notes along with your files.

Enable Design Notes in Site Definition dialog box

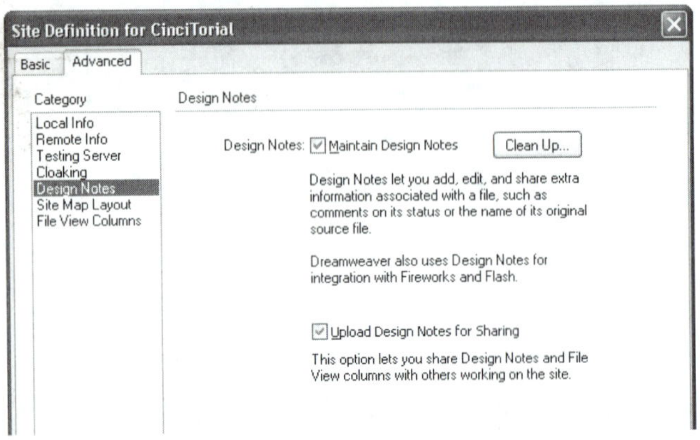

Note: *See Chapter 2 for information on site setup. Typically, the Design Notes options are selected by default when you define a site using the Site Definition wizard.*

- Add Design Notes to a page using the File>Design Notes command on the menu bar. Or click the File Management button on the Document toolbar and select Design Notes from the menu.
- On the Design Notes dialog box's Basic Info tab, you can specify the page's status, insert the current date, and add comments (see illustration at the top of the next column).
  - Click the Status list arrow to display a list of status options, including draft, revision1, and final.
  - Click the date icon to insert the current date in the Notes box.
  - Type comments or insert other necessary information in the Notes text box.

Add basic Design Note information

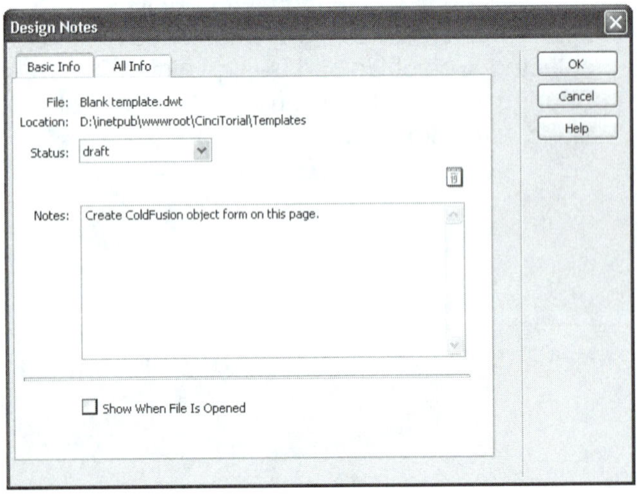

- If you want the Design Notes to appear each time the page opens, select the Show When File Is Opened checkbox.
- To see more Design Note information, click the All Info tab. This tab shows information as sets of **keys** and values. In the illustration below, status, notes, and author are keys. The = sign separates a key from its value.

Add new keys on All Info tab

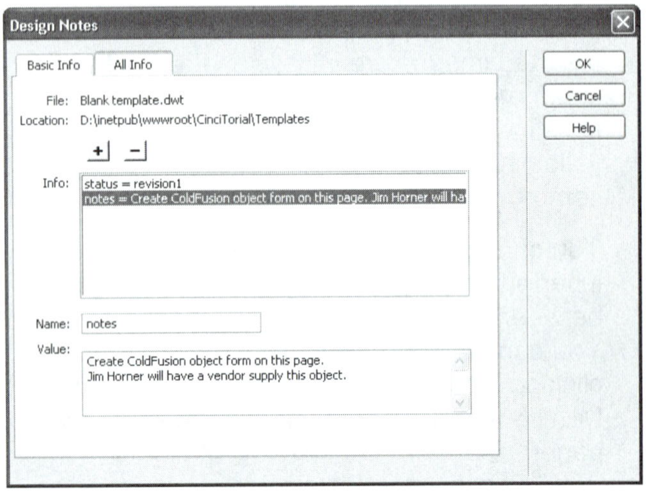

- Add new keys (such as *author* in the illustration above) by clicking the + button. The Name and Value boxes at the bottom of the tab empty so you can type the name of the new key and its value.
- Select a key/value combination in the Info list and click − to remove the key/value.
- In addition to Web pages, design notes can also be added to objects such as image files.

Viewing Design Notes

- The same steps used to create a design note can be used to view a design note. However, to easily see that a page has a design note attached to it, expand the Site panel.
- Design notes that are attached to a Web page or object are shown with a note icon in the Local Files pane of the expanded Site panel window.
- To open the note, double-click the icon.

Procedures

Create New Template

Using existing page

1. Click **File** .... Alt+F
2. Click **Save As Template**.... T

OR

- Click the **Make Template** button in the Templates tab of the Insert bar.

3. Type name for template.
4. Click [Save].
5. Edit and modify formats as desired.
6. Save template after editing.

Create Editable Region

1. Select text or graphic to make editable or position insertion point in area of page to make editable.
2. Click the **Editable Region** button in the Templates tab of the Insert bar.
3. Supply name for editable area.

   ✓ *To remove an Editable Region, select the region by right-clicking its tab and then clicking Remove Tag.*

   ✓ *Make an editable area noneditable by selecting it and clicking Modify>Templates> Remove Template Markup.*

Apply a Template

Apply when creating page.

1. Click **File** .... Alt+F
2. Click **New** .... N
3. Click Templates tab.
4. Select desired template.
5. If desired, select **Update Page when Template Changes** option.......................... Alt+U
6. Click [Create]

Apply to existing page.

1. Click **Modify**................ Alt+M
2. Click **Templates**.......... E, E
3. Click **Apply Template to Page** .... →, A
4. Select the desired template.
5. Click [Select].

OR

- Drag template name from the Assets panel to page.

Detach Page from Template

1. Click **Modify**................ Alt+M
2. Click **Templates**.......... E, E
3. Click **Detach from Template** .... →, D

Edit Template

From Site panel

1. Open the Template folder.
2. Double-click the template file.
3. Make changes to editable and noneditable regions as desired.

From Assets panel

1. Click the **Templates** category.
2. Double-click the template file.

OR

   a. Select the template.

   b. Click the **Edit** button.

3. Make changes to editable and noneditable regions as desired.

Delete Template

From Site panel

1. Open the Template folder.
2. Right-click the template file.
3. Click **Delete**.

From Assets panel

1. Click the **Templates** category.
2. Right-click template file.
3. Click **Delete**.

OR

2. Select template.
3. Click **Delete** button.

Update Template Pages

After making changes to template

- Click [Update] in Update Template Files dialog box to update all files that use the template.

OR

If files have not been updated after changes

1. Click **Modify**................ Alt+M
2. Click **Templates** .... E, E
3. Click **Update Current Page**.............. →, C

   OR

   Click **Update Pages**........... U

Add Items to the Library

Ctrl + Shift + B

1. Select object.
2. Click **Modify**................ Alt+M
3. Click **Library** I
4. Click **Add Object to Library** .... O

OR

1. Click **Window**............. Alt+W
2. Click **Assets**........................ A
3. Click **Library** category.
4. Select and drag item from the Document window to the lower pane in the Library.
5. Type a name for the new item.

Insert Library Item on Page

1. Position insertion point where library item should appear.
2. Select library item in Library pane.
3. Click Insert.

OR

- Drag library item from Library pane to desired location on page.

Modify Library Item

From Assets panel

1. Click **Library** category.
2. Double-click the library item.

OR

   a. Select the library item.
   b. Click the **Edit** button.
3. Make changes to library item as desired.

Delete Library Item

From Assets panel

1. Click **Library** category.
2. Right-click template file.
3. Click **Delete**.

OR

4. Select library item.
5. Click **Delete** button.

Update Library Items on Pages

After making changes to library item

- Click Update in Update Library Items dialog box to update all files that use the template.

OR

If items have not been updated after changes

1. Click **Modify** .... Alt+M
2. Click **Library**...................... I
3. Click **Update Current Page** C

   OR

   Click **Update Pages** .... P

Enable Design Notes

1. Click **Site** .... Alt+S
2. Click **Edit Sites** .... E, E, Enter
3. Click name of site to edit.
4. Click Edit... .
5. Click **Design Notes** in Category list.
6. Select **Maintain Design Notes** checkbox, if necessary Alt+M
7. Select **Upload Design Notes for Sharing** if desired Alt+U
8. Click OK
9. Click Done to close the Edit Sites dialog box.

View Design Notes

1. Expand the Site panel.
2. Double-click (**Note icon**) in the Notes column of the Local Files pane.

Add Design Notes to Page

1. Select the desired Web page or object.
2. Click **File** .... Alt+F
3. Click **Design Notes** .... G
4. Click **Status** list arrow and choose status for page.
5. Click icon to add current date to Notes box.
6. Type comments in Notes box.
7. Select **Show When File Is Opened** checkbox to see Design Notes each time file opens.
8. Add new key:
   c. Click **All Info** tab.
   d. Click +.
   e. Type name for key in Name box.
   f. Type value for key in Value box.
   g. Click OK.
9. Select a key and click − to delete it if desired.

Exercise Directions

1. Start Dreamweaver.
2. Open the **CinciTorial** site.
3. To save time, you want to create a template that contains a space for the logo link to the Home Page, a formatted Heading 2, and a placeholder for a navigation bar. Create the template as follows:
   - Open **contactus.htm**. This page already has the formatted Heading 2 in place.
   - Create a new template from this page and name it **cinci_page**.
   - Position the insertion point to the left of the heading and press the **Enter** key to create a new line.

   ✓ *To avoid error messages, work in Code and Design view so that you can select the <p> and <h2> tags as well as the text between them when you create the editable regions.*

   - Move up into the new line and type **Logo**.
   - Position the insertion point at the end of the Heading 2 heading, press the **Enter** key, and type **Navigation**.

   ✓ *Don't worry about the formats of the paragraphs you have just typed. You will change these formats below.*

   - Create editable regions from each of the three lines in the template, using the names **Logo**, **Heading 2**, and **Navigation**.
4. Format the editable regions as follows.

   ✓ *Try this shortcut. Right-click anywhere in the text and click Paragraph Format from the shortcut menu and select the desired format.*

   - Format the Logo editable region with the Paragraph format.
   - Format the Heading 2 editable region with the formats you used for Heading 2 on other pages, if necessary.
   - Format the Navigation region with Paragraph formatting. If necessary, change the font to **Default Font** and the font color to black.
5. Remove the Contact Us page title in the Document toolbar.
6. Save and close the <<Template>> page. If you are asked to update, do so. (No pages will be changed.)
7. Open **contactus.htm** and apply the **cinci_page** template to this page.
8. The Inconsistent Region Names dialog box opens because the page already has content. Click Document body, and then choose **Heading 2** to receive the existing content on the page.
9. Enter the page title **Contact Us** for this page.

   ✓ *The previous page title disappeared when you applied the template, because the template does not have a page title.*

10. Create a new page that uses the **cinci_page** template. Name the page **specialties.htm** and give it the page title **Our Specialties**.
11. Replace the Heading 2 placeholder with **Our Specialties**.
12. You forgot you wanted to use the **puzzle.gif** background on all new pages. Open the **cinci_page** template and apply the **puzzle.gif** background to the <<Template>> document.
13. Save and close the template. Update the pages with the revised template.
14. Now that you have basic formatting in place for **contactus.htm** and **specialties.htm**, detach these pages from the template.
15. Display the Library pane in the Assets panel and add—and update—items to the Library as follows:
    - Open **index.htm** and drag the logo image to the Library. Name it **Logo**.
    - Open **people.htm** and drag the small logo that links to the home page to the Library. Name it **Home link**.
16. Create a new library item named **Copyright** that contains the text **Copyright © CinciTorial Co. All rights reserved.** If you are asked to update, do so. (No pages will be changed.)

    ✓ *Dreamweaver may display a note about special characters. You can ignore the warning.*

17. Insert library items as follows:

- Insert the **Home link** library item in place of the Logo placeholder on **contactus.htm** and **specialties.htm**.
- Insert the **Copyright** library item below the last paragraph of type on all pages in the site.

  ✓ *Make sure the copyright library item is left aligned on all pages. You may need to adjust HTML code in the Code view or Code inspector.*

  ✓ *In the contactus.htm and specialties.htm documents, the Copyright library item should go under the Navigation bar placeholder.*

18. Cut the *Last update* paragraph on **index.htm** and delete it on **services.htm**. You will add this information to the **Copyright** library item.
19. Modify the Copyright library item to include the color #990033 and no shading. Paste the cut *Last update* information following the *All rights reserved* sentence.
20. Don't update pages automatically. Instead, view each page in the site and update it to see the change to the library item.
21. Save and close each page after you update it.
22. Open **contactus.htm** and create the following Design Note information:
    - Set the status as **draft**.
    - Insert the following comment: **Create form on this page.**
    - Add a new key named **author** and assign the value **Ellen**.
23. Open **specialties.htm** and create the following Design Notes:
    - Set the status as **draft**.
    - Insert the following comment: **Create table on this page**.
24. Expand the Site panel and view the design notes.
25. Open **index.htm** and add the words **Our Specialties** below the list of links. Use these words to create a link to **specialties.htm**.
26. Test the Web site in the browser and make sure all links work from and to the Home Page. Your Contact Us page should look similar to Illustration A.
27. Close the browser.
28. Close any open pages.
29. Exit Dreamweaver.

Illustration A

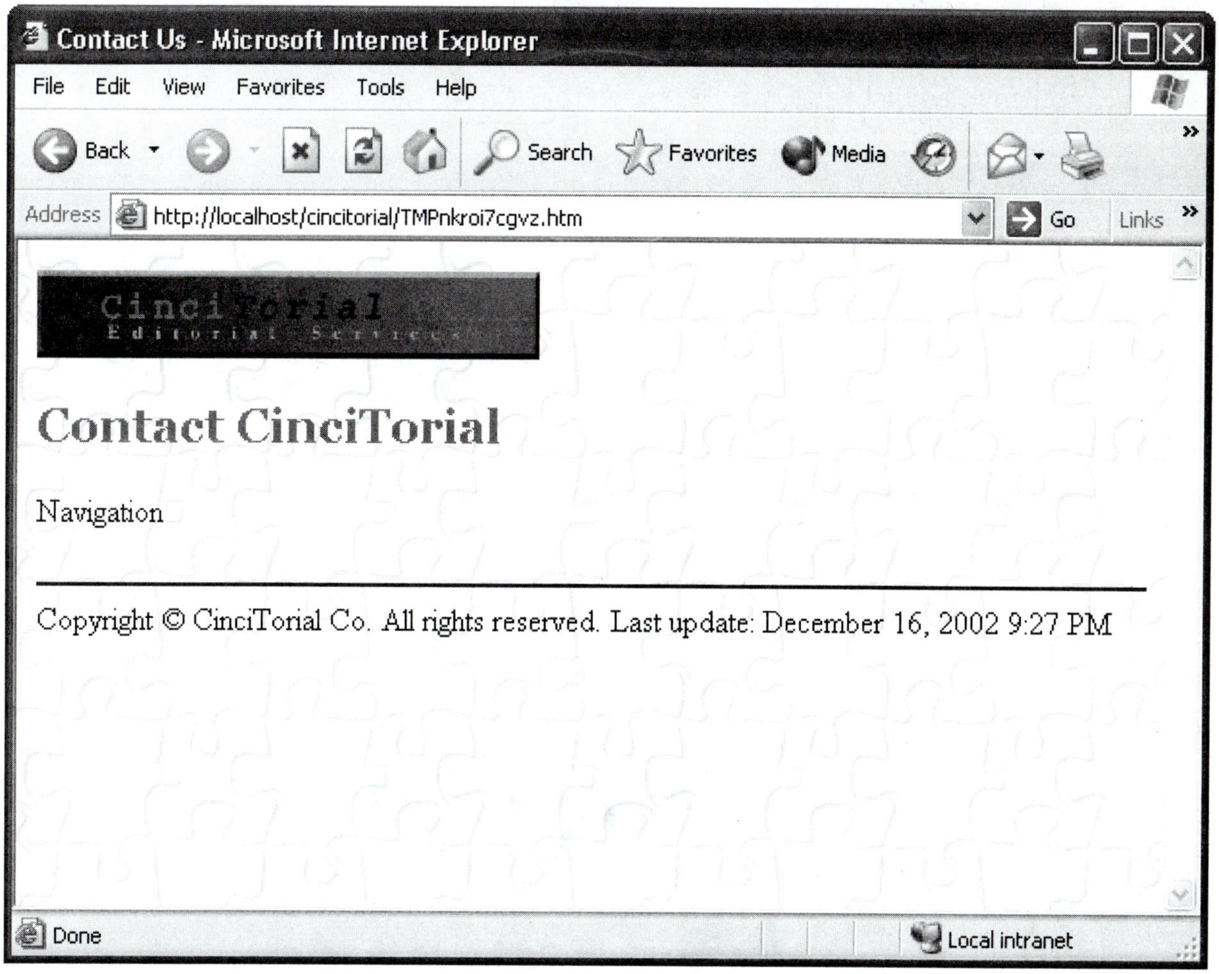

Next Chapter

chapter

8

Tables and Navigation Bars

A table in a Web document is the best and most structured way to organize graphics, text, and other objects such as forms in your Web pages. A table can be designed to be an obvious part of the page—as an object itself—or invisible so that it simply supports nested elements such as graphics. You can use a table to structure a Dreamweaver navigation bar, which supplies links to pages in a Web site.

In this chapter, you'll learn how to:

- Create and restructure a new table
- Format a table with borders, background colors, and images
- Create a Dreamweaver navigation bar

About Tables

- Tables are used on Web pages to organize related data in a grid made up of **rows** and **columns**. A table may consist of only a few rows and columns, or it may be used to organize an entire Web page.
- Though there are other, more elaborate ways of organizing Web page data, such as the layers and frames you will learn about in Chapters 11 and 12, tables provide the most dependable framework for Web page layout. All browsers can display the HTML codes used to create tables, so if you want to make sure your page layout will work for all visitors, structure it using a table.

  Note: *You will use a table to create a page layout in Chapter 9.*

- Once a table has been inserted on a Web page, it can be restructured very easily. Change the look of a table by adjusting row height or column width, adding or deleting rows or columns, or merging or splitting **cells** (a cell is the intersecting point of a row and a column).
- You can modify a table's appearance by inserting images, modifying border width and color, and adding background color or images to table cells. In addition to the obvious formatting commands and tools available for tables, you can also use the Tag inspector or Assets panel to change table appearance.

Create a Table

- Create a table on a Web page using the Insert bar or a menu bar command. Position your insertion point where the table should appear and then use one of these methods:
  - Click the Insert Table button on the Common tab, the Layout tab, or Table tab of the Insert bar.
  - Use the Insert>Table command on the menu bar.

  Note: *You can also draw a table in Layout view. You will work with Layout view and table drawing tools in Chapter 9.*

- The Insert Table dialog box opens after you perform either of these actions (see illustration below). In this dialog box, you can specify the number of rows and columns for the new table.

Insert Table dialog box

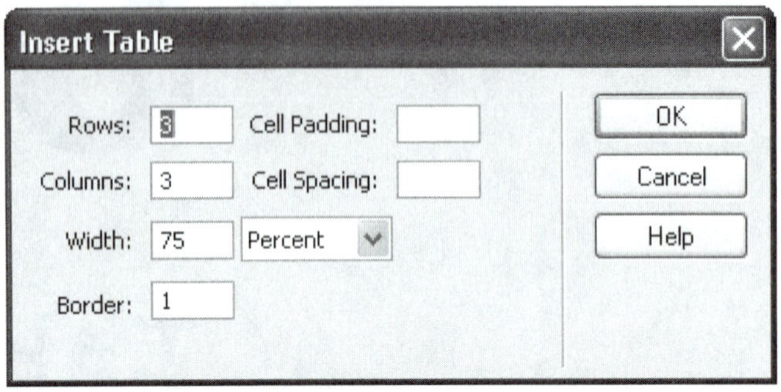

Note: *The Insert Table dialog box shows the settings chosen for the last table. Make sure you check* all *settings in the Insert Table dialog box before clicking OK.*

- You can specify a width for the table as it is being created. Type a width in the Width box in the Insert Table dialog box and choose to measure that width either as a percent of the page width or in pixels.
- By using the percentage value in the Width text box, you can maintain the ratio of table to page text when the page is viewed in different types of browsers. Using pixel values ensures that the table will be exactly the same physical size in any browser or screen resolution.
- Either measurement option is appropriate for tables used to format the entire Web page. A pixel value, however, is the best choice for tables that you don't want to be resized in the browser.
- You can also select border width in the Insert Table dialog box. Border width is measured in pixels.

  Tip: *Leaving the Border box empty results in a borderless—or invisible—table that can be used to format an entire Web page or other data.*

New table on Web page

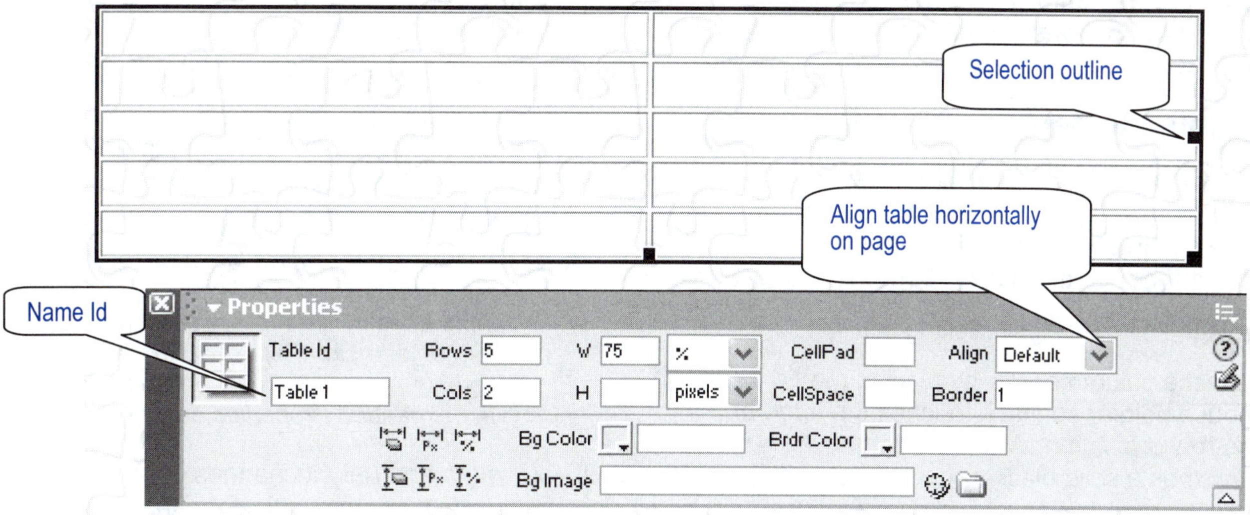

- If desired, you can insert values for **cell padding** and **cell spacing**. Cell padding is the distance between cell text and a cell border. Cell spacing is the amount of space between cells.

  Tip: *You can change these values at any time after creating a table using the Properties panel.*

- A new table displays on the Web page with default border options (see illustration above) if you have specified a border width. The table is selected when inserted.
- While the table is selected, you can use the Properties panel to make a number of changes to the table:
  - Identify (name) the table if desired.
  - Change the number of rows and columns in the table.
  - Change the width and/or height of the table in percentage of page width or pixel measurements.
  - Specify cell padding and cell spacing.
  - Specify a border width (or delete the border measurement to remove borders altogether).
  - If the table is less than the full page width, you can use the Align list to center, left align, or right align the table in the page.
- In the expanded portion of the Properties panel, you will find properties relating to the table's appearance. You can change column widths and row heights, add border and background colors—or a picture to be used as a table background. (Individual cells can have backgrounds, too, allowing for creative effects.)

  Note: *You will learn about borders and backgrounds later in this chapter.*

Insert Text and Images in Table

- To enter text in a table, click in a table cell and begin typing. Use the Tab key or an arrow key to move from cell to cell in the table.
- Format text in a table cell just as you would on a Web page using the buttons and other options on the Properties panel. You can change font style, size, and color; adjust alignment; and even insert links in table cells.
- You can also insert an image in any table cell using the same procedure as for inserting an image on a Web page. If the image is larger than the table cell, the cell automatically expands to accommodate the image.

Adjust Table Structure

- Once you have inserted the basic table structure on a Web page, you can make a number of changes to it to accommodate data as you begin to add content.

- As you adjust table structure, you will find it helpful to display the History panel so you can view your adjustments. You can easily undo a whole series of actions from this panel.

Select Table Elements

- To make some structural and formatting modifications, you need to select a portion of the table or the entire table. Use these guidelines for selecting table elements:
  - Select a single cell by clicking in it.
  - Select a column or row by placing the mouse pointer so that it touches the edge of the row or column. When the pointer becomes a solid black arrow pointing either downward or to the right, click the mouse button to complete the selection (see illustration below).

Selected column

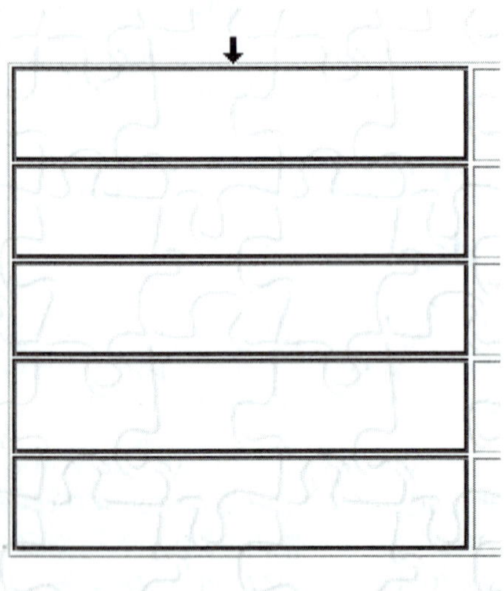

- To select noncontiguous elements, such as cells, rows, and columns in a table, hold the Ctrl key and make the desired selections.
- To select the entire table, click on any outside border with either the four-headed arrow pointer or the sizing pointer, or click inside the table and then click the <table> tag in the tag selector on the left side of the status bar.

Change Cell Width and Height

- You can easily resize column widths or row heights by clicking on a column or row border and then dragging to the desired size. You can also resize table elements precisely in the Properties panel in order to fit graphics, text, and other objects.
- Click in a cell and type a value in the W (Width) and/or H (Height) box in the expanded Properties panel. All cells in a column change when a new width is entered, and all cells in a row change when a new height is entered.

  Note: *If you want the cell value in percentages rather than in the default pixels, immediately follow the value with a percentage sign (%). You can also use the pixel-to-percentage conversion buttons in the expanded Properties panel.*

- If your width and height changes do not look the way you want, you can select the table and use the Clear Row Heights or Clear Column Widths buttons on the expanded Properties panel. Clear Row Heights returns any rows to their default height. Clear Column Widths reduces column width to exactly fit the widest entry in the column.

  Tip: *If you prefer to use menu commands, you can select the table and use Modify>Table>Clear Cell Heights or Clear Cell Widths to adjust column height and width.*

Insert and Delete Rows and Columns

- You may need to add or delete rows and columns after you have created a table. You can insert a new row as you are adding content to a table by simply pressing the Tab key when you are in the last cell of the table.
- To add a new row elsewhere in the table or a new column, use the commands on the Modify>Table submenu:
  - Click Modify>Table>Insert Row to insert a new row above the currently selected cell.
  - Click Modify>Table>Insert Column to insert a new column to the left of the currently selected cell.
  - Click Modify>Table>Insert Rows or Columns to open the Insert Rows or Columns dialog box (see illustration below) where you can specify a number of rows or columns and their position.

Select number of rows or columns to insert

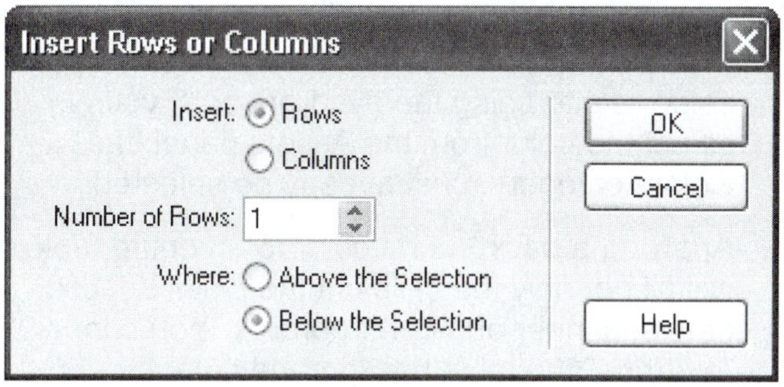

Tip: *You can also access these commands by right-clicking in a cell and then clicking Table on the shortcut menu.*

- To delete a row or column, click in it and then press the Delete key.

Split and Merge Cells

- Tables are generally considered symmetrical elements, with rows stacked on rows, cells stacked on cells. Although this is beneficial for tabular or mathematical data, you may need to split and merge the cells to emphasize headers, labels, and other design elements.
- When you **split cells**, you break one cell into more than one column or row. When you **merge cells**, you combine more than one cell to create a single, larger cell.
- To split a cell, select the cell and then click the Splits cell button on the Properties panel (or use the Modify>Table>Split Cells command on the menu bar). The Split Cell dialog box opens to allow you to split the cell into the desired number of rows or columns (see illustration below).

Split cell into rows or columns

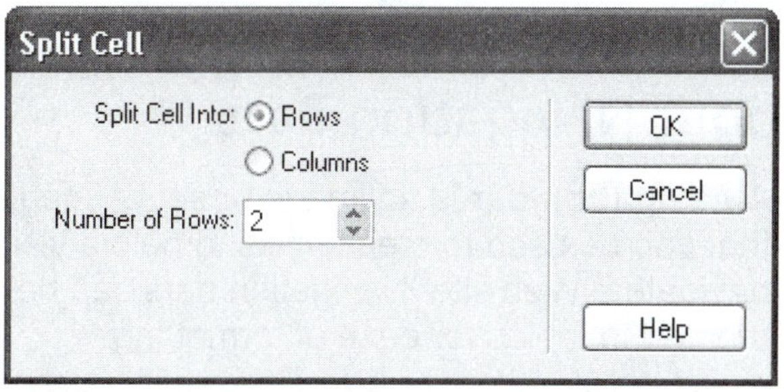

- To merge cells, select the cells and click the Merges selected cells button on the Properties panel (or use the Modify>Table> Merge Cells command on the menu bar).

Span Rows and Columns

- The Modify>Table submenu also features commands for merging columns or rows so that they span across one or more columns or down one or more rows. In the illustration below, for example, the text has been set to span down one row.

Text spans down one row

Editor Specialities	

- Use the Modify>Table>Increase Row Span or Increase Column Span to span rows or columns.
- Choosing a span command causes the current cell to merge with the one to its right (if you span columns) or below it (if you span rows). Increase the span by issuing the command more than one time.
- Use the Decrease Row Span or Decrease Column Span command to decrease the number of rows or columns spanned.
- Spanning is much the same as merging, but it is easier to do "on the fly" than merging. If you decide you want text to span three columns rather than two, for example, just increase the span. Decreasing the span is likewise easier than splitting a cell you have already merged.

Note: *You can achieve interesting effects with tables if you do some experimenting. For example, you can nest a table within a table cell to provide more layout options.*

Modify Borders and Backgrounds

- New tables usually display default gray borders and no background (the page background displays in the table cells). To improve the look of a table, you can modify the weight and color of the table borders and add a color or background image to the table or cells.

Set Border Colors

- Note that a Dreamweaver table displays two sets of borders around cells to give a three-dimensional look. You have two options for applying color to these borders:
  - You can use a single color for all borders in the table.
  - You can set one color for the outside table border and another color for individual cells in the table. (Or give each cell its own border color, if desired.)

Caution: *Cell border colors may not appear as desired in all browsers. See information on targeting browsers in Chapter 17.*

- To set table border colors, first select the entire table and then click the Brdr Color box to open the color palette and pick the color.

Note: *You can also type the hexadecimal value for any color in the provided text box or select a color scheme already used in the site from the Colors category in the Assets panel by first clicking on the Brdr Color box clicking on the desired color in the Assets panel with the eyedropper tool.*

- To set cell border colors, click in the cell to which you want to apply the color. Click the Brdr color box to display the color palette.
- You may need to experiment with border colors to find a combination that provides visual appeal without overwhelming the table text.

Caution: *Empty cells may not display all border lines when viewed in a browser. To prevent this, insert an invisible object such as a nonbreaking space in an empty cell from the Characters tab on the Insert bar or by pressing Ctrl+Shift+Spacebar.*

Add Background Color to Cells

- Color cell backgrounds in a Web page can draw the eye to information you want emphasized. You can add a color background to one cell, a row, a column—or even the entire table.
- Select the table element you want to add color to and then click the Bg Color box on the Properties panel. Then choose a color from the color palette using the eyedropper. If you select the color from the Assets panel, the Colors category must already be selected.
- Applying a background color to an entire table will fill not only the cells but the small spaces between inner and outer borders. You can "override" the table background color by applying color to individual cells, but the table background color will still show in the border spaces.
- Take care when choosing background colors for table cells. A dark color may make text difficult to read. If you want to use a dark cell background, change text color to white or light yellow to contrast with the background.

Insert Background Image in Cell

- You can select background images for your table or individual cells to add visual interest in much the same way that you add background images that tile for entire Web pages.
- Select the table elements you want to format with the background image. In the Bg box on the Properties panel, type the path to the image, or use the Point to File icon or Browse for File button (or Background URL of cell button) to locate the image.
- You can insert any Web graphic into a table cell or cells, from texture GIFs to JPG photographs, which, if smaller than the cell, tile inside the table cells like page backgrounds do. Make sure, however, that the image you choose does not overwhelm any text in the table.

About Navigation Bars

- A **navigation bar** is an image or set of images that can be used to create links to help a visitor navigate a Web site. Navigation bars can be created in tables for ease of formatting.

Note: *Simple navigation bars can also be created with text in tables. There are many of these already preformatted in the Navigation folder in the Snippets panel.*

- The images in a navigation bar change according to actions taken by a site visitor. For example, a navigation bar button changes color when a visitor rests the mouse pointer on the button.

  Note: *The navigation bar buttons that change color use the Swap Image behavior. You will learn more about behaviors in Chapter 14.*

- You can provide up to four images for each element in a navigation bar:
  - Up: This image is the one that displays when a page opens.
  - Over: This image displays when the mouse pointer moves over the element.
  - Down: This image displays when the navigation bar element is clicked.
  - Over While Down: This image displays if the pointer is moved over the element after it has been clicked.
- Each navigation bar element can be linked to a page in the site or another Web site. The navigation bar can be inserted horizontally or vertically on the page.
- After you create a navigation bar, you can copy it from page to page in a Web site to provide a consistent navigation structure for all pages.

Insert Navigation Bar dialog box

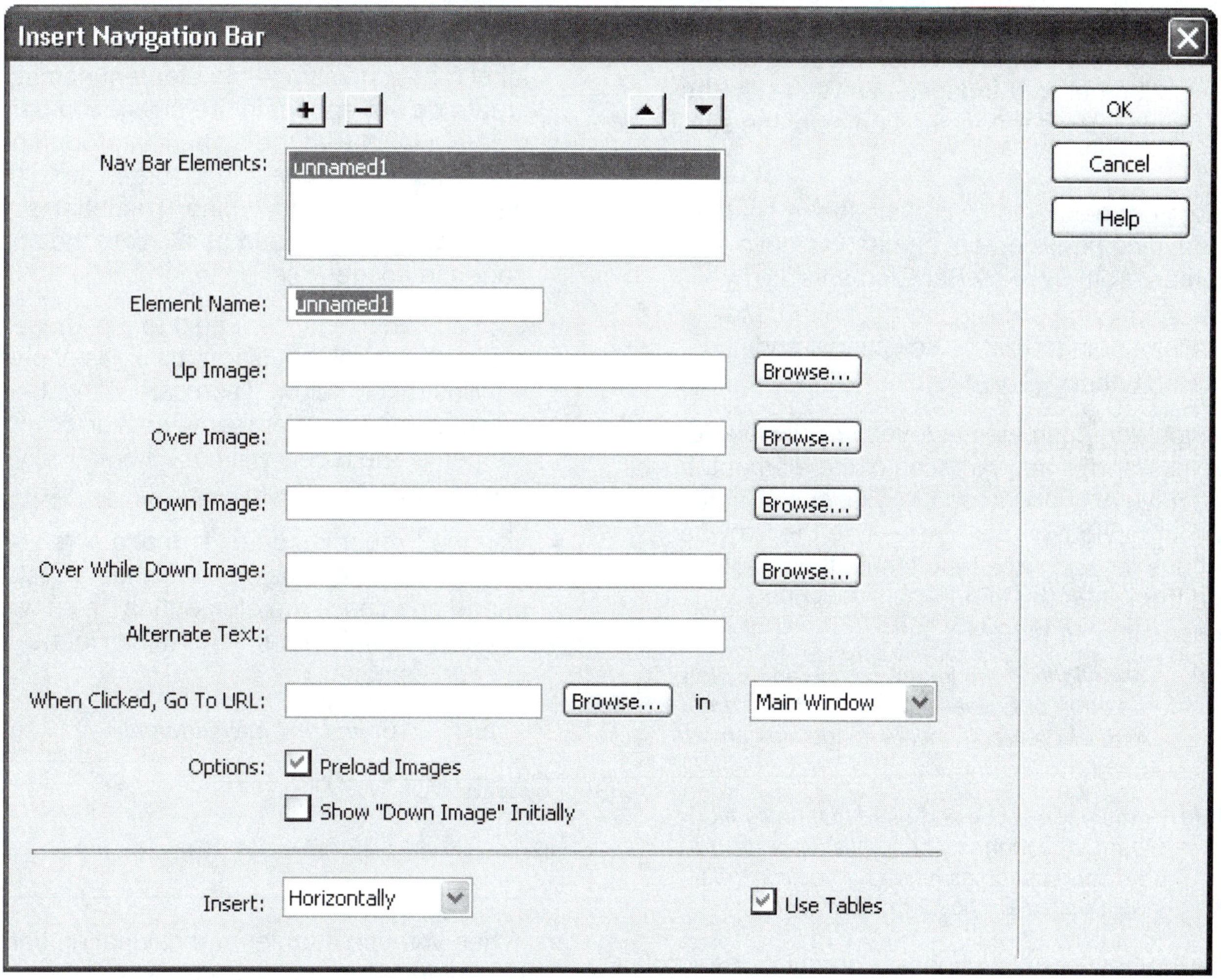

Create Navigation Bar

- To create a new navigation bar, click the Insert Navigation Bar button on the Common tab of the Insert bar, or use the Insert>Interactive Images>Navigation Bar command on the menu bar.
- The Insert Navigation Bar dialog box opens (see illustration above) with a default unnamed element displayed in the Nav Bar Elements list.
- A navigation bar **element** is the image that will appear in the navigation bar. Each element must have a unique name.
- To add the first navigation bar element, replace the *unnamed1* default element with your first navigation bar element. When creating a navigation bar to link pages in a Web site, the elements should reflect the names of the site's pages.
- Add other elements by clicking the + button and typing new element names. Remove an element from the Nav Bar Elements list by selecting it and clicking the – button. Move an element in the list by selecting it and clicking either ▲ or ▼.
- As you add each element, you specify images for the various appearances of the element. If you have only one image to use, specify it for all four navigation bar states. Use the Browse buttons for each image to locate the image, and then save the images with the other images in your site.

Tip: *A navigation bar image can be a GIF file of a button or bullet—although virtually any kind of Web-compatible image file can be used.*

Note: *An image of the sort used in a navigation bar that changes when a visitor performs an action such as hovering or clicking is also called a* rollover *image.*

- For the best results, choose a graphic for each selection—Up, Over, Down, and Over While Down. Be creative and use different images, each a different color, for the four states. If you have only one image to use, select it for each image state.
- For each element, type a relative or absolute address in the When Clicked, Go To URL text box, or use the Browse button to locate the page or site that should open when the element is clicked.
- You can choose to insert the navigation bar horizontally (the default) or vertically on the page, and in a table or freestanding. Inserting the navigation bar in a table gives you access to the table formatting options you have already learned about in this chapter.
- After you click OK to finish the navigation bar, you can modify it on the page. Adjust column widths, for example, if the navigation bar uses a table.
- Unless the images chosen for the navigation bar contain labels, you will need to supply a label for each image—the element names you create do not appear in the navigation bar. To create a label with the same link properties as the image, select the image, press the right arrow key, and begin typing. The label is automatically formatted as a link to the same page the image is linked to.
- Or, you can simply click next to the image and type a text label that is not a link, as shown in the illustration below. Take care with labels if you decide to reorder the navigation bar elements: the labels will not automatically "travel" with the images.
- Use the Properties panel to make sure you have the correct label for an image. (Click the image and check the element name shown just to the right of the image thumbnail in the Properties panel.)

Completed navigation bar

- When you use a table for a navigation bar, you cannot format the table in the same ways you format other tables. You cannot, for example, add cell borders, although you can change the background color of cells or the entire table.

- To modify a navigation bar after creating it, click anywhere in the navigation bar and use the Modify>Navigation Bar command on the menu bar.
- Creating a navigation bar in a Web site with a number of pages can take time. Fortunately, after you create the navigation bar you can select it, copy it, and paste it on other pages in the site. You can also make it part of a template so that it appears whenever a document is created with the template.
- You can also copy the navigation bar and then create a new library item. The copied navigation bar is automatically “pasted” in the Library when you name the new library item.
- There are several advantages to making a navigation bar a library item. Not only is it then easy to insert on other pages, but it cannot be changed accidentally on a page.
- Most important, when new pages are added or old pages deleted, the navigation bar can be modified in the library and then updated easily on all pages.

Procedures

Create Table
Ctrl + Alt + T

1. Position insertion point at location for new table.
2. Click **Insert** .... Alt + I
3. Click **Table** .... T

   OR

   - Click (**Insert Table** button) on Common (or Layout or Tables) tab on Insert bar.
4. Specify number of rows and columns.
5. Specify width as percentage of page width or in pixels.
6. Specify border width and cell padding and spacing.
7. Click OK.

Align Table

1. Select entire table (see below).
2. Click **Align** list arrow in Properties panel.
3. Select desired alignment.

Insert Text and Images in Table

- Click in cell and begin typing.
- Use Tab or arrow key to move from cell to cell.
- Use buttons and features on Properties panel to change format, font, size, font style, color, and alignment of text.
- Insert images as on any page using **Insert>Image** menu command or on Common tab of Insert bar—or drag from Assets panel.

Select Table Elements

- Select cell: click in cell.
- Select noncontiguous cells: click in first cell, hold down Ctrl, and click other cells.
- Select column or row: position mouse pointer just above column or just to left of row (pointer becomes a solid black arrow) and click.
- Select table: Click on table border or click in the table and then click the <table> tag in the tag selector on the status bar.

Change Cell Width and Height

- Drag a column or row border in the direction to resize.

OR

1. Click in cell to resize.
2. Expand Properties panel, if necessary.
3. Type desired width in **W** text box on Properties panel.
4. Type desired height in **H** text box on Properties panel.

Return to Default Row Height

- Select table and click (**Clear Row Heights** button) on Properties panel to restore default row height.

Return to Default Column Width

- Select table and click (**Clear Column Widths** button) on Properties panel to set column width to accommodate widest entry in column.

Delete Rows and Columns
Ctrl + Shift + M, Ctrl + Shift + -

1. Click in row or column to delete.
2. Press **Delete** key.

Insert Rows and Columns
Ctrl + M, Ctrl + Shift + A

1. Position insertion point in cell below where new row should appear or to right of where new column should appear.
2. Click **Modify** .... Alt + M
3. Click **Table** .... T
4. Click **Insert Row** .... N

   OR

   - Click **Insert Column** C

   OR

   a. Click **Insert Rows or Columns** I

   b. Select **Rows** or **Columns**.

   c. Type or choose number of items.

   d. Select location for new items either above or below selection.
5. Click OK.

Split Cells
Ctrl + Alt + S

1. Click in cell to split.
2. Click **Modify** .... Alt + M
3. Click **Table** .... T
4. Click **Split Cell** .... P

   OR

   - Click (**Splits cell** button) on Properties panel.

In Split Cell dialog box

5. Select **Rows** or **Columns**.
6. Type or choose number of rows or columns to create.
7. Click OK.

Merge Cells
Ctrl + Alt + M

1. Select cells to merge.
2. Click **Modify** .... Alt + M
3. Click **Table** .... T
4. Click **Merge Cells** .... M

   OR

   - Click (**Merges selected cells** button) on Properties panel.

Span Text in Rows and Columns

1. Click in cell to span.
2. Click **Modify** .... Alt + M
3. Click **Table** .... T
4. Click **Increase Row Span** .... R
   to span down one row.

   OR

   Click **Increase Column Span** .... A
   to span to right across one column.
5. Repeat to span additional rows or columns.
6. Click **Decrease Row** .... W
   Span or **Decrease Column Span** .... U
   to remove span.

Set Border Colors

1. Select entire table.
2. Set same-color borders in Properties panel:
   a. Click **Brdr Color** box.
   b. Select color with eyedropper.
3. Set cell border colors:
   a. Click in cell.
   b. Click **Brdr** box.
   c. Select color with eyedropper.

   ✓ *When selecting a color from Assets panel, the Color category pane must be in view.*

Add Background Color to Cells

1. Click in cell to add background color to, or select table or group of cells.
2. Click **Bg Color** box and select color for background.

   OR

   Type hexadecimal value for color in box to right of color box.

Insert Background Image in Cell

1. Click in cell to add background image to, or select table or group of cells.
2. Type relative or absolute address for background image in **Bg** text box.

   OR

   a. Click (**Background URL of cell** button) on Properties panel and navigate to image.
   b. Click image and click OK.

Create Navigation Bar

1. Position insertion point at location to insert navigation bar.
2. Click **Insert**................ Alt + I
3. **Interactive Images**...... N, →
4. Click **Navigation Bar**........, G

   OR

   Click (**Insert Navigation Bar** tool) on Insert bar.
5. Type name of first element for navigation bar.
6. Type path to image for Up image, or click Browse... and navigate to image.
7. If necessary, save image in current site.
8. Select other or same image for Over, Down, and/or Over While Down images.
9. Type path for page to link to in **When Clicked, Go To URL** box, or click Browse... and navigate to page.
10. Click + to add elements or − to remove elements.
11. Use ▲ or ▼ to move elements in list.

    ✓ *To make changes to a navigation bar, click in it and then use the **Modify**> **Navigation Bar** menu command.*

Exercise Directions

1. Start Dreamweaver.
2. Open the **CinciTorial** site.
3. Open **specialties.htm**.
4. Create a blank paragraph below the Navigation placeholder and above the library item.
5. Type the following paragraph:

   CinciTorial editors have worked with most widely used software applications. Each editor has areas of specialization, as shown in the table below. All three editors are certified in one or more applications.
6. Press the **Enter** key to create a new paragraph.
7. Create a new table at the insertion point consisting of 5 rows and 2 columns. Set the table width at 75 percent of the page width. Set the border at **1** if necessary.
8. Drag the border between the two columns about 1" to the left. Center the table.
9. Format the table heading area:
   - Click in the first cell and type **Editor Specialties**.
   - Click to the left of the text and insert the image **book.gif** from the Data folder and save it in your image folder.

   ✓ *Save all images in the site's images folder. When you create additional elements, navigate to this folder and select the bullet images.*
   - Resize the image so it is 88 pixels wide and 40 pixels high. Use Bottom alignment.
   - Use the column span command to make the heading span both columns.
   - Format the text as Heading 4 and change its color to #990033. Insert a space between the image and the heading.
10. Change the background of the entire table to white (#FFFFFF).
11. Using Illustration A as a guide, insert text in the next 4 rows of the table as follows:
    - Use the split cells feature to split the 3 cells below the *Word Processing* cell into three columns.
    - Adjust column width as necessary to display the names on one line.
    - Insert the bullet characters using the Insert> Special Characters>Other command. Change the character size to **4** and its color to #990033. Copy the bullet character and use Paste to insert it elsewhere in the table.
    - After entering the bullets for Caitlin, press the **Tab** key repeatedly to create 13 more new rows. Merge the three smaller cells in the appropriate rows to create one wider cell for the *Spreadsheets, Databases, and Programming* headings.
    - Enter the remaining text and characters.
12. Merge the empty cells above the names in the first column.
13. Format the table as follows:
    - Use Illustration A as a guide for boldfacing and centering table text.
    - Adjust column widths for the split columns as necessary to look attractive.
    - Change the table border width to **2**. Set a border color of #003399.
    - Fill the subject heading cells (such as *Word Processing, Speadsheets*, etc.) with background color #CCFFFF and change the font color to #990033.
    - Fill the application heading cells (such as *Word, Quattro Pro,* and *ColdFusion*) with background color #0066CC and change font color to white (#FFFFFF) in these cells.
    - Select all cells in the first column and apply the background image **blueshade.jpg** from the Data folder. Make sure you do not select the column. You want to exclude the table's first row.
    - Enter a nonbreaking space (use the Insert Non-breaking Space button on the Characters tab of the Insert bar or press Ctrl+Shift+Spacebar) in any empty cells.
14. Save the page.
15. Delete the Navigation placeholder near the top of the page.
16. Create a navigation bar as follows:
    - For the first element, type the name **contact**.
    - For the Up Image, browse to the Data folder and select **bluebullet.gif**. For the Over image, select **maroonbullet.gif**. For the Down image, select **tealbullet.gif**.
    - Link the element to **contactus.htm**.

- Add additional elements named **people**, **services**, **specialties**, and **praise**. Use the same images given above for the Up, Over, and Down images of all elements.
- Link the elements to **people.htm**, **services.htm**, **specialties.htm**, and **praise.htm**, respectively.
- Move the **praise** element up in the list until it is below **people**.
- Click **OK** to create the navigation bar.

17. Change the size of the table that contains the navigation bar images to 434 pixels wide.
18. Type the following labels for each image, from left to right: **Contact**, **People**, **Praise**, **Services**, **Specialties**. (See illustration on page 98.)

    ✓ *Click to the right of the image and begin typing. If the label becomes a link, delete it and try again.*

19. Boldface the labels and change their color to #990033.
20. Set the width of the first four cells in the navigation bar table at about 82 pixels wide.
21. Copy the completed navigation bar.
22. Select the navigation bar and click Modify>Library>Add Object to Library.In the Library pane name the library item **Nav bar**.

    ✓ *If you are asked to update library items, do so.*

23. Insert the **Nav bar** library item below the first heading on **contactus.htm** (remove the Navigation placeholder), **people.htm**, **services.htm**, and **praise.htm**. Save each file after you add the navigation bar.
24. Open **index.htm** and preview it in the browser. Check navigation to and from all pages in the site.
25. Close the browser.
26. Display the site map in the expanded Site panel, dragging the frame border to display the entire map.
27. Click the + symbol next to each page to check links to other pages.
28. Close any open pages.
29. Exit Dreamweaver.

Illustration A

CinciTorial
Editorial Services

Our Specialities

● Contact ● People ● Praise ● Services ● Specialities

CinciTorial editors have worked with most widely used software applications. Each editor has areas of specialization, as shown in the table below. All three editors are certified in one or more applications

Editor Specialties

	Word Processing		
	Word	WordPerfect	StarOffice
Jim Horner	•	•	•
Caitlin Preston	•	•	•
	Spreadsheets		
	Excel	Quattro Pro	StarOffice
Jim Horner	•	•	•
Caitlin Preston	•		•
	Databases		
	Access	Paradox	StarOffice
Jim Horner	•	•	•
Caitlin Preston	•		•
Tyler Meadows	•		
	Programming		
	ColdFusion	Java	HTML
Caitlin Preston	•	•	
Tyler Meadows	•	•	•

Copyright © CinciTorial Co. All rights reserved. Last update: December 16, 2002 9:27 PM

Chapter

9 Advanced Table Features

Tables may be used to organize information or used to lay out an entire Web page. Using a table for page layout allows you to create a sophisticated design that will display in all browsers. If you have tabular data stored in another application, you can import it to create a table in Dreamweaver. After importing the data, you can sort it and format it.

In this chapter, you'll learn how to:

- Create a table for page layout
- Use Layout view
- Import tabular data to create a table
- Sort a table
- Automatically format a table
- Insert table-related tags

Use a Table for Page Layout

- Tables are useful not only for organizing data on a Web page but also for laying out a page's content. An advantage to using a table for page layout is that all browsers can display tables. Laying out a page with a table allows you to create a complex page design without the use of sophisticated layout features such as frames or layers that do not display in all browsers.

  Note: *You will learn how to create frame pages and layers in later chapters.*

- Creating a table for page layout is the same process as creating a table to organize data, except that you work on a larger scale to fill the page. For best results, maximize the Document window and collapse unnecessary panels before you begin creating the page layout.
- Make sure the table uses the full page width (100 percent of page width). You can then insert rows or columns and merge as necessary to create areas to insert text and images.
- You can apply color and design to the page creatively by adding a background color or image to specific table cells. When laying out an entire page, you will probably not want to use table borders, but applying a cell border to an individual cell can draw attention to its content.

Layout View

- **Layout view** can be selected by clicking the Layout tab in the Insert bar. The Standard View and Layout View 

buttons allow you to toggle between the two views.
- Layout View allows you to "draw" a layout on a page using *layout tables* and *layout cells* (see illustration below). This feature gives you a great deal of flexibility in creating and positioning cells precisely where you need them within the table.
- After you create a layout table and layout cells, you can move or resize cells by dragging. You can specify exact dimensions for cells or let them "stretch" to conform to the browser window's size.

Layout view showing layout table and a layout cell

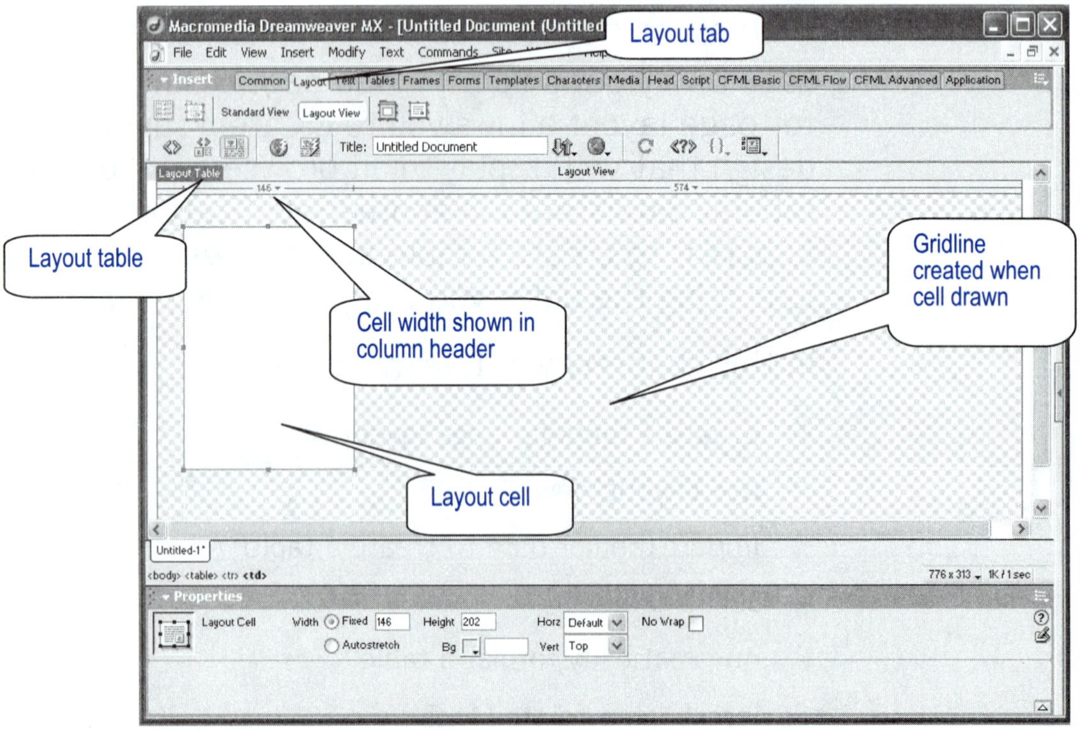

- Before you can draw a layout table or layout cells, you must switch to Layout view by clicking the Layout View button in the Layout tab of the Insert bar.
- You will not notice a change in the page after you switch to Layout view, but the Draw Layout Cell and Draw Layout Table buttons become active in the Layout tab.
- The first time you switch to Layout view, Dreamweaver displays the dialog box shown in the illustration below to give you further information about Layout view.

Dreamweaver supplies information about Layout view

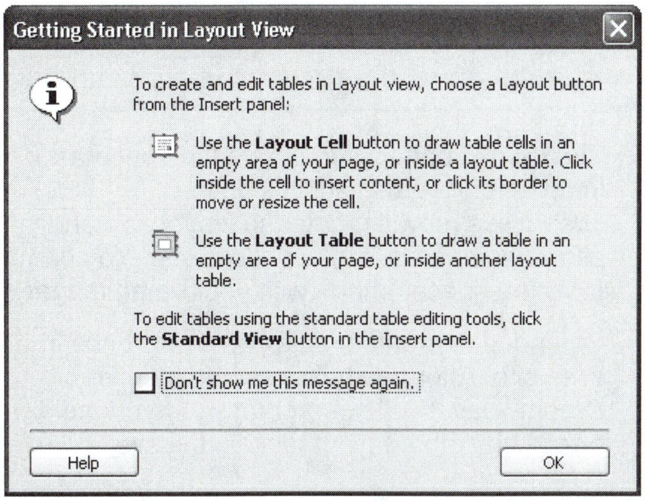

Tip: *If you don't want to see this message each time you switch to Layout view after you start Dreamweaver, select the* Don't show me this message again *checkbox.*

Draw a Layout Table

- Begin a new page layout by drawing a layout table. You should create the first layout table the full size of your page. You can create other layout tables within the first layout table.

  Note: *You can draw a layout cell without first drawing a layout table; Dreamweaver will automatically create the layout table to surround the layout cell.*

- Draw a layout table by clicking the Draw Layout Table button on the Insert bar and then use the crosshair pointer to drag the outline of the table on the page. This procedure is the same as drawing an object in a program such as Word or Paint.
- The new layout table displays a green border with sizing handles and a green tab containing the label *Layout Table*. The table's width in pixels is shown in the column header area at the top of the table. The table area itself is light gray.
- You can modify the table width by dragging a sizing handle or you can use the Width and Height boxes in the Properties panel to set exact measurements. You can also adjust cell spacing and cell padding values just as you do in a standard table to adjust spacing between cells and cell borders.
- If a layout table appears on a page by itself, you do not have to take any special step to select it. Because the table is the only object on the page, it is selected by default.
- Once you insert cells in the table, the table itself is deselected. If you have inserted the table on a page with other content (or within another layout table), you can deselect the table by clicking on other page content.
- To select the table again, click on its green outline or its green tab.

Draw Layout Cells

- Use the same general method to draw layout cells. Click the Draw Layout Cell button on the Objects panel and use the crosshair pointer to draw the cell anywhere on the page or within the layout table.
- Dreamweaver automatically creates a grid of rows and columns in the remaining portion of the layout table relative to the inserted cell (see the illustration on the previous page). You can use this grid to guide you in inserting other cells.
- The changes you can make to a layout cell depend on whether the cell is *active* or *selected*.
- To make a cell *active*, click in it. An active cell displays a light blue border and a white background. When a cell is active, you can add content to it by typing text at the insertion point or by pasting text. Insert graphics in the cell just as you would in a standard table.

- To *select* a layout cell, move the pointer on the border (the border turns red when the pointer is on it) and then click the border. When selected, the cell border displays sizing handles on the light blue border.
- When a cell is selected, you can change its background color and the horizontal and vertical alignment of its content.
- Modify a selected cell's width by dragging its border or using the Properties panel's Width and Height boxes. You can also specify the autostretch option for a selected cell, as discussed below.

Use Autostretch

- Tables and columns within tables can be sized to fixed widths or you can use the **autostretch** feature. Autostretch allows a table column (or the entire table) to resize automatically to fill the browser window.
- Typically, you will use both fixed width columns and an autostretch column in a table. Use fixed widths for columns that contain cells you want to remain the same size, such as those containing images, a menu, or links. Use the autostretch column for text that can wrap flexibly.

  Note: *Only one column in a table can be set to autostretch.*

- Fixed-width columns display the width in pixels in the cell's column header in the table border. Autostretch columns display a wavy line in the column header to indicate that the size can change.
- To make a column autostretch, select a cell in the column and select the Autostretch option in the Properties panel. Or, click the down arrow in the column header and choose Make Column Autostretch from the menu.
- If you have not used the autostretch feature previously in the current site, Dreamweaver asks if you want to create a spacer GIF file to insert in the fixed width columns (see illustration below). The spacer image prevents fixed width columns from resizing, allowing the autostretch column to adjust freely in the browser window.

Dreamweaver suggests a spacer file

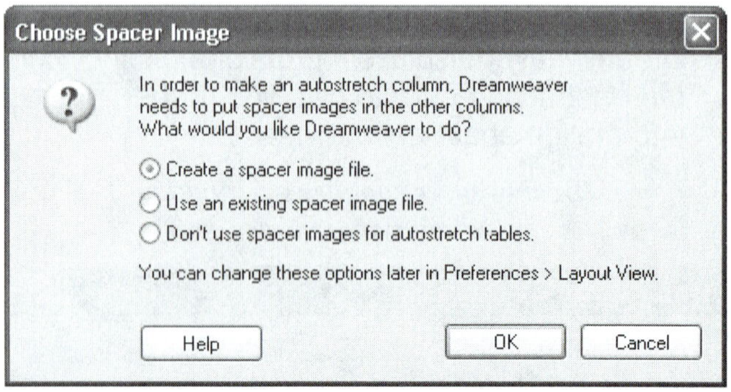

- The default option is to create the spacer image file. If you select this option, Dreamweaver will create the file for you and allow you to save it in your Web site. You can save the spacer image with your other images.
- You need to create a spacer file only once in a Web site. After you have created the file, Dreamweaver will not prompt you to create one in any other layout table in the site.

Format Layout Cells

- You can apply some formats to layout cells in Layout view using the Properties panel. You can, for example, adjust cell width and height, apply a background color, and set both horizontal and vertical alignment. You can also, if desired, prevent text from wrapping in the cell, a good choice if you have a list of links in a cell that you want to display on one line.
- You can apply standard table formats to layout cells by clicking the Standard View button in the Layout tab of the Insert bar to display the layout table as a standard Dreamweaver table.
- You then have access to the same formatting options as for a standard table, such as cell borders and backgrounds, fonts and styles, and so on.

Import Table Data

- You may think that most tables are created from scratch on a Web page. However, with collaborative projects, you will also use existing data from a word processing program or spreadsheet to create a table. Importing can eliminate data entry errors or the tedium of reentering long columns of numbers.
- Data to import must be saved in a **delimited format**. That is, columns must be separated by delimiters such as commas, tabs, semicolons, or colons.

Caution: *Dreamweaver can use spaces as delimiters, but you may need to do a lot of cleanup on the table if you are importing text with spaces between words.*

- Most spreadsheet and word processing applications allow you to save a file in a delimited form. Save a word processing document using the TXT format or a spreadsheet using the CSV format.
- Such formats save only the data, so formatting such as fonts and font styles will not be imported. These can be applied easily in Dreamweaver.
- Use the File>Import>Tabular Data command to import the data into a new table. Or click the Tabular Data  button on the Common tab of the Insert bar displays the Import Tabular Data dialog box (see illustration below).

Import Tabular Data dialog box

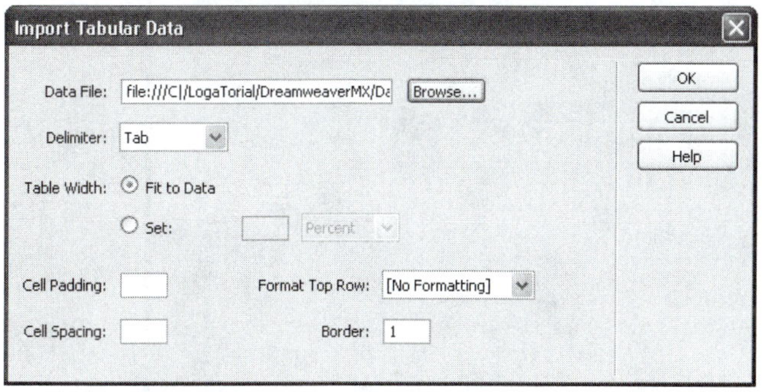

- Use the Browse button to locate the file to import. If necessary, choose from the Delimiter list the delimiter format used in the file you want to import.

Note: *Dreamweaver will recognize some common file types such as CSV and set the delimiter automatically.*

- As when creating a table from scratch, you can choose formats such as size, cell padding, cell spacing, and border width.
- Note in the illustration of the Import Table Data dialog box above that Dreamweaver will also fit the table cells to the imported data and allow you to choose a font style for the top row.

Sort Table Data

- You can sort table data by row or column to further organize your data. Data presented in alphabetical or numerical order can be easier for visitors to read and understand.
- To sort data in a table, click in the table and use the Commands>Sort Table command on the menu bar to open the Sort Table dialog box (see illustration below).

Sort Table dialog box

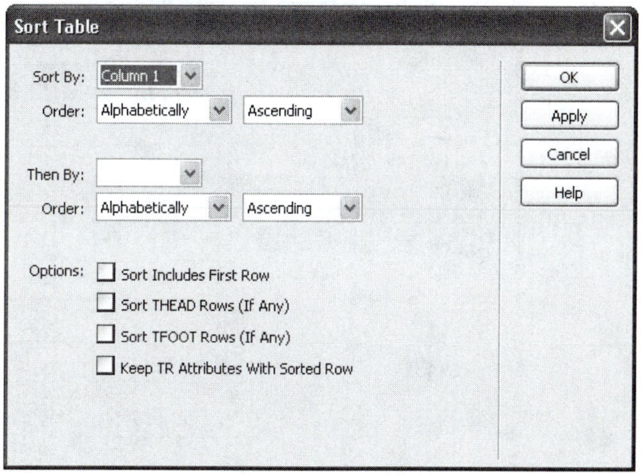

- Select a column to sort by (or select more than one column) and choose to sort Alphabetically or Numerically. You also can set the direction of the sort as Ascending (A to Z, 1 to 10) or Descending (Z to A, 10 to 1).
- If you do not want to sort the first row of the table along with the remaining rows, make sure the Sort Includes First Row checkbox is *not* selected.

- The Sort THEAD and TFOOT rows options apply to special tags that contain one or more rows used to repeat the headers or footers of tables that will printout on more than one page. They are not covered in this book, but typically you would not want to sort them.
- Select Keep TR Attributes With Sorted Row if you want to keep the table's attributes (color, images, spanning, split, and so on).
- You cannot sort data in a table that has spanned columns or rows. If you know you want to sort data and also want to create spanned columns or rows, sort the data first.

Use Format Table Command

- If you do not want to spend time creating an attractive look for a table, you can use Dreamweaver's Format Table feature. Format Table provides a number of color schemes you can customize to format your table.
- Use the Commands>Format Table command to open the Format Table dialog box (see illustration below). This dialog box contains a list of predesigned formats in a variety of colors and patterns.

  Note: *Although you can use the Format Table feature to format a page layout table (including one created in Dreamweaver's Layout view), the formats are more appropriate for use with a table that organizes data.*

- Choose a color scheme from the list and see how it looks applied to the sample table in the dialog box. You can use the options at the bottom of the dialog box to customize the format.
- For example, change row colors, adjust the pattern by which row colors alternate, apply font style and alignment of the top row or left column, and modify background and border options.

Select table formats in the Format Table dialog box

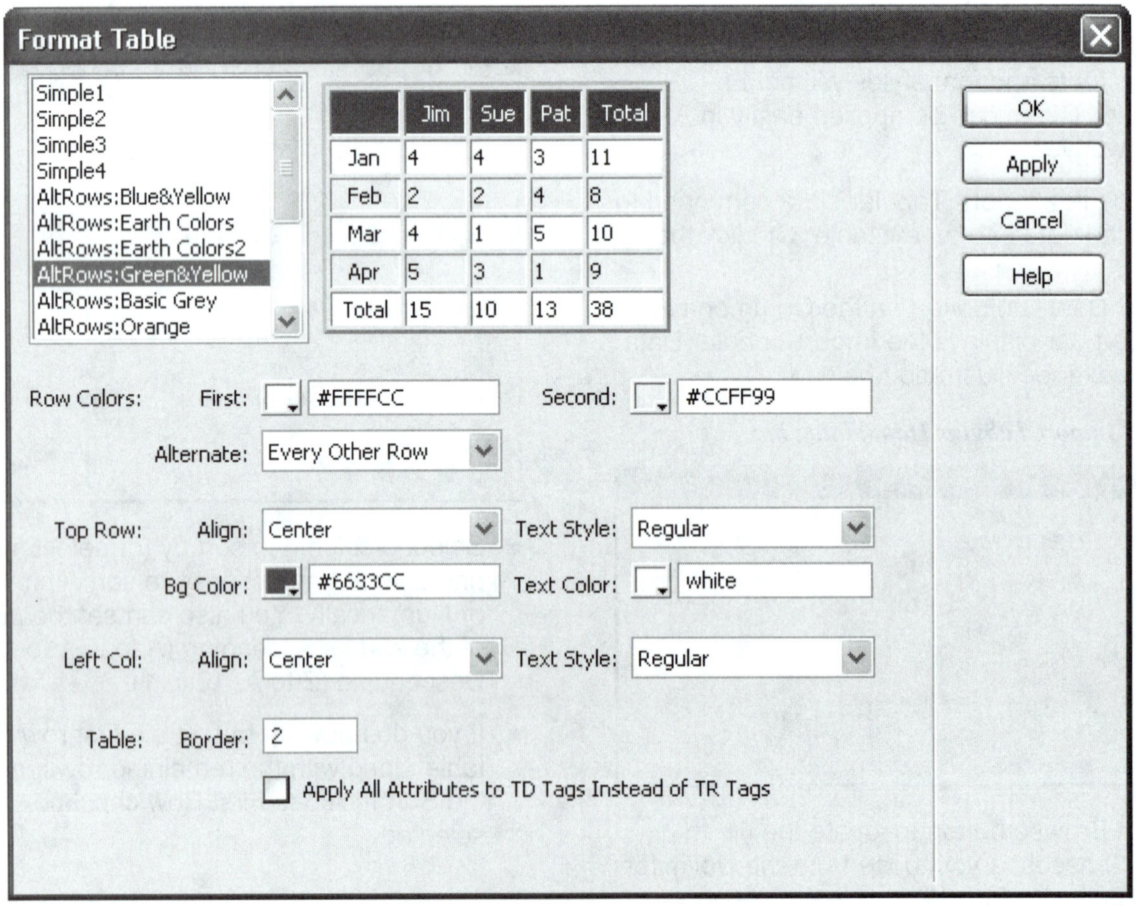

Insert Table-Related Tags

- Dreamweaver provides tools for editing—and even creating—tables in Show Code and Show Code and Design views. The Table tab in the Insert bar is for inserting table-related tags (see illustration).

Table tag tools

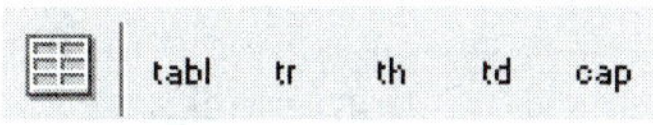

- If you click the Tables tab in Design view, you will see an active table button. The table tag buttons, however, will be illegible. When these buttons are active in one of the code views, you can click on them or drag them into the code view to insert <table> tags that create the basic table structure. There are also tags for creating rows (<tr>), headings (<th>), data (<td>), and captions (<caption>).
- Captions are text that appears outside of the table, but ares part of the table structure.
- You can also insert table-related tags with a menu command, Insert>Table Objects.

Procedures

Switch to Layout View

1. Click the Layout tab in the Insert group pane.
2. Click Layout View (**Layout View** button.
3. Click OK if necessary to close dialog box.
4. When finished working in Layout view, click Standard View (**Standard View** button).

Draw Layout Table

1. Click (**Draw Layout Table** button) in Layout tab of Insert bar.
2. Hold down mouse button and drag crosshair pointer to create table's outside border.
3. Release mouse button when table is desired size.

Draw Layout Cell

1. Click (**Draw Layout Cell** button) in Layout tab of Insert bar.
2. Hold down mouse button and drag crosshair pointer to create cell of desired size.
3. Release mouse button.

   ✓ *If you have not already created a layout table when you draw a layout cell, Dreamweaver will automatically create the table for you.*

Modify Layout Table or Cell Dimensions

1. Click on outside border of table or cell to select it.
2. Drag a border to resize.

   OR

   - Use Width and Height boxes in Properties panel to set exact dimensions.

Use Autostretch

1. Select cell to autostretch.
2. Click **Autostretch** option in Properties panel.

   OR

   - Click down arrow in column header in table border for column to autostretch and select **Make Column Autostretch**.
3. Choose **Create a spacer image file** in Choose Spacer Image dialog box.
4. Save spacer image in site's images folder.

Import Table Data

1. Position insertion point at location for imported table.
2. Click **File** .... Alt+F
3. Click **Import** I
4. Click **Tabular Data** .... T

   OR

   - Click (**Insert Tabular Data** tool) in Common tab of Insert bar.

   OR

   - Click **Insert**............ Alt+I
   - Click **Table Objects** .... →, A
   - Click **Import Tabular Data** .... T
5. Type path to data file or click Browse... and navigate to data file.
6. Specify delimiter if necessary.
7. Set table width, cell padding, cell spacing, border width, and format for top row, if desired.

   ✓ *Data file must be saved as delimited text, with columns separated by a delimiter such as commas, tabs, semicolons, or colons.*

Sort Table Data

1. Click in table to sort.
2. Click **Commands** .... Alt+C
3. Click **Sort Table** .... S
4. Choose column(s) to sort by.
5. Specify alphabetical or numerical sort.
6. Choose Ascending or Descending sort.
7. Select options to include first row in sort and keep attributes after sort.

Use Format Table Command

1. Click in table to format.
2. Click **Commands** .... Alt+C
3. Click **Format Table** .... F
4. Select format style.
5. Customize style to format specific rows and columns as desired.

Insert Table-Related Tags

1. Click Table tab in Insert bar.
2. Click (**Show in Code View** button) or (**Show in Code and Design View** button)
3. Click the desired tag button or drag it into code view pane of Document window.

   OR

   - Click **Insert**............ Alt+I
   - Click **Table Objects** .... →, A
   - Click the desired tag button or drag it into code view pane of Document window.

Exercise Directions

1. Start Dreamweaver.
2. Open the **CinciTorial** site.
3. If necessary, open a new, blank page. Save the page as **mission.htm** with the page title **Our Mission**.
4. Create the page layout table shown in Illustration A as follows:
   - Switch to Layout view. Draw a layout table the full width of the page.
   - Draw a layout cell in the upper-left corner of the layout table that is 200 pixels wide and 300 pixels high.
   - Draw the remaining cells as shown in Illustration A. The first cell in the second column should be about 75 pixels high.
   - Make the right column an autostretch column.
   - Select the table and set cell spacing at **7**.
5. Add content to the layout table as follows:
   - In Cell 1 (see Illustration A), insert the image **Laura_Brater-Reidel.jpg** from the Data folder. Save the image in your images folder.
   - Resize the image to 200 pixels wide and 300 pixels high.
   - In Cell 2, insert the **Home link** library item and center it horizontally in the table cell.
   - In Cell 3, insert the text shown in Illustration B. Use the Heading 2 format for the centered heading.
   - In Cell 4, insert the following text and center it:

     We dedicate this site to Laura Brater-Reidel, the smartest one in the family.
   - In Cell 5, type the text **Quality products on time at a fair price.** Center the text horizontally and apply the Middle vertical alignment and the Heading 4 style.
   - Fill Cell 5 with the background color #336699 and change the text color to white.
6. Drag Cell 5 upward about a quarter of an inch. If two new cells appear below the cell you moved, remove them in Standard view.
7. Preview the page in the browser.
8. Switch back to Standard view and click the Common tab in the Insert bar.
9. Save and close the page.
10. Open **index.htm** and position the insertion point after the *We build computer books* heading at the top of the page. Press the **Enter** key and type **Read Our Mission Statement**. Link this text to **mission.htm**.
11. Save the changes to **index.htm**.
12. Open **praise.htm**. Scroll to the bottom of the page click to place the insertion point to the left of the *Back to Top* link.
13. Import the tabular data contained in **contacts.txt** stored in the Data folder. Choose to fit the table to the data and make sure **Tab** appears as the delimiter.
14. Sort the table data in ascending order according to the first column. Do not include the first row in the sort.
15. Use the Format Table command to apply formats to the table. Choose a format style and customize it as desired.
16. Insert a new column to the left of the current first column. Type the following text in the first cell of the new column:

    Contact our best clients for more info on our services.
17. Span this text down all rows in the column and boldface the text.
18. Adjust the first column width to 85 pixels, and adjust other column widths to best fit their data, if necessary.
19. Adjust the font color if necessary.
20. Switch to Show Code and Design View.
21. Locate the first table tag, <table border="2">.
22. Type a caption tag after the <table border="2"> tag that reads **Our Clients**.
23. Format the caption in bold.
24. Save and close any open pages.
25. Exit Dreamweaver.

Illustration A

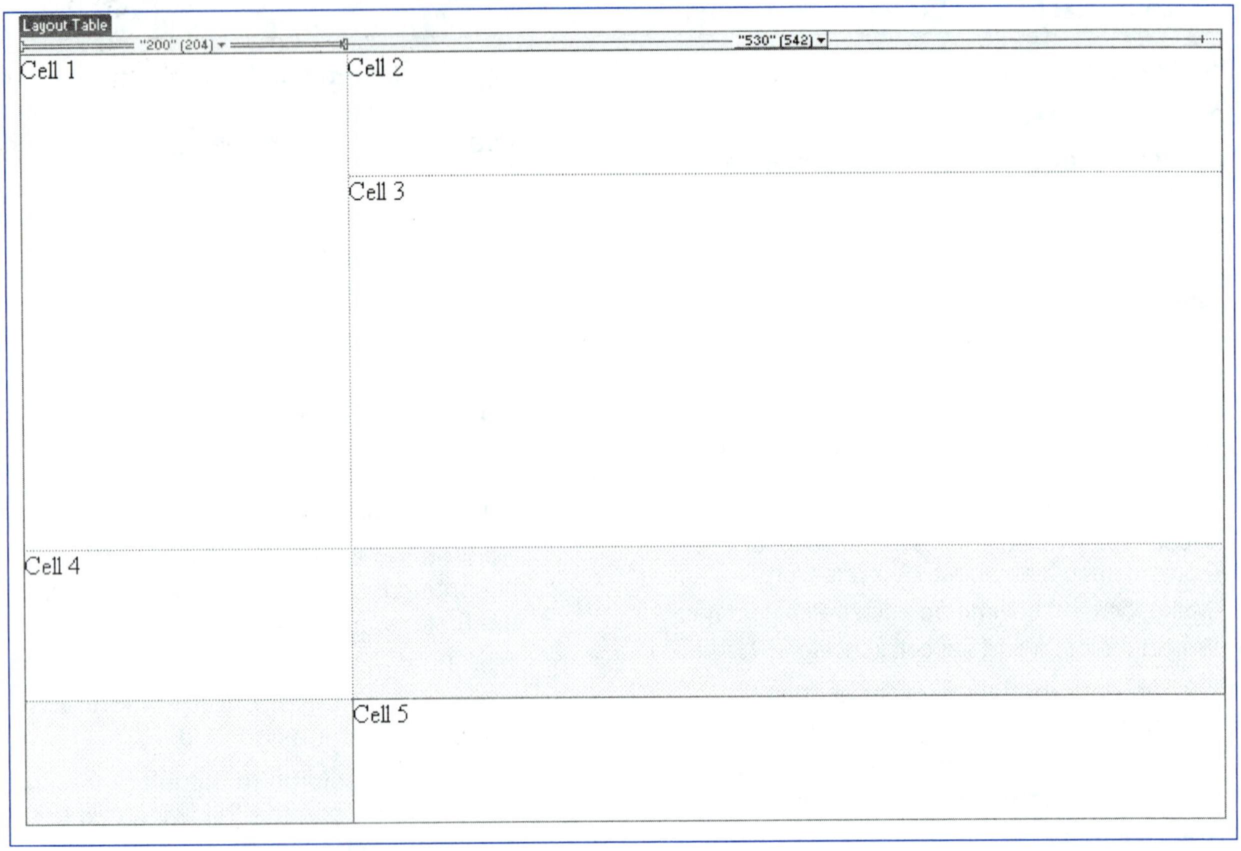

Illustration B

Our Mission Statement

Every job is an important job.

At CinciTorial, we believe every job is an important job. No matter how big. No matter how urgent. When you work with CinciTorial staff, you can rest assured we'll do our best for you. We learn from every job and every client, and you benefit from that learning process.

Next

Chapter

▶▶

Chapter

10

Create Forms

Creating a form in Dreamweaver MX is a simple process that uses many of the skills you already have, such as inserting tables and inserting and formatting text. With careful coordination, you can test and use your form on your computer, an intranet, or on the Web using your testing server and ColdFusion.

In this chapter, you'll learn how to:

- Create a form
- Insert form objects such as drop-down lists, single-line and multiple-line text boxes, radio buttons, checkboxes, and submit and reset buttons
- Link a ColdFusion form to an Access database
- Test a form

About Forms

- You can use a **form** to collect information from visitors to your Web site. You can create forms for surveys, contact information, feedback, searching, ordering products, or even an online job interview.
- Forms can vary greatly in complexity, but all forms consist of a form area in which you insert form fields such as text boxes, radio buttons, and submit buttons. The skills you learn in this chapter will enable you to create both simple and complex forms in Dreamweaver.
- A Dreamweaver form requires two components: the HTML code for the form objects, and a **script** or **application** on the Web site server to process the information that visitors insert in the form's fields.

  Note: *You will learn more about scripts and applications later in this chapter.*

Create a Form

- Create a form using commands on the Insert menu or using buttons from the Forms tab on the Insert bar (see illustration).
- It is a good idea to insert a descriptive paragraph or caption above the form to make the purpose of the form clear. You can also use this paragraph to give specific directions for filling out the form if necessary.
- With the insertion point where you want the form to begin, use the Insert>Form command on the menu bar, or click the Form button in the Forms tab of the Insert bar.

  Tip: *Before beginning your form, display the Forms tab in the Insert bar and launch the Properties panel if necessary.*

- A red dashed outline appears on all sides of the insertion point and as wide as the page. This outline marks the borders of the form. The Properties panel allows you to specify information about the form (see illustration on the next page).
- You should name the form using the Form Name text box. If you know the path to the script or application file that will be used to process the form data, enter it in the Action box.
- The Method list choices are used to define the way the form data will be handled. If you are not sure what method will be used by your script, leave the setting as POST (the default setting for a new form).
- For certain kinds of forms, such as the kind that send personal data and credit card information, there are also advanced properties to select. The Enctype drop-down list lets you specify the type of data encoding that is submitted to the server for processing. The Target drop-down list allows you to choose a window in which to display data returned by a form handler application.
- To create a tidy-looking form, you can insert a table directly in the form area. Using a table allows you to align labels and form fields and maintain that alignment on any browser.

  Note: The Label button on the Form tab inserts the <label> tag. If used in forms created in tables, it requires special coding to associate it with the form input object that it labels beyond the scope of this book. The <label> tag is more easily used in forms that are not created in tables—and can be "read" by text-to-speech browsers used by vision-impaired people.

- If you do not want to insert a table, you can align form elements using the Spacebar, although this method does not guarantee that the alignment you create in Dreamweaver will look the same in the browser.
- Once your form area is set up, you are ready to enter form objects: **labels** and **form fields**. Labels are text words or phrases that tell a visitor what kind of information to enter. Form fields are the boxes and buttons visitors type in or click to supply information.

Forms tab on Insert bar

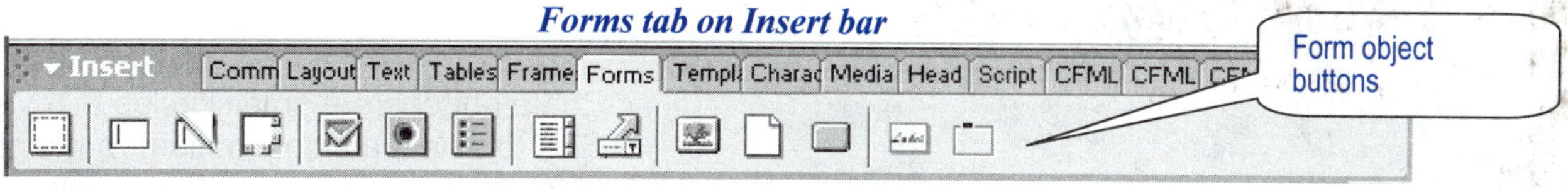

Properties for a new form

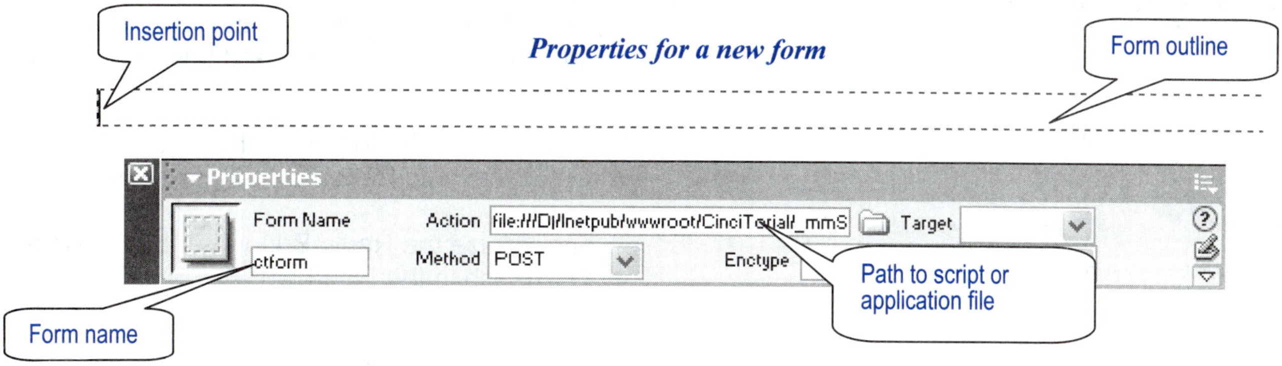

- Dreamweaver supplies a number of different form fields you can add to a form, but you will use the following five fields most often:
  - *Text fields* allow the visitor to type text in a box. A text field can consist of a single line or multiple lines.
  - *Radio buttons* allow the visitor to choose only one option from a group of options.
  - *Checkboxes* enable a visitor to select an option or select more than one option from a group of options.
  - *List/menu fields* give visitors a list or menu of options to choose among.
  - *Buttons* and *Button Groups* perform a specific action when a visitor clicks them.

Insert Single-Line Text Fields

- Single-line text fields are used to hold a modest amount of text data that can appear on one line, such as names, e-mail addresses, and street addresses.
- Insert a single-line text field using the Insert>Form Objects>Text Field command on the menu bar. Or, click or drag the Text Field 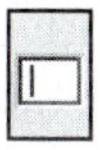 button on the Forms tab of the Insert bar.
- Dreamweaver inserts the default text field and the Properties panel displays properties for the field. See the illustration on the next page

Note: *The illustration shows a table that has already been created and a label for the text field. Creating a text field will not automatically create its label, too.*

- When first inserted, a form field is selected so you can modify its properties. To change properties later, simply click the form field.
- You should supply a name for every field in a form. The script or application used to handle the form data uses these field names—as well as the name you give to your form—to store data correctly. The field name should be only one or two words. If you use two words, join them with an underscore, such as street_address.
- You can specify how many characters wide the field should be, as well as how many characters it can hold.
- If your data is being stored in a database, you will need to make sure that your fields are not incompatible with the size and type of data used by the database.
- If you want the field to show an **initial value** (text that displays each time the form is opened, such as *Type full name here*), insert this text in the Init Val box in the Properties panel.
- The Password  option is selected for text boxes in which passwords are typed so that onlookers cannot see the form user's password, which appears as a series of black dots as shown here .

- The table below shows examples of labels, names, and field widths you might use in a form.

Field Label	Field Name	Width
Mailing Address	mail_address	60
City	city	45
State	state	3
Zip Code	zip	15
Country	country	45
E-mail Address	e_dress	30
Phone Number	phone	15

Insert Radio Buttons

- Radio buttons are small circles that visitors click to select a single option from a group of options. Radio buttons allow simple selections to supply data. If you have ever participated in an online poll, you have used this kind of form object.
- Insert a radio button using the Insert>Form Objects>Radio Button command on the menu bar. Or use the Radio Button button on the Forms tab in the Insert bar.

Single-line text field

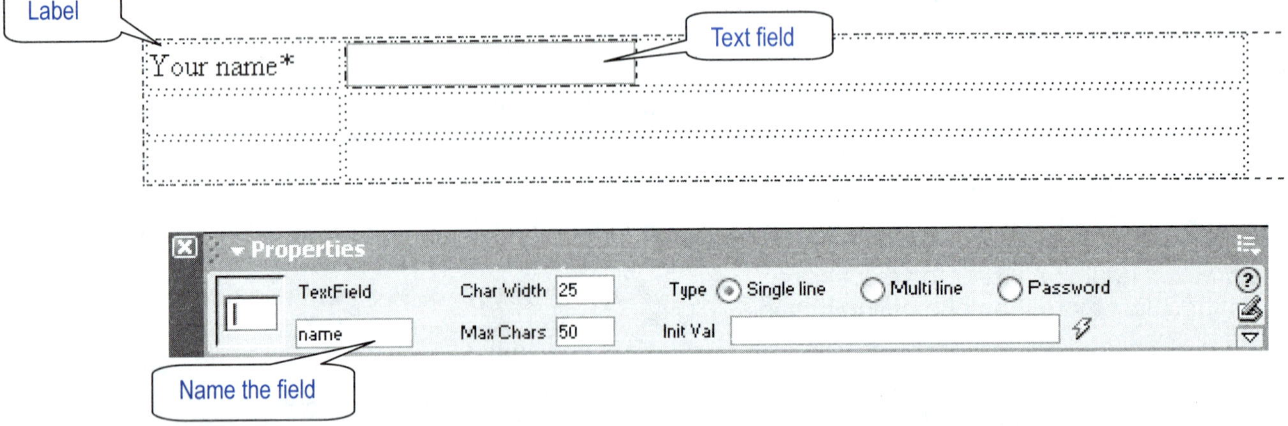

Radio button field

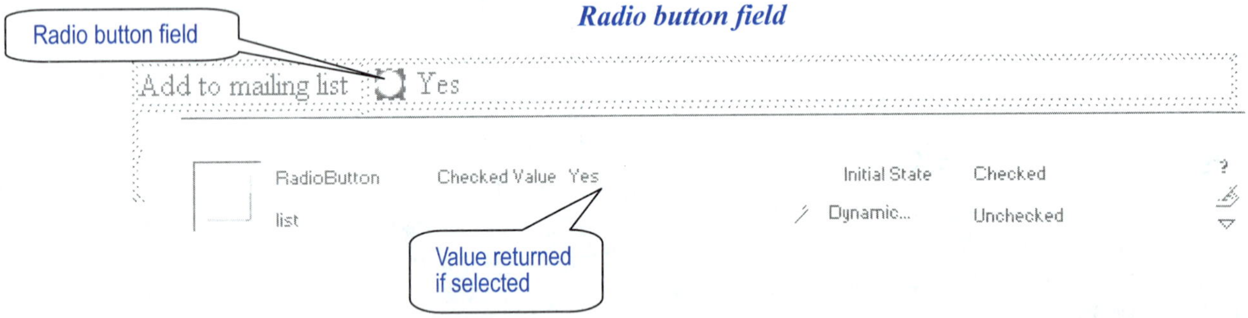

- Dreamweaver inserts the radio button and the Properties panel shows properties for the radio button field (see illustration on next page).
- Because each radio button functions as part of a group of buttons, all radio buttons in the group must have the same name. Only the **value** changes for each button. The value entered in the Checked Value box is the data that will actually be shown in the form results
- For example, if you create a group of three radio buttons for a credit card field, each button will be named card_type, but one button will have the value *MasterCard*, another will have the value *Visa*, and the third may have a value such as *Discover*. (Creating grouped buttons is discussed in the next topic.)
- If a visitor selects the *Visa* radio button, the form results will show an entry of *Visa* for the card_type field.

- If you want one of the radio buttons to be selected each time the form opens, select the Checked initial state option. Visitors will still be able to change their selection even if one radio button is selected by default.

Insert Radio Groups

- A radio group allows you to create two or more radio buttons quickly either on separate lines or in a table.
- Insert a radio button group using the Insert>Form Objects>Radio Group command on the menu bar. Or, click the Radio Group button on the Forms tab of the Insert bar.
- In the Radio Group dialog box, you can enter a name for the radio group. In the Radio Buttons list, two buttons are created by default. To customize the button labels, simply click on the label name and enter your own. Then click on the value to type in a custom value (see illustration).

Radio Group dialog box

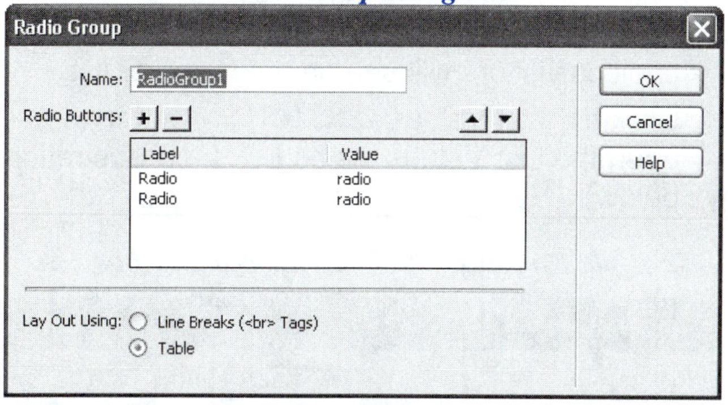

- Type the item labels (the radio button items visitors will see in the form) and a value for each label. The value is the data that will be sent to the server when the form data is recorded. Values should be similar to item labels, with no spaces or capital letters.
- Use the + button to enter additional labels and values (or simply press Tab to create a new label). Press the ▲ and ▼ buttons to change the radio group order.
- To remove a list item, select the item and click the − button.
- You can lay out a radio group either in separate lines or in a table by selecting the desired Lay Out Using option

Insert Checkboxes

- Checkboxes are much like radio buttons, but checkboxes can stand alone in a form or be grouped to allow visitors to make more than one selection from several options.
- Insert a checkbox using the Insert>Form Objects>Check Box command on the menu bar. Or, use the Checkbox button on the Forms tab of the Insert bar.
- Dreamweaver inserts the checkbox and the Properties panel displays properties for the field (see illustration on the next page).
- Name the checkbox as for any other form field if it is standing alone in the form. If you are offering visitors a number of selections, give each checkbox the same name, as when creating radio buttons, to create a group of checkboxes.
- For grouped checkboxes, make sure each checkbox has a unique value. This value is usually similar to the label used for the checkbox. Because a visitor can select more than one checkbox, the form results can show multiple values for the checkbox field name.
- As for radio buttons, you specify whether checkboxes are checked by default when the form opens.

Tip: *Checkboxes are usually not checked by default, to save visitors from unintentionally choosing an option.*

Insert Lists and Menus

- Dreamweaver's List/Menu field allows you to place several options on a scrollable list or drop-down menu. Visitors click the list or menu to display choices and then select one (or more, if you allow multiple selections).
- Lists and menus are generally used for three or more options. For fewer options, radio buttons or checkboxes are preferred.

Checkbox form field

List/Menu form field

- Using a list or menu can save room in a form because the options are stored in one field rather than in multiple radio buttons or checkboxes.
- Insert a list or menu using the Insert>Form Objects>List/Menu command on the menu bar.

  Or, use the List/Menu button on the Forms tab in the Insert bar.
- Dreamweaver inserts the List/Menu field and the Properties panel displays properties for the field (see illustration above).
- The List/Menu field is only a few characters wide when first inserted. Its final size is determined by the choices you add to the list or menu.
- Name the field as for other form fields. Then you must choose whether to create a menu or a list:
  - A menu displays a single choice by default and drops down when clicked to display a menu of choices. Visitors can select only one choice.
  - A list can display more than one choice by default, and visitors can scroll the list to see additional choices. Visitors may be allowed to select more than one choice.
- If you choose to create a list, you can specify the height of the list (that is, how many items will display by default) and select the Allow multiple checkbox to let visitors choose more than one option from the list.
- For both menus and lists, you must create the choices visitors will see on the menu or list. Click the List Values button to open the List Values dialog box (see illustration below).

Add choices in the List Values dialog box

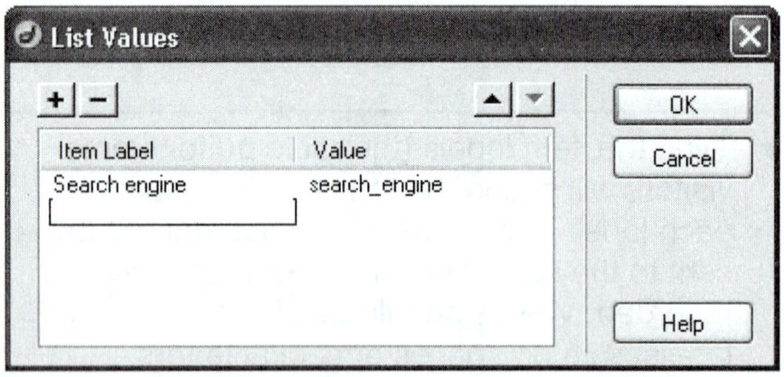

- Type the item labels (the actual list items visitors will see in the form) and a value for each label. As in other form objects, the value is the data that will be sent to the server when the form data is recorded.
- Use the + button to enter additional labels and values (or simply press Tab to create a new label) and the ▲ and ▼ buttons to change the list order.

- To remove a list item, select the item and click the [–] button.
- If desired, you can select one of the choices to appear in the list or menu box (if Height is set to 1). Expand the Properties panel, if necessary, and click the desired label in the Initially Selected box (see illustration below).

Select an item for default display

- If you do not select one of the choices to appear initially, Dreamweaver displays the first choice in the list when the form is opened in the browser.

Specify properties for multiple-line text field

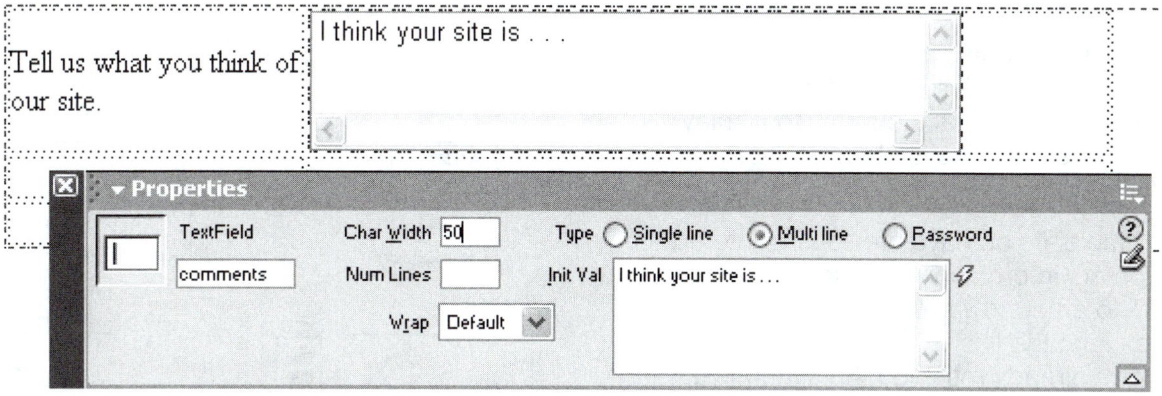

Insert Multiple-Line Text Fields

- As you have already learned, text fields are used for single-line entries. Text fields can also be set to allow for multiple-line entries. A multiple-line text field can be used to request more information from site visitors or allow them to answer questions.
- Use a Text field to create a multiple-line text field. In the Properties panel, select the Multi line option. The Properties panel then activates additional properties for the multiple-line field (see illustration above).
- As for other Text fields, you must specify a name. You can also specify a width in characters and the number of lines visitors can use for their comments.

  Tip: *Defining the character width and number of lines allows you to limit user responses to a reasonable length.*

- You can change the way text wraps in the multiple-line text field, but the Default option is suitable for most form uses.
- The Init Val text box allows you to enter an initial value text to ask a question or make a request

Insert Buttons

- You must give your site visitors a way to send or clear (reset) the information they have provided in the form. Use Dreamweaver's Button fields to create Submit and Reset buttons.
- Insert a button using the Insert>Form Objects> Button command on the menu bar. Or, use the Button button on the Forms tab in the Insert bar.
- Dreamweaver inserts a Submit button by default (see illustration on next page). You will generally accept the default properties for this button.
- To insert another button to be used for resetting or clearing the form, use the same procedure. You will then need to change the button's name to reflect its purpose, change its label, and choose the appropriate action (Reset form for a Reset button).

  Note: *The text you type in the Label box is the label that will appear on the button in the form.*

Dreamweaver inserts Submit button

Dynamic Data

- The Properties panels for the different form objects can also be linked to database recordsets. This allows the forms to display data from the recordset instead of users entering data.
- For example, if you have previously entered your contact information in a form—and needed to enter new data—your name, address, and the like would already be entered if the form already retrieved the dynamic data from its database.
- Dynamic data can be linked by clicking the Dynamic [Dynamic...] button or button in the Properties panel.
- How form objects are configured with dynamic data is beyond the scope of this text. However, you can press F1 and read about dynamic data in Dreamweaver Help.

Form Handling

- Forms you create in Dreamweaver require special software to process them: either a script such as CGI or an application such as ColdFusion.
- When a visitor enters information into a form and clicks the submit button, the information is sent to the Web site server, where it is processed on the "server-side"—which means inside the server itself or on another computer networked to the server.
- This processing means that the responses made by the Web site visitor are automatically entered into a database.
- The script or application may also generate a response page to indicate that the information has been accepted—or to indicate that there is a problem (see illustration).

How Form is processed

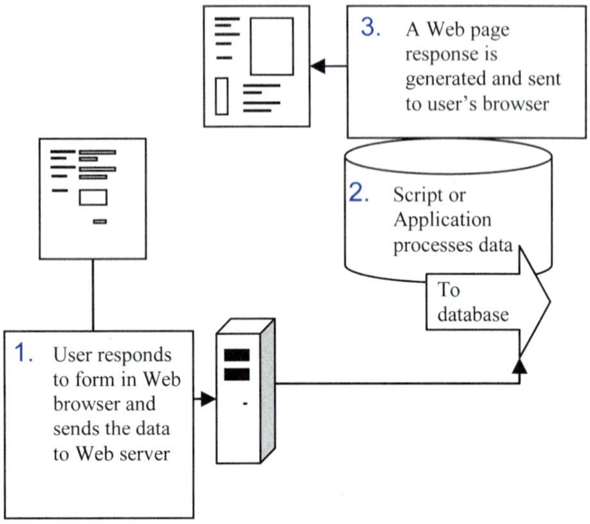

Scripts

- Scripts are special software such as CGI (Common Gateway Interface) script. The server-side script should reside on the server to which a Web site is published.
- You can see an example of a **CGI script** in the illustration below.

CGI script for a form

```
###########################################################################
sub try_again
  {
     print "Content-type: text/html\n\n";
     print <<__W3__;

     <H1>Missing Data!</H1>
     <B>Please press the back button and fill in
     all required fields!<P></B>

__W3__
     exit;
  }

###########################################################################
sub answer_back
 {

    $subject = "Thank you";
    $msgtext="";
  if ($fields{'automessage'} ne "") {
    open (AM,"< $fields{'automessage'}");
    while (<AM>) {
      chop $_;
      $msgtext .= "$_\n";
    }
    close(AM);
  }
```

- There are client-side forms, too. These are forms that have the script written into the Web page that contains the form. JavaScript and VBScript are used to process the form before the data is sent to the Web server that collects the data.
- Your ISP, network administrator, or intranet server may already have CGI scripts incorporated on your server. You can also find "generic" freeware or shareware CGI scripts on the Internet.

Note: *Creating CGI scripts is beyond the scope of this course. To learn about CGI scripts, search the Internet for CGI tutorials.*

Applications

- Applications servers are composed of scripts and typically can support more complexity than CGI scripts. They use a ColdFusion page, JavaServer Page (JSP), or Active Server Page (ASP) to process a form.
- The application that you use to build your forms depends on whether the Web server on which you publish your Web site supports and utilizes the application.

Test a Form

- After creating a form, you should test it to make sure your values are set up correctly. If your form is linked to a script or application, you can display the form in the browser and fill in the form fields. Your form results will show you if you need to modify your fields or values.
- Dreamweaver MX ships with a single-user developer's copy of ColdFusion that allows you to create and test Web sites that use dynamic data forms.

Testing ColdFusion Forms

- Open the Application panel group and click the Server Behaviors tab. Note that there are up to six steps that are—or have to be— completed before you can use a database and a form (see illustration).

Server Behaviors panel before choosing a recordset

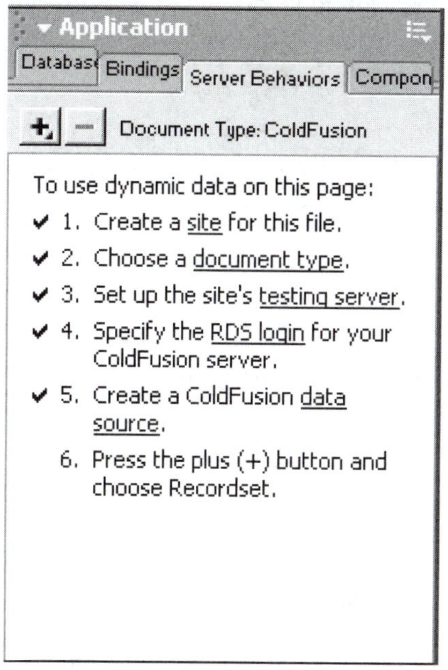

- If any of these steps are not checked, you will need to click on the link in the step and perform the required setup tasks. Typically, if you have already selected ColdFusion as the application used by your testing server, at least the first three steps are checked, and you need only create a login password and select a data source.
  - **1. Create a site for this file.** If this step is not checked, you are not working with the CinciTorial Web site. Clicking the link opens the Site Definition wizard.
  - **2. Choose a document type.** Clicking this link opens the Choose a Document Type dialog box. If necessary, select ColdFusion as the document type. If steps 4 through 6 were missing before, they appear when you select the document type.
  - **3. Set up the site's testing server.** Clicking this link opens the Site Definition Advanced tab for configuring the Testing Server. Select ColdFusion as the Server Model if necessary and select Dreamweaver MX Pages Only in the This site contains list box. Select your access protocol—FTP or Local/Network.
  - **4. Specify the RDS login for your ColdFusion server.** Clicking this link opens the Login to ColdFusion Remote Server Development Services dialog box. Type a password and click OK if necessary.

- **5. Create a ColdFusion <u>data source</u>.** Clicking this link opens the Web browser. Enter your ColdFusion Administrator password and click Login.
- In the Data Sources page, under Add New Data Source, type a database source name for the database. Then select the desired driver from the Driver list and click Add.
- Depending on the kind of driver you select, you will open a Web page in which you can navigate to and select the database after clicking the Database File Browse Server button.
- After selecting the desired database file, click Apply.
- Back in the database page, change any other configurations as desired and click Submit.
- In the Connected Data Sources table, make sure that the selected database is listed in the Data Source Name column. Then make sure that *ok* appears in the Status column and close the Data Sources page.
- The database is added to sample databases that ship with Dreamweaver. If you want to see which databases are configured to work with the application you are using (for example, ColdFusion), open the Databases panel in the Application panel group (see illustration).

Databases panel

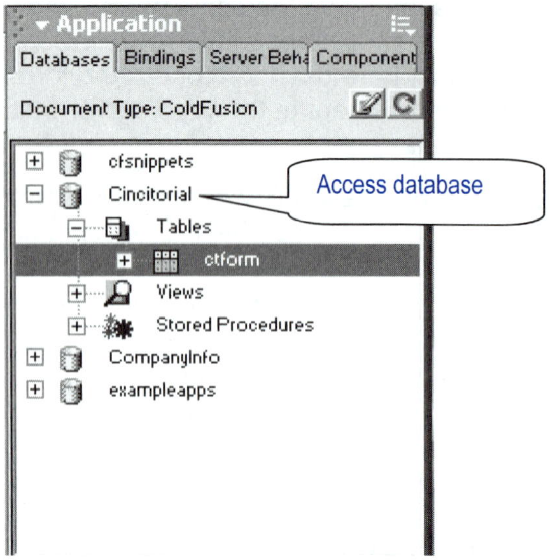

Enter Data from a Form

- There are many ways to make a variety of forms and databases work together. For example, a simple form that writes its data as a record into an Access database can be configured by Selecting the form itself—not an individual form object—and clicking the + button in the Server Behaviors panel and selecting Insert Record.
- In the Insert Record dialog box, verify that the form's name appears in the Submit Values From list box. Then click the Data Source list arrow and select the desired database.
- In the Insert Into Table list box, verify that the table that contains the desired recordsets is selected.
- In the Columns list, you will see that the fields in the form's data table "get" their values from corresponding fields with the same names of the form objects in the form (see illustration).

Columns list shows correspondence between database and form field names

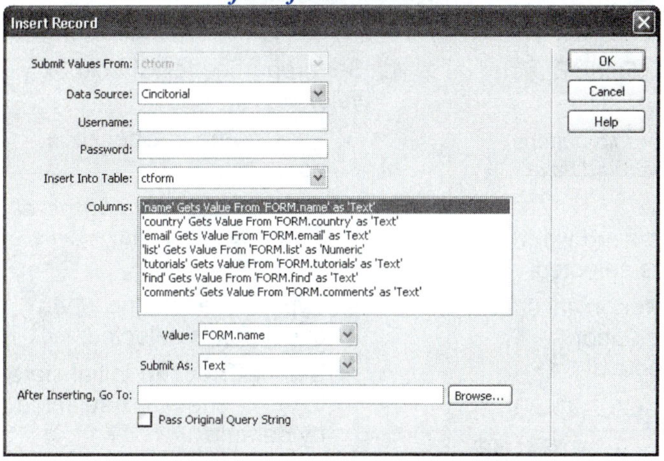

- In some instances, the data that is typed into a form is not compatible with its field in the database. Click the Value list arrow and select the first field's value, then click the Submit As list arrow and select how the data should be submitted. For example, you may want a checkbox to submit its data as text—not as a Yes or No response, which is the default submission method for this kind of form object.
- Even if you don't have a script for your form, you should preview it in the browser to check its appearance. By entering sample data in the form, you can determine if your text fields are wide enough or positioned logically in the form.

Procedures

Create Form Area

1. Position insertion point where form will begin.
2. Click **Insert** .... Alt+I
3. Click **Form** .... F

OR

- Click or drag (**Form** button) on Forms tab of Insert bar.

4. Set properties for form:
   - Type form name.
   - Type script or application file name in **Action** box, or click and navigate to location of script.
   - Specify method if necessary.

Insert Single-Line Text Field

1. Click **Insert** .... Alt+I
2. Click **Form Objects** .... B
3. Click **Text Field** .... T

OR

- Click or drag (**Text Field** button) on Forms tab of Insert bar.

4. Set properties for Text field:
   - Type name in TextField box.
   - Type value for field width.
   - Type value for maximum characters.
   - Type initial value if desired.

Insert Radio Buttons

1. Click **Insert** .... Alt+I
2. Click **Form Objects** .... B
3. Click **Radio Button** .... R

OR

- Click or drag (**Radio Button** button) on Forms tab of Insert bar.

4. Set properties for Radio Button field:
   - Type name in RadioButton box.
     ✓ *In group of radio buttons, all buttons should have same name.*
   - Type value to send when radio button is selected.
   - Select **Checked** initial state to show radio button selected by default.

Insert Radio Group

1. Click **Insert** .... Alt+I
2. Click **Form Objects** .... B
3. Click **Radio Group** .... G

OR

Click or drag (**Radio Group** button) on Forms tab of Insert bar.

4. Specify items for radio group:
   a. Type a group name in RadioButton box.
   b. Type label for first item.
   c. Press Tab and type value.
   d. Click + to add items to list or − to remove items.
   e. Click ▲ or ▼ to reorder list.
5. Select the desired **Lay Out Using** option:
   a. Click **Line Breaks** to place the radio buttons on lines with <br> tags.
   b. Click **Table** to place radio buttons in table.

Insert Checkboxes

1. Click **Insert** .... Alt+I
2. Click **Form Objects** .... B
3. Click **Check Box** C

OR

- Click or drag (**Checkbox** button) on Forms tab of Insert bar.

4. Set properties for Checkbox field:
   - Type name in Checkbox box.
     ✓ *In group of checkboxes, all boxes should have same name.*
   - Type value to send when checkbox is selected.
   - Select **Checked** initial state to show checkbox selected by default.

Insert Drop-Down List

1. Click **Insert** .... Alt+I
2. Click **Form Objects** .... B
3. Click **List/Menu** L

OR

- Click or drag (**List/Menu** button) on Forms tab of Insert bar.

4. Set properties for List/Menu field:
   - Type name in List/Menu box.
   - Select **Menu** or **List**.
   - For **List**, specify number for **Height** and if desired select **Allow multiple** checkbox.
5. Specify items for list:
   a. Type a group name in RadioButton box.
   b. Type label for first item.
   c. Click List Values... .
   d. Type label for first item.
   e. Press Tab and type value.
   f. Click + to add items to list or − to remove items.
   g. Click ▲ or > ▼ to reorder list.
6. Set initial selection by expanding Properties panel, if necessary, and choosing item from **Initially Selected** list.

Insert Multiple-Line Text Field

1. Click **Insert**................ Alt+I
2. Click **Form Objects** .... B
3. Click **Text Field**................ T

OR

- Click or drag (**Text Field** button) on Forms tab of Insert bar.

4. Set properties for multiple-line Text field:
   - Type name in TextField box.
   - Type value for field width.
   - Select **Multi line** option.
   - Type value for number of lines in text box.
   - Type initial value if desired.
   - Change wrap option if desired.

Insert Buttons

1. Click **Insert**................ Alt+I
2. Click **Form Objects** .... B
3. Click **Button**...................... B

OR

- Click or drag (**Insert Button** button) on Forms tab of Insert bar.

4. Set properties for Button field:
   - For Submit button, leave all default properties as is.
   - For Reset or other button, type button name.
   - Type label to appear on button.
   - Select **Reset form** action for Reset button.

Select Data Source for ColdFusion Form Page

1. Open the Application panel group and click the **Server Behaviors** tab.
2. If any of these steps are not check-marked, you will need to click on the link in the step and perform the required setup tasks:
   - **1. Create a site for this file.** If this step is not checked, you are not working with the CinciTorial Web site. Clicking the link opens the Site Definition wizard.
   - **2. Choose a document type.** Clicking this link opens the Choose a Document Type dialog box. If necessary, select ColdFusion as the document type.
   - **3. Set up the site's testing server.** Clicking this link opens the Site Definition Advanced tab for configuring the Testing Server. Select ColdFusion as the Server Model if necessary and select MX Pages Only is selected in the This site contains list box.
   - **4. Specify the RDS login for your ColdFusion server.** Clicking this link opens the Login to ColdFusion Remote Server Development Services dialog box. Type a password and click **OK** if necessary.
3. Click the link in step 5, Create a ColdFusion data source.
4. Your Web browser will launch. Enter your ColdFusion Administrator password and click Login.
5. In the Data Sources page, under Add New Data Source, type a data source name, then select a database driver in the Driver list. Click Add.
6. In the driver type page, click the Database File Browse Server button and navigate to the desired database file in the Browse Server page.
7. Select the database file and click Apply.
8. In the database driver type page, click Submit.
9. In the Connected Data Sources table, make sure the selected database file is listed in the Data Source Name column. Then make sure that *ok* appears in the Status column.
10. Close the Data Sources page.
11. Select the desired form by clicking its red outline.
12. Click + in the Server Behaviors panel and select Insert Record.
13. In the Insert Record dialog box, verify that the form name appears in the Submit Values From list box.
14. Click the Data Source list arrow and select the desired database source name.

    ✓ *If you don't see the data source name, open the Databases panel and click the Refresh button.*

15. Click the Insert Into Table list arrow and select the desired table.
16. Make changes to the values that will be submitted to the database in the Value and Submit As list boxes.
17. Click **OK**.

Test a Form

F12

1. Save page that contains form............ Ctrl+S
2. Click **File** .... Alt+F
3. Click **Preview in Browser**........................... P
4. Select browser, if necessary.
5. Test form by entering sample data and clicking Submit button to send data.

   ✓ *You may receive an error page after you click Submit if you have not yet attached a script or are not connected to the server.*

Exercise Directions

Part I - Create the Form

1. Start Dreamweaver.
2. Open the **CinciTorial** site.
3. Open **contactus.htm**. On a new paragraph below the navigation bar, type the following text:

   To learn more about CinciTorial, fill out the form below and click Submit. We'll respond to your submission within 24 hours.
4. Display the Forms tab on the Insert bar.
5. Insert a form below the paragraph you just typed.
6. Name the form **ctform**. Set the Method setting to POST if necessary.

   ✓ *You do not need to enter anything in the Action text box at this point. You will do so when you set up your form's database and test it on your server.*
7. Create a table within the form as shown in Illustration A, with 11 rows, 2 columns, no border, and cell padding of 2. The table should be 90 percent of page width and the first column should be 30 percent of the table width. Merge cells as shown.

   ✓ *With the insertion point in the form outline, click the Insert>Table menu command.*
8. In the first table cell, type **Fields marked with * are required!** Format the text in bold using the #990033 color.

   ✓ *Refer to Illustration C as you create the labels and form fields in the steps below.*
9. Insert single-line form fields as follows:
   - In the next row, type a label **Your name*** in the left column. Insert a text field in the right column. Name it **name** and specify a width of 35 characters and a maximum of 50 characters.
   - In the next row, type a label **Country*** in the left column. Insert a text field named **country** in the right column with the same properties as the *name* field.

   ✓ *The field names must be typed exactly as shown, since they correspond to the field names in the Access database that you will use to test your form.*
   - In the next row, type a label **Email address*** in the left column. Insert a text field named **email** in the right column with the same properties as the *name* field.
10. Insert radio group:
    - In the next row, type **Add your name to our mailing list?** in the left column.
    - In the first row opposite the merged cell, insert a radio button named **list**. Type the label **Yes**. Press Tab and type the value **TRUE**.

    ✓ *The value TRUE (and FALSE) are interpreted by the database as Yes (and No)*
    - In the row directly beneath, insert another radio button with the same name, **list**. Type the label **No**. Press Tab and type the value **FALSE**.
    - Select the **Table** as the layout and click **OK**.
11. Insert checkboxes:
    - In the next row, type **What kinds of tutorials do you need?** in the merged cell in the left column.
    - In the first row opposite the merged cell, insert a checkbox named **tutorials**. Type the value **suites**. Click to the right of the checkbox and type the label **Office suites**.

      ✓ *Resize the Office suites row if necessary to match the two below it.*

      ✓ *Make sure the Unchecked option is selected for all checkboxes.*
    - In the row directly beneath, insert another checkbox with the same name, **tutorials**. Type the value **web**. Click to the right of the checkbox and type **Internet & Web publishing**.

      ✓ *Using the same name for all checkboxes tells the form script they are part of a group.*
    - In the row directly beneath, insert another checkbox with the same name, **tutorials**. Type the value **programming**. Click to the right of the checkbox and type **Programming**.

12. Insert the drop-down list:
    - In the left column of the next row, type **How did you find us?**
    - In the right column, insert a List/Menu field named **find**. Choose the **Menu** option and click the **List Values** button.
    - Insert the following labels and values:

Search engine	search_engine
Professional publication	publication
ExpoPub	expopub

    - Select *Search engine* as the initially selected item.
13. Insert the multiline text box:
    - In the left column of the next row, type **Tell us what you think of our site**.
    - In the right column, insert a Text field named **comments** and select the **Multi line** option.
    - Specify a width of 50 characters and 5 lines.
    - Type the initial value **I think your site is . . .**
14. Insert Submit and Reset buttons:
    - In the right column of the last row, insert a Button field. Make no changes to the button's properties.
    - Click to the right of the button and insert a second button.
    - Change the new button's name to **reset**, type the label **Reset**, and select the **Reset form** option.
15. Save your changes to this page and preview it in the browser. Your form should look similar to Illustration C.

    ✓ *You may need to adjust the first column width to match the illustration.*

    ✓ *When you create a form and ColdFusion has been selected as the testing server application, your new form will automatically be generated as a ColdFusion page with the .cfm file extension. The .htm version of the page is closed during this process.*

Part II – Testing Your ColdFusion Form

16. Copy the **cincitorial.mdb** Access file to your hard drive if necessary or locate it on the network.
17. Open the Application group panel and click the **Server Behaviors** tab.

    ✓ *Note that there are up to six steps that have to be completed before you can use a database and a form. If your CinciTorial Web has been set up correctly to work with ColdFusion, the first three or four steps should be check-marked. If any are not, click the link and perform the required setup task.*

18. Create a ColdFusion data source (step 5) for the form using **Cincitorial** as the Data Source Name in the ColdFusion Administrator**.** Select Microsoft Access for the database driver. Specify cincitorial.mdb as the Database file (browse to it, if necessary) and click Submit to update the data source.
19. Select the form by clicking its red outline. Its Properties panel will appear.
20. Click + in the Server Behaviors panel and select **Insert Record**.
21. In the Insert Record dialog box, verify that the ctform appears in the Submit Values From list box.
22. Click the Data Source list arrow and select Cincitorial.

    ✓ *You may need to refresh the Databases panel to see the Cincitorial data source.*

23. In the Insert Into Table list box, verify that the table ctform is selected.
24. Notice that the type of data for FORM.tutorials is Checkbox, Y,N. This is the default setting and will not enter the desired data in the database record field. Click the Value list arrow and select the first FORM.tutorials item and then click the Submit As list arrow and select Text.
25. Repeat this for the other two FORM.tutorial entries in the Value list. Your Columns list should look like Illustration B.
26. Click **OK**.
27. Notice that the form changes color in the Dreamweaver Document window. It is now light blue, indicating that an action has been set for the form.
28. Verify that <cfoutput>#CurrentPage# </cfoutput> appears in the Action box of the ctform Properties panel.
29. Preview the contactus.cfm page in your Web browser.

30. Enter the following response in the appropriate form fields in the following table. Your form should look like the one in Illustration C.

Your name*	Todd Tedesco
Country*	Canada
Email address*	ttedesco@maplexpo.org
Add your name to our mailing list?	Yes
What kinds of tutorials do you need?	Office suites, Internet & Web publishing, Programming
How did you find us?	ExpoPub
I think your site is . . .	Fantastic! I can't wait to build my own Dreamweaver site.

31. Click **Submit**.
32. Open the cincitorial.mdb database to verify that the data has been recorded in the ctform table.
33. Close the table.
34. Enter your name and vary your responses.
35. Have one or more other students type responses—or create fictional ones of your own.
36. Review the new entries in the ctform table.
37. Close and save the contactus.cfm document.
38. In the Site panel, delete the unneeded contactus.htm document.
39. **Optional.** If you or your classmates would like to create a form that can be used by the text-to-speech browsers of the vision-impaired in your community, refer to the Reference panel and study the examples for inserting the <label> tag using the FOR code to associate the label with the field name of the form object that is being labeled. With the approval of your instructor, you can edit your form to use the <label> tag in a code view.
40. Close Access.
41. Close Dreamweaver.

Illustration A

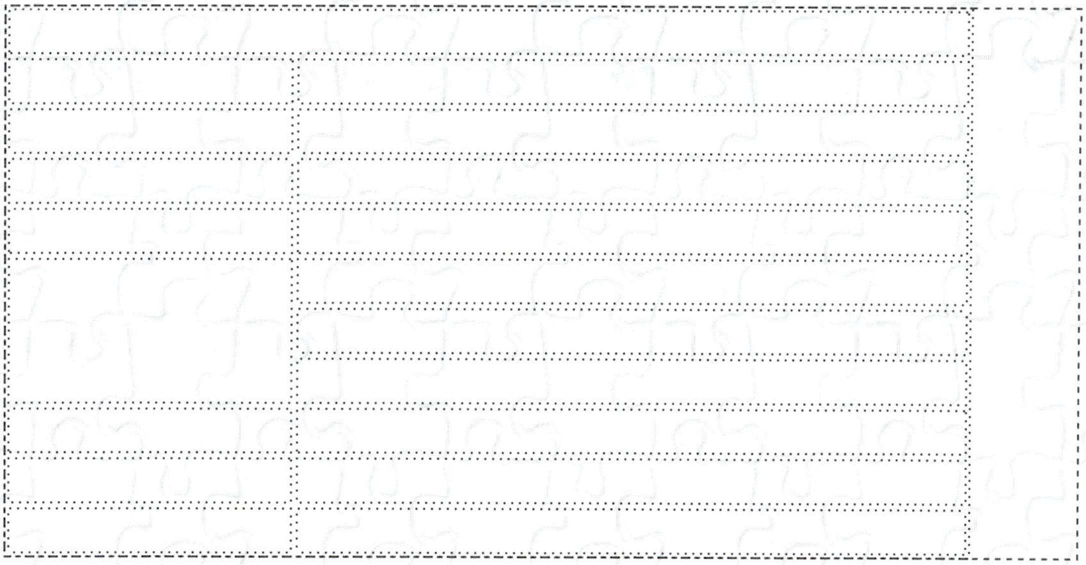

Illustration B

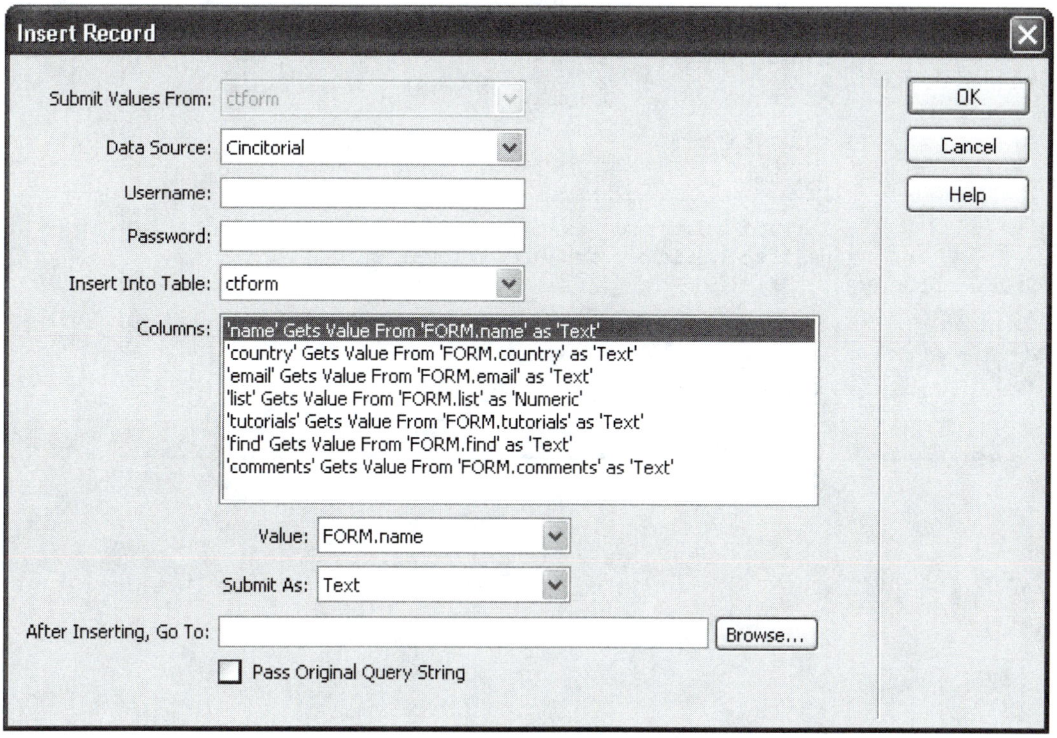

Illustration C

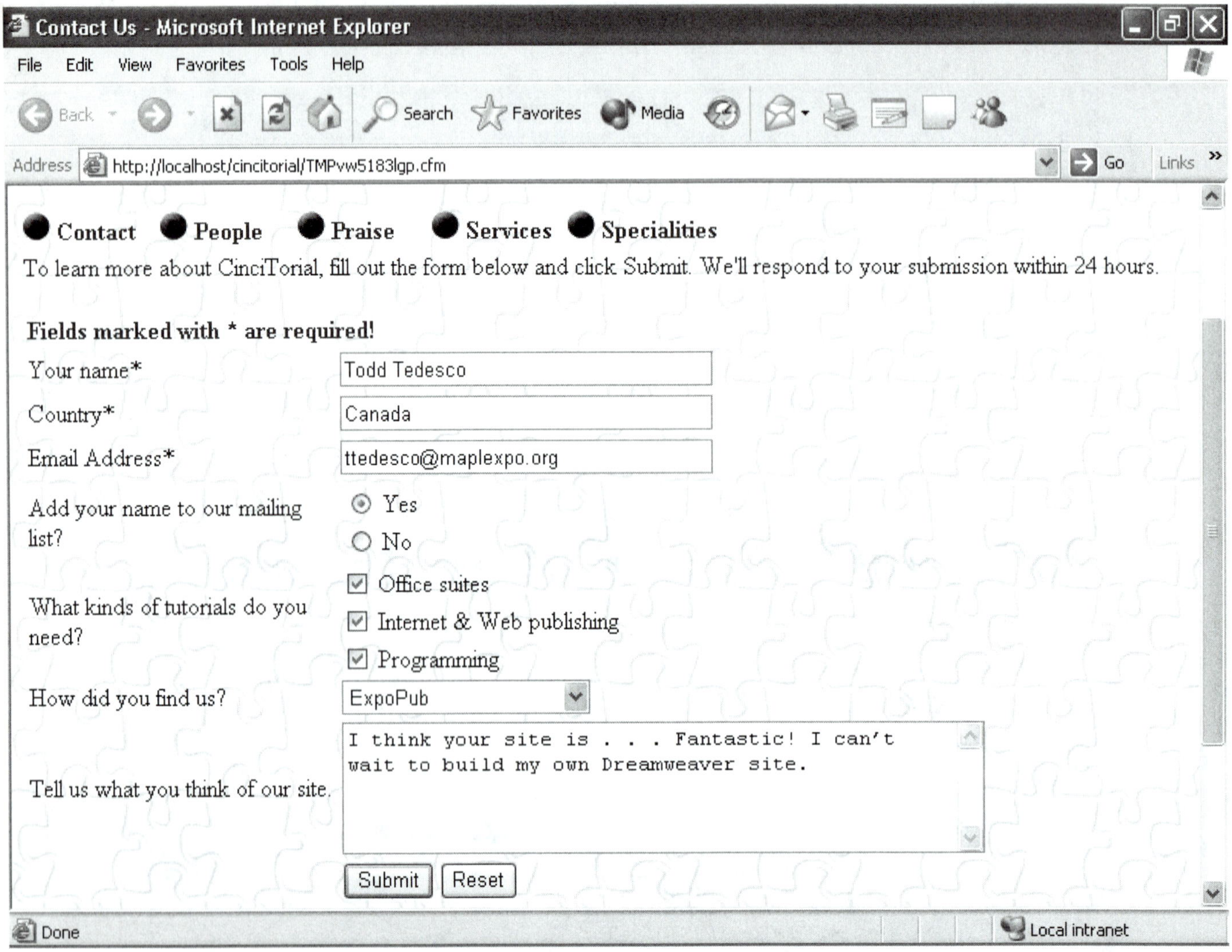

Chapter

11

Layering for Design Flexibility

Layers make it possible for Web designers to create overlapping or perfectly aligned images, text boxes, and other objects. Newer browsers support layering, giving designers an alternative to using tables to lay out a Web page. Layers not only enhance the appearance of a Web site, they also enhance its functionality, directing the visitor's eye to important content, links, images, and so on.

In this chapter, you'll learn how to:

- Create layers
- Size and position layers
- Add content to layers
- Manipulate layers
- Control layer visibility

About Layers

- A **layer** is simply a container for Web page content. Any content you can add to a Web page, you can insert in a layer.
- Layers can contain text, graphics, multimedia objects such as sounds, and even other layers. You can overlap them for creative layouts (see illustration below) or convert them to a table if you're not sure your target browsers can display layers.

Portion of Web page containing layers

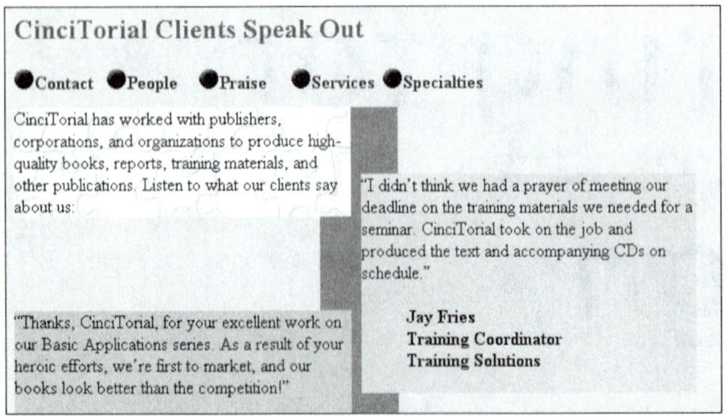

CinciTorial Clients Speak Out

●Contact ●People ●Praise ●Services ●Specialties

CinciTorial has worked with publishers, corporations, and organizations to produce high-quality books, reports, training materials, and other publications. Listen to what our clients say about us:

"I didn't think we had a prayer of meeting our deadline on the training materials we needed for a seminar. CinciTorial took on the job and produced the text and accompanying CDs on schedule."

Jay Fries
Training Coordinator
Training Solutions

"Thanks, CinciTorial, for your excellent work on our Basic Applications series. As a result of your heroic efforts, we're first to market, and our books look better than the competition!"

- A real value of using layers is that layers can be positioned precisely on a Web page, so your creative design will look the same on any browser that supports layering.

  Note: *Layers are robust Web design elements that require Netscape 4.0 or Internet Explorer 4.0 and higher.*

Insert Layers

- You can insert a layer on a Web page using any of three methods:
  - Insert a layer using a menu command.
  - Drag a layer from the Common or Layout tab of the Insert bar.
  - Draw a layer using the Draw Layer button on the Common or Layout tab of the Insert bar.
- To use a menu command to insert a layer, place the insertion point where you want the layer and use the Insert>Layer command on the menu bar.

  Note: *The placement can be an approximation, since the layer can be dragged to any position on the page.*

- Dreamweaver inserts a default-sized layer at the position of the insertion point, as well as a **layer marker** to indicate the point where the layer was inserted (see illustration below).

New layer on Web page

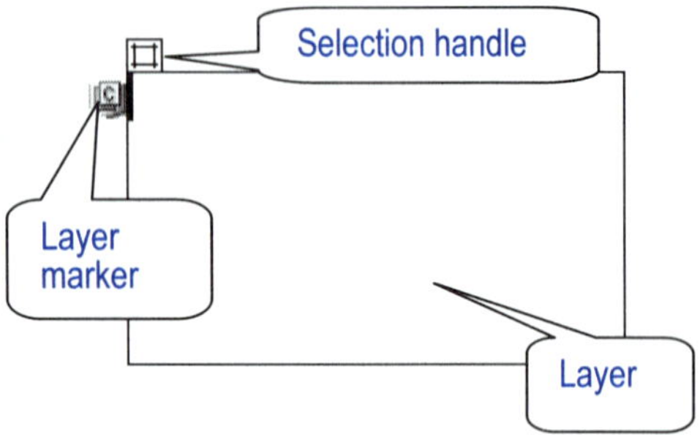

- The remaining two methods of inserting a layer use the Draw Layer button on the Common and Layout tabs of the Insert bar. You can drag the button to the page and release it where you want the layer to insert a default-sized layer. Or, you can click the button and then use a crosshair pointer to draw the layer the desired size (see illustration below).

Draw a layer the desired size

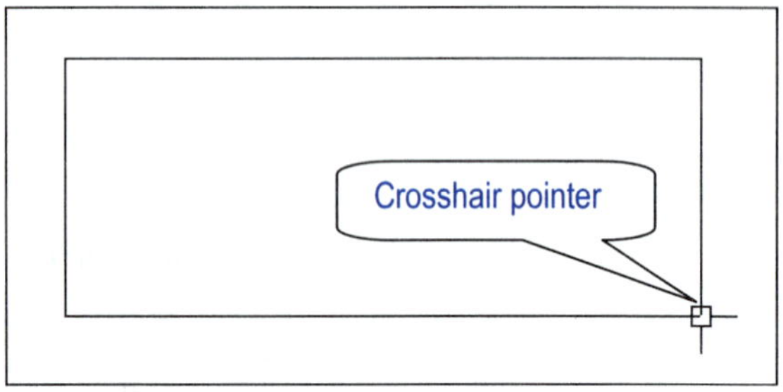

Size and Position Layers

- You can easily adjust the size and location of a layer by dragging. Or, you can use the Properties panel to size and position a layer precisely using pixel measurements and coordinates.
- Before you can change the size or location of a layer, you must select it. Select a layer by
  - Clicking its layer marker.
  - Clicking its selection handle.
  - Clicking its outside border.

Drag to Resize or Relocate

- The easiest way to resize a layer is to click one of the handles on its selected border and drag in the direction you want to resize. Use this method to create a rough layout with your layers. Or, if you have only one or two layers on a page, this method may be sufficient for final sizing.
- You can also use dragging to move layers to new positions after they have been inserted. Drag the selection handle or click on the outside border of a layer and drag with the four-headed arrow pointer.
- Dreamweaver places a <div> tag at the location where you insert a layer. This tag will remain in its original position in the HTML code no matter where you move the layer.
- If you are not happy with your changes to a layer, you can easily delete it. Just select the layer and click the Delete key.

Size and Position Layers Precisely

- To size or position a layer precisely, use the Properties panel. The Properties panel allows you to specify width and height measurements and coordinates for the top left corner of the layer (see illustration on the bottom of the page).
- The L (Left) coordinate measures the distance from the left edge of the page. The T (Top) coordinate measures the distance from the top of the page. Using these positioning coordinates ensures that a layer will appear at the same location in any browser.
- Measurements are in pixels (px) by default. You can also use percentages for size measurements or picas (pc), points (pt), inches (in), millimeters (mm), centimeters (cm), or percentages (%) for the positioning coordinates by using the common symbol or abbreviation for each measurement.
- Your ability to reposition layers freely will depend on whether you have enabled overlap. You can control overlap in the Layers panel.

  Note: *You will learn more about overlap later in this chapter.*

  Tip: *You will find it easier to position layers if you maximize the Document window and collapsing unneeded panels or panel groups.*

Use the Layers Panel

- After you have inserted multiple layers on a page, you can use the Layers panel—a panel in the Advanced Layout panel group—to work with the layers on your workspace. Launch this panel using the Window>Others>Layers command on the menu bar.
- The Layers panel (see illustration below) shows the names of the layers on the page and the order in which they are stacked (the Z column).

Layers panel and layers

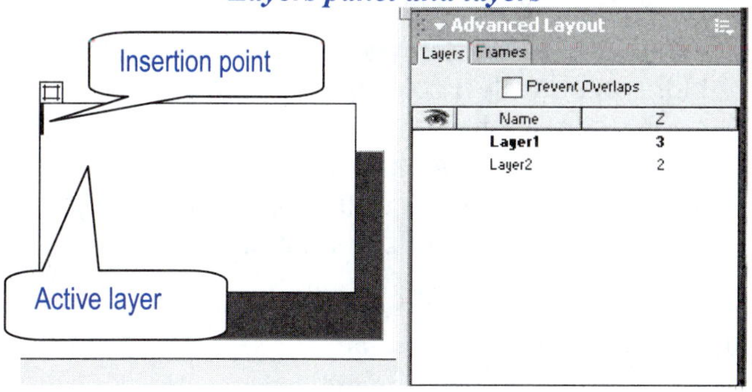

Use Properties panel to size or position precisely

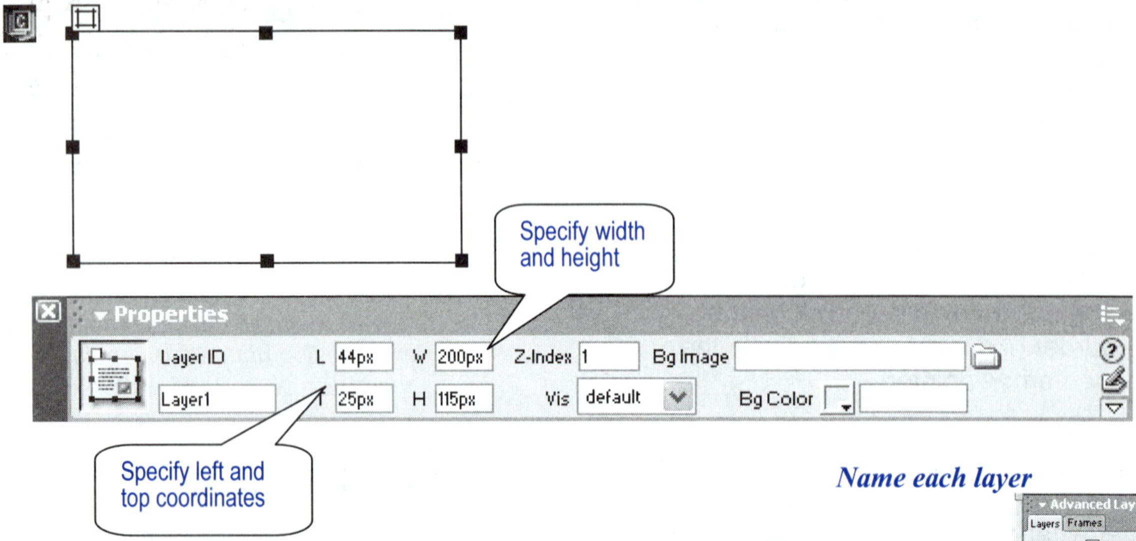

Note: *When you create your first few layers, their Z numbers reflect the order in which the layers were created. As you change the stacking order, the Z number reflects a layer's position in the stack.*

- The Layers panel display changes as you work with layers. When you *activate* a layer by clicking anywhere inside it, the layer's name is boldfaced in the Layers panel. An active layer is ready for you to enter text or an image and has an insertion point in the upper-left corner.
- When you select a layer, the layer name is highlighted with a color band in the Layers panel (see illustration below). You can select a layer by clicking its name in the Layers panel. This is a very helpful feature when your page contains many overlapping layers.

Name Layers

- When you have a number of layers on a page, you can help yourself remember what each one contains by naming the layers.
- Name a layer by typing a name in the Layer ID text box on the Properties panel. As you create names, they appear in the Layers panel (see illustration in the next column).

Name each layer

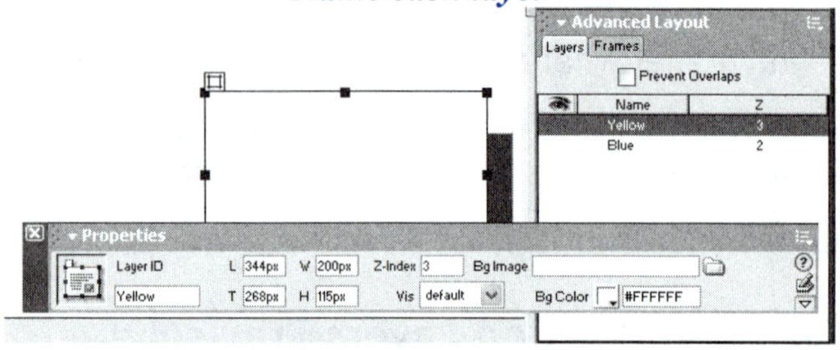

Tip: *You can also double-click on the name of the layer in the Layers panel and change the name there, or right-click the selection handle or layer marker of a selected layer, choose ID . . ., and then type the layer name in the Change Attribute dialog box.*

Add Content to Layers

- Layers can contain any type of HTML content that you can insert on a Web page. Besides adding text or images, you can format a layer with a background color or image.

Insert Text

- To insert text in a layer, click inside the layer to activate it and begin typing at the insertion point. The layer behaves very much like a text box in a word processing application. For example, as you resize the layer, the text wraps to conform to the new shape.
- You can also insert text in a layer by cutting or copying it from another location and then pasting it in the layer. After inserting and formatting the text, you can resize the layer to

fit neatly around the text (see illustration on next page).

Enter text in a layer by typing

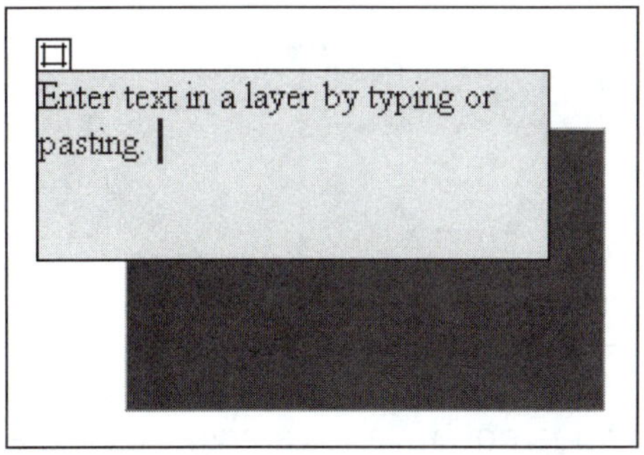

- If you want to add padding around the text—as in a table cell or a text box in a word processing program—you need to insert a table in the layer that consists of one row and one column. Then you can type or paste text into the table cell.

Insert Images

Inserting an image in a layer is no different from inserting it on any Web page. Activate the layer by clicking in it and then use the Insert>Image command on the menu bar or the Image  button on the Common tab of the Insert bar to insert the image.

- An image in a layer may be formatted just like any image on a Web page (see illustration below). You can resize the image, change its alignment, add a border to it, and so on.

Insert image in layer

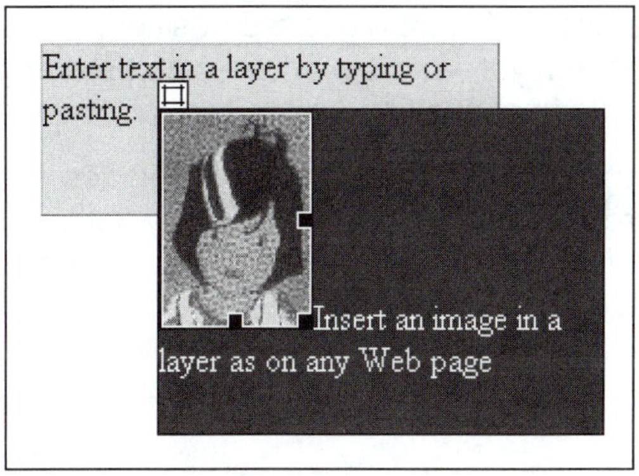

Add Background Color or Image

- Using the Properties panel, you can add color and background images to a layer to provide contrast with the background of the Web document.
- You must select a layer to display properties for background color or image in the Properties panel.
- Use the Bg Color button to display the familiar palette of background colors. Use the Bg Image box to type the name of the image to use, or click the Browse for File button to navigate to the background image file.

Manipulate Layers

- You can manipulate multiple layers on a page to create special effects. For example, you can insert layers within layers to hold related content or images. Before you begin manipulating layers, you need to decide whether your layers can overlap on the page.

Set Overlap Options

- By default, Dreamweaver allows you to overlap layers. This means that you can drag one layer on top of another or partially obscure one layer with another one.
- For some layouts, you will want to prevent layers from overlapping, as, for example, when text in one layer describes images in a layer next to it.
- Control layer overlap in the Layers panel. If you click the Prevent Overlaps checkbox, you will not be allowed to overlap one layer on another.

Change Stacking Order

- When you do overlap layers, you may need to adjust the **stacking order** from time to time. Layers are stacked on a page in the order they are created, from the first layer (designated by default as Layer1) on the bottom to subsequent layers on top (see illustration at top of next column).

Stacked layers on a page

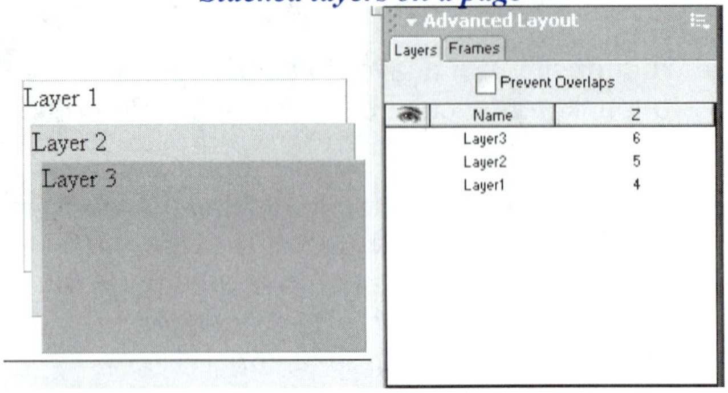

- The stacking order is also called the **Z-index**. The bottommost layer is given a Z-index number of 1, and subsequent layers receive incrementally higher numbers. To change the stacking order of a layer, you change its Z-index number.

  Note: *It is possible to assign the same Z-index number to more than one layer.*

- You can change a layer's Z-index number by clicking it in the Z column of the Layers panel and typing a new number. Or, type a new stacking order number in the Z-Index box on the Properties panel.
- You can also change stacking order by selecting a layer name in the Layers panel and dragging it to the desired level in the Layers panel's stack.

Nest Layers

- Just as it sounds, a *nested* layer is a layer inserted inside an existing layer. You can use the same methods to insert a layer on a Web page to insert a layer in another layer.

  Caution: *If you draw the layer with the crosshair generated by the Draw Layer button, you must press Alt to nest the new layer if nesting is turned off in Layers preferences in the Preferences dialog box.*

- The layer in which you insert a nested layer is called the *parent layer*. The nested layer is called the *child layer*. The child layer's layer marker appears within the parent layer, and the child layer is listed underneath the parent layer in the Layers panel (see illustration at top of next column).

Nested layer created in Layer3

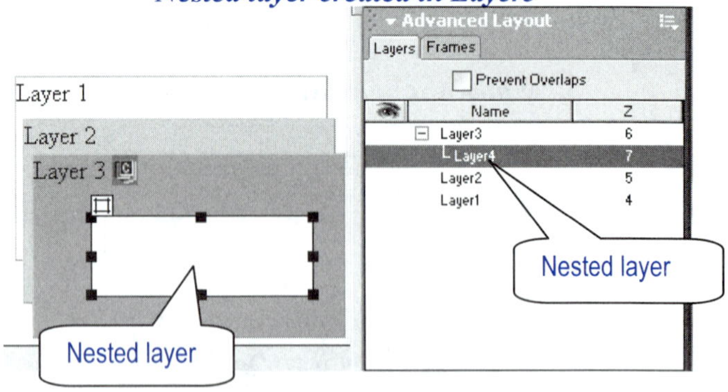

- Though created within a parent layer, the child layer does not have to remain within the parent layer. It can be moved outside of the nested layer without its ceasing to be a nested layer.
- Click the minus sign next to a parent layer in the Layers panel to hide child layers. Click a plus sign to display child layers.
- You can click on the nested layer's name in the Layers panel and drag it out of the parent layer to break the nested relationship.
- To create or restore nesting in the Layers panel, press Ctrl and then drag the layer's name over the name of the desired parent layer. When the parent layer is outlined—selected—release the mouse button to create the nesting relationship.
- Nested layers can be stacked in the Layers panel just like other layers. A nested layer can even be nested within another nested layer.
- You can also nest or restore nesting in the Document window by clicking the layer's layer marker and then dragging it inside the target parent layer, releasing the mouse button when the anchor is in the desired position. The nested layer—or its marker—can be dragged into its final position as desired.
- A child layer inherits certain properties of the parent layer, such as the visibility setting (see the next section for more information on visibility).

Control Layer Visibility

- Making a layer or layers invisible can be helpful to "quiet" the on-screen complexity of a Web page so that you can work on one layer at a time.
- Controlling visibility also allows you to test the page with different layouts, since an invisible layer remains hidden when previewed in a Web browser.
- You can control layer visibility from the Layers panel or the Properties panel.
- To hide a layer in the Layers panel, click to the left of the layer's name to display the closed eye icon. When the eye is closed, the layer is hidden (see illustration below).

Layer3 is hidden

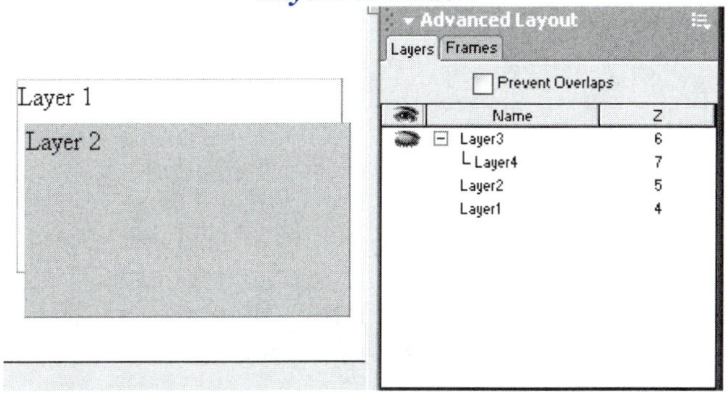

- Note in the illustration above that the child layer inserted within Layer3 is also hidden. The child layer inherits the visibility setting of its parent layer.
- Click the closed eye icon next to the layer to show a hidden layer. The closed eye icon changes to an open eye icon .

  Tip: *To hide or show all layers at the same time, click the eye column heading until the desired view is achieved. To reset to the blank default mode, click on the individual eye icon until it is removed.*

- Using the Properties panel gives you greater control over visibility settings for nested layers. Select a layer and click the Vis list arrow on the Properties panel to see a list of visibility attributes:
  - Select *hidden* to make the layer and its contents invisible.
  - Select *visible* to make the layer and its contents visible.
  - Select *inherit* to determine the layer's visibility based on the parent layer's visibility setting.
  - The *default* setting typically provides the same attributes as the *inherit* setting.
- Using the Vis list, you can set a child layer's visibility to differ from that of its parent. For example, you can make the child layer visible while the parent layer is hidden.

Advanced Layer Properties

- With a layer selected, click on the expansion arrow of the Properties panel to see advanced settings that control the appearance and functionality of layers in different browsers. (See illustration on next page.)
- By default, Dreamweaver creates CSS layers that use the div tag. (Span is another CSS layer tag.) Most browsers, including Internet Explorer, Netscape Navigator, and Mozilla, will support div-tagged CSS layers.
- To tailor a site specifically for Netscape browsers, you can change the default div tag option to layer and ilayer tags. These tags will work only in the Netscape browser—or the open-source browsers based on it, such as Mozilla and Phoenix.

  Note: *The layer and ilayer tags for building Netscape layers have their own settings. Consult Dreamweaver Help for additional information.*

- The Overflow (CSS layers only) property controls the layer's behavior when the layer's content is larger than its size. Choose from the following options:
  - *Visible* increases the layer's size so that all content is visible. The layer expands down and to the right.
  - *Hidden* maintains the layer's size and crops any content that does not fit. No scroll bars are provided.
  - *Scroll* adds scroll bars to the layer regardless of whether the contents exceed the layer's size.
  - *Auto* makes scroll bars appear only when the layer's content exceeds its boundaries.

- Use the Clip settings to control the size of layer content by specifying in pixels (or another measurement system) how much content to remove from each side of the layer. This is useful when an image is too large for the layer. Dreamweaver does not resize layers to fit graphic images, and with this feature, you can crop parts of an image that do not contribute to your page.

Convert Layers to Tables

- Pre-version 4 browsers do not support layers. However, Dreamweaver offers an option to convert a layer layout to a table so that the page can be viewed by any browser version.

Caution: *Before converting a layer layout to a table, you must unnest nested layers and make sure layers do not overlap.*

- To convert layers to a table, use the Modify>Convert>Layers to Table command.

Advanced layer properties

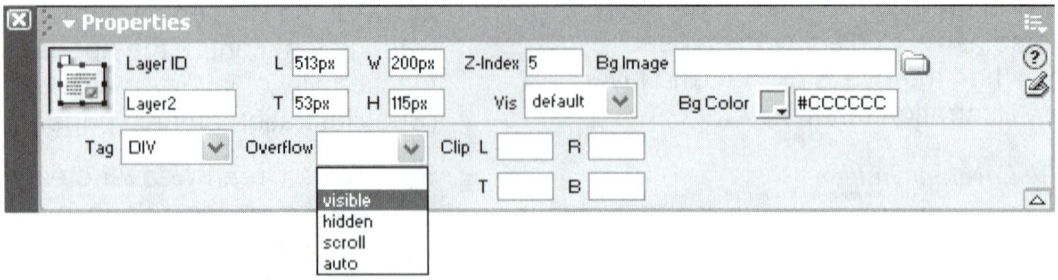

Note: *Transparent GIFs are invisible GIF images used to adjust layout.*

- The Convert Layers to Table dialog box (see illustration below) gives you a number of options for the conversion.

Convert Layers to Table dialog box

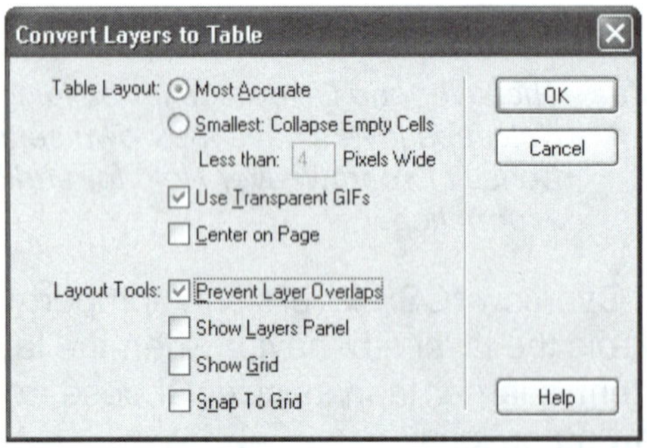

- *Most Accurate* creates a table cell for every layer. Additional table cells are created to replace the original spacing between layers.
- *Smallest: Collapse Empty Cells* specifies that the layers' edges should be aligned if they are positioned within the number of pixels entered in Pixels Wide box. This option results in a table with fewer empty rows and columns.
- *Use Transparent GIFs* fills the table's last row with transparent GIFs. This allows for tables that are consistent in appearance from browser to browser.

- The resulting table layout may still need some work to merge cells and reposition content (see illustration below), but this option is still much faster than recreating a layout.
- It is also possible to convert a table to layers. In this process, each cell becomes a layer.

Layers converted to a table.

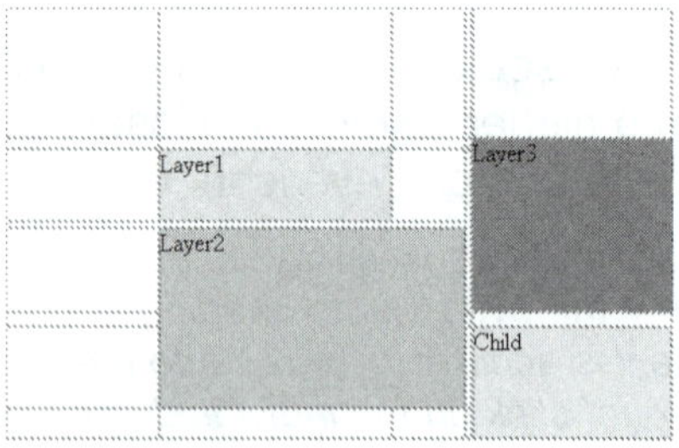

Looking Ahead

- Dreamweaver allows you to work with layers in other ways. In Chapter 15, you will learn about timelines, a Dreamweaver feature that allows you to create animation without special ActiveX controls, Java applets, or plug-ins. You create the animated effect by changing the position, size, visibility, and stacking order of layers and images in a series of frames over time.

Procedures

Insert Layers

1. Position insertion point where layer should appear.
2. Click **Insert** .... Alt + I
3. Click **Layer** .... Y, Enter

OR

- Drag (**Draw Layer** button) from Common or Layout tabs of the Insert bar to Document window and release mouse button.

OR

1. Click (**Draw Layer** button) on Common or Layout tabs of the Insert bar.
2. Draw layer of desired size at desired location.

Select a Layer

- Click layer marker.
- Click layer selection handle.
- Click outside border of layer.

Drag to Resize or Relocate

To resize a layer

1. Select layer.
2. Click on a black handle on any side of selected layer and drag in direction to resize.

To move a layer

1. Select layer.
2. Click on selection handle or outside border.
3. Drag layer to new location.

Size and Position Layers Precisely

To resize precisely

1. Select layer.
2. Type exact width in **W** text box on Properties panel.
3. Type exact height in **H** text box on Properties panel.

To position precisely

1. Select layer.
2. Type measurement from left edge of page in **L** text box on Properties panel.
3. Type measurement from top of page in **T** text box on Properties panel.

Display Layers panel
F2

1. Click **Window** .... Alt + W
2. Click **Others** .... O
3. Click **Layers** .... Y

Name Layers

In Layers panel

1. Double-click layer name.
2. Type new name.

In Properties panel

1. Select default name in **Layer ID** box.
2. Type new name.

In Document window

1. Right-click on the layer's selection handle or layer marker.
2. Click **ID** in the shortcut menu to open the Change Attribute dialog box.
3. Type new name in the **Id** text box.

Insert Text

1. Activate layer by clicking inside layer.
2. Begin typing at insertion point.
   OR
   Paste cut or copied text at insertion point.

Insert Images
Ctrl + Alt + I

1. Activate layer by clicking inside layer.
2. Click **Insert** .... Alt + I
3. Click **Image** I

   OR

   Click (**Image** button) on Common tab of the Insert bar.
4. Format image as on any Web page.

Add Background Color or Image

Insert background image

1. Select layer.
2. Click in **Bg Image** box on Properties panel and type path to image.
   OR
   Click (**Browse for File** button) on Properties panel and navigate to image.

Insert background color

1. Select layer.
2. Click **Bg Color** box and select color from palette.
   OR
   Type hexadecimal value for color in **Bg Color** text box.

Set Overlap Options

1. Display Layers panel.
2. Select **Prevent Overlaps** checkbox to prevent overlap.
3. Clear **Prevent Overlaps** checkbox to allow overlap.

Change Stacking Order

In Layers panel

- Click **Z-index** number and type new number.
- Select layer name and drag to new position in name list.

In Properties panel

- Select **Z-Index** number and type new number.

Nest Layers

1. Activate layer that will become parent layer.
2. Insert child layer using one of the appropriate methods listed in these Procedures.

   ➸ *If you drag or draw the nested layer using the Draw Layer button, press* Alt *to nest the new layer if nesting is turned off in Layers preferences in the Preferences dialog box.*
3. Format nested layer as any other layer.

Change Visibility

To hide layer

1. Select layer to hide.
2. Click to left of layer name in Layers panel to display icon.

   OR

   Click **Vis** list arrow on Properties panel and select **hidden**.

To show hidden layer

- Click icon in Layers panel.

  OR

  Click **Vis** list arrow on Properties panel and select **visible**.

To give child layer parent layer's visibility setting

- Click **Vis** list arrow on Properties panel and select **inherit**.

Convert Layers to Table

1. Reorganize any nested layers and adjust layers to prevent overlap.
2. Click **Modify** .... Alt+M
3. Click **Convert** C
4. Click **Layers to Table** L
5. Select options for table display.

Exercise Directions

1. Start Dreamweaver.
2. Open the **CinciTorial** site.
3. Open **praise.htm**. You will create layers on this page to hold the page's text paragraphs.
4. Display the Layers panel and clear the **Prevent Overlaps** checkbox if necessary.

   ✓ *As you create the layers and the new layout, refer to Illustration A to guide you. To make it easier to work with layers, maximize your page. But first drag the Layers panel from its docked position and place it in a handy, unobstrusive position.*
5. Click to the left of the first text paragraph on the page.
6. Use the Insert menu to insert a new layer. Name this layer **intro**. Click outside the layer to deselect it.
7. Because layers cannot be padded, you will want to insert a table inside the layer. Click Insert>Table and create a table that has one row and one column. Set the width to 100% and the cell padding to 2.
8. Select the first paragraph on the page and cut it using the right-click and Cut command from the shortcut menu.
9. Activate the *intro* layer and paste the cut text into the table that was inserted into the layer.
10. Resize the layer to be about 4" wide and 2" high. Insert the **puzzle.gif** image from your images folder as a background image.

    ✓ *Do not insert 4in and 2in in the W and H boxes respectively. You will set the sizes precisely later in the exercise.*
11. As you cut text from this page, other paragraphs will move up and get in the way of your layers. You will need to insert blank paragraphs to make space for layers. Hide the *intro* layer and click below its layer marker at the left edge of the page. Press the **Enter** key twice to insert space.
12. Display the *intro* layer again.
13. Draw a second layer to the right of the *intro* layer. Name this layer **training**.
14. Resize the *training* layer to be about 4" wide and 2" high, and move it so the top of the layer lines up with the middle of the *intro* layer.
15. Insert a one-celled table as in step 7.
16. Select and cut the praise paragraph and client information for Training Solutions (this includes the quote and the contact's name, title, and company).
17. Paste the cut text into the table inserted in the *training* layer. Add a background color to this layer using #CCFFFF. Resize the layer if necessary to fit the text.
18. Add two more blank paragraphs at the left edge of the page to take the place of the cut text. (In other words, position the insertion point and press the **Enter** key twice.)
19. Draw a third layer about 4" wide below the *intro* layer and aligned about halfway down the *training* layer. Name this layer **lion**.
20. Insert a one-celled table as in step 7.
21. Cut the praise paragraph and client information for Lion Press and paste this text into the table inserted in the *lion* layer. Apply a background color of #99FFFF to the layer.
22. Draw a fourth layer below the *training* layer and name it **quentin**.
23. Insert a one-celled table as in step 7.
24. Cut the testimonial and client information for Quentin-Stevens and paste this text into the table inserted into the *quentin* layer. Apply a background color of #66FFFF to the layer.
25. Draw a fifth layer below the *lion* layer and name it **peters**.
26. Insert a one-celled table as in step 7.
27. Cut the last praise paragraph and client information and paste it into the table inserted into the *peters* layer. Apply a background color of #00CCCC to the layer.
28. Add blank paragraphs at the left edge of the page as necessary to move the link and the table down past the last layer.

29. Make the following adjustments to size and position in pixels:
    - For the *intro* layer, set Left to 9 and Top to 160. Set Width to 300 and Height to 91.
      ✓ *Don't worry if the text obscures the navigation bar. It will look correct in the browser.*
    - For the *training* layer, set Left to 318 and Top to 217. Set Width to 300 and Height to 115.
    - For the *lion* layer, set Left to 9 and Top to 335. Set Width to 300 and Height to 115.
    - For the *quentin* layer, set Left to 318 and Top to 449. Set Width to 300 and Height to 115.
    - For the *peters* layer, set Left to 9 and Top to 567. Set Width to 300 and Height to 115.
30. Add the "stripe" layer down the center of the page as follows:
    - Beginning about ½" from the right edge of the *intro* layer, draw a new layer from the top of the *intro* layer to just below the *peters* layer. The layer should overlap the left edge of the *training* layer about ½". (See Illustration A.)
    - Name the layer **stripe** and add background color of #FF6666.
    - Fine-tune the size and position: Set a Left measurement of 281 and a Top of 160. Set a Width of 70 and a Height of 625.
31. Change the stacking order so the *stripe* layer has a Z-index number of **1**.
32. Draw a final layer to the right of the *peters* layer and name it *link*. Apply the background color #FFCC66.
33. Set the Left measurement at 318, Top at 661, Width at 280, and Height at 90.
34. Create a nested layer within the *link* layer and name the child layer *picture*.
35. Insert the **CPreston.jpg** image in the child layer. Resize the picture to 51 by 66 pixels, and then resize the *picture* layer to fit closely around the image.
36. Create another nested layer within the *link* layer to the right of the picture. Name the layer *linktext*.
37. Type the following text in the *linktext* layer: **For more information on our staff, click the picture.**
38. Create a link from the image in the *picture* layer to **people.htm**.
39. Save your changes and preview the page in the browser.
40. If necessary, return to Dreamweaver and add space under the layers to move the table and the *Back to Top* link down so they do not obscure the layers.
41. Close the browser.
42. Close any open pages.
43. Exit Dreamweaver.

Illustration A

CinciTorial
Editorial Services

CinciTorial Clients Speak Out

● Contact ● People ● Praise ● Services ● Specialities

CinciTorial has worked with publishers, corporations, and organizations to produce high-quality books, reports, training materials, and other publications. Listen to what our clients say about us:

"I didn't think we had a prayer of meeting our deadline on the training materials we needed for a seminar. CinciTorial took on the job and produced the text and accompanying CDs on schedule."

Jay Fries
Training Coordinator
Training Solutions

"Thanks, CinciTorial, for your excellent work on our Basic Applications series. As a result of your heroic efforts, we're first to market, and our books look better than the competition!"

Maggie Jenkins
Senior Editor
Lion Press

"We've worked with CinciTorial since the beginning, and we've always found them to be highly professional as well as downright fun. We plan to continue to use their development and production services into the next century."

Tyler Stanislowski
Production Manager
Quentin-Stevens Inc.

"We know when we hand a project over to CinciTorial that it will come back to us on time and ready for the printer. We feel very fortunate to work with their great people."

Lennie Makarios
Project Coordinator
Peters Press

For more information on our staff, click the picture.

Our Clients

Contact our best clients for more info on our servinces	Client	Contact	E-mail
	Lion Press	Maggie Jenkins	Maggie_Jenkins@lionpress.com
	Peters Press	Lennie Makarios	lmakarios@peterspress.com
	Quentin-Stevens	Tyler Stanislowski	tylerstan@qspub.com
	Training Solutions	Jay Fries	jfries@trainingsolutions.com

Back to Top

Next Chapter

Chapter

12

Frame Pages

A frame page allows you to display several Web pages at the same time in specified areas on the page. You can set up links in a page in one frame to open pages in another frame or create many other kinds of layouts and uses for frames. Dreamweaver's tools make frame page building easy. You only need to plan the layout and choose the content.

In this chapter you will learn how to:

- Create a frameset and frames
- Use the Frames tab and Frames panel
- Add content to frames
- Set up frame and frameset properties
- Set frame links and targets
- Modify page properties

About Frame Pages

- The term *frame page* is used to describe a page that contains several **frames**. Frames are regions on an HTML page that contain a specific HTML page.
- In Dreamweaver, a frame page is known more properly as a **frameset**. The frameset has a name and a page title, but its only content is the frame definitions.
- Each frame in a frameset contains a page that has its own name and page title. Pages displayed in frames consist of text, images, and links just like any other Web page and can be formatted with backgrounds, styles, and other effects.

Create a Frameset

- You have two options for creating a new frameset:
  - Create a new page that you split into frames manually.
  - Apply a predefined frameset to a new or existing document.

Insert Frames Manually

- If you want to control the number and location of frames in a new page, insert the frames yourself. Use the Modify>Frameset command on the menu bar and then select the desired type of split from the Frameset submenu:
  - Split Frame Left and Split Frame Right insert a border that divides the page or current frame in half vertically.
  - Split Frame Up and Split Frame Down insert a border that divides the page or current frame in half horizontally.
- The distinctions between these split directions are more relevant if a frame already contains content. The existing content always moves into the new frame, so choose the split type that will keep your content where you want it.

Tip: *If you inadvertently choose the wrong split type, simply use the Edit>Undo command to reverse the split.*

- After you click a split type, Dreamweaver displays the frame border on the page (see illustration below). You can drag this border to adjust the size of the frame.

New page divided into two frames

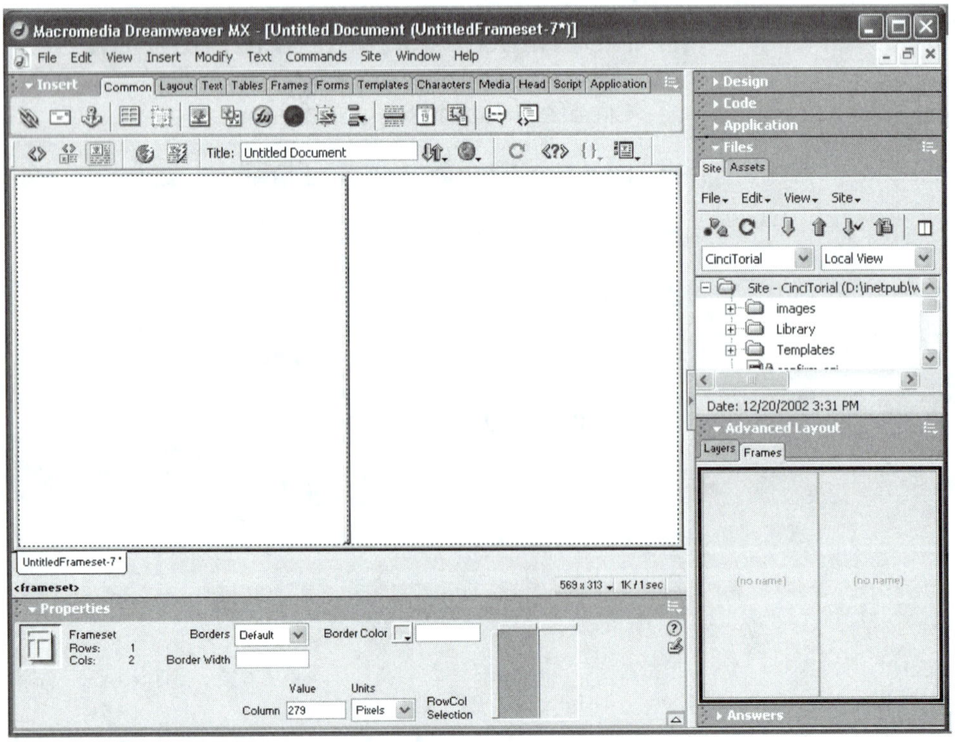

- The Frameset Properties panel also displays to allow you to change the frameset's properties.

  Note: *You will learn more about changing frameset properties later in the chapter.*

- To further split a frame, click in that frame to activate it and use the Modify>Frameset submenu commands. You can continue to split frames until you have established all the frames for the frameset.

  Caution: *Create only two or three frames in a frameset. More than three frames can make the page look confusing.*

Use Frames Tab in Insert Bar

- Dreamweaver offers thirteen predefined framesets on the Frames tab in the Insert bar (see illustration below).
- The first four frameset layouts are similar to the basic left, right, up, and down splits. There are also nested framesets—frames within frames—and a top and bottom frameset. Place the mouse pointer on the frameset buttons to see their descriptive tooltip
- You can use these predefined framesets on either a new blank page or a page that already contains content. The blue-shaded area of these framesets represents the page's existing content, making it easy to see how your existing page will look with other frames around it.
- You can use these framesets on a whole page or within a specific frame to further subdivide a frame.

Activate or Select a Frame

- Working with frames will require you to know how to activate and select frames. Some operations, such as adding content, require the frame to be active. Other operations, such as changing frame properties, require the frame to be selected.
- To *activate* a frame, simply click in it to position the insertion point. When a frame is active, you can add and format content, save the frame's page, and apply page properties such as background color and a page title.
- To *select* a frame, hold down the Alt key and click in the frame. The frame's borders show a dotted outline to let you know the frame is selected (see illustration at the bottom of the page).
- A selected frame also displays frame information in the Properties panel, such as the frame's name, source, and border options.
- The distinction between activating and selecting is extremely important when working with frames. If you find you cannot perform a specific operation, check the Procedures section at the end of this chapter to make sure whether you should activate or select a frame.

Frame tab has basic and complex frame layouts

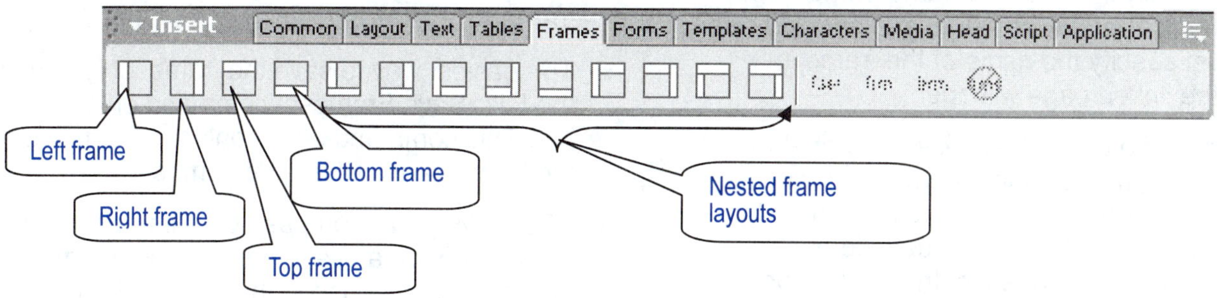

Frame1 is selected

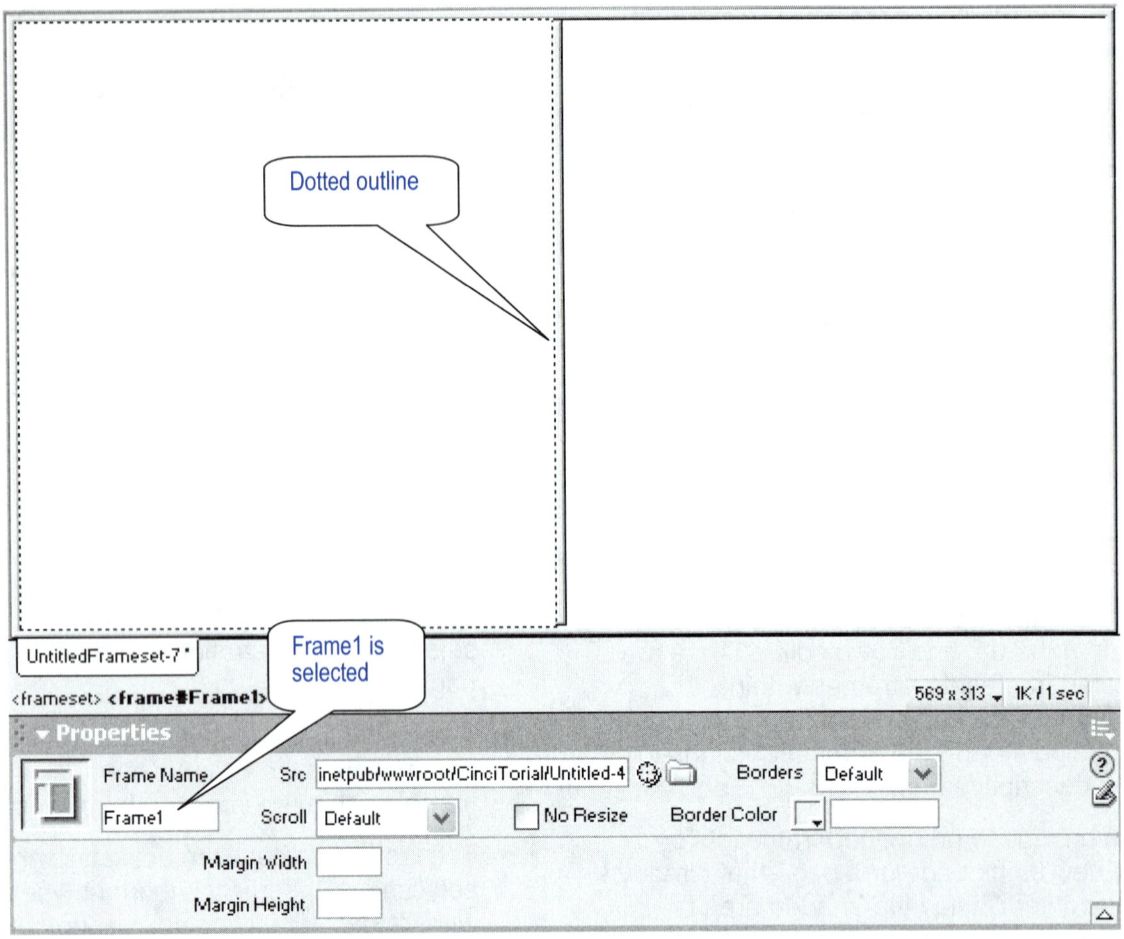

Name a Frame

- You will find it helpful to name the frames you create (or change the default names Dreamweaver supplies).
- It is especially important to name frames if you want to link from one frame to another because you must specify the name of the frame in which the linked page will open.
- Name a frame using the Properties panel. *Select* the frame, click in the Frame Name text box (see illustration on the bottom of the previous page), and type the desired name. Frame names should reflect the content or function of a frame. A frame that holds a logo at the top of a page, for example, might be named *logo*.

Save Framesets and Frames

- Saving a frameset and its frames pages can be confusing for first-time Dreamweaver users, because the frameset page itself and each frame's page must be named and titled.
- The easiest way to save the frameset is to use the File>Save Frameset command on the menu bar. This command saves only the frameset, not the frame pages within the frameset.
- After saving the frameset, be sure to give the frameset page a title in the Page Properties dialog box. If you issue the Modify>Page Properties command directly after saving the frameset, you can be certain the page title applies to the frameset, not one of its frames.

  Note: *You can also type a new page title in the Document toolbar's Title box.*

- If you intend to create new content in a frame, you must also name and title the page in that frame. You can do so by clicking in the frame to *activate* it and issuing the File>Save Frame command.
- As you work with the frameset, use the File>Save Frameset command often to save changes to the frameset and its frames. You can also save changes to a specific frame by clicking in it to activate it and then clicking Ctrl + S.

  Tip: *Save changes to all frames at once using the File>Save All command.*

  Note: *Remember, if the page name within parentheses in the title bar shows an asterisk, changes have been made since the last save. This is your signal to save again.*

Add Content to Frames

- You have two choices for adding content to a frame in a frameset:
  - You can simply begin typing in the frame to insert content in the frame, or you can paste text that has been copied or cut from another location.

    Tip: *Remember, you must* activate *a frame before you can add content to it.*

  - You can link the frame to an existing Web page. When the frameset is opened, that Web page appears in the frame.
- If you intend to link a frame to a Web page, you can save time by creating that Web page before creating the frameset.
- As you begin to add content to frames, you will find the Frames panel in the Advanced Layout group panel extremely useful to manipulate the frames. Launch the Frames panel using the Window>Others>Frames command on the menu bar.
- The Frames panel (see illustration in next panel) shows the frame layout of the frameset and the names you have assigned each frame.

Frames panel

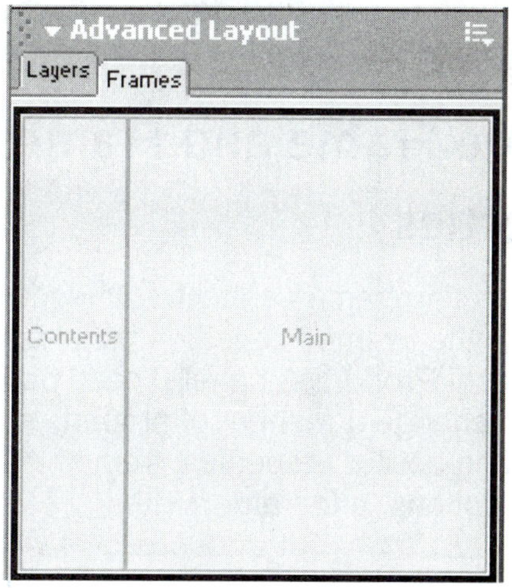

- You can quickly select any frame in the frameset by clicking the corresponding frame in the Frames panel. This operation can be faster than the Alt + click method of selecting a frame.

Set Frame Source

- If you want an existing Web page to open in a frame, you must specify that page as the frame's *source*. Specify a frame source in the Properties panel.
- *Select* the frame to link to a source and type the address of the source page in the Src text box on the Properties panel. You can also click the Browse for File button and navigate to the source page

  Tip: *Or, click the Point to File icon and drag it to the desired source page in the Files panel.*

- Dreamweaver assumes that you will choose a Web page from the current site folder, but you can select a page at any Internet address.
- The Src text box displays the name of the source page and the page immediately opens in the selected frame (see illustration on next page).
- The Src text box will not be empty when you begin this operation. It will contain a placeholder name (such as UntitledFrame-2) for the HTML document set up in the frame when the frame was created.

- If you choose to create a new Web page in the frame, you rename this default placeholder name when you save the frame's page.

Change Frame and Frameset Properties

- By selecting frames and the frameset, you display the Frame Properties panel and the Frameset Properties panel. These panels allow you to change a number of properties, including border properties, frame resize and scroll options, and frame width.

Modify Frame Properties

- In addition to setting a name for a frame and specifying its source, you can change scroll settings, resize options, border properties, and frame margins.
- The frame's Scroll setting controls the display of scroll bars in the frame.
  - Select No if you want to prevent scroll bars from displaying. This setting is suitable for frames that have little content.
  - Select Yes or Auto to display scroll bars if the frame's page is longer than the frame's depth. Auto will cause scroll bars to appear automatically if the browser window is resized.
  - The Default setting uses whatever the browser's setting is, which is typically Auto.
- Selecting the No Resize checkbox prevents users from dragging the frame's borders in the Web browser to resize the frame.

Link frame to source page

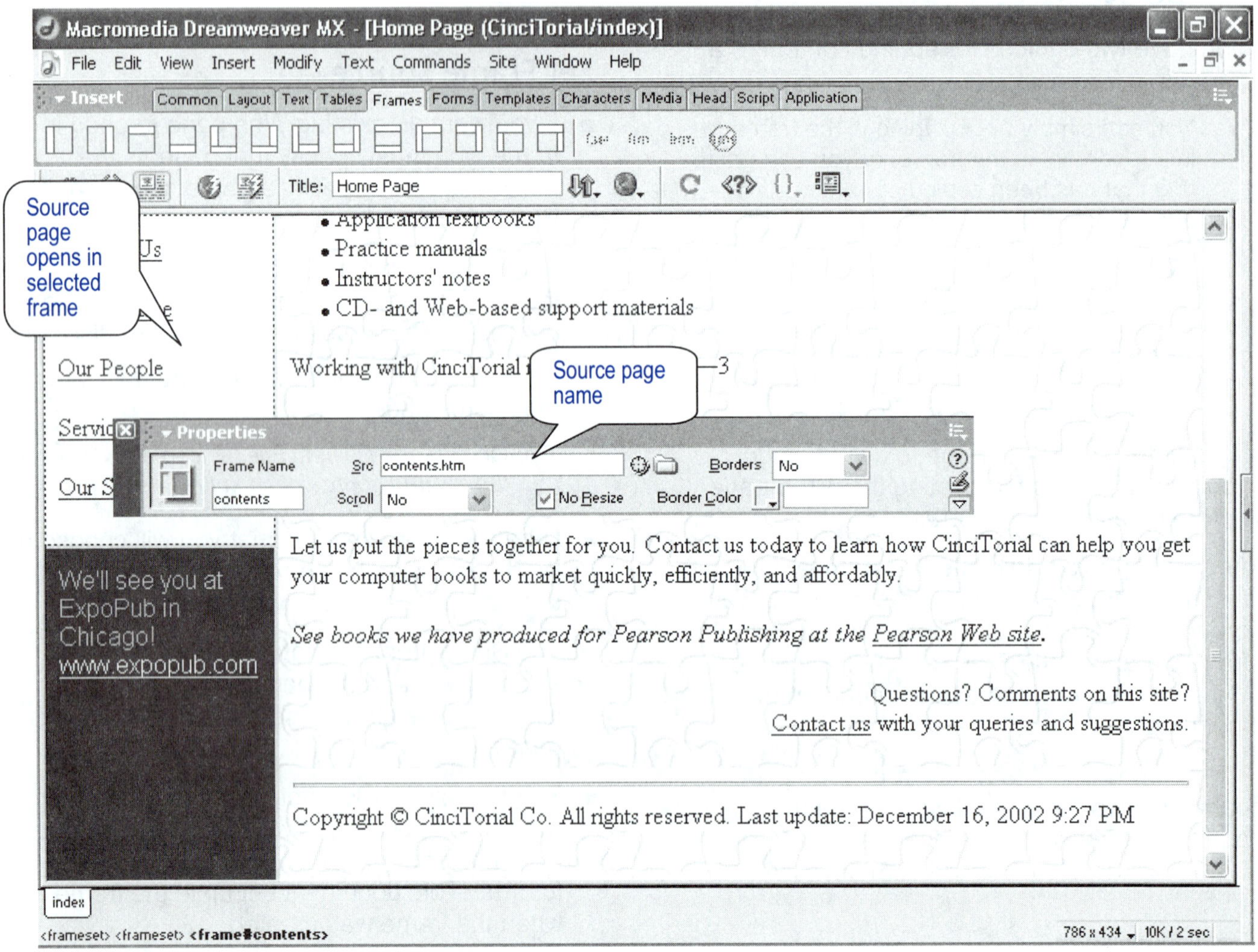

- You can set border options for each frame in a frameset as well as the frameset itself. Frame border properties override frameset border properties, however.
  - Select Yes from the Borders drop-down list to display borders for the active frame.
  - Select No to remove borders. To remove all borders in a frameset page, you must select the No option for each frame.
  - Selecting Default will display or suppress borders depending on the browser's default setting, which is usually Yes.
  - Use the Border Color palette to choose a border color.
- Setting border options for frames can require patience. If you apply one color border in one frame and another in an adjoining frame, for example, only one of the border colors will display. You may need to experiment with frameset and frame border options to achieve a desired effect.
- If you expand the Frames Properties panel, you can set margins—space between the borders and the frame's content—in pixels for frame width and height.
- If you create a frameset using a predefined frameset, the Scroll setting is No and No Resize is selected by default for the new, empty frame or frames. The main frame, which contains existing text, has no scroll or resize limitations. You can modify these settings, however, as discussed previously.

Modify Frameset Properties

- To change frameset properties, you must select the entire frameset rather than one of its frames. Select the frameset using one of these options:
  - If borders are displayed in the frameset, click any border.
  - In the Frames panel, click the heavy border that surrounds all frames.
- The Frameset Properties panel (shown in its expanded form in the illustration on the next page) allows you to specify border options for the entire frameset and set a width for each frame.
- Choose which frame you want to work on in the RowCol Selection window. The selected frame is shaded.
- You can specify whether the frameset will display borders, the border color, and the border width.

  Note: *If you create a frameset using a predefined frameset, the frameset is set to the No Borders option. You must delete the 0 from the Border Width box to display the borders for the frames.*

- In the expanded area of the Frameset Properties panel, specify the width of a frame in pixels or percent. You can also set a relative size for a frame that will change depending on the size of the browser window.

Set Frame Target for Links

- A common use for frames in a frameset is to insert links in one frame that open pages in other frames. For example, you may insert a list of links like a table of contents in a frame at the left side of a page. Clicking a link in the left frame opens a page in the main frame of the frameset.
- When you create a link from text or an image in one frame that will open a page in another frame, you must tell Dreamweaver which frame to open the page in.
- As you have set up links throughout this course, you have probably been aware of the Target box associated with the Link box in various dialog boxes and panels.

Frameset Properties panel

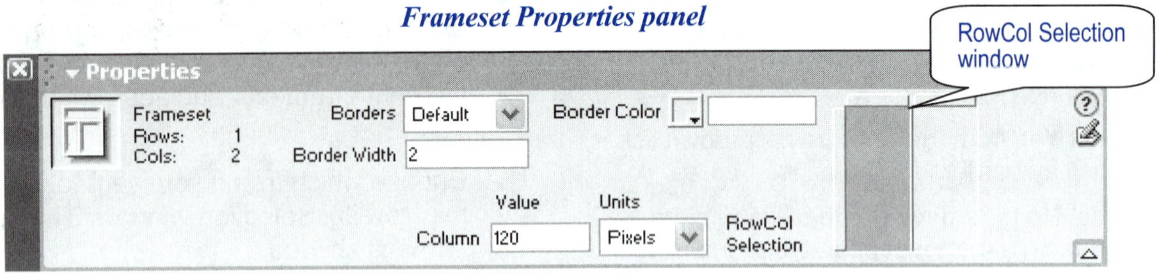

Select a target for link

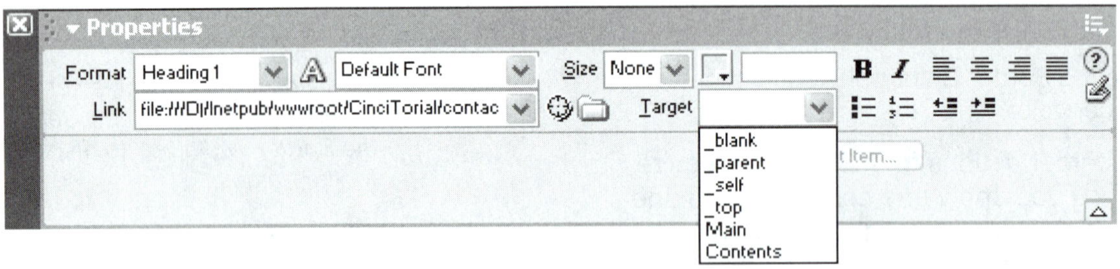

- You use the Target list options (see illustration above) in the Properties panel to tell Dreamweaver which frame to open a linked page in.
- To set up a link from one frame to another, follow this procedure:
  - Select the text or image that will be used for the link.
  - In the Link text box in the Properties panel, specify the page that will open when the link is clicked.
  - Click the Target list arrow to display a list of the frames in the current frameset (see illustration above).
  - Select the frame in which you want the page to open.
- In addition to the frames in the current frameset (such as Main, Contents), the Target list includes four other default targets: _blank, _parent, _self, and _top. Use these targets as follows:
  - Choose the _blank target to open the linked page in a new browser window while also keeping the current browser window open.

    Tip: *This is a good choice if you are linking to a page outside your Web site.*
  - Choose _parent to open the linked page in the current frameset, replacing all frames.
  - Choose _self to open the linked page in the frame that also contains the link, replacing all content in this frame.
  - Choose _top to open the linked page in the outermost frameset, replacing all frames.
- If you have only one frameset on a page, _parent and _top function in the same way. If you have more than one frameset in a page, _parent replaces the frameset of the current frame and _top replaces all framesets on the page with the linked page.
- Consider the use of each frame on your page as you set up links. If you have a frame that functions as a contents area, it should never display other content. The main frame on the page should be used to display the main content of the site.

  Note: *Target settings are most important when working with frames. You can, however, use the _blank Target setting with any link on any kind of Web page to open the linked page in a new browser window.*

Preview a Frameset

- Before you can preview a frameset, you must save all frames and the frameset itself.

- You can click in each frame you have modified and use the Ctrl + S shortcut to save changes, and use the File>Save Frameset command on the menu bar. Or simply use the File>Save All command to save everything at once.
- If you have not saved all elements of the frameset before issuing the Preview in Browser command (or pressing F12), Dreamweaver displays the dialog box shown below.

Prompt to save changes

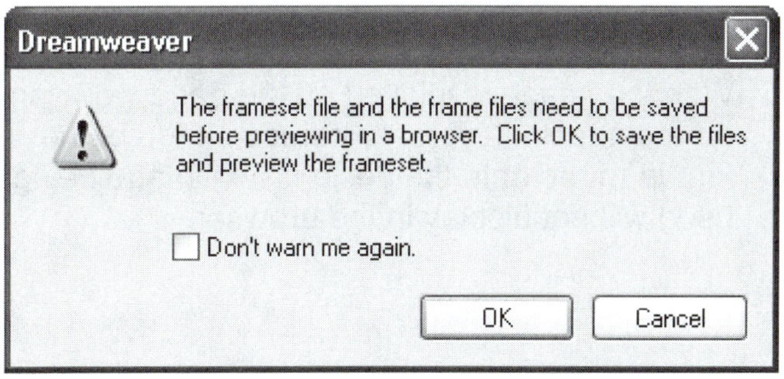

- Clicking OK saves all frameset elements so you can preview your frameset page.
- If you are using a remote testing server or the RDS service on your computer, you may also see another dialog box that precedes the one advising you to save all frameset elements (see illustration).

Prompt to view frameset locally

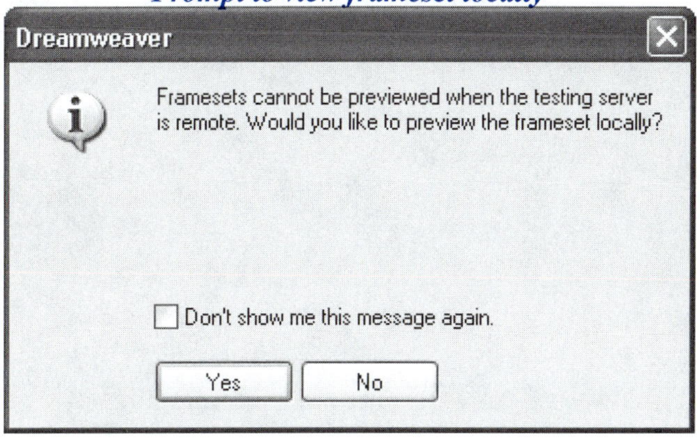

- Click Yes to view the frameset locally.

Modify Page Properties

- So far, you have used the Page Properties dialog box to create page titles, apply background images, and choose page background colors.
- You can use the options in the Page Properties dialog box (see illustration below) to make other changes to a page's properties that can improve or control the page's appearance.

Modify page properties in the Page Properties dialog box

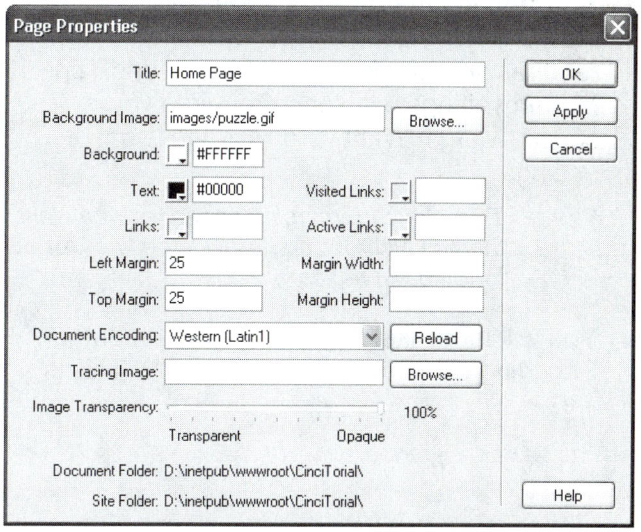

- The default text color is black (#000000), because black supplies the best contrast to most background colors. You can, however, choose any color for text using the Text color box. Try a dark blue color, for example, for a colorful contrast to a white background.
- An easy way to customize a page's appearance is to change the color used for links. The default link color is a bright blue.
- The Page Properties dialog box lets you choose three different colors for a link:
  - Use the Links color box to choose the color that will display when you first insert a link on a page, before it has been used.
  - The Active Links color box lets you choose the color that will display when a visitor actually clicks on a link.
  - Use the Visited Links color box to select the color that will display after a link has been clicked.

- Choosing different colors for these three states does more than provide additional color and interest on a page. If you choose different colors for Links and Visited Links, visitors to your site can also track which links they have already visited on a page.
- You can add margins to pages using the four margin setting boxes. Internet Explorer requires you to specify Left Margin and Top Margin settings; Netscape requires you to specify Margin Width and Margin Height settings.

  Tip: *To make sure margins appear as you want them in all browsers, provide settings for all four margin boxes.*

- You will most likely accept the Document Encoding choice of Western (Latin1). This is the encoding used for characters on the page. You can choose from many other encoding options, however, such as Japanese, Chinese, and Cyrillic.
- If you would like to use a design created in a graphics program as a basis for page layout, you can "trace" the design using options in the Page Properties dialog box.
- Specify the file name of the image you want to trace and then use the Image Transparency slider to determine how transparent you want the image to appear.
- With the image displayed on the page, you can create a table, layers, or frames on top of the image to recreate the design. The image being used will not display in the browser.

Procedures

Create a Frameset

In new, blank page

1. Click **Modify** .... Alt+M
2. Click **Frameset** .... F
3. Click desired type of split:
   - **Split Frame Left** L
   - **Split Frame Right** .... R
   - **Split Frame Up** .... U
   - **Split Frame Down** .... D
4. Insert additional frames to achieve final layout.

OR

In new, blank page or in existing page

1. Display Frames tab in the Insert bar, if necessary.
2. Click or drag predefined frame layout from Frames panel to Document window.

Activate or Select Frame

Activate frame

- Click anywhere in frame to position insertion point.

Select frame

- Hold down Alt and click in frame.

OR

- Click frame name in Frames panel.

OR

- Click Frameset Properties panel's RowCol Selection window.

Select Frameset

- Click any frame border in the frameset, if borders are displayed.

OR

- Click border that surrounds frames in Frames panel.

Name a Frame

1. Select frame to name.
2. Click in Frame ID text box and type one-word name.

Save and Title Frameset

Ctrl + S

Immediately after creating frameset

1. Click **File** .... Alt+F
2. Click **Save Frameset** .... S
3. Type name for frameset as for any other Web page.
4. Click Save.
5. Click **Modify** .... Alt+M
6. Click **Page Properties** .... P
7. Type page title as for any other Web page.

Save Frame

Ctrl + S

1. Activate frame to save.
2. Click **File** .... Alt+F
3. Click **Save Frame** .... S
4. Type desired page name.
5. Click Save.

Save Changes to Frames

1. Click **File** .... Alt+F
2. Click **Save All** L

Display Frames panel

Shift + F2

1. Click **Window** .... Alt+W
2. Click **Others** .... O
3. Click **Frames** .... F

Add Content to Frame

- Activate frame and type text or paste text cut or copied from other location.
- Modify frame's page properties as for any other Web page.

Set Frame Source

1. Select frame to link to source.
2. Click in **Src** box on Properties panel and type address of source page.

   OR

   - Click (**Browse for File** button) on Properties panel and navigate to address of source page.

Modify Frame in Properties panel

1. Select frame to modify.
2. Specify name for frame.
3. Link frame to source page.
4. Set Scroll property:
   - Choose No to prevent scroll bars from displaying.
   - Choose Yes or Auto to display scroll bars when necessary.
   - Choose Default to use browser's scroll default.
5. Select **No Resize** to prevent visitors from resizing frame in browser.
6. Set Border options:
   - Choose Yes to display border.
   - Choose No to suppress border.
   - Choose Default to use browser's border preference.
   - Click **Border Color** button to display palette and choose border color.
7. Expand Properties panel to set margin width and/or margin height.

Modify Frameset Properties

1. Select frameset.
2. Set Borders options:
   - Choose Yes to display borders in frameset.
   - Choose No to suppress borders.
   - Choose Default to use browser's border preference.
   - Specify border width in pixels or type 0 to remove all borders.
   - Click **Border Color** button to display palette and choose border color.
3. Expand Properties panel to click frame to modify in RowCol Selection window.
4. Specify width for frame in **Column** box and choose units of measurement from **Units** list.

Set Frame Target for Links

1. Click in link to select it.
2. Specify page to link to.
3. Click Target list arrow and select frame name from current frameset or default target such as _blank, _parent, _self, or _top.

Preview a Frameset
F12

1. Click **File** .... Alt+F
2. Click **Save All Frames** L
3. Click **File** .... Alt+F
4. Click **Preview in Browser** .... P, P, →
5. Select browser.
6. If Dreamweaver displays alert box to save frameset elements, click OK.

Modify Page Properties
Ctrl + J

1. Click **Modify** .... Alt+M
2. Click **Page Properties** .... P
   - Click the **Text** color box and choose a new color for all text on the page or in a frame.
   - Click the **Links** color box and choose a color that will display when a link is first inserted.
   - Click the **Active Links** color box and choose a color that will display when a link is clicked.
   - Click the **Visited Links** color box and choose a color that will display after a link has been clicked.

Exercise Directions

1. Start Dreamweaver.
2. Open the **CinciTorial** site. You will create a new frameset page with a contents frame at the left to hold links that will open the Web site's pages in a main frame. You will name the frameset **index.htm** so it will operate correctly as the site's home page.
3. Make the following preparations:
   - Open **index.htm** and cut from the page the series of links beginning with *Contact Us*.
   - Use the default untitled new, blank page and paste the cut links on the page. Save the page as **contents.htm** with the page title **Contents**.
   - Change the page title for the **index.htm** page to **Welcome to CinciTorial**.
   - Save and close **contents.htm** and **index.htm**.
   - In the Site window, rename the **index.htm** as **home.htm**.
   - Do *not* update links, since you will be creating a new **index.htm** page.
4. Open **home.htm**. If necessary, display the Insert bar and click Frames tab.
5. Click the Left Frame 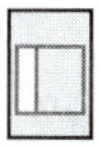 button to create a new frame to the left of the current page content.
6. Save the new frameset as **index.htm** and supply the page title **Home Page**.
7. Name the new frame **contents** and the frame that holds existing text **main**.
8. Select the *contents* frame and set its source as **contents.htm**. The links you cut from the previous **index.htm** page open in the frame.
9. Use the Page Properties dialog box to make the following property changes to the **contents.htm** page in the *contents* frame:

   ✓ *To make these changes, activate the frame by clicking in it.*

   - Apply the lightest yellow background color (#FFFFCC).
   - Change the color for active links to #990033 and the color for visited links to #009999.

   ✓ *Because you did not change the Links color, you will not see changes to link colors until you use the links in the browser.*
10. Select the frameset and specify a width for the *contents* frame of 120 pixels. (Use the RowCol Selection window in the Frameset Properties panel to select the proper frame.)
11. Activate the *contents* frame by clicking in it and split this frame so the links remain at the top of the frame.
12. Name the new frame **blurb**.
13. Save the new frame's page as **blurb.htm** and title it *blurb*.
14. In the blurb frame, type the following information as shown, breaking them with a line break <br>:

    We'll see you at ExpoPub in Chicago!

    www.expopub.com
15. Adjust the *blurb* frame's width and height to eliminate scroll bars and set the Scroll property to **No**. Format the frame and its content as desired.
16. Remove borders on all frames.
17. The links in the *contents* frame's list are already set to the correct pages. Specify the **_top** frame as the target for each link.
18. Create a link from the www.expopub.com URL in the *blurb* frame to **http://www.expopub.com**. Use the **_blank** link target.
19. You will need to make some changes to links that have already been inserted on **home.htm**:
    - Change the target for the *Read Our Mission Statement* link to **_top**.
    - Change the target for the *Pearson Web site* link to **_blank**.
20. Save the frameset and each frame you have modified.
21. Preview the **index.htm** frameset page in the browser and test all links. Your frameset should look similar to Illustration A.

    ✓ *The www.expopub.com link is not "live," but you can see how the link opens another browser window.*
22. Close all browser windows.
23. Close any open pages.
24. Exit Dreamweaver.

Illustration A

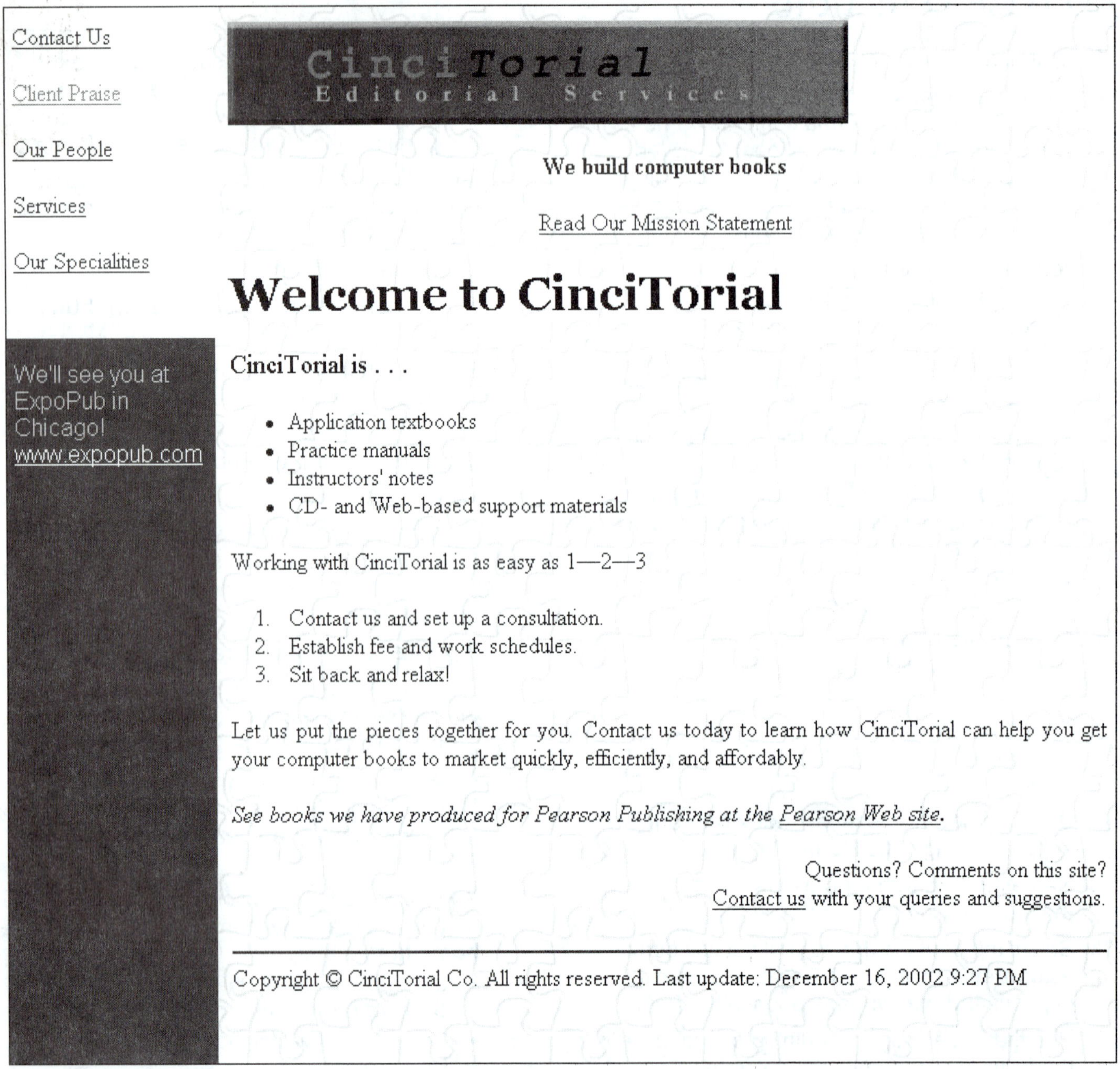

We build computer books

Read Our Mission Statement

Welcome to CinciTorial

CinciTorial is . . .

- Application textbooks
- Practice manuals
- Instructors' notes
- CD- and Web-based support materials

Working with CinciTorial is as easy as 1—2—3

1. Contact us and set up a consultation.
2. Establish fee and work schedules.
3. Sit back and relax!

Let us put the pieces together for you. Contact us today to learn how CinciTorial can help you get your computer books to market quickly, efficiently, and affordably.

See books we have produced for Pearson Publishing at the Pearson Web site.

Questions? Comments on this site?
Contact us with your queries and suggestions.

Copyright © CinciTorial Co. All rights reserved. Last update: December 16, 2002 9:27 PM

Chapter

13

Styles and Style Sheets

Use styles to capture formatting for text elements that can easily be applied to other pages in the Web site. You can create custom Cascading Style Sheet (CSS) styles for a specific page or an external CSS style sheet that can be used throughout the Web site. HTML styles provide another way to quickly and consistently format text. You can create your own HTML styles to use on demand for any page you build with Dreamweaver.

In this chapter, you will learn how to:

- Create custom CSS styles
- Create an external CSS and add styles to it
- Create and use HTML styles
- Use Design panel group to work with styles
- Open Web sites

About Styles and Style Sheets

- A **style** is a collection of formats that controls the appearance of text on a Web page. A style may be applied to selected text or to entire paragraphs of text. There are several advantages to creating and using styles:
  - After you take a few moments to define a style, you can quickly apply its formats to elements on one or more pages in a Web site.
  - You can change a style's formatting and, depending on the style type, automatically or manually update all elements formatted with that style.
  - Employing styles throughout a Web site ensures consistency in text elements from page to page.
  - Again depending on the style type, styles may be used not just in one Web site but also in other Web sites, so the time it takes to create styles saves time in the long run.
- A collection of styles created for a page or a Web site is called a **style sheet**. Using a style sheet, you can format a number of text elements quickly and easily. Dreamweaver supports **Cascading Style Sheets (CSS)**, style sheets developed specifically for use in Web design.

  Note: *Cascading Style Sheets work in recent browser versions such as Internet Explorer 4, Netscape Navigator 4, Mozilla 1.0 and later. Earlier browser versions do not support CSS formatting.*
- You have three options for creating and applying styles in Dreamweaver:
  - Create a *custom* CSS containing styles that can be applied to text on a single page of a Web site.
  - Create an *external CSS* containing one or more styles that can be linked to all pages in a Web site.
  - Modify existing *HTML* styles or create new HTML styles that can be used throughout a Web site.

Create Custom CSS Styles

- Dreamweaver's custom CSS styles can be applied to any text on a Web page, regardless of the text's HTML tag. This means a custom CSS style can be applied both to characters and to paragraphs.
- You create, apply, and manage CSS styles using the CSS Styles panel. Use the Window>CSS Styles command on the menu bar to display the panel.

  Note: You can also click on the Launcher if this preference is selected.
- The CSS Styles panel (see illustration below) lists all CSS styles that have been defined for or linked to the current page. It also allows you to toggle between the Apply Styles pane and the Edit Styles pane of the CSS Styles panel.
- You can only apply styles in the Apply Styles pane. You can edit styles in either the Apply Styles or Edit Styles pane.

>CSS styles displayed in the CSS Styles panel

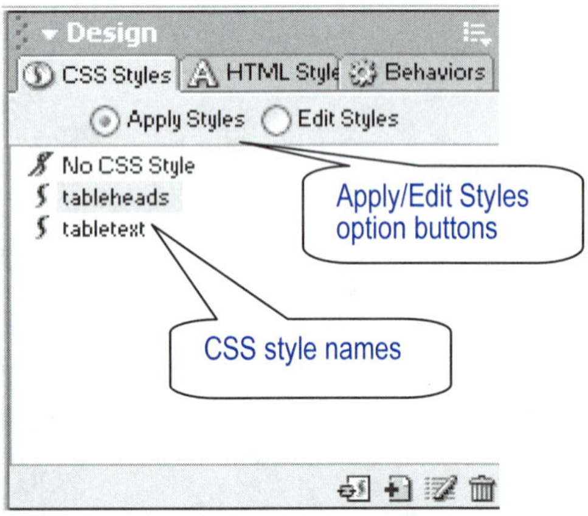

- To create a new CSS style (in either pane), click the New CSS Style button in the CSS Styles panel to open the New CSS Style dialog box (see illustration on next page).

New CSS Style dialog box

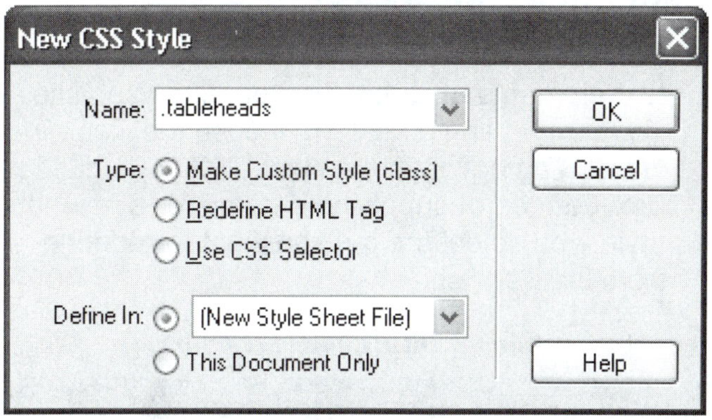

- Choose the type of style to create:
  - The *Make Custom Style (class)* option allows you to create a CSS style that can be applied to either a selection (or range) of text or to a paragraph (block) of text using the class attribute.
  - The *Redefine HTML Tag* option allows you to choose a specific HTML tag (such as h1) and modify the tag with your own formats.
  - The *Use CSS Selector* option lets you define formats for a specific combination of tags or tags that contain the ID attribute.
- Dreamweaver allows you to define a style for the current document only (that is, the current page only) or create a new style sheet file in which to store new styles.
- If you choose the option to define styles in a new style sheet file, Dreamweaver allows you to name and save the style sheet to create an *external style sheet*. You will learn more about external style sheets later in this chapter.

Create and Apply Custom Styles

- Select the *Make Custom Style (class)* option in the New CSS Style dialog box to create a new custom CSS style.
- You must then type a new name for the style in the Name text box. Custom CSS style names must begin with a period (.). If you forget to insert the period at the beginning of the style name, Dreamweaver will add it for you automatically.
- Select This Document Only to create a style sheet in the current document.
- Clicking OK in the New CSS Style dialog box opens the CSS Style definition dialog box for your new style (see illustration below). You can define formats in eight different categories.

Define formats for new custom style

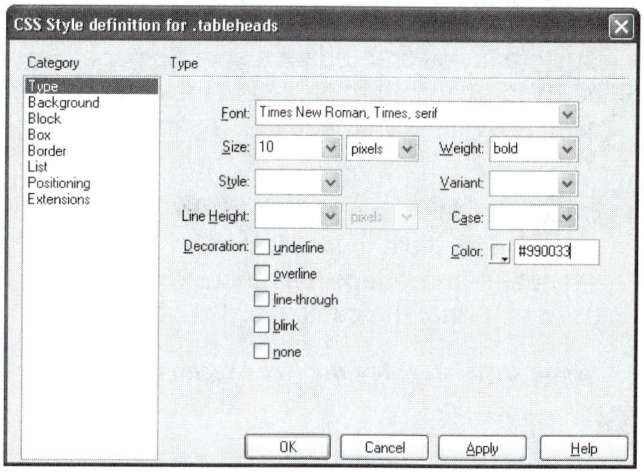

- You will use the options in the Type category most often when creating new text formats. You can select the desired font, size, style, weight, and color.

  Note: *You can choose from nine different measurement types for font size, including pixels, points, picas, and inches. Dreamweaver uses pixels as the default measurement.*

- Use the Background category to set a background color or image for the style. If you select a background image, you can tile it on the page using the Repeat option in the Repeat list.
- Use the Block category to set vertical and horizontal alignment options. You can also create indents in this category.
- The Box, Border, List, Positioning, and Extensions categories offer settings that are supported by most browsers in use today.
- Custom styles display in the CSS Styles panel. To apply a style to text on the page, click in or select existing text, or position the insertion point where you intend to begin typing new text, and select the style name in the panel.
- If you mistakenly apply a style, click the No CSS Style No CSS Style option in the CSS Styles panel to remove style formatting.

- Edit a custom style by double-clicking it in the CSS Styles panel or by clicking the style and then clicking the Edit Style Sheet button to open the CSS Style definition dialog box. After you make changes and click OK, all text formatted with that style updates immediately to show the new formats.
- Custom styles created for a specific page can be used *only* on that page, but they can be used anywhere on that page, as many times as desired.
- Custom styles are stored in the Head section of the page. Note in the illustration below the <style> </style> tags that enclose the tags used to format the custom styles.

Custom styles stored in the Head section of the page

- You also can see an icon representing the custom CSS styles if you select the Head Content option from the View menu. Click the CSS Styles icon to open the CSS Properties panel. Click on the Edit Style Sheet [Edit Style Sheet...] button on the Properties panel to open the Edit Style Sheet dialog box (explained in more detail in the next section.)

Redefine HTML Tags

- You can modify standard HTML tags to format text elements uniquely for a page or Web site. To redefine an HTML tag, choose the *Redefine HTML Tag* option in the New CSS Style dialog box. Instead of supplying a name for a new style, you select the tag you want to redefine from the Tag list.

Choose HTML tag to redefine

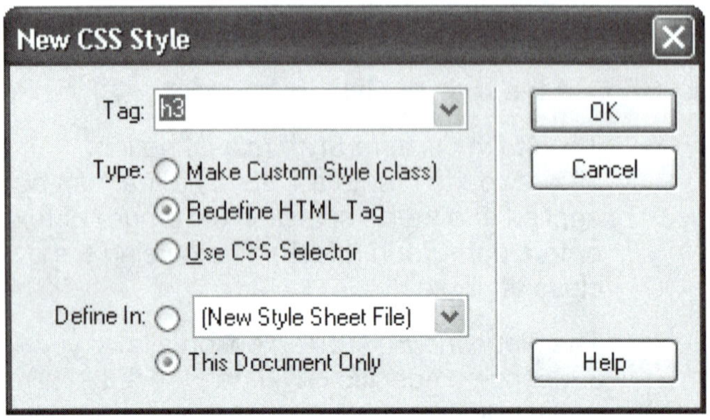

- Choose formats for the HTML tag in the Style definition dialog box, just as when creating a custom CSS style.
- After you redefine an HTML tag, apply the new tag just as you would ordinarily apply the HTML format. Apply paragraph and heading formats from the Properties panel's Format list, for example, or apply a redefined unordered list tag using the Unordered List button on the Properties panel or the Text>List>Unordered List command.
- Redefined HTML tags are stored in the Head section of the page along with other custom styles created for that page (see illustration at left).
- As with a custom CSS style, if an HTML tag is redefined for a specific page, it displays its new formats *only* on that page.
- Redefined HTML tags do not appear in the CSS Styles panel, because they are not CSS styles. You can view all styles, both CSS and HTML, by clicking the Edit Styles option button in the CSS Styles panel—or by opening the current style sheet.

- Use the Text>CSS Styles>Edit Style Sheet command on the menu bar. Or click the Edit Styles Edit Styles option in the CSS Styles panel toolbar, select the Web page name, and then click the Edit Style Sheet button.
- The Edit Style Sheet dialog box (see illustration below) displays all custom and HTML styles. Click on a style to see its formats.

Edit Style Sheet dialog box

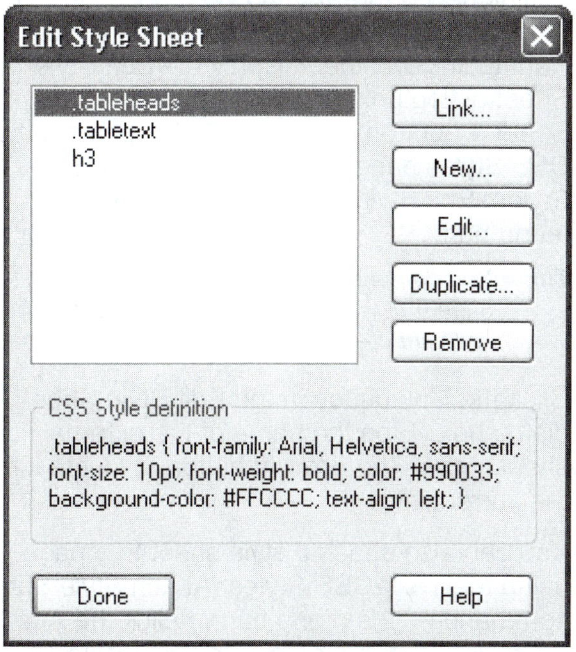

- You can use this dialog box to create new styles, edit existing styles, duplicate styles (a good option if you want to create a style very similar to another style), or delete (remove) a style.

Note: *You can also delete a style by selecting it in the CSS Styles panel and clicking the Delete CSS Style button.*

Dreamweaver CSS Reference

- You can get additional help with CSS styles on the Reference panel. Click the Book list arrow and select O'REILLY CSS Reference, and then choose a style you want information on (see illustration below).

CSS styles Reference panel

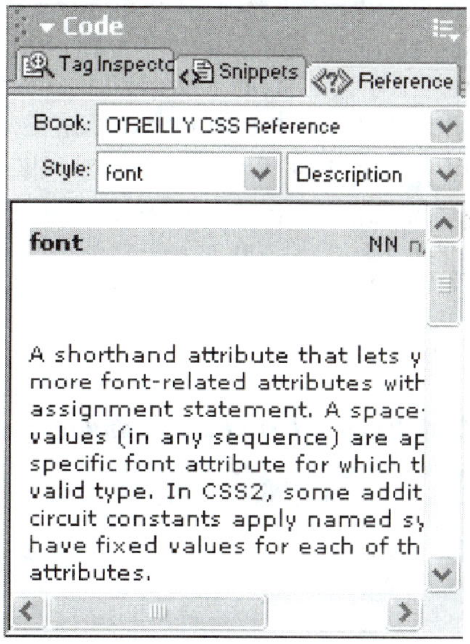

Create External Cascading Style Sheet

- If you want to apply styles to several Web pages in a site, you need to create an **external style sheet**. An external style sheet is so called because it is a separate, or external, file in a Web site. After you create the external style sheet and link it to the site's pages, any change you make to the external style sheet's styles will immediately be reflected in all pages linked to the style sheet.
- External style sheets have the file extension .css. After the style sheet itself has been saved, you add styles to it just as when creating custom styles or redefining HTML tags.

Caution: *You cannot simply save a Web page as a .css page. It cannot be linked to a Web page and will generate an error if this is tried.*

Save New External Style Sheet

- As you have seen already, Dreamweaver allows you to create an external style sheet any time you use the New CSS Style dialog box to define a custom style or redefine an HTML tag. You can also create an external style sheet from the Edit Style Sheet dialog box.

- Begin the process by opening the Edit Style Sheet dialog box shown at the top of the previous column. Click the Link button to open the Link External Style Sheet dialog box (see illustration below). If Dreamweaver asks you if you want to create the style sheet, click Yes.

  Note: *You can create an external style sheet with any page displayed, even one that already contains custom CSS styles. The custom styles, however, will not be included in the external style sheet.*

Link External Style Sheet dialog box

- In the File/URL box, type a name for the new style. Include the file extension *.css* and make sure the Link option is selected.
- After you click OK, the new style sheet name appears in the Edit Style Sheet dialog box, as shown in the illustration below. Select the style sheet name and click the Edit button.

New style sheet name

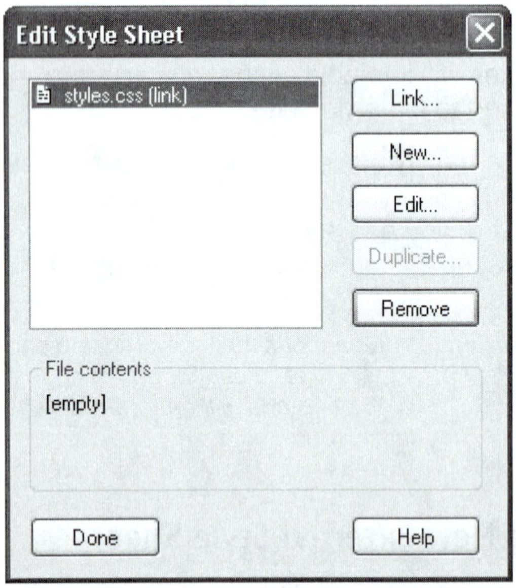

- Another copy of the Edit Style Sheet dialog box launches with the name of the external style sheet in the title bar. Click the New button to open the New CSS Style dialog box. Here you can choose to create custom styles or redefine HTML tags, as you learned earlier.
- After you add styles to the style sheet, you must save to store the style sheet's styles in your root folder. Click the Save button in the Edit Style Sheet dialog box with the name of the external style sheet in the title bar, and then click Done in the original Edit Style Sheet dialog box to save the style sheet.

Link Web Document to External Style Sheet

- To link new or preexisting Web documents to an external style sheet, open the page you want to link and then display the Edit Style Sheet dialog box by clicking the Edit Style Sheet button in the Edit Styles pane of the CSS Styles panel. Or, use the Text>CSS Styles>Edit Style Sheet command on the menu bar.

  Tip: *You do not have to link the style sheet to the page that was active when you created the style sheet—it is already linked to that page.*

- Click the Link button in the Edit Style Sheet dialog box. Type the name of the external style sheet, or use the Browse button to locate it in the current site.
- You can also attach a style sheet to a page using the Text>CSS Styles>Attach Style Sheet command on the menu bar, or click the Attach Style Sheet button on the CSS Styles panel. You then choose the style sheet in the Link External Style Sheet dialog box.
- You will normally choose the Link option in the Link External Style Sheet dialog box. If you select the Import option, the styles are directly imported into the document rather than linked to the external file. This option is suited for Web documents that might be used outside of the Web site in which the .css file resides.
- The linked style sheet is now available to format your document. You can use the styles shown in the CSS Styles panel (or in the Format list on the Properties panel for redefined HTML tags) to apply formats just as when you create custom styles.

- The HTML code that controls the link to an external style sheet is stored in the Head section of a page. If you examine the page's code, you will see code similar to this:

```
<link href="tut_styles.css"
rel="stylesheet" type="text/css">
```

- If you choose to view the Head Content panel at the top of the Document window, you will see the link to an external style sheet represented by a link icon. Click on the icon to open a Link Properties panel.
- You can usually apply CSS styles by simply clicking in any text paragraph and choosing the style from the CSS Styles panel. To apply a style to a portion of text, select it first.
- You can have both an external style sheet and custom styles available for a specific Web page (see illustration below) or even link more than one style sheet to a page.

Both external and custom styles can be applied

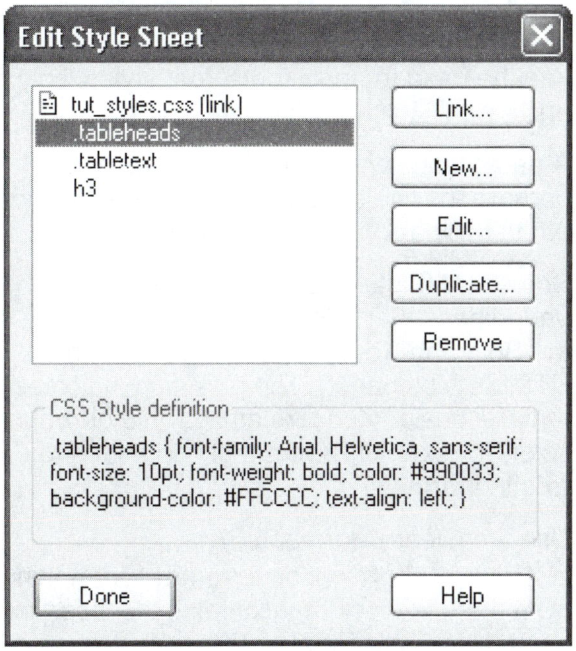

- The CSS Styles panel makes clear which styles belong to the external style sheet and which are defined for the current page only. The external style sheet styles have a "link" to left of the style name (see illustration in next column).

CSS Styles panel

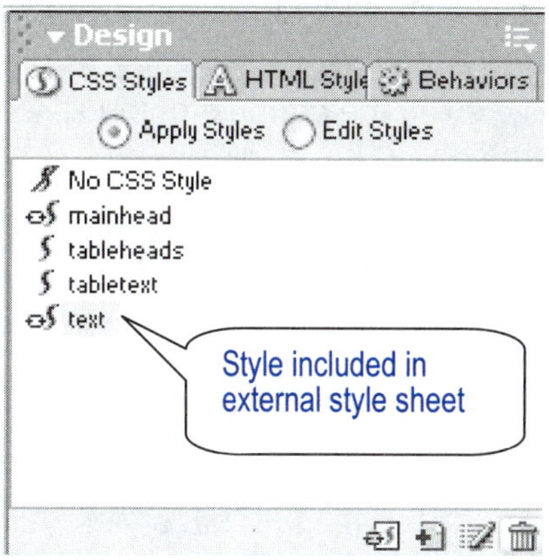

Modify and Update Styles

- The styles in an external style sheet can be edited the same way as custom styles. These changes, once saved, update applicable attributes in any Web page that is linked to the style sheet, which makes for efficient, **global** style revisions.

Advanced CSS Features

- Style sheets supply a great deal of flexibility for formatting pages in a Web site. You can link an external style sheet to a template so that the styles are applied along with other template elements. Or, you can create custom styles for an editable area in a template.

  Note: *You may need to tweak HTML code in the template to make sure the styles are applied correctly to the editable areas.*

- One of the great benefits of creating an external style sheet is that it can be used in any number of Web sites. You simply link to the style sheet from any site, saving to your current site's root folder when prompted.
- It is possible to apply more than one style to a text element, but doing so can lead to style conflicts. Style conflicts can give unexpected results because of the way browsers read the conflicting style tags.
- Browsers use the following rules to resolve style conflicts:
  - When two different styles are applied to the same text, browsers will display all attributes for both styles, unless the attributes conflict

directly (for example, one applies a blue color and the other applies a purple color).

- In the case of such a conflict, the browser will display the attribute of the style closest to the text in the HTML code.
- Attributes from CSS styles will override HTML tag styles.

Work with HTML Styles

- An alternative to creating an external CSS is modifying or creating HTML styles. An **HTML style** is defined by one or more HTML tags.
- Though the trend in Web design has been toward using CSS styles rather than HTML styles to apply site-wide formatting, older legacy browsers (pre-version 4.0) that do not support CSS can read HTML styles. Thus, Web designers who need to create Web sites for a wide variety of browsers need to know how to create and modify HTML styles.
- Like the CSS styles in an external style sheet, HTML styles can be applied to any page in a Web site or to pages in other Web sites.
- Unlike CSS styles, HTML style formatting does not update automatically if you change the style. You must reapply the HTML style each time you update it.

Use the HTML Styles Panel

- You apply, edit, and manage HTML styles from the HTML Styles panel (see illustration in next column)—which is included in the same Design panel group that includes the CSS Styles panel. Display the HTML Styles panel using the Window>HTML Styles command on the menu bar.

Tip: *If you have the CSS Styles panel open, click the HTML Styles tab in the Design panel group to display HTML styles.*

HTML Styles panel

- By default, Dreamweaver does not display any predefined HTML styles in its HTML Styles panel.
- Notice in the illustration above that some styles are preceded by an underlined letter *a* and others by a paragraph symbol (¶). Unlike CSS styles, HTML styles are classified as either *selection* or *paragraph* styles.
- A selection style applies to selected text, such as a word or phrase. This type of formatting may be used to apply fonts, font styles, colors, and so on.
- A paragraph style applies to an entire paragraph. The style may include font formats but usually also includes alignment options.
- Some HTML styles are preceded by the underlined letter *a* followed by a plus sign (see the Bold and Red styles, for example, in the HTML Styles panel). The plus sign indicates that the designated formatting (bold or red color, for example) will simply be added to existing formats.
- Use the Clear Paragraph Style Clear Paragraph Style option to remove formatting from the text block that contains the insertion point. Use Clear Selection Style Clear Selection Style option to remove formatting from selected text. These options will remove formatting applied with the Properties panel as well as with the HTML Styles panel.
- You can create new HTML styles or modify existing styles. New styles display in the HTML Styles panel.

Create New HTML Style

- You have several options for creating a new HTML style:
  - Click the New Style button on the HTML Styles panel to open the Define HTML Style dialog box.

    Note: *Or, click the Text>HTML Styles>New Style command on the menu bar.*
  - Click in text that contains the formats you want to use for the new style and then click the New Style button on the HTML Styles panel to open the Define HTML Style dialog box.
  - Right-click an existing style in the HTML Styles panel and select Duplicate on the shortcut menu to open the Define HTML Style dialog box.
- When creating a new style by any of these methods, you must supply a name for the style and specify how it is to be applied (to a selection or to a paragraph). (See illustration below.)

Create new HTML style

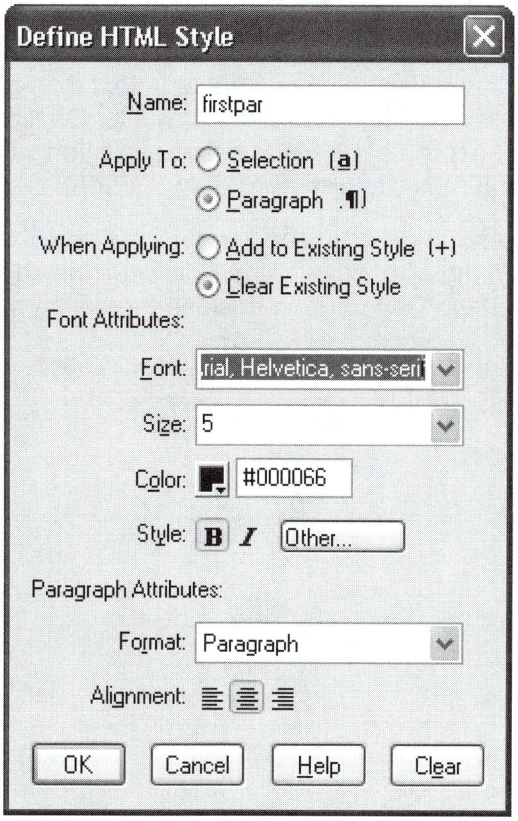

- You must also determine whether the style will be added to the existing style or whether the existing style should be cleared before the new style is applied.
- Generally speaking, you would add to an existing style if you are changing only one or two formats; for example, adding italic or color emphasis. When creating a more complex style, it is best to clear any existing style first.
- If you have clicked in formatted text you want to use for a new style, those formats will display in the Define HTML Style dialog box. Otherwise, you can select the desired font and paragraph attributes for the new style.

  Note: *If you specify Selection as the method of application, the Paragraph attributes are unavailable.*

Modify Existing HTML Style

- Modify an existing HTML style by double-clicking it in the HTML Styles panel to open the Define HTML Style dialog box.
- When modifying an existing style, you will usually not change how the style is applied (to a selection or to a paragraph) or whether it is added to an existing style or replaces that style.
- You can change both font attributes and paragraph attributes for any HTML style. Select a font, size, color, and style; an HTML paragraph or heading format; and an alignment option.

  Note: *To reset the attributes of the Define HTML Style dialog box to the default options, click the* Clear *button.*
- After you edit the style, you must reapply it to any selection or paragraph already formatted with the style to see the new formats.

Share HTML Styles

- An advantage to creating HTML styles is that you can share your HTML styles with other sites or users. HTML styles are saved in the Library folder of your site in a file named styles.xml (see illustration on next page).

Styles are stored in Library folder

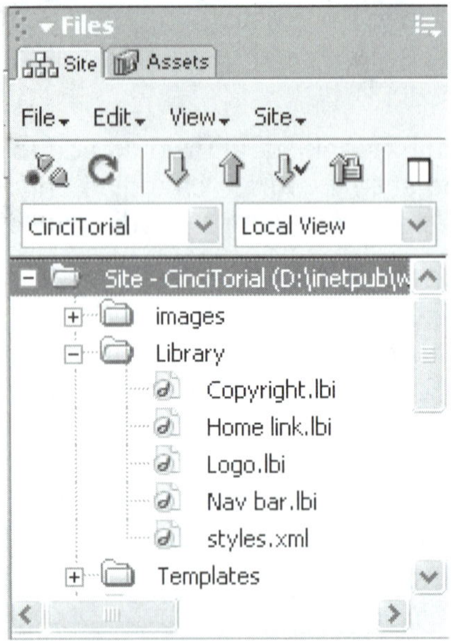

- You can work with this file like any other file in the Site window. Copy the file and paste it in another Web site, for example, to make it available in another site.

Open Web Sites

- As you work with Dreamweaver, you will probably create a number of Web sites in various folders on your local drive. By default, Dreamweaver opens the last Web site you worked on when you start the program.
- You can open a different Web site from the Site panel. Click the drop-down list in the Site panel's toolbar—either in its expanded window or collapsed panel form—and select the desired Web site (see illustration below).

Click a Web site to open it in Site panel toolbar

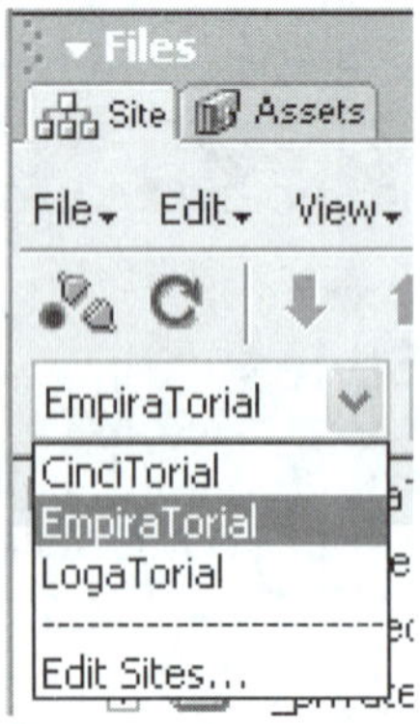

- When you open a Web site this method, the Site window's contents change to the selected site. You can then open pages or other objects directly from the Site panel.
- If you want to edit the settings for a site, Click Edit sites in the drop-down list. Or use the Site>Edit Sites command on the menu bar, select the desired site, and then click the Edit button. You can change any of the existing settings for each category.

Choose site to edit in Define Sites dialog box

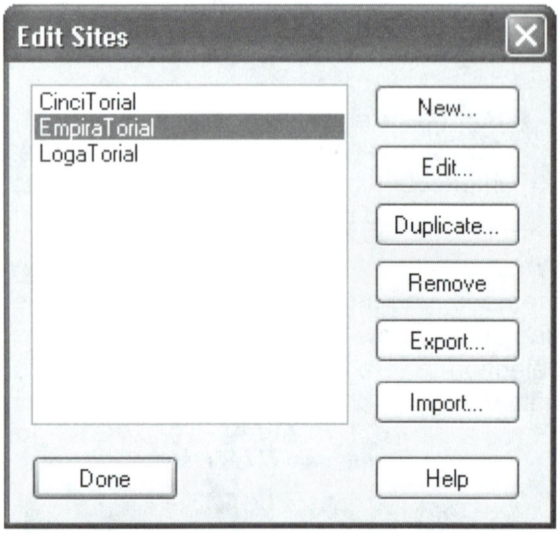

- You can also duplicate a site in this dialog box, remove a site, or create a new site. Duplicate a site to create a backup or to save effort when creating a site with similar layout or text.
- After you have finished editing or otherwise working with a site in the Edit Sites dialog box, click the Done button to close the dialog box.

Procedures

Display CSS Styles panel
Shift + F11

1. Click **Window** .... Alt + W
2. Click **CSS Styles** .... Y

OR

- Click on Launcher.

Create and Apply Custom Styles to Current Page Only
Ctrl + Shift + E

1. Click **Text** .... Alt + T
2. Click **CSS Styles** C
3. Click **Edit Style Sheet** .... E
4. Click New... .

OR

- Click (**New CSS Style** button) on CSS Styles panel.

In New CSS Style dialog box

5. Choose **Make Custom Style (class)** option.
6. Type name for style preceded by period.
7. Choose **This Document Only** option.
8. Click OK .
9. Select options from the **Type**, **Background**, and **Block** categories as desired.
10. Click in paragraph to style, or select text.
11. Click style name in CSS Styles panel.
12. Click No CSS Style (**No CSS Style**) to remove style.

Redefine HTML Tags and Apply

Follow steps for creating custom style through step 4.

5. Choose **Redefine HTML Tag** option.
6. Select tag from **Tag** drop-down list.
7. Click OK .
8. Select options from the **Type**, **Background**, and **Block** categories.
9. Click in paragraph to style.
10. Display Properties panel, if necessary.
11. Click Format list and select redefined HTML style.

View Style Sheet for Current Page

1. Click **Text** .... Alt + T
2. Click **CSS Styles** C
3. Click **Edit Style Sheet** .... E

OR

4. Click Edit Styles (**Edit Styles** option button) in the CSS Styles panel.
5. Select Web page or style sheet in file tree.
6. Click (**Edit Style Sheet** button) on CSS Styles panel.

OR

- Double-click the Web page or style sheet in the CSS Style panel.

Create and Save New External Style Sheet

1. Click **Text** .... Alt + T
2. Click **CSS Styles** C
3. Click **Edit Style Sheet** .... E
4. Click Link... .
5. Type name for new external style sheet, including .css extension, in File/URL text box.
6. Click OK .

✓ *If you are prompted to create the style sheet, click **Yes**.*

7. Select style sheet name in Edit Style Sheet dialog box.
8. Click Edit... .
9. Click New... to add new style to sheet.
10. Select **Make Custom Style (class)** or **Redefine HTML Tag** option, and see procedures at left to create or redefine styles.
11. When finished creating styles, click OK .
12. Click Save .
13. Click Done .

Link Web Document to External Style Sheet

1. Open page to link to external style sheet.
2. Click **Text** .... Alt + T
3. Click **CSS Styles** C
4. Click **Edit Style Sheet** .... E
5. Click Link... .
6. Type name of external style sheet, including .css extension in File/URL text box.

   OR

   - Click Browse... and navigate to style sheet.
7. Click OK ..
8. Click Done .
9. Apply styles from CSS Styles panel as for custom styles.

OR

1. Open page to link to external style sheet.
2. Click **Text** .... Alt + T
3. Click **CSS Styles** C
4. Click **Attach Style Sheet**... A

OR

- Click (**Attach Style Sheet** button) on CSS Styles panel.
5. Select style sheet in Link External Style Sheet dialog box.
6. Click OK .

Delete a Style or Style Sheet

1. Click **Text** .... Alt + T
2. Click **CSS Styles** C
3. Click **Edit Style Sheet** .... E
4. Click style sheet to remove (or style sheet that contains a style that you want to remove).
5. Click [Remove] to remove the style sheet.

   OR

   - Click [Edit...].
   - Click style to remove.
   - Click [Remove].
   - Click [Save].
6. Click [Done].

OR

1. Select the style or style sheet in CSS Styles panel.
2. Click Delete CSS 🗑 button.

Display HTML Styles Panel
Ctrl + F11

1. Click **Window** .... Alt + W
2. Click **HTML Styles** L

OR

- Click HTML Styles tab [HTML Styles] in CSS Styles panel.

Create New HTML Style

1. Click (**New Style** button) on HTML Styles panel.

   OR

   - Click in formatted text to be used as style and click (**New Style** button) on HTML Styles panel.

   OR

   - Right-click existing style to copy on HTML Styles panel and click **Duplicate** on shortcut menu.

   OR

   a. Click **Text** .... Alt + T

   b. Click **HTML Styles** .... T

   c. Click **New Style** .... N
2. Type name for new style.
3. Determine if style will apply to selection or paragraph.
4. Specify whether style will be added to existing style or replaces (clears) it.
5. Select font and paragraph attributes.
6. Apply new style from HTML Styles panel like any other HTML style.

Modify Existing HTML Style

1. Double-click style in HTML Styles panel.

   OR

   - Right-click style and click **Edit** on shortcut menu.
2. Choose new font and paragraph attributes as desired.
3. Reapply modified style to any text or paragraph originally formatted with the style.

Share HTML Styles

1. Display Site panel.
2. Open Library folder to see HTML style sheet (for example, **styles.xml**).
3. Click **Edit** .... Alt + E
4. Click **Copy** C
5. Paste copied style sheet in Library folder of new Web site.

Open Web Sites

In Site panel toolbar

- Click drop-down list [Site: CinciTorial] (Expanded)

  OR
- [CinciTorial] (Collapsed)
- Select a site to open it.

Exercise Directions

1. Start Dreamweaver.
2. CinciTorial is preparing to launch a new Web site that contains online tutorials for popular applications. In this exercise, you will create the new Web site and set up styles for its pages. Begin by creating the Web site using the Site Definition wizard in Dreamweaver:
   - Define a new site named **tutorials** with the online folder as the local root folder.
   - Select ColdFusion as your server technology.
   - Choose to edit locally on your computer and change the new folder's default name from *tutorials* to **online**. Store this new folder within the folder that contains the cincitorial folder for the **CinciTorial** site (for example, in the c:\inetpub\wwwroot folder if you are using Microsoft PWS or IIS server).

   ✓ *Do NOT create the folder within the cincitorial folder.*

   - Select None for the remote server option.
3. In Dreamweaver, open **contents.htm** and **index.htm** from the Data folder and save them to the new Web site folder.
4. Set **index.htm** as the site's home page.
5. Activate **index.htm**. Use the Properties panel to check the link in the second line. Note that it is an absolute link that refers to the Data folder. In the Properties panel's Link box, modify the link to read **contents.htm**.
6. Activate **contents.htm** and modify the link in the second line in the Properties panel to read **home.htm**.

   ✓ *There is currently no home.htm page. You will fix this link in the last chapter of the book.*
7. Display the CSS Styles panel.
8. Create a new custom style named **.tableheads**. Choose to create the style for this document only. Use the following formats for the style:
   - From the Type category, choose Times New Roman font, 10-point size, bold weight, and color #990033.
   - From the Background category choose the lightest yellow background color (#FFFFCC).
   - From the Block category, choose the center Text Align option.
9. Apply the **.tableheads** custom style to *Word* and *WordPerfect* in the table on this page.
10. Create a second custom style named **.tabletext**. Create the style for the current document only. Use the following formats:
    - From the Type category, choose Arial font and 10-point size.
    - Use the lightest blue background color (#CCFFFF).
11. Apply the **.tabletext** custom style to all entries in the right column of the table.
12. Redefine the h3 HTML tag to be Arial, 10 point, bold and italic, and the dark blue color #000066.
13. Use the Properties panel to apply the Heading 3 style to the *Word Processing* head above the table.
14. Click in one of the table cells using the **.tableheads** style and edit the style to use the Arial font and left alignment and note how both headings formatted with the style immediately update.

    ✓ *If your insertion point is in another paragraph or table cell when you edit the style, your revised style will be applied to that paragraph. If necessary, reapply the correct style to the paragraph or table cell.*
15. Create a new external style sheet named **tut_styles.css**. Add the following styles to the style sheet:
    - Create a custom style named **.mainhead** that uses Times New Roman, 24-point, bold weight, and a cranberry color such as #CC0033.
    - Redefine the H2 HTML tag to use Times New Roman, 18-point, bold weight, and a slate blue color such as #336699.
    - Create a custom style named **.text** that uses Arial, 12-point, and a dark blue color such as #000099.
16. Save the style sheet and then click the **Done** button, if necessary.
17. Make sure both pages in the Web site are linked to the **tut_styles.css** style sheet.

18. Apply styles on the pages as follows:
    - On **index.htm**, apply **.mainhead** to the first heading (*Welcome to …*).
    - Apply the redefined Heading 2 to the word *Contents* near the bottom of the page (not to the link at the top of the page).
    - Apply the **.text** style to the three paragraphs that begin with ellipses (. . .) and the paragraph below the *Contents* heading.
    - On **contents.htm**, apply Heading 2 to *Table of Contents* and **.text** to the paragraph below that heading.
19. You have decided the blue text is not effective. Change the **.text** style's color to black. Note the style changes on both pages.
20. In the HTML Styles panel, create a new HTML style as follows:
    - Name the style **firstpar**.
    - Choose the Paragraph option and clear existing styles.
    - Select the Arial font and size 5.
    - Select a very dark blue color, such as #000066.
    - Choose the Paragraph format and center alignment.
21. Apply the **firstpar** style to the *CinciTutorial is* paragraph on **index.htm**.
22. The **firstpar** formats are not quite right. Change the size to 4 and alignment to left.
23. Note that the paragraph does not show the new formats. Reapply the style to the paragraph.
24. Save changes and preview this page in the browser. It should look similar to Illustration A.
25. Close any open pages.
26. Exit Dreamweaver.

Illustration A

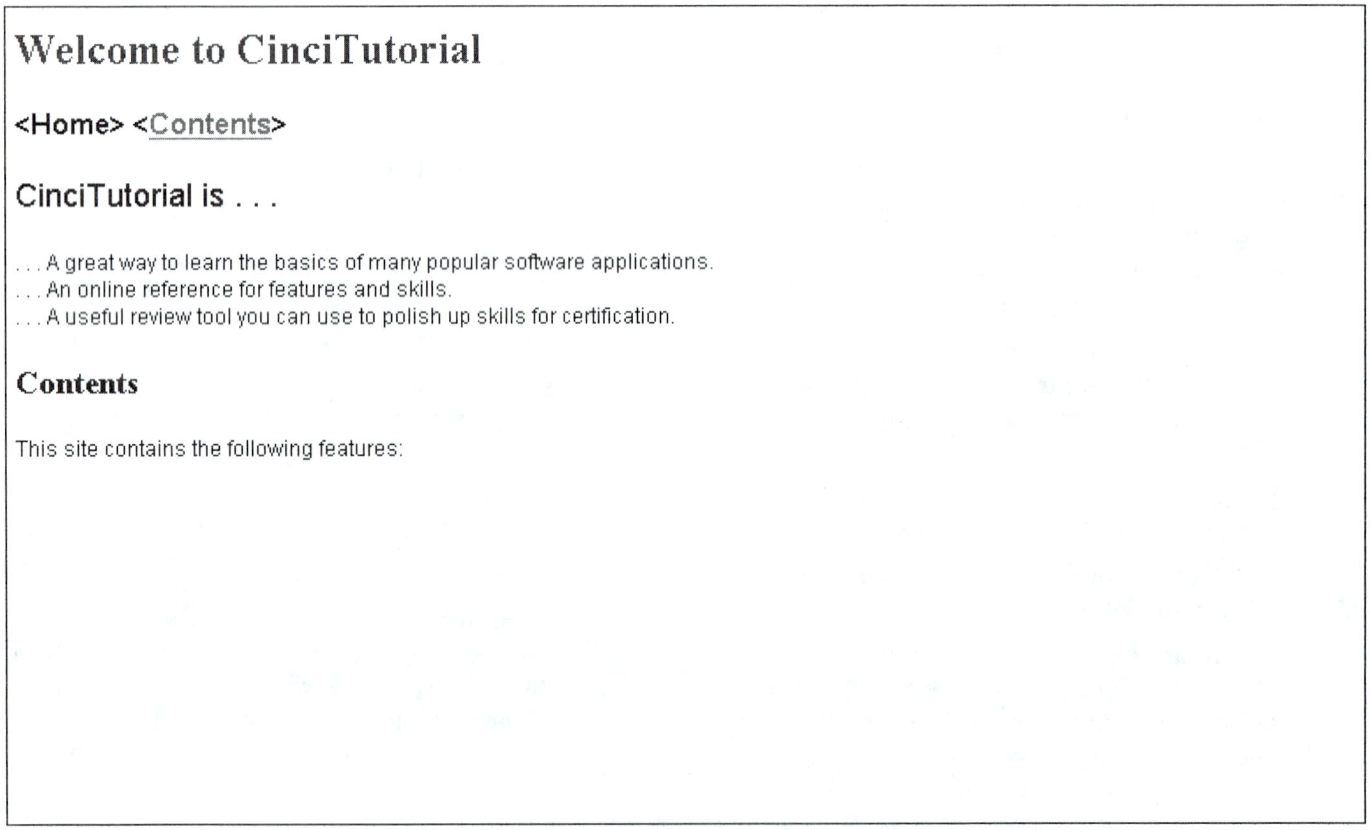

Chapter

14

Behaviors

You may have noticed a third member of the Design panel group: Behaviors. In Dreamweaver, behaviors are browser actions that occur when users interact with a Web page. If you have ever visited a Web site and noticed a "pop-up," a stripped-down Web browser window that opens with an advertisement, that's a behavior. This chapter describes a selection of behaviors commonly used in Web design.

In this chapter, you will learn how to:

- Use the Behaviors panel
- Select and configure common behaviors
- Change a behavior
- Remove a behavior

About Behaviors

- A Dreamweaver **behavior** is an interactive feature that takes place in a browser. When a particular **event** occurs (such as the loading of a page), an **action** takes place. Actions are prewritten JavaScripts that perform specific tasks, such as loading a document window or playing a sound or movie.
- To attach a behavior, you must select an object on a Web page (or an entire Web page) and then specify both the action and the event that triggers the action. More than one action can be attached to the same event. You attach and control behaviors using the Behaviors panel.

Use the Behaviors Panel

- Launch the **Behaviors panel** using the Window>Behaviors command on the menu bar, click the Show Behaviors button on the Launcher—or click the Behaviors tab Behaviors in the Design panel group.
- The Behaviors panel lists events and actions (see illustration below) for the currently selected page element. You use this panel to add or remove behavior actions.

Behaviors panel

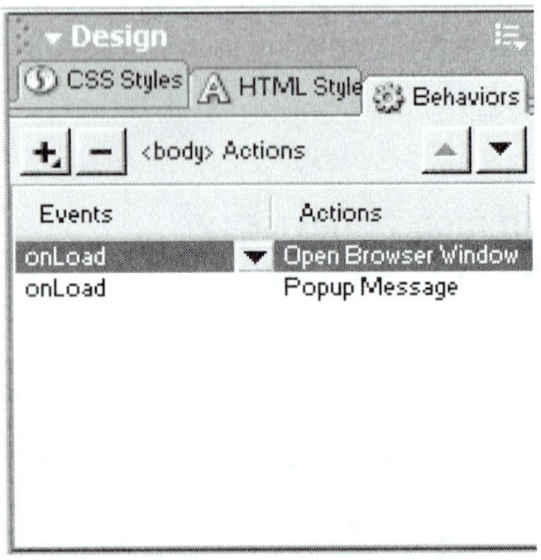

- You use the same general process to attach all Dreamweaver behaviors: select the object to attach the behavior to, choose an action, and then specify the event that will trigger the action.

Select Object

- Behaviors can be attached to an entire document, to links, to images, to form fields, and to some other HTML objects. Before you can attach a behavior to an object, you must select the object.
- Select an entire document using the Edit>Select All command on the menu bar, or use the Ctrl + A keyboard shortcut. Select other objects such as links or images by clicking in them.
- You can verify what object you have selected by looking at the Behaviors panel's title bar. The title bar displays the currently selected object's HTML tag. The illustration in the previous column, for example, shows the <body> tag in the title bar, indicating that the entire page (or Body section) is selected.

Select Action

- Before you begin attaching behaviors, specify a browser version in Dreamweaver by clicking the Actions button, click Show Events for, and choose a browser version from the submenu.
- Setting the browser version saves you from attaching actions that will not work properly in your chosen browser.

  Note: *Dreamweaver's behaviors are written to work in all Microsoft Internet Explorer and Netscape 4.0 browsers as well as the new open-source browsers such as Mozilla. Many behaviors will also work correctly in version 3 browsers, however, which is the default setting.*

- To select a behavior to attach to the selected object, click the Actions button in the Behaviors panel. Dreamweaver displays a list of actions that can be attached to the currently selected object. Not all actions are available for all kinds of selected objects. For example, some behaviors can be used only with layers.

- After you select an action from the list, a dialog box opens to allow you to set **parameters** for the action. The parameters you set are specific to each action. For the Popup Message action, for example, you type the message that will pop up in a message window (see illustration below).

Popup Message parameter dialog box

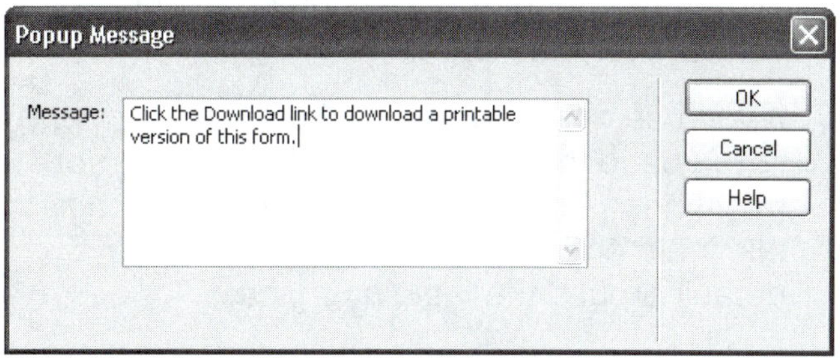

- Once parameters have been set, the action displays in the Behaviors panel's Actions list. You can then specify an event to trigger the action.

Select Event

- Dreamweaver chooses a default event for some types of selected objects. When an entire page is selected, for example, the default event is onLoad, which means the action will take place when the page is downloaded by a browser (opened).
- If you don't want to use the default event, click the list arrow in the Events column of the Behaviors panel. Dreamweaver displays a drop-down list of available events you can choose among (see illustration below).

Select event to trigger action

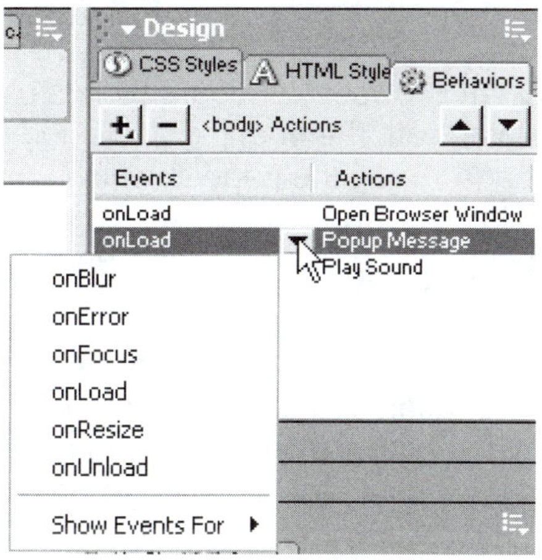

Tip: *If you do not see the list arrow, click on an entry in the Events column to select it and activate the list arrow.*

Note: *The Events list also includes the Show Events for command, allowing you to tailor a specific action to a browser version.*

- If more than one action is specified for an event, actions take place in the order in which they are listed in the Actions column. You can change the order in which actions occur by selecting an action and clicking the ▲ or ▼ button.
- Dreamweaver offers over 30 events. Events available at any one time depend on the selected object, browser version, and action.

Note: *To see a list of all the Dreamweaver events, consult Dreamweaver's Help files for Behaviors: click Help>Using Dreamweaver, or with the Behaviors panel selected, click* *and then click Help in the panel menu.*

- Some of the most commonly used events are described in the table below.

Event	Event occurs . . .
onBlur	When selected object stops being the focus of user interaction (for example, when a user clicks outside of an object such as a form field).
onClick	When user clicks specified object.
onDblClick	When user double-clicks specified object.
OnError	When a browser error occurs during a load.
onFocus	When selected object becomes focus of user interaction (for example, when a user clicks in an object such as a form field).
OnLoad	When a page or image finishes loading.
OnMouseOver	When user moves mouse over top of specified object.
onUnload	When user leaves a page.

- Some actions, such as Swap Image, are available only for certain events, such as clicking a link. When you select an action of this type, the event displays in parentheses.

Dreamweaver Actions

- Dreamweaver includes more than 20 actions you can use to perform various tasks. Not all actions are available for all selected objects. Actions unavailable for a specific object are grayed out on the Actions list.

  Note: *To see a list of all the Dreamweaver actions, consult Dreamweaver's Help files for Behaviors.*

- Some of Dreamweaver's actions perform advanced tasks beyond the scope of this book. The sections below describe several common actions that you can easily implement in any Web site.
- Because actions are designed to display in a browser, you will not see any evidence of the action in Dreamweaver. Preview the pages to which you have attached behaviors in a browser to see the behaviors in action.

Open Browser Window Action

- If you have spent any time browsing on the World Wide Web, you have probably seen behaviors similar to Dreamweaver's Open Browser Window action. This action launches a new browser window containing a specified Web page (document), a common way to display advertising—such as a pop-up window—or additional information.
- Such content draws the user's attention and forces the user to interact with the Web site by viewing and then closing the second browser window.
- The browser window typically lacks the controls that you normally associate with your Web browser, such as scroll bars, toolbar buttons, and menus. The only controls may be the minimize and close buttons.
- Setting up the Open Browser Window action requires a bit of advanced planning and production. You must decide what size to make the content that will display in the new browser window and then create the content before setting up the behavior.
- You can use the skills you already have to create content for your open-browser action. For example, if you want to create a 400 × 400 pixel advertisement, you can simply create it in a 400 × 400 pixel table.
- You can create such content in other applications, too, such as Adobe Photoshop and Adobe Illustrator. Illustration programs allow for richer graphical content and greater control over the image.
- If you use a table or illustration for the content of the page that will open in the browser, you might need to adjust the margins of the page to eliminate any white space that appears by default around the table or image.
- Make this adjustment in the page's Page Properties dialog box (see illustration below). Set the margins to 0 in all four margin boxes to eliminate any default white space in any browser.

Set margins at 0

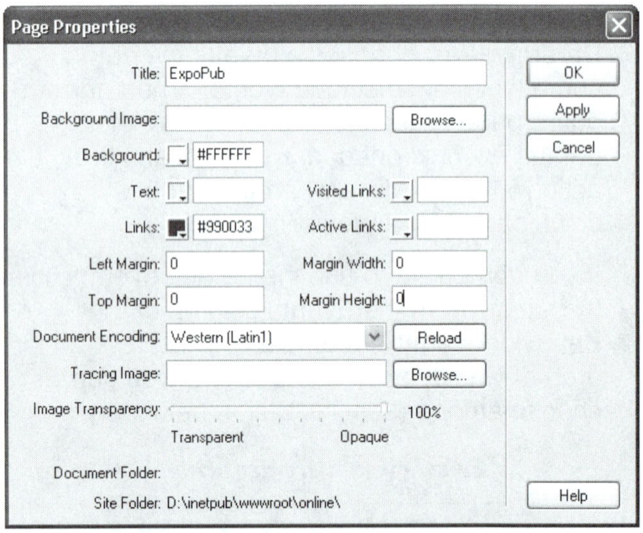

- The Open Browser Window action is usually associated with the opening or closing of a Web page. Open the page to which you will attach this behavior and select it, making sure the <body> tag appears in the Behaviors panel's title bar.
- In the parameters dialog box for the action (see illustration at the top of the next page), specify the address of the page to open in the browser window and the browser window's width and height.

Open Browser Window parameters

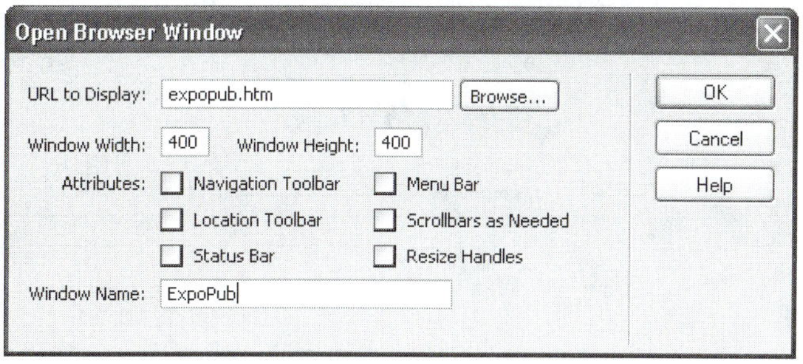

- Typically, this Web page will be contained in your Web's root folder so that the page is available when you publish to a Web server. However, it can be stored in another Internet or intranet server. Include the full path for the file in the URL to Display text box if it is in another location.
- You can select attributes depending on how much interaction you want to allow your visitors. For example, if visitors need to take further action from the browser window, you can select the Menu Bar or Navigation Toolbar attribute.
- The Open Browser Window action is most logical when a page opens or closes, so you will generally use the onLoad or onUnload event for the action.

Play Sound Action

- The Play Sound action attaches a sound file to a selected Web page or page element. Sounds can add multimedia interest to a Web site, but remember that some visitors may not have or want to use sound capability. So, it is a good practice not to include important information in a sound file unless it can also be read in a Web document, too.
- Even very short sound files can also add significantly to the size of a Web page, resulting in a longer download time even for visitors who have a broadband connection. Web designers should consider file size and download time when attaching a sound behavior.
- As for any other behavior, first select the object to which you will attach the sound. You can choose an object such as a button, a link, or the entire page.
- After you select the Play Sound action in the Behaviors panel, the parameter dialog box for this action opens to allow you to select the sound file (see illustration below). This file should be stored in your root folder.

Select sound file

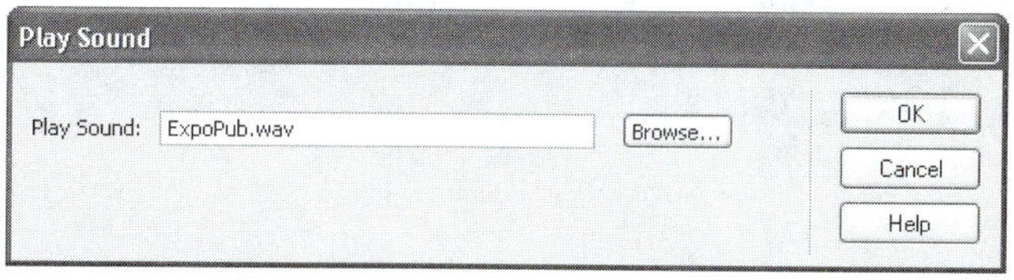

- Dreamweaver does not allow you to control how many times the sound file plays or what application is used to play it. The default media player may even open rather than play in the browser when the event triggers the action.
- The event you choose for the Play Sound action will depend on what object you have selected. Sounds are often played when a page loads or unloads.

Note: *The sound file may play automatically in the browser or you may have to click a button to play the file.*

Popup Message Action

- Dreamweaver offers several actions that relay text content to the visitor, including popup messages and the four Set Text behaviors.
- A popup message is a JavaScript alert that displays a message in a dialog box (see illustration below). The visitor can read the message and click the OK button to close it.

Popup message in alert box

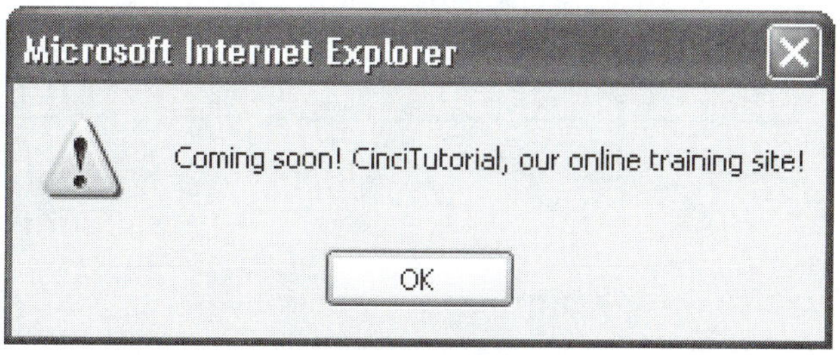

- Popup messages can be used to supply additional information about a button or link or alert the visitor to some aspect of the Web site content.

- Creating a popup message is easy: After selecting the object to which the message action will be attached, choose Popup Message on the Actions list and type the message in the parameters dialog box (see illustration below).

Type message that will pop up

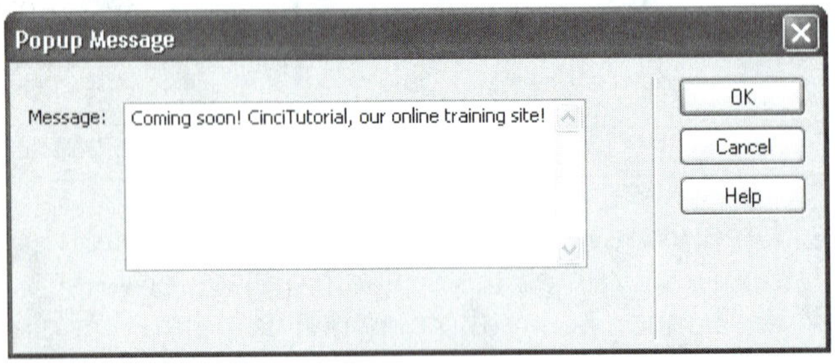

- You then need only select the event to trigger the message. Popup messages work well with any Web page event.

Set Text Actions

- Dreamweaver's Set Text actions offer four options for inserting text in various page elements.
- The Set Text of Frame action allows you to select an object in a frame and then replace the contents of that frame with new HTML content (see illustration below).

Replace text in a specific frame

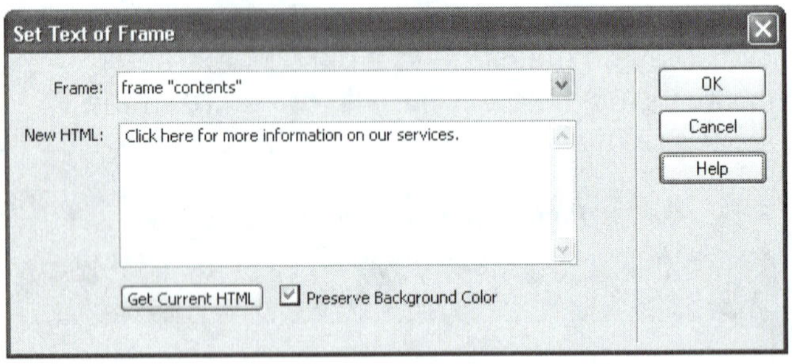

- The Set Text of Layer action lets you choose a layer on a page and replace its existing text with new text (see illustration below).

Set text in a layer

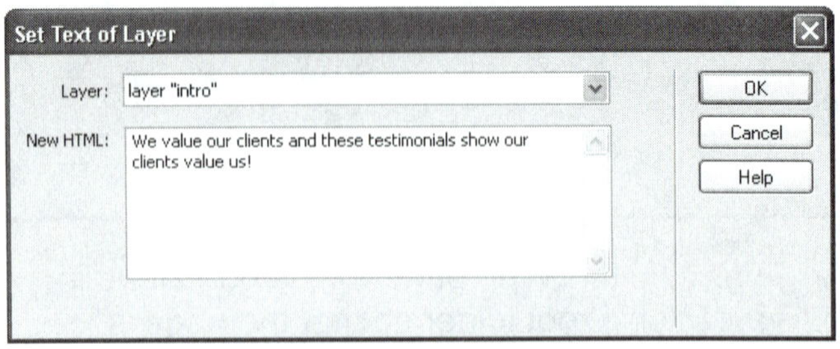

- The Set Text of Text Field action lets you insert text that will appear in a form's text field (see illustration below). To set the text to appear when a visitor clicks in the field, use the onFocus event. To display the text when the visitor moves to another field, use the onBlur event.

Set text for a text field

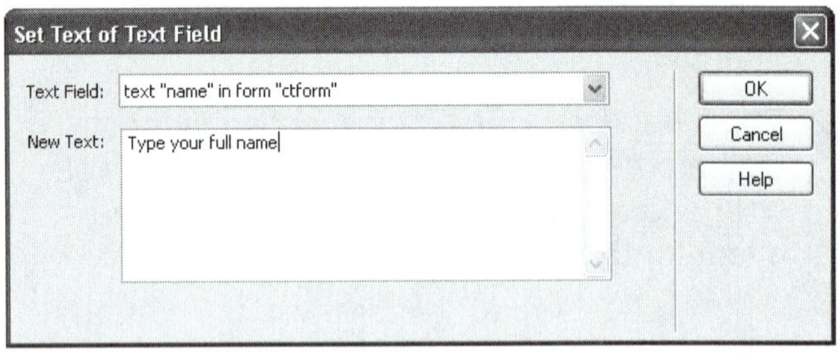

- The Set Text of Status Bar action offers a way to use that space to communicate with Web visitors. The status bar can display the destination of a link or information about the content of a Web page (see illustration below).

Set text to appear in the status bar

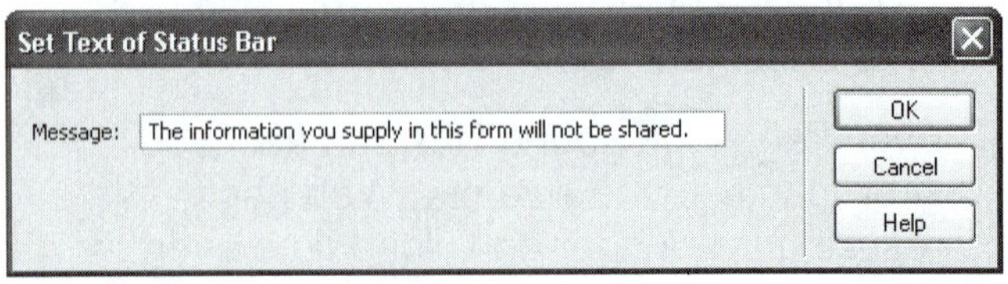

- You can attach this action to an entire page or to a specific link or button (for example, in a form). The designated message displays at the lower-left corner of the browser window, in the status bar (see illustration below).

Text displays in status bar

Swap Image Action

- The Swap Image action can be used for creative interactive effects. When an image is set to *swap*, it changes to another image when the visitor's mouse pointer crosses the image.
- GIF buttons or bullets, for example, can be set up to appear to change colors or shape. You accomplish this by swapping out an image that is virtually the same as the original image except for a change in color or shape.
- The Swap Image action can *restore* itself after the mouse has passed over it, or it can remain changed to indicate to visitors that they have referenced the image or content associated with the image—which adds user friendliness to an otherwise visual effect.
- Attach the Swap Image action by selecting the image to swap and choosing Swap Image from the Actions list.

  Note: *Dreamweaver provides a Swap Image Restore action, but this action is added automatically when you select Swap Image. You do not have to choose it unless the Swap Image Restore action is accidentally deleted from the Behaviors panel.*

- In the parameters dialog box, browse to locate the image that will swap with the selected image (see illustration at the top of the next column). Both images should be stored in your Web site's images folder.

Set source of image to swap

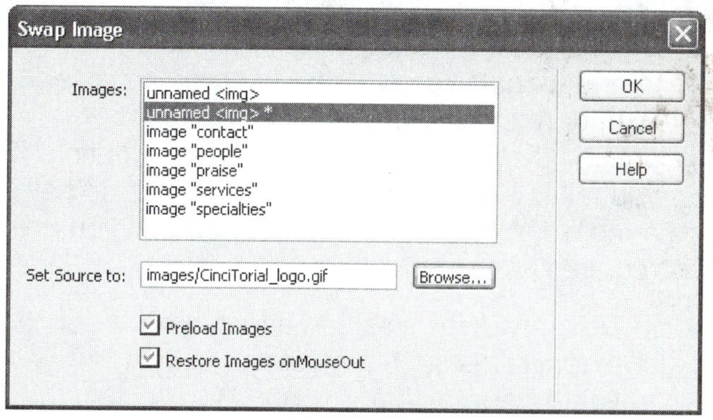

- Note the two checkboxes in the parameter dialog box. Make sure these options are selected to load images with the page and restore the original image after the mouse pointer leaves the swapped image.
- In the Behaviors panel, you will see that two actions have actually been attached: Swap Image and Swap Image Restore (see illustration below).

Two actions control the swap

- Also note that the events are enclosed in parentheses to indicate that these events are appropriate for links. You have actually linked the image to a new source. When the visitor's mouse pointer rests in the swap image, it displays the pointing finger that designates a link (see illustration below).

Swap image in browser

Validate Form Action

- If you have ever used a commercial or informational Web site that features an order form or mail-list form, you have probably noticed that certain fields require information. If you fail to supply information in a required field, a message displays to remind you that you are required to fill in that field.
- In Dreamweaver, you can attach a behavior that generates such a message using the Validate Form action.
- Click in the field you want to validate and select the Validate Form action from the Actions list. The Validate Form parameter dialog box opens with a list of the named fields in the current form (see illustration below).

Validate form fields

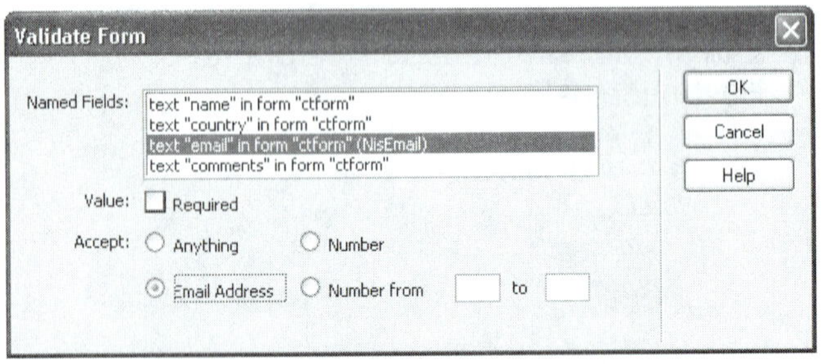

- Select the Required checkbox to require an entry in a field. After you select this checkbox for a field, the field information displays (R) as shown in the illustration above.
- If the field requires a certain type of data entry, specify the required entry type with the Accept options:
  - *Anything* allows any entry, such as names, addresses, and so on.
  - *Email Address* allows one e-mail address to be entered in the field. The e-mail address must have the proper SMTP syntax indicated by the @ symbol.
  - *Number* allows numbers, including decimals.
  - *Number from . . . to . . .* allows a specific range of numbers.
- If you choose a specific data entry option, the field name in the Named Fields list displays an abbreviation of the option, such as (NisNum) for a field with a numerical data entry type. If an entry is required, the *N* is replaced by *R*. A field that requires an e-mail entry will display (RisEmail).
- Each time you open the Validate Form parameter dialog box, the first form field in the Named Fields list is selected by default, even if you have selected another field in the form. You must take care to choose the correct field in the Named Fields list.
- The default event for a Validate Form action is onBlur. This means that the message will display after the visitor leaves the field that has validation applied.
- Though you can set validation rules for all fields at one time in the parameter box, you should not do so because error messages may display for fields the visitor has not yet visited. Instead, create a separate validate action for each field.

  Note: *You can create more than one different action for each field, however.*

- Test your validation rules by displaying the form page in the browser and leaving out required information or supplying incompatible information. As you leave a field, or when you submit the form, you will see error messages similar to the ones shown below.

Validation error messages

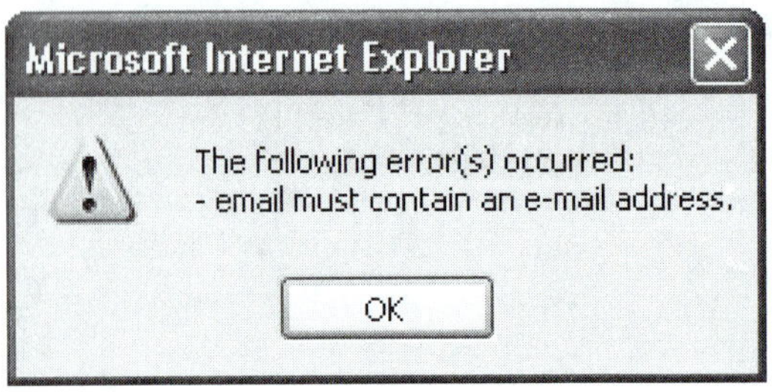

Other Dreamweaver Actions

- As discussed earlier, not all of the behaviors that ship with Dreamweaver are covered in this chapter. Timeline actions are discussed in the next chapter. Shockwave and Flash actions are discussed in Chapter 16. Use Dreamweaver Help to learn more about the other behavior actions.

Modify or Remove Attached Actions

- To modify an action, simply double-click the action in the Behaviors panel to launch the parameter dialog box. You can change any of the parameters you originally set.
- You can also easily change the event that triggers the action by clicking the Events drop-down list arrow and selecting a different event.
- However, the events that Dreamweaver chooses for you by default are typically the ones that work best with the browser or browsers you have selected for your behavior.
- To remove an attached behavior, select the object or page to which the action is attached to see the actions in the Behaviors panel. Then select the action to be removed and click the Delete Actions – button in the Behaviors panel.

Procedures

Display Behaviors panel

F8 (Shift + F3 in Dreamweaver 4)

1. Click **Window** .... Alt + W
2. Click **Behaviors** .... E

OR

- Click Show Behaviors button on Launcher.

Attach Behavior to Object

1. Select object to which behavior will be attached.

   OR

   Select entire page ...... Ctrl + A
2. Click + (**Actions** button) on Behaviors panel.
3. Select action from Actions list.
4. Specify settings in action's parameter dialog box.
5. Accept default event in Behaviors panel, or click Events' list arrow and select new event from drop-down list.

Open Browser Window Action

Before attaching the behavior

1. Create Web page that contains the content that will display in the new browser window.
2. Click **Modify** .... Alt + M
3. Click **Page Properties** .... P
4. Type **0** for all four margins if necessary.

Attach the behavior

1. Select object or page to which the behavior will be attached.
2. Select **Open Browser Window** from Actions list.
3. Type URL of page to open in browser window in **URL to Display** text box.

   OR

   Click Browse... and navigate to page.
4. Set values for Window Width and Window Height.
5. Type name for window and select any additional attributes.
6. Specify event for action if necessary.

Play Sound Action

1. Select object or page to which the behavior will be attached.
2. Select **Play Sound** from Actions list.
3. Type name of sound file in **Play Sound** text box.

   OR

   Click Browse... and navigate to file.
4. Specify event for action if necessary.

Popup Message Action

1. Select object or page to which the behavior will be attached.
2. Select **Popup Message** from Actions list.
3. Type message in **Message** text box.
4. Specify event for action if necessary.

Set Text Actions

Set Text of Frame

1. Select page to which the behavior will be attached (the page must include frames).
2. Select **Set Text** from Actions list and **Set Text of Frame** from submenu.
3. Select the frame in which text will be set from the Frame drop-down list.
4. Type new HTML text in **New HTML** text box.

   OR

   Click Get Current HTML to display and modify current frame content.
5. Select **Preserve Background Color** if desired.
6. Specify event for action if necessary.

Set Text of Layer

1. Select page to which the behavior will be attached (page must include layers).
2. Select **Set Text** from Actions list and **Set Text of Layer** from submenu.
3. Select layer in which text will be set in the Layer drop-down list.
4. Type text for layer in **New HTML** text box.
5. Specify event for action if necessary.

Set Text of Status Bar

1. Select object or page to which the behavior will be attached.
2. Select **Set Text** from Actions list and **Set Text of Status Bar** from submenu.
3. Type message that will appear in the status bar in **Message** text box.
4. Specify event for action if necessary.

Set Text of Text Field

1. Select text field in form to which the behavior will be attached.
2. Select **Set Text** from Actions list and **Set Text of Text Field** from submenu.
3. Select field name from **Text Field** list, if necessary.
4. Type text to appear in field in **New Text** text box.
5. Specify event for action if necessary.

Swap Image Action

1. Select image to which the behavior will be attached.
2. Select **Swap Image** from Actions list.
3. Type source file name in **Set Source to** text box.

   OR

   Click [Browse...] and navigate to location of image file.
4. Select **Preload Images** to load images with the page.
5. Select **Restore Images onMouseOut** to automatically restore the original image after the mouse pointer moves away from the image.
6. Specify event for action if necessary.

Validate Form Action

1. Select form field to validate.

   ✓ *Apply validation actions to each field separately.*
2. Select **Validate Form** from Actions list.
3. Select field from **Named Fields** list.
4. Select validation options:
   - Select **Required** checkbox to make entry required.
   - Select **Anything** option to allow any entry.
   - Select **Email Address** option to require proper format for e-mail address entry.
   - Select **Number** option to require an entry in digits (including decimals).
   - Select **Number from** and specify low and high values for range entry.
5. Specify event for action if necessary.

Modify Behavior

1. Select object or page to which the behavior is attached.
2. Double-click action in Behaviors panel.
3. Make any necessary changes to parameters.
4. Change event if desired.

Remove Behavior

1. Select object or page to which the behavior is attached.
2. Click action in Behaviors panel to select it.
3. Click [–] (**Delete Actions** button) in Behaviors panel.

Exercise Directions

✓ *For best results, Show Events for IE 6.0*

1. Start Dreamweaver.
2. Open the **CinciTorial** site.
3. Open **expopub.htm** from the Data folder and save it with the cincitorial root folder.
4. Prepare the page for use:
   - Display page properties for the **expopub.htm** page and set all margin options to **0**.
   - Insert the **Logo** library item in the blank paragraph below the link on the page.
   - Click the logo and then click the **Detach from Original** button in the Properties panel to detach the image from the library so you can resize it.
   - Resize the logo image to 257 pixels wide by 44 pixels high.
5. Select the entire document.
6. Attach the Play Sound action to the same page. Use the **ExpoPub.wav** sound file from the Data folder (save the sound file in your root folder) and use the **onMouseOver** event.

   ✓ *If you cannot use settings for Internet Explorer 6.0, use the onUnload event instead.*
7. Save and close the page.
8. Open **people.htm** and display the Behaviors panel. Choose to create behaviors for 4.0 and later browsers.
9. Select the entire page. Note that an action already has been attached to this page to preload existing images.
10. Attach the Open Browser Window action to this page as follows:
    - Select **expopub.htm** as the URL to display.
    - Set the Window Width and Window Height measurements to **400**.
    - Type **ExpoPub** as the Window Name.
    - Make sure the **onLoad** event displays in the Events column of the Behaviors panel.
11. Save changes and close the page.
12. Open **services.htm** and select the entire page. Create a popup message that will display the following text when the page closes: **Coming soon! CinciTutorial, our online training site!**
13. Save and close the page.
14. Open **home.htm**. Set up the Swap Image action on this page as follows:
    - Click the logo at the top of the page and detach it from the Library.
    - Click the image again to select it (make sure the <img> tag appears in the Behaviors panel's title bar).
    - Choose the **Swap Image** action and browse to select **CinciTorial_logo_blue.gif** from the Data folder. (Save this image in your images folder.)
    - Note that both the Swap Image and Swap Image Restore actions have been added to the Behaviors panel.
15. Save and close the page.
16. Open **contactus.cfm**. Click in the *name* form field to select it.
17. Use the Set Text of Text Field action to insert the following message in the form field: **Type your full name**. Use the onFocus event.
18. With the *name* field still selected, use the Set Text of Status Bar action to display the following message: **The information you supply in this form will not be shared.** Use the onBlur event.
19. With the *name* field still selected, use the Validate Form action to specify that this field is required. Verify that the onBlur event is chosen for the action.
20. Use the Validate Form action to require an entry in the *country* field. (Be sure to select the "country" field in the Named Fields list.) Use the onBlur event.
21. Require an entry in the *email* field and specify the **Email Address** option. Use the onBlur event.
22. Save changes to all open pages. Open the **index.htm** page and preview it in the browser.

23. Test your behaviors:
    - Click the *Our People* link to see your Open Browser Window behavior and hear the sound file. Your browser window should look similar to Illustration A.

      ✓ *The sound file may not work in Preview in Browser mode. Try opening your site outside of Dreamweaver by entering http://localhost/cincitorial in the Address bar or whatever the URL is for your testing or remote server.*

      ✓ *You may need to play the sound file by clicking a button. You will need speakers and a sound card to hear the sound.*
    - Close the ExpoPub window and click the *Services* link in the navigation bar to open the Our Services page.
    - Click the logo link at the top of the page and view the popup message box that displays as you unload Our Services.
    - Click **OK** to close the popup message box.
    - Point to the logo at the top of the Home Page to see the image swap.
    - Click the *Contact Us* link to open the Contact Us page. Click in the first form field to see the text message. Replace the message with your name and press **Tab** to move to the next field. Notice the message in the status bar.
    - Press **Tab** again to see the message informing you that the Country field requires an entry.
    - Type **USA** in the Country field.

      ✓ *When you leave the E-mail address field to type the country, an error message will display to tell you an entry is required in the Email field. Click OK and proceed.*
    - Type your first name in the *E-mail address* field. You should receive a message telling you to enter an e-mail address in the field.
    - Supply a correct e-mail address in the field.
24. Close the browser and any open pages.
25. Exit Dreamweaver.

Illustration A

Chapter

15

Timelines

Have you ever wondered how Web designers create those animated banner ads at the top of a Web page? Dreamweaver's timeline feature allows you to create similar animation effects using the Timelines panel and layers.

In this chapter, you'll learn how to:

- Use the Timelines panel
- Create a rotating banner ad using the Timelines panel
- Create an animation using the Timelines panel
- Record a layer's path to create an animation
- Test animations
- Edit and remove animations

About Timelines

- **Timelines** create animation by changing the position, size, visibility, and stacking order of layers. For example, you can animate images to move them from one position to another, show and hide layers to make text or images appear and disappear, and even generate slideshows.

  Note: *If you have already created an animation in Macromedia Flash—or want to learn Flash one day—you will find that creating timelines is a similar process.*

- Timelines can also be used to control object behaviors. Use a timeline, for example, to change the source of an image or launch a behavior at a specific time after a page is loaded rather than rely on a visitor to trigger the behavior event.
- Timelines can move only layers. To make text or images move, they must be inserted in a layer.

Use the Timelines panel

- You create and control timelines using the **Timelines panel**. Display the Timelines panel using the Window>Others>Timelines command on the menu bar.
- The Timelines panel looks different from other Dreamweaver panels (see illustration below).
- You can equate this panel to a recording device; much of its terminology is similar to that of a sound or media recorder.
- The current timeline name (Timeline1 by default) is shown in the Timeline pop-up menu. You can create more than one timeline on a page. Display the timeline you want to work with by selecting its name in the pop-up menu.
- The Timelines panel displays a grid of **frames** that track the duration of behaviors and animations.
  - At the top of the panel is the *Behaviors channel* used to set timing for behaviors.
  - At the bottom of the panel are the *animation channels*, used to display *animation bars* for layers and images.
- The *playback head* shows which frame of the timeline is currently displayed on the page. You can drag the playback head to any frame in the timeline. The current frame number is also shown at the top of the panel.
- As you create an animation or control a behavior in the Timelines panel, you set a duration for the effect of a specific number of frames.
- Frames are displayed in the browser at a designated speed. The default, 15 frames per second, is a good speed for most browsers.

  Note: *Increasing the number of frames per second causes the animation to play faster.*

Timelines panel with no animations shown

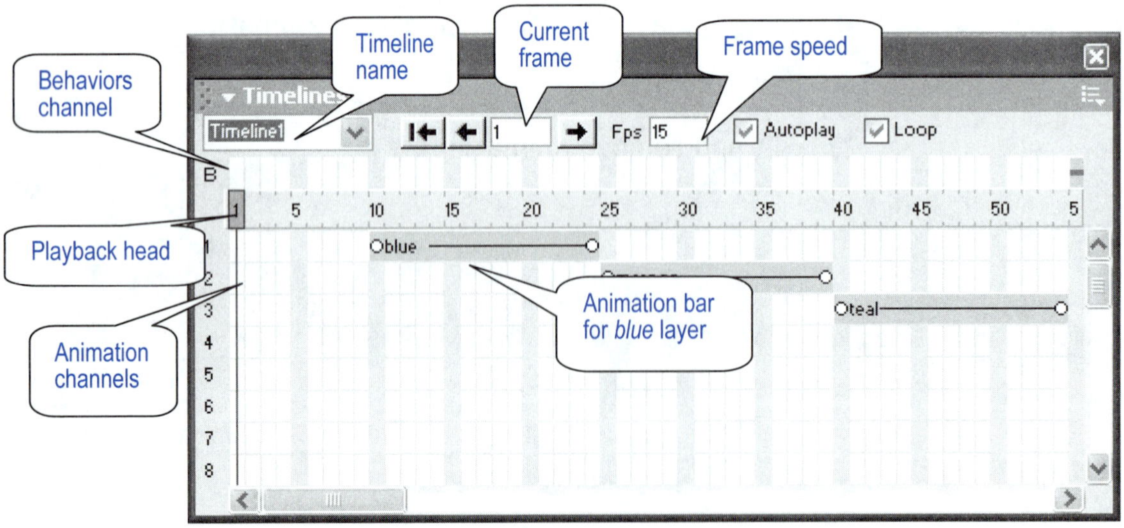

Create a Rotating Banner Ad Using the Behaviors Channel

- You can use the Show-Hide Layers behavior and the Behaviors channel to create a *rotating banner ad*, a popular way to display two or more images in the same location on a Web page.

  Note: Banner ads, *as the term suggests, are frequently used to display advertising or corporate information in image form.*

- To make use of the Show-Hide Layers behavior, the banner ad must consist of two or more layers of the same size that occupy the same position on the page.

  Tip: *This same method can be used to create slideshows, using a larger number of images rather than the two or three used for a typical banner ad.*

Stack and Hide Layers

- Use the Properties panel to position the layers at the same coordinates. Use the Layers palette to make sure the layer you want to display when the page loads is on top of the stack.
- Use the Layers palette or the Properties panel to set the top layer as visible and all other layers as hidden. Recall that you can easily do so by clicking the eye icons in the Layers palette (see illustration below).

Set visibility properties for banner layers

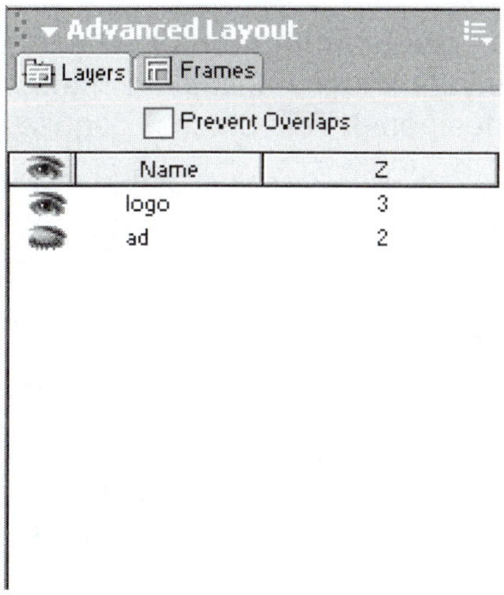

Note: *Assign the highest Z index number to the layer you want to show when the page is loaded. Stacking order does not matter for other layers because they will be controlled by the Show-Hide Layers action.*

- Your layers are now ready to be incorporated into a timeline.

Attach Behavior to Timeline

- Because you use a behavior to create a banner ad, you control the banner ad's function in the Behaviors channel of the Timelines panel. The Behaviors channel consists of a grid of frames, each of which represents a fraction of a second of time.

  Note: *The fractional time depends on the frame speed. At a frame speed of 15, each frame is 1/15 of a second.*

- To attach a behavior to the current timeline, double-click in the frame where you want the behavior to begin. For example, to start the behavior 15 seconds after the page is loaded, double-click in frame 15.
- Dreamweaver displays an alert box reminding you how to add a new behavior from the Actions list (see illustration below). Dreamweaver also opens the Behaviors panel if it is not already displayed.

Reminder dialog box

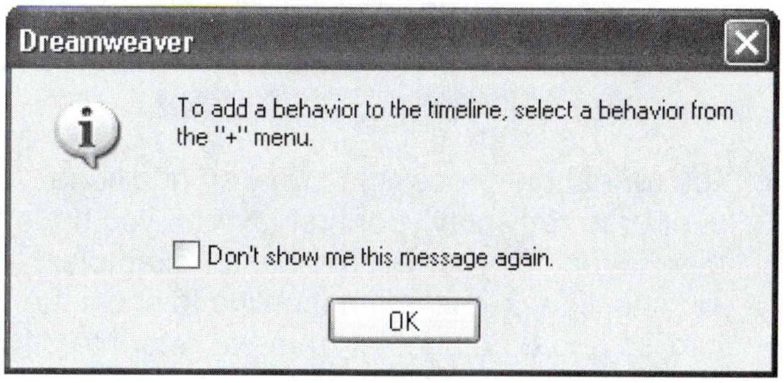

- Click OK to close the alert box. In the Behaviors panel, click the Actions [+] button and choose the Show-Hide Layers action. In the Show-Hide Layers parameter dialog box (see illustration on next page), you designate which layer to show and which to hide.

Specify show/hide settings

- Remember that your visitors will see the top layer of your stack when the page loads. So when you attach the Show-Hide Layers action, you will usually hide the top layer that visitors have already seen, as shown in the illustration above.
- The Behaviors channel shows a horizontal marker in the frame where the behavior begins, and the Behaviors panel lists the action and event (see illustration below).

First behavior attached to timeline

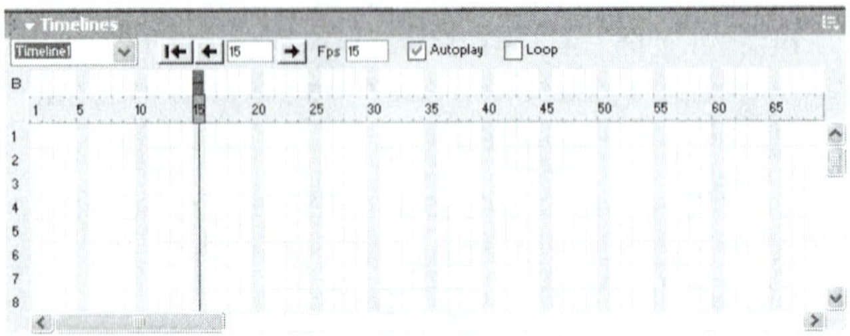

- You repeat the process to show an additional layer or to redisplay your first layer. If you have three layers for your banner ad, for example, you specify a frame in the timeline to show the third ad and then another frame to return to your first layer.

Set Playback Options

- The Timelines panel has two checkboxes that help you control the playback of a timeline.
- Select the *Autoplay* ☑ Autoplay checkbox to play the timeline automatically when the page loads. When you select this checkbox, Dreamweaver displays the alert box shown below to let you know the onLoad event has been created for the timeline.

Autoplay generates an onLoad event

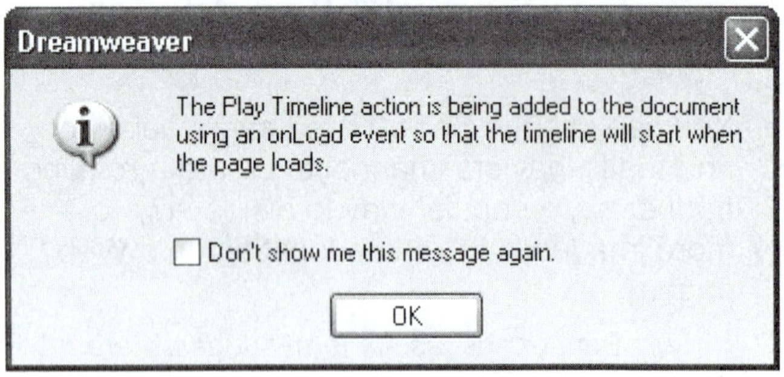

- Select the Loop ☑ Loop option to play the timeline over and over while the page is open in the browser. When you select this checkbox, Dreamweaver displays the alert box shown below to give you more information about the loop settings.

Loop alert box

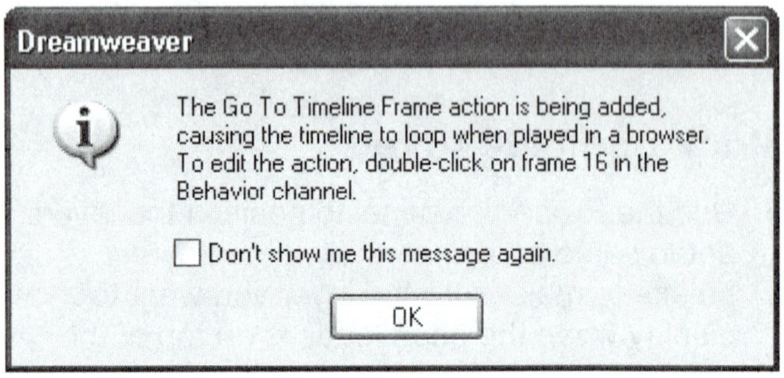

- If you want to limit the number of times the timeline loops, double-click in the frame referenced in the alert box to change settings.

Create Animations Using Timeline Channels

- You can create **animations** in Dreamweaver using layers and the animation channels in the Timelines panel. This process is quite simple:
  - Position the layers on the page where you want them to appear at the start of the animation.
  - Add the layers to the Timelines panel.
  - Drag the layers to their ending positions.
- Before beginning this process, you must have all layers required for the animation in place on the page and the Timelines panel open.

Add Layers to Timeline

- To create an animation, you must add the layer that will move to an animation channel in the Timelines panel. Select the layer and use one of these methods:
  - Click Modify>Timeline>Add Object to Timeline on the menu bar. The animation bar for the layer is added to the first available channel starting in frame 1.
  - Right-click the *selected* layer and click Add to Timeline on the shortcut menu. The animation bar for the layer is added to the first available channel starting in frame 1.
  - Drag the layer into the Timelines panel and drop it in the frame where you want the animation to begin.

Tip: *When working with small layers, it can sometimes be difficult to tell if the layer is selected. Try clicking or right-clicking the layer marker rather than the layer itself to select it.*

Tip: *Also, the size of the Timelines panel can overwhelm the Document window. Undock it and resize it approximately to the size you need. You may also want to collapse panel groups and the like to increase your workspace. You can also collapse and expand the docked Timelines panel by clicking its collapse/expand button.*

- Any of these methods generates the alert box shown below, telling you what attributes the Timelines panel can animate.

Alert box displays when layer added to timeline

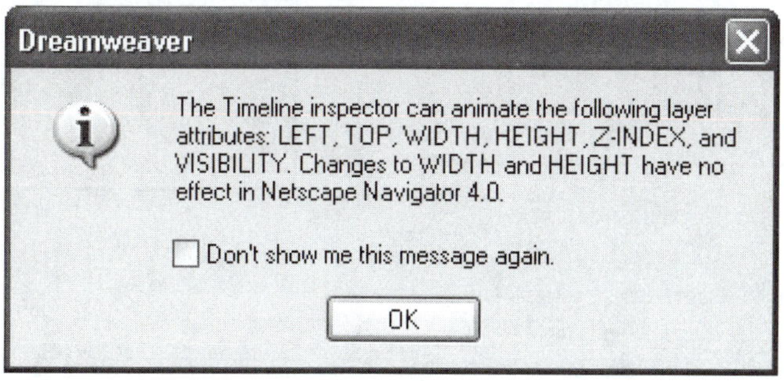

- When you add a layer to the timeline, you create an **animation bar** for that layer (see illustration below). The animation bar contains the layer's name. The small circles at the beginning and end of the animation bar are called **keyframes**.

Animation bars in timeline

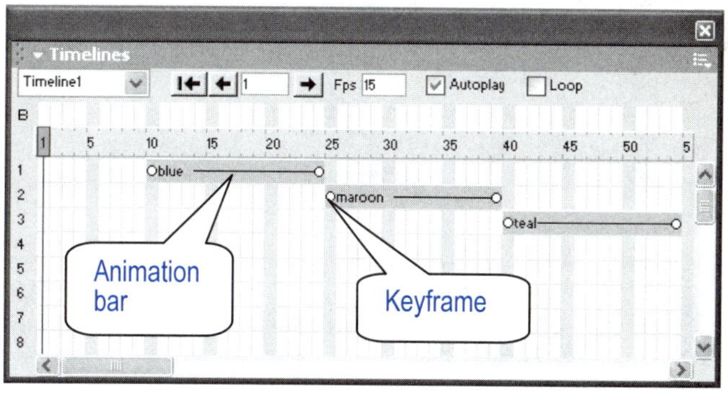

- If the animation bar does not display where you want the animation to begin, click it to select it and drag it to the correct frame.
- Dreamweaver specifies a default duration for the animation of 15 frames. You can increase or decrease duration by dragging the end keyframe left or right in the grid.

Animate Layers

- To animate a layer that has been added to the timeline, use the following process:
  - In the Timelines panel, click the ending keyframe of the layer you want to animate. This action selects the layer on the page.
  - Drag the layer on the page from its starting location to the location where you want it to appear when the animation ends. (See illustration on next page.)
  - Release the mouse button after you have positioned the frame at its ending location.
- Dreamweaver sets a straight path from the starting position to the ending position. You will learn later in the chapter how to make the animation's path appear to curve.

Drag layer to its ending position

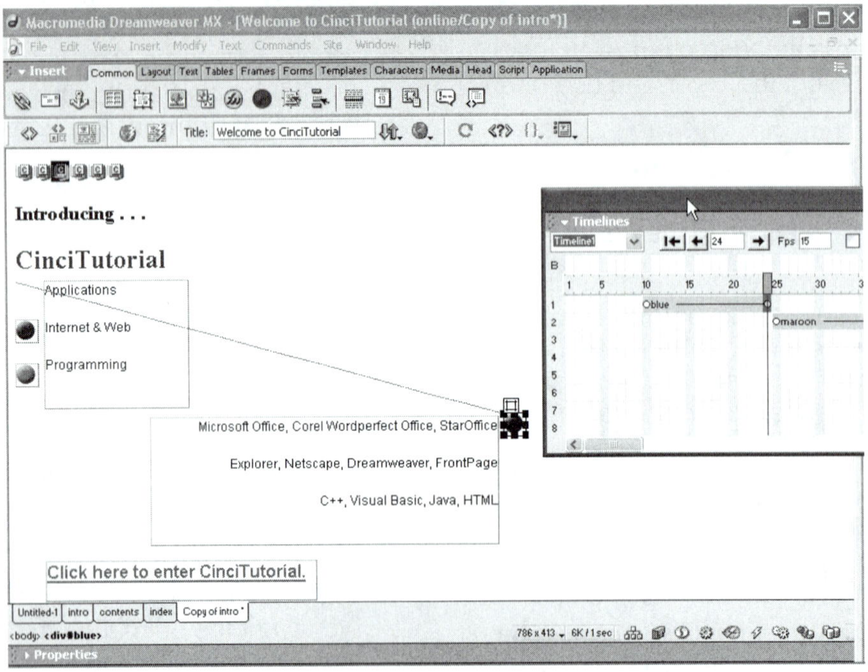

Set Playback Options

- You have the same playback options for animations as for behaviors. Select Autoplay to play the animation automatically after the page loads.
- You can also select the Loop option, but use care when looping an animation that your page does not look too "active."

Create Curving Animations

- By adding one or more keyframes to an animation bar in a timeline, you can create animations that appear to move in a curve.
- To add a keyframe to an animation bar:
  - Select the animation bar to which you want to add a keyframe.
  - Click at the point where you want to add the keyframe—that is, at the point where the animation will appear to curve.
  - Use the Modify>Timeline>Add Keyframe command on the menu bar.
  - Or, right-click the selected animation bar where you want to add the keyframe and select Add Keyframe from the shortcut menu.

Note: *Insert additional keyframes in the animation bar to add other curves.*

- To adjust the curve, click the new keyframe and then drag the layer object to the point at which it will curve (see illustration below).

Position layer to create curve

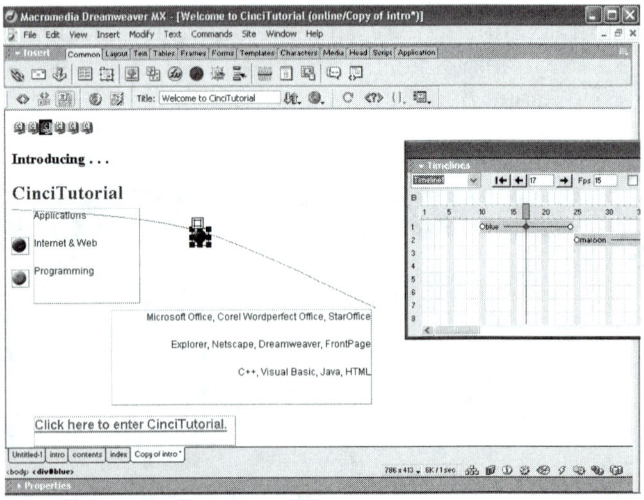

- You may need to test your animation in the browser several times to adjust the curve to your satisfaction.

Record a Layer's Path

- You can use the Record Path (or Record Path of Layer) command to "draw" the path you want your animation to take. This method automatically adds the keyframes required to move the layer over a path that can be straight, curved, multiangled, or circular—the complexity is up to you.
- Begin this process by selecting the layer you want to record. You do not have to add the layer to the timeline.
- Then, right-click the selected layer and click Record Path on the shortcut menu or use the Modify>Timeline>Record Path of Layer command on the menu bar.
- You must then drag the layer to define the path. As you drag, a dotted line shows you the path you are creating (see illustration below).

Record a layer's path

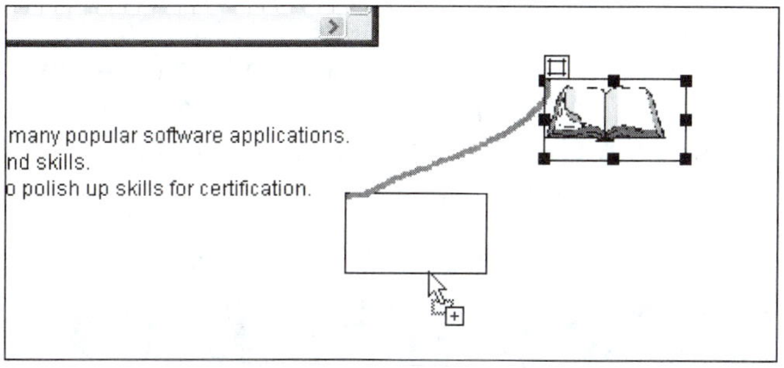

- The recorded path is automatically added to the Timelines panel, with keyframes representing each change of direction. You can select keyframes to adjust the path, just as when creating a curved path.
- Drawing a layer's path using this method requires a steady hand and usually some cleanup. You will probably want to keep the path short for these reasons.

Change Image and Layer Properties with Timelines

- Timelines can be used to change image and layer properties. Use this method, for example, to change the color of the bullet images used in this chapter's exercise by switching the source file for each image.
- To change an image's properties using a timeline, you can add the image directly to the timeline without first inserting it in a layer.
- The only animation option you have when adding an image directly to the timeline is to change its source. Dreamweaver will remind you of this with the message shown below.

Warning when adding image to timeline

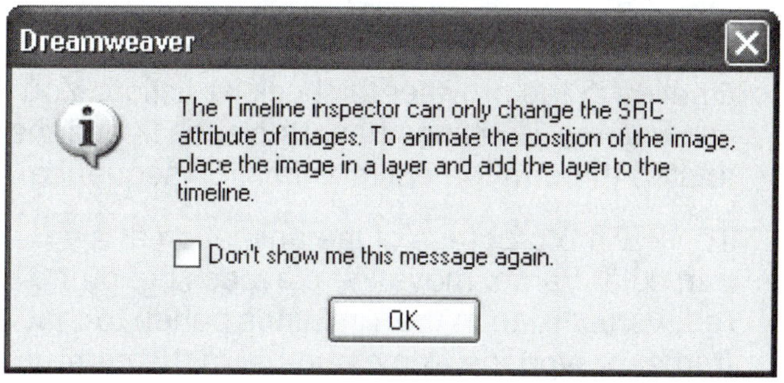

- Add an image to a timeline using the same procedure as for adding a layer: select the image and then drag it to the timeline or use a menu command to insert it.

  Tip: *When dragging an image to the timeline, you may inadvertently resize it. To make sure your image remains the same size, select the image and then use the Modify>Timeline>Add Object to Timeline command.*

- To change the image's source, select the keyframe where the source change should occur. In the Properties panel, type the new source name or use Browse for File to select the file.
- The same method can be used to change the properties of layers using timelines. Use the Layer Properties panel and Layers panel to change the visibility of the layer, to change its size, and to change the stacking order at different intervals on a timeline.

Edit Timelines in Timelines Panel

- After you have set up timelines, you can edit them easily in the Timelines panel. For example, you can drag beginning, ending, or any other keyframes to increase or decrease the duration of an animation (or a segment of the animation).
- Similarly, you can drag the horizontal lines (–) in the Behaviors channel to change the time when a behavior begins or ends.

- If desired, change the default timeline name by selecting the default name in the Timelines panel's pop-up menu and typing a new one.

  Note: *Or right-click anywhere in the Timelines panel, select Rename Timeline, and enter a new name in the Rename Timeline dialog box.*

Test Timeline Frame by Frame

- You don't need to preview an animation timeline in the browser to check its action. You can use the Timelines panel's playback options to step through the entire animation sequence.
- To view the progress of the animation at a particular frame, move the playback head (the red, vertical line in the Timelines panel) to that frame, or type the frame number in the current frame box.
- To view the animation step by step, use the direction buttons in the Timelines panel. The Rewind button moves the playback head to frame 1. The Play button moves the playback head one frame forward, and the Back button moves the playback head one frame backward.
- Hold down the Play or Back button, or drag the playback head, to play or rewind the animation.

  Note: *To see exactly where an animation will appear in the finished Web page, however, you should use the browser to preview the animation effects.*

Remove Frames, Objects, and Timelines

- Dreamweaver gives you precise control over removing timeline elements.
  - Use Remove Frame to delete a single frame from the timeline.
  - Use Remove Object to remove a layer from a timeline channel.
  - Use Remove Behavior to remove a behavior from the Behaviors channel.
  - Use Remove Keyframe to eliminate a keyframe from an animation bar.
  - Use Remove Timeline to remove an entire timeline.
- Access these commands by selecting an element and then right-clicking or clicking Modify>Timeline and then the desired command.

  Caution: *Don't confuse removing an object in a timeline channel with removing a timeline. Remove Timeline removes an entire timeline that could consist of a number of objects.*

Change Object in Timeline

- If desired, you can change the object in a timeline animation using the Change Object command on the shortcut or Modify>Timeline menu. The Change Object dialog box (see illustration below) allows you to select a different layer object to animate.

Change an object in an animation

- Changing the animation, however, will not remove the layer from the Web document. If this is necessary for the proper function and appearance of an animation, select and delete the unneeded layer.

Procedures

Display Timelines panel

Alt + F9

1. Click **Window** .... Alt+W
2. Click **Others** .... O
3. Click **Timelines** .... T

Create Rotating Banner Ad

Before creating the banner ad, create all images required for the ad and insert them in layers.

1. Use the Properties panel to position ad layers in the desired location on the page.
   - ✓ *All the layers in the banner ad must occupy the same position on the page.*
2. Use the Layers panel or the Properties panel to set visibility options for the layers.
   - ✓ *All layers but the top layer should be hidden.*
3. Display the Timelines panel.
4. Double-click in the frame where you want to begin displaying a different layer.
5. Click OK to close the alert box.
6. Click + (**Actions** button) in the Behaviors panel to add behavior.
7. Select **Show-Hide Layers**.
8. Specify layer(s) to show and hide.
9. Repeat process to show/hide other layers in other frames in the timeline.
10. Select **Autoplay** and **Loop** checkboxes to automatically play and repeat behavior.
11. Click OK after selecting each checkbox to add actions and events for Autoplay and Loop.

Create Animation Using Timeline Channels

Before creating animation, create all images or text used for animation and insert them in layers.

1. Display the Timelines panel.
2. Select the layer to be animated.
3. Click **Modify** .... Alt+M
4. Click **Timeline** .... M
5. Click **Add Object to Timeline** .... A

   OR

   - Right-click selected layer and click **Add to Timeline**.

   OR

   - Drag layer into Timelines panel to proper channel and drop.
6. Click OK to close alert box.
7. Drag animation bar if necessary to proper location on timeline.
8. Click ending keyframe for layer in Timelines panel.
9. Select and drag layer to its ending position.
10. Select **Autoplay** checkbox to play animation automatically.

Select Animation Bar

- Click on animation bar.
  - ✓ *When selected, animation bar becomes darker.*

Add a Behavior to Timeline

1. Display Timelines panel.
2. Click in a frame in Behaviors channel.
3. Click **Modify** .... Alt+M
4. Click **Timeline** .... M
5. Click **Add Behavior to Timeline** .... B

   OR

   - Right-click frame in Behaviors channel and click **Add Behavior**.
6. Click OK to close alert box.
7. Use the Behaviors panel to choose an action and event.
8. Select **Autoplay** checkbox to play timeline automatically.

Add Keyframe

F6

1. Select animation bar in which to add keyframe.
2. Click at position on animation bar to add keyframe.
3. Click **Modify** .... Alt+M
4. Click **Timeline** .... M
5. Click **Add Keyframe** .... D

OR

1. Right-click on selected animation bar at location to add keyframe.
2. Select **Add Keyframe** from shortcut menu.

Create Curving Animations

Add layers to timeline as directed at left.

1. Select animation bar of layer to curve.
2. Click at position on animation bar to add curve.
3. Add keyframe.
4. Click new keyframe to select and drag layer to adjust its position.
5. Add additional keyframes as necessary to control curve.

Record a Layer's Path

1. Select layer to animate.
2. Click **Modify** .... Alt+M
3. Click **Timeline** .... M
4. Click **Record Path of Layer** .... R

   OR

   Right-click selected layer and click **Record Path**.
5. Drag layer to define path.
6. Adjust layer's path if necessary.

Change Image Source with Timeline

1. Drag image to Timelines panel.
   ✓ *Image must not be in layer.*
2. Add keyframe where image source will change, if necessary.
3. Display Properties panel, if necessary.
4. Click keyframe where image source will change.
5. Type new image source file name in **Src** text box on Properties panel.

   OR

   - Use (**Browse for File** button) on Properties panel to navigate to image file.

Name Timeline

1. Click **Modify** .... Alt+M
2. Click **Timeline** .... M
3. Click **Rename Timeline** I
4. Type new name.

OR

1. Click default timeline name in Timelines panel's pop-up menu.
2. Type new name.

OR

1. Right-click anywhere in Timelines panel.
2. Click **Rename Timeline**.
3. Type new name in Rename Timeline dialog box.

Create New Timeline

1. Click **Modify** .... Alt+M
2. Click **Timeline** .... M
3. Click **Add Timeline** .... T

OR

1. Right-click anywhere in Timelines panel.
2. Click **Add Timeline**.
   ✓ *To switch the view in the Timelines panel to display a different timeline, click the list arrow to display the pop-up menu and select the timeline you want to display.*

Test Timeline Frame by Frame

- Click (**Rewind** button) on Timelines panel to move playback head to first frame.
- Click (**Play** button) to move animation forward one frame.
- Click (**Back** button) to move animation backward one frame.
  ✓ *Hold down Play or Back button to see animation over more than one frame.*

OR

- Drag playback head to see animation in motion.

Remove Frames from Timeline

1. Select animation bar to edit.
2. Click **Modify** .... Alt+M
3. Click **Timeline** .... M
4. Click **Remove Frame** .... E

OR

- Right-click selected animation bar and select **Remove Frame**.
  ✓ *Use the same initial steps to select Remove Keyframe and Remove Behavior.*

Remove Objects from Timeline

1. Select animation bar of object to remove.
2. Click **Modify** .... Alt+M
3. Click **Timeline** .... M
4. Click **Remove Object** .... M

OR

- Right-click selected animation bar and select **Remove Object**.

Remove Timeline

1. Select the timeline you want to remove from the drop-down list in the Timelines panel.
2. Click **Modify** .... Alt+M
3. Click **Timeline** .... M
4. Click **Remove Timeline** L

OR

- Right-click anywhere in Timelines panel and select **Remove Timeline**.

Change Object in Timeline

1. Select animation bar of layer to change.
2. Click **Modify** .... Alt+M
3. Click **Timeline** .... M
4. Click **Change Object** C

OR

- Right-click selected animation bar and select **Change Object**.

5. Select new object to animate.

Exercise Directions

1. Start Dreamweaver.
2. Open the **tutorials** site.
3. Create a new folder in the site named **images**.
4. In Windows Explorer, copy the following files from the **cincitorial** Web folder's images subfolder to the online folder's images subfolder: **bluebullet.gif**, **maroonbullet.gif**, **tealbullet.gif**, and **CinciTorial_logo.gif**.
5. Open **index.htm**. Create the content for a banner ad as follows:
   - Position the insertion point at the left of the main heading and insert a layer using the Insert>Layer command.
   - Name the layer **logo**.
   - Insert **CinciTorial_logo.gif** in the layer and adjust the size of the layer to surround the image.
   - Create a second layer named **ad** and insert **CinciTorial_ad.gif** from the Data folder. (Save the image in your images folder.)
6. Position and stack the layers:
   - Set the Left measurement at 8 and the Top at 4 for *both* layers.
   - Insert a blank paragraph above the *Welcome* heading to move it down beyond the layers.
   - Adjust the stacking order if necessary so that the red logo is on top.
   - Make the *logo* layer visible and hide the *ad* layer.
7. Attach the behavior for the layers:
   - Display the Timelines panel and double-click in frame 15 of the Behaviors channel.
   - Click OK to close the alert box. In the Behaviors panel, select the **Show-Hide Layers** action.
   - Hide the *logo* layer and show the *ad* layer.
   - Double-click in frame 30, select the **Show-Hide Layers** action, hide the *ad* layer, and show the *logo* layer.
8. In the Timelines panel, select the **Autoplay** and **Loop** checkboxes and click **OK** to add both events.
9. Name the timeline **Logo**.
10. Save and preview the page in the browser to see the banner ad in operation.
11. Open **intro.htm** from the Data folder and save it in the **tutorials** Web site.
12. Attach the **tut_styles.css** style sheet to this page, if necessary, which should result in the text on the page being formatted. If this does not happen, format the first line with the **Heading 2** style, the second with the **mainhead** style, and the text in the layers with the **text** style.

    ✓ *To make it easy to work with animations on this page, maximize the page.*

13. Use the Properties panel to check the *Click here to enter CinciTutorial* link. Change the link in the Properties panel to read **home.htm** if necessary.
14. Insert the **bluebullet.gif** in the **blue** layer (next to the text *Applications*), the **maroonbullet.gif** in the **maroon** layer (next to *Internet & Web*), and the **tealbullet.gif** in the **teal** layer (next to *Programming*).
15. Drag the *blue* layer to the first animation channel in the Timelines panel and drop it so it begins at frame 10.

    ✓ *If desired, undock the Timelines panel and resize it to make it easier to work in the Document window.*

16. Drag the *maroon* layer to the timeline and drop it at frame 25 of channel 2. Drag the *teal* layer to the timeline and drop it at frame 40 of channel 3.
17. Select the *blue* layer's ending keyframe and then drag the layer just to the right of the last layer on the page and aligned with the *Microsoft Office, Corel WordPerfect Office,* StarOffice text (see Illustration A).
18. Select the ending keyframe for the maroon layer and then drag the maroon layer to align with the end of the next line of text and then do the same with the remaining bullet.
19. Select the **Autoplay** checkbox if necessary and then preview your animation in the browser.
20. If the **Loop** checkbox is selected, remove the checkmark. Your page should look similar to Illustration A at the end of the animation.

21. Add keyframes to each animation bar and create a curve for each bullet path. Test your animations in the browser and adjust as necessary to achieve a pleasing effect.
22. Save and close the page.
23. On the **index.htm** page, create a new layer named **book** and insert in it the **book.gif** image from the Data folder. (Save the image in your images folder.)
24. Reduce the size of the image to 70 pixels by 35 pixels, and reduce the size of the layer to fit closely around the image.
25. Position the layer at a Left measurement of 518 pixels and a Top measurement of 186.

    ✓ *Or use a measurement that will align the book with the first paragraph of text when viewed in the browser.*

26. Add a new timeline to the page named **Book**.
27. Issue the Record Path command and then drag the layer down to the right of the third paragraph as shown in Illustration B.
28. Specify the **Autoplay** option and deselect the Loop option if necessary. Then preview your animation in the browser. Make any adjustments desired to the path.
29. Open **contents.htm** and place the insertion point in the first blank paragraph above the *Table of Contents* heading if necessary.
30. Format the new paragraph with the Paragraph HTML format.
31. Insert in the new paragraph the **bluebullet.gif**, **maroonbullet.gif**, and **tealbullet.gif** images in a row, with five nonbreaking spaces between each image.
32. Add each image to the Timelines panel in separate animation channels, beginning in frame 1 of each channel. End each animation bar at frame 30.
33. Add a new keyframe in each animation bar at frame 15.
34. Set new image sources as follows:
    - For image1 (the blue bullet), change the image source at the frame 15 keyframe to **maroonbullet.gif**. Change the image source at the frame 30 keyframe to **tealbullet.gif**.
    - For image2 (the maroon bullet), change the image source at frame 15 to **tealbullet.gif** and at frame 30 to **bluebullet.gif**.
    - For image3 (the teal bullet), change the image source at frame 15 to **bluebullet.gif** and at frame 30 to **maroonbullet.gif**.
35. Select the **Autoplay** and **Loop** checkboxes. Preview the page to see how the bullets change colors automatically.
36. Save and close the page.
37. After having reviewed all your animations, you decide the book animation on **index.htm** does not add much to the page. Delete the Book timeline and the *book* layer.
38. Close the browser.
39. Save and close all open pages.
40. Exit Dreamweaver.

Illustration A

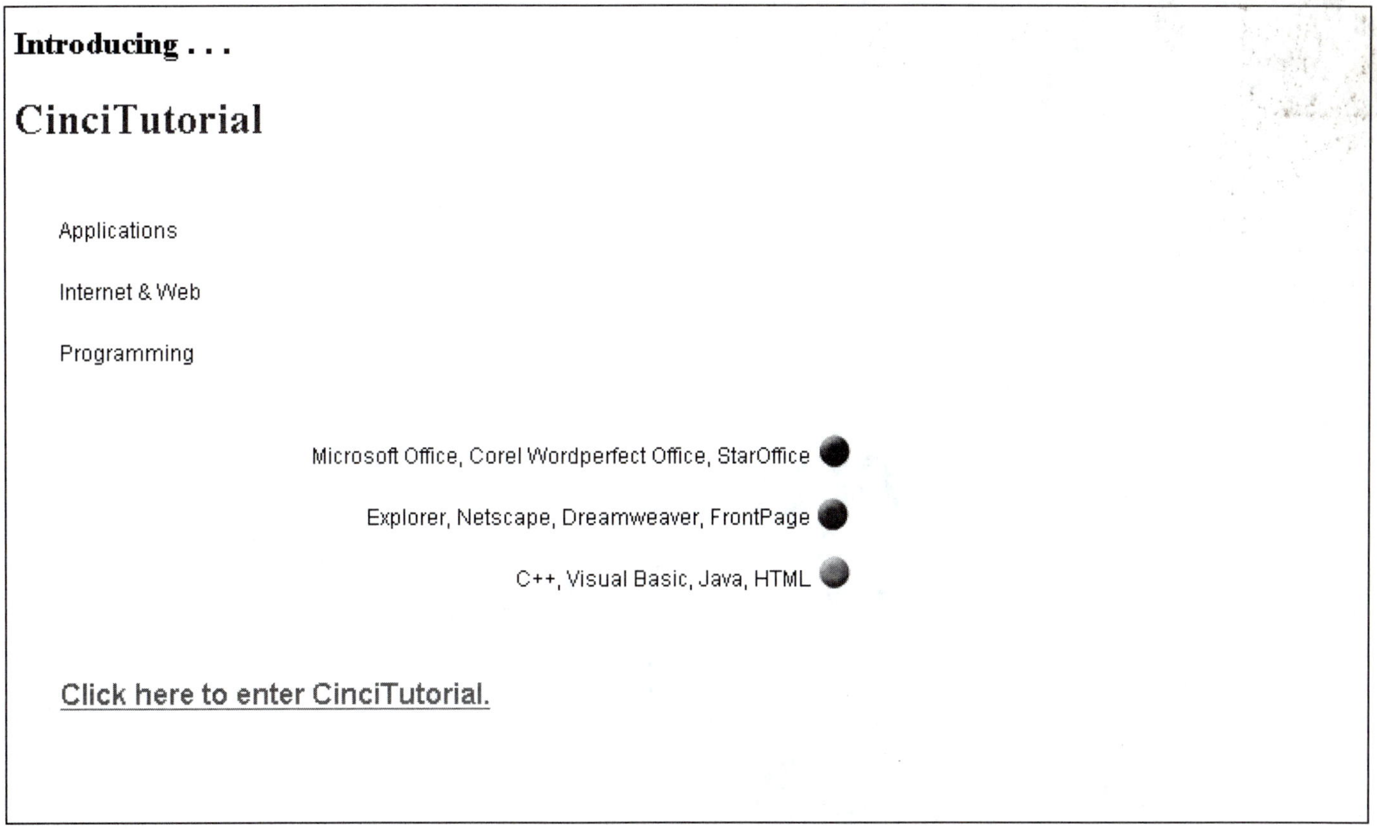

Illustration B

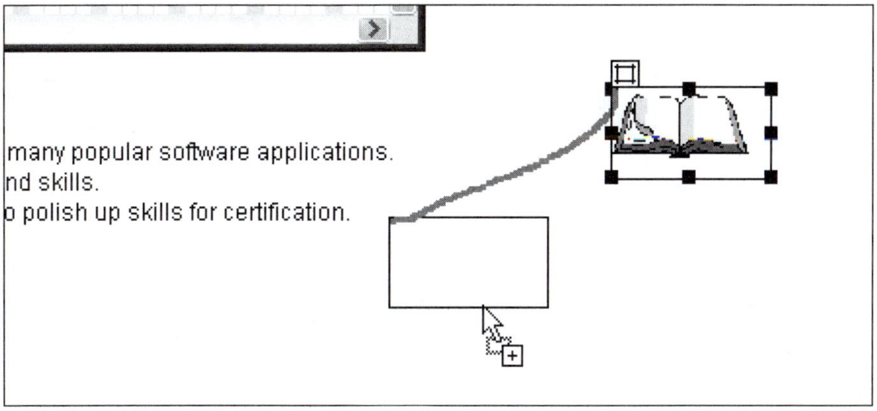

Next Chapter

▶▶

Chapter

16

Multimedia Objects

Multimedia files—sound, action, video, and interactive elements such as games—can add new levels of impact, creativity, and interest to a Web site. Macromedia Shockwave and Flash movie files, as well as other kinds of multimedia files, can easily be added to Web documents.

In this chapter, you'll learn how to:

- Insert Flash and Shockwave movie files
- Modify and view movies
- Insert Flash buttons and Flash text
- Embed Java applets, ActiveX objects and controls, and Netscape Navigator plugins

About Multimedia Files

- **Multimedia** files present information in the form of video sequences, animations, illustrations, and sounds. The Media tab on the Insert bar provides buttons for inserting several popular types of multimedia files. These files include Flash movies and objects, Shockwave movies, Java applets, ActiveX controls, and **plugin** files that require Netscape Navigator plugins that are also used by the Mozilla browser.

  Note: *The Common tab also has buttons that allow you to insert Flash objects—and illustrated objects created with Macromedia Fireworks HTML illustration application ( ).*

  Note: *The Shockwave button can also be used to insert QuickTime movies as well.*

- Creation of multimedia files is beyond the scope of this book. Use of a number of Dreamweaver plugins likewise requires programming skills not covered in this chapter. This chapter concentrates on inserting, modifying, and playing Flash and Shockwave movies, which are readily available on the Internet.

  Note: *If you have access to a program such as Flash, you can create your own Flash movies—and in Dreamweaver MX, you can create Flash buttons and Flash text directly in Dreamweaver, which is covered in this chapter.*

Insert Flash or Shockwave Movie

- Macromedia Flash files are designed to deliver low-bandwidth animations and presentations. Your online audience can view a Flash movie with the Macromedia Flash Player, which is a free download.
- Macromedia Shockwave Director files are much larger. They are designed for a more powerful online multimedia experience that can combine graphics, sound, animation, text, and video.
- When you insert a **Flash** or **Shockwave** file, Dreamweaver uses two sets of HTML tags to provide support for multiple browsers. The object tags are supplied for Microsoft browsers and the embed tags are supplied for Netscape browsers.
- Shockwave files (identified by extensions .dcr, dxr, and .dir) and Flash movies (identified by the .swf extension) can be added to a Web document using menu commands or buttons on the Media tab of the Insert bar.
- Position the insertion point on the page where the movie is to appear and then use the Insert>Media>Flash or Insert>Media> Shockwave command on the menu bar.
- Or, click the Flash button or the Shockwave button on the Media tab of the Insert bar.

  Note: *The movie can be inserted directly in the document or in a layer in the document.*

- After you insert the multimedia file and save it in your current Web site, Dreamweaver displays a gray placeholder for the object. If you have the Properties panel displayed, it shows properties for the selected multimedia object (see illustration at the bottom of the page).
- The process for inserting Flash movies and Shockwave movies is identical. Dreamweaver allows you to change more properties with Flash movies than with Shockwave movies, however.

Media object buttons on the Media tab

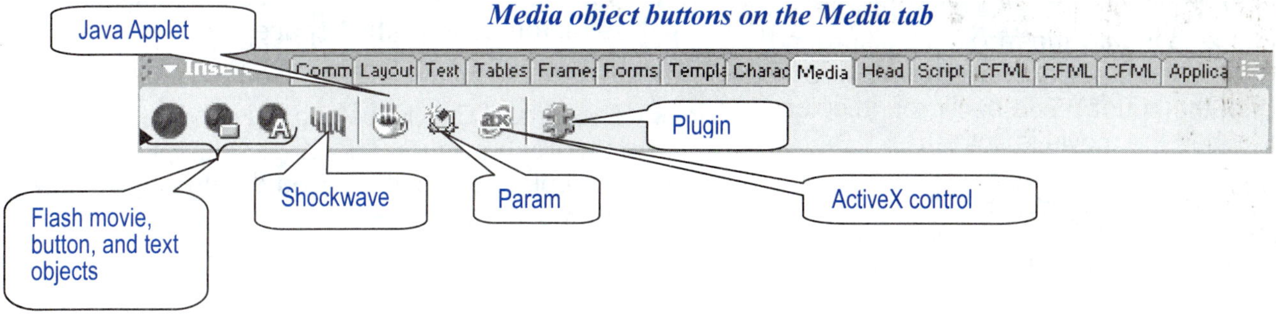

Flash file placeholder

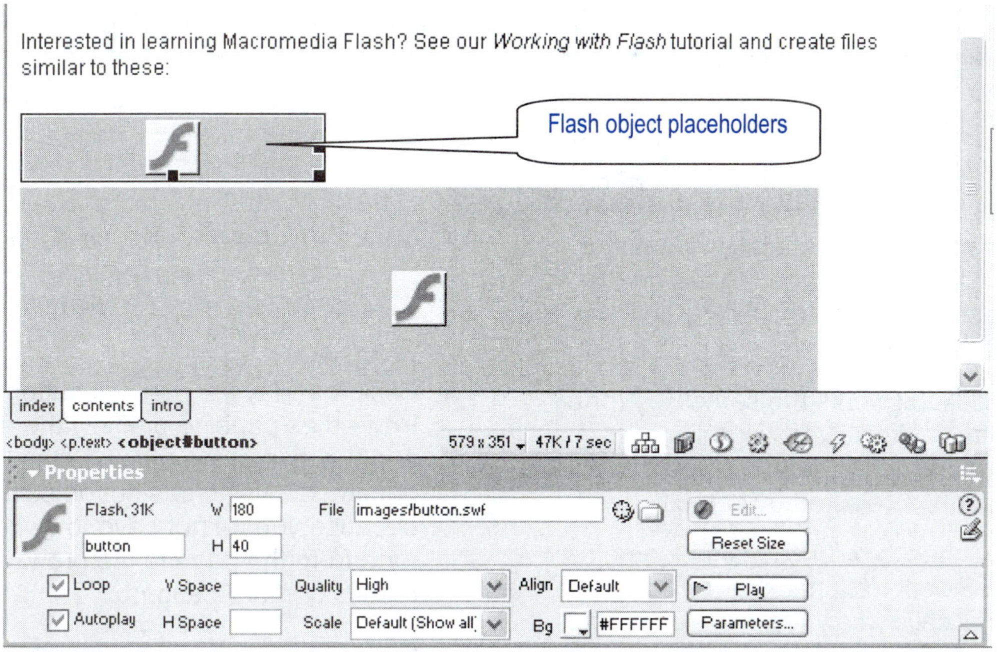

- The size of the placeholder is determined by the original size of the multimedia object. You can change the object's size using sizing handles or the Properties panel.
- Dreamweaver displays a gray placeholder labeled to identify the media file type. For miscellaneous kinds of plugins, a gray puzzle piece is displayed. More information, specific to the media object or plugin, is also available in its Properties panel.

Modify and Play Movie

- You can use the Flash or Shockwave Properties panel to modify the appearance and performance of the movie in the Web document. Dreamweaver also includes a Play button ([Play]) on the Properties panel to allow you to play a movie without previewing the page in a browser—and stop it, too.
- The Properties panel displays by default several properties that will look familiar to you from other graphic objects (see the illustration of the expanded Properties panel for a Flash movie on the next page).
- Use the Name text box to identify the movie for scripting purposes. Specify an exact size for the movie in pixels using the W and H text boxes. You can click the [Reset Size] button after making a sizing change to restore the object to its original size.
- The File text box shows the path to the movie file. You can enter a path in this box, point to the file in the Site or Asset panel, or click the Browse for File icon to navigate to a file.
- Use the Align options to determine how the movie is aligned in the Web document. You have the same options as for any other image.

- Use the Bg button to display a color palette you can use to modify the movie's background color (or type the hexadecimal equivalent to the right of the button). The background color appears when the movie is active.
- If you have inserted a Flash button or Flash text object, the Edit  button will be active so that you can edit the object file.
- Use the V Space and H Space text boxes to set an amount of white space in pixels above, below, and on both sides of the movie.
- The default Quality setting of High is adequate for most browsers. The other settings (for example, Low) can be used depending on how the movie was made.

Dreamweaver Flash movie properties

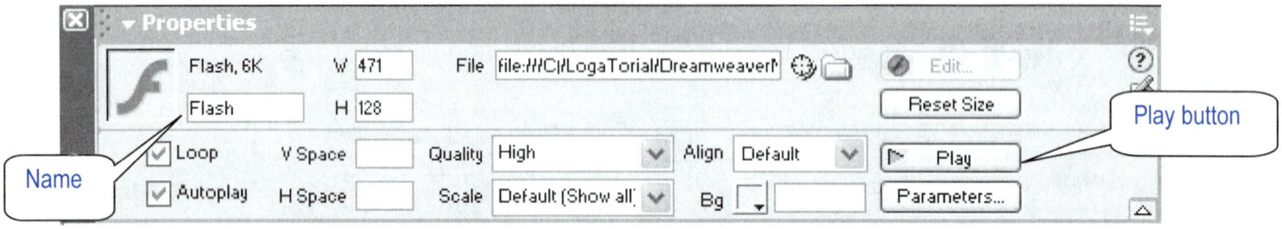

- The Scale property sets the scale parameter for the object and embed tags. This is an advanced setting also determined by how the movie is created in Flash.
- The Loop checkbox works the same way for a movie as for a timeline. Selecting this checkbox causes the movie to play over and over. This option is selected by default.
- The Autoplay checkbox functions the same as in a timeline. Select this checkbox to play the movie automatically when the page loads. This option is selected by default.
- If you prefer to control the movie using a behavior, deselect this checkbox. Make sure the movie is named and then use the Control Shockwave or Flash behavior to set up controls for the movie (see illustration below).

Control a movie using a behavior

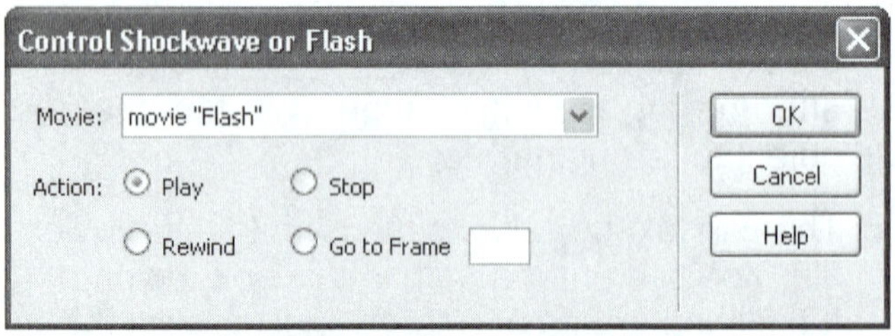

- Click the Parameters button to launch a dialog box that allows you to enter additional movie parameters. These advanced settings are beyond the scope of this book, but you can consult Dreamweaver Help for more information.

Note: *The param button on the Media tab inserts a <param> tag using the Tag Editor dialog box. It is used for applying parameters in code view.*

- Click the Play  button in the Properties panel to preview the appearance and function of the plugin in the Web document. Using this button saves time because you do not have to switch back and forth from the page to the browser to see results of modifications.
- Click the Stop  button to turn off the movie. You must click this button even after the movie stops playing to restore the gray placeholder and make further modifications.

Insert Flash Buttons and Flash Text

- Dreamweaver includes two features that can add visual interest as well as functionality to Web pages: Flash buttons and Flash text. When you use these features, you create your own Flash objects without having to leave Dreamweaver.

Insert Flash Button

- Dreamweaver includes a set of predesigned Flash buttons that you can customize and insert on your Web pages. These buttons (see illustration below) are not only graphically interesting but functional ways to navigate a site.

Flash button on a Web page

- Flash buttons have additional appeal because of their interactive effects. When the mouse pointer is over a Flash button, most buttons changes their appearance. Each type of button has its own special effects, such as a color change or a moving part.
- To insert a Flash button, use the Insert>Interactive Images>Flash button command on the menu bar, or click the Insert Flash Button  button on the Media tab of the Insert bar. Dreamweaver opens the Insert Flash Button dialog box shown at the top of the next page.
- Choose a button style from the Style list, which offers over 40 different Flash buttons. (Some buttons have the same appearance except for color.) You can then type the text that will appear on the button and choose the font and size for the text.

Tip: *The buttons can only fit so much text—typically only a few words. Keep your labels short—and sweet!*

Insert Flash Button dialog box

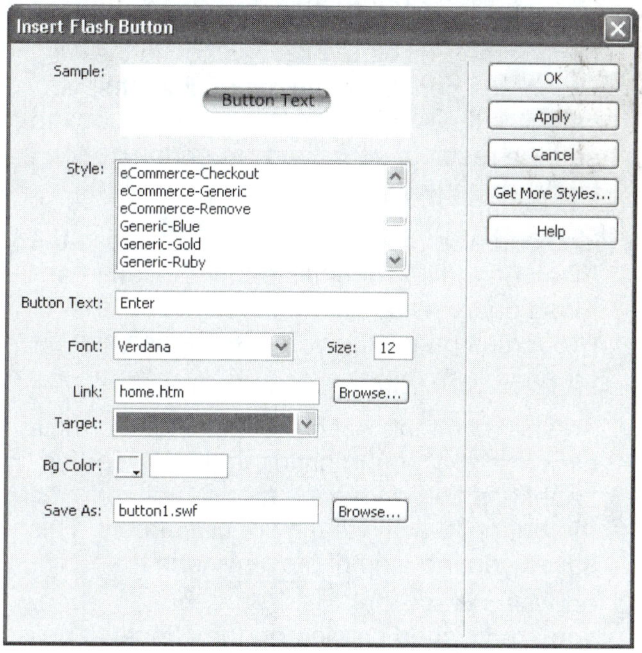

- Dreamweaver suggests a font and size for each button style. If your system does not have the default font for a particular button, Dreamweaver displays a message at the bottom of the dialog box to let you know you do not have the font. You can then choose a different font from the Font list.
- You can also change the Font and size as desired even if your system has the default font. Choose a new font from the Font list and type a new size in the Size box.

Note: *The Sample button in the dialog box will not change as you make changes in the dialog box.*

- Flash buttons are designed to work like links, so you can type in the Link box or browse to locate the page that will open when the button is clicked. You can also specify a target for the linked page.
- If you want to surround the button with a background color other than the default white, use the Bg box to choose a new color. The background color displays as a rectangle of color behind the Flash button.
- Dreamweaver suggests a default file name for the Flash button. You can change the default name in the Save As text box if desired.

- To modify a Flash button, double-click it to open the Insert Flash Button dialog box again or click the Edit button in the Properties panel. As you make changes, you can click the Apply button in the dialog box to see the result of your changes on the button on the Web page.
- You can also make some modifications in the Flash button's Properties panel. Because a Flash button is actually a Flash movie, the Properties panel shows the same settings as for any Flash movie.
- To see a button's special effects, for example, click the Play button in the Properties panel and then move the mouse pointer over the button to activate the special effects. This saves you the step of previewing in the browser. Press the Stop button when you are finished previewing the effects to be able to make further modifications to the button's properties.

Insert Flash Text

- Dreamweaver's Flash text feature allows you to create a short Flash movie that consists of text only. As for a Flash button, you can use this text as a link to another page or Web site, or you can use it simply to create a special text effect on a page.
- Flash text changes color when the mouse pointer rests on it. This effect occurs whether or not the text is linked to another page. Such an effect is called a *rollover* effect, because it occurs when the mouse "rolls over" the object.

  Tip: *Use the Insert>Interactive Images>Rollover Image menu command when using two image files.*

- To create a Flash text movie, use the Insert>Interactive Images>Flash Text command on the menu bar, or click the Flash Text button on the Media tab of the Insert bar. Dreamweaver opens the Insert Flash Text dialog box shown at the top of the next page.
- Choose a font, font size, font style, and alignment for the Flash text object. Use the Color box to select the initial color for the text in the object and the Rollover Color box to choose the color that displays when the mouse pointer rests on the object.
- Type the Flash text itself in the Text box. As you can see by the dimensions of this box, you can create a word, phrase, or entire paragraph if desired. Note that the Text box does not have a wrap feature. If you want text in a paragraph to wrap, you must press the Enter key to start new lines.

Insert Flash Text dialog box

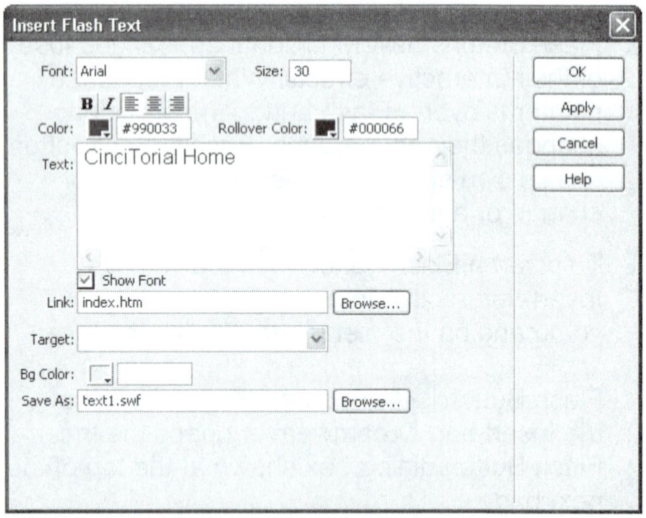

- With the Show Font checkbox selected, text in the Text box displays in the font you have chosen. Using this feature can help you judge how your Flash text will look on the page.
- As for a Flash button, you can create a link for the Flash text to open, specify a target, and select a background color. You can also save the Flash text object with a file name other than the default shown in the Save As text box.
- Double-click a Flash text object to make further changes in the Insert Flash Text dialog box—or click the Edit button in the Properties panel. As for a Flash button, you can use the Apply button to see how your changes look on the page and the Properties panel to "play" the movie.
- Roll the mouse over the text to see the color change take effect after clicking the Play button, and click Stop when you have finished.

Other Multimedia Plugins

- You can use the same techniques used to insert Shockwave and Flash movies to insert other plugin types from the menu bar or the Media tab of the Insert bar by clicking the appropriate button.

  Note: *In Dreamweaver, some plugins appear in the Special category of the Media tab of the Insert bar.*

- Use the Applet button on the Media tab of the Insert bar to insert **Java** applets. An **applet** is a small application that can be embedded in a Web page.
- For example, an applet can be used to insert Web site counters that tabulate the number of "hits" or visits your site receives, visual effects, games, Web site tools, and so on.
- Use the ActiveX button to insert **ActiveX** components. Formerly known as OLE controls, ActiveX components function like browser plugins to perform specific tasks. They are typically used for buttons, forms, and the like.
- ActiveX components run only in Windows-based Internet Explorer. They will not work in a Macintosh environment or in Netscape browsers.
- If you need to insert a file that requires a Netscape plugin to play properly, use the Plugin button.
- All of these objects are created in other programs—some of which require programming skills—and are beyond the scope of this course. Your instructor can, however, provide you with, or help you locate, files that you can use.

  Tip: *You can also use a Web browser search engine and type in keywords such as "free Java applets," "free ActiveX controls," and so on to obtain such files to insert in your Web pages.*

Procedures

Insert Flash or Shockwave Movie

Ctrl + Alt + F, Ctrl + Alt + D

1. Position insertion point where movie should appear on page.
2. Click **Insert** .... Alt + I
3. Click **Media** .... M, M, →
4. Click **Flash** .... F
   or **Shockwave** .... S

OR

- Click (**Flash**) or (**Shockwave**) button on the Media tab of Insert bar.

5. Navigate to file location in Select File dialog box.
6. Click media file and click OK.
7. Store file in current Web site when prompted.

   ✓ *You can use these steps to insert any media plugin—Java applet, ActiveX, Netscape plugin—on the Media tab of the Insert bar.*

Play Movie

1. Click movie to select placeholder, if necessary.
2. Click Play in expanded Properties panel to play movie in Web page.
3. Click Stop in expanded Properties panel to stop playing movie.

Modify Movie

1. Click movie to select placeholder, if necessary.
2. Change properties as follows:
   - Type name for movie in Name text box.
   - Set exact width and height in **W** and **H** text boxes.
   - Specify or locate media file in **File** text box.
   - Set vertical alignment for movie in **Align** list box.
   - Change background color using **Bg** button (or type hexadecimal value).
   - Set space above and below and on each side of movie using **V Space** and **H Space** text boxes.
   - Set quality in **Quality** list box.
   - Specify continuous play by selecting **Loop** checkbox.
   - Set the movie to play when the page loads by selecting the **Autoplay** checkbox.

Insert Flash Button

1. Click **Insert** .... Alt + I
2. Click **Interactive Images** .... N
3. Click **Flash Button** .... →, F

OR

- Click (**Flash Button** button) on Media tab of the Insert bar.

4. Customize the button:
   - Choose a button style.
   - Enter text to label button.
   - Select new font and size if desired.
   - Type or browse to page to link to button.
   - Specify target if necessary.
   - Select background color for button.
   - Save button with default or other file name.
5. Click OK.

Insert Flash Text

1. Click **Insert** .... Alt + I
2. Click **Interactive Images** ... N
3. Click **Flash Text** .... →, L

OR

- Click (**Flash Text** button) on Media tab of the Insert bar.

4. Create Flash text:
   - Choose a font and size.
   - Choose font style and alignment, if desired.
   - Choose color for initial text and rollover color.
   - Type text for object.
   - Type or browse to page to link to text.
   - Specify target if necessary.
   - Select background color for text.
   - Save text with default or other file name.
5. Click OK.

Modify Flash Button or Flash Text

1. Double-click Flash button or Flash text.

OR

- Click the Flash button or Flash text.
- Click the Edit Edit... button in the Properties panel.

2. Change properties in the dialog box and click OK.
3. Change other properties in the Properties panel.

Exercise Directions

1. Start Dreamweaver.
2. Open the **tutorials** site.
3. Open **contents.htm** and place the Insertion point on the last blank paragraph. There should be a blank line between the new paragraph you will create in step 4 and the bottom of the table (see Illustration A).
4. Format the paragraph with the **text** style and type the following text:

   Interested in learning Macromedia Flash? See our *Working with Flash* tutorial and create files similar to these:
5. Insert the **button.swf** Flash file from the Data folder below the new paragraph. Save the file in your images folder.
6. Name the object **button** in the Properties panel and make sure the **Loop** and **Autoplay** checkboxes are selected.
7. Change the size of the button to 180 pixels wide and 40 pixels high.
8. Click [Play] to play the button movie. Click **Play** on the button to hear the music and **Stop** when you have finished listening.
9. Note that the button is surrounded by a light-blue background. Click [Stop] to stop the movie and display the placeholder again.
10. Change the background color of the movie to white (#FFFFFF).
11. Play the movie again to see the new background color.
12. Insert three nonbreaking spaces to the right of the button movie placeholder.

    ✓ *Use the Character tab of the Insert bar to quickly insert nonbreaking spaces—or press Ctrl+Shift+Space.*
13. Insert the **flash.swf** Flash file from the Data folder to the right of the button, with the three nonbreaking spaces between the two media inserts. Save the **flash.swf** file in your images folder.

    ✓ *Increase the Document window size if desired by collapsing unneeded group panels.*
14. Name the object **flash** in the Properties panel.
15. Change the Alignment to **Top** and deselect the **Loop** and **Autoplay** checkboxes.
16. Attach the **Control Shockwave or Flash** behavior to the entire page and select the **flash** movie to control. Set the behavior to play the movie onLoad.

    ✓ *Note that these instructions give the same result as autoplaying the movie but allow you to see how movies can be controlled using behaviors.*
17. Save the changes and preview the page in the browser to see the **flash** movie play once as the page is loaded. The bottom of your page should look similar to Illustration A after the movie plays.

    ✓ *Your **flash** movie may display below the **button** object, depending on the width of your browser window.*
18. Open **intro.htm**.
19. In the last layer on the page, which contains the link *Click here to enter CinciTutorial*, delete the link and leave the insertion point in the layer.
20. Insert a Flash button in the layer and customize it as follows:
    - Choose the **Glass-Turquoise** style.
    - Type the button text **Enter CinciTorial**.
    - Change the font to **Arial** and the size to **12** if necessary.
    - Type the link **index.htm**.
    - Save the button as **enter.swf**.
21. Close the dialog box and use the Properties panel to name the button **enter**.
22. "Play" the button: rest the mouse pointer over the button to see its color change.
23. The button's label is too long. Modify the button so that its label reads only **Enter**. Change the size of the label to **14**.
24. Click to the right of the Flash button and press the **Enter** key to create a new paragraph in the layer.

25. Insert a Flash text movie and modify the properties as follows:
    - Change the font to **Arial** and the size to **24**.
    - Change the Color setting to **#990033** and the Rollover Color setting to **#000066**.
    - Type the following text in the Text box: **CinciTorial Home**.
    - Type a link to the **index.htm** page in your cincitorial folder on your hard drive.

      ✓ *Be sure to type the link. You cannot browse to this location and have the text link correctly.*
    - Save the Flash text movie as **homelink.swf**.
26. In the Properties panel, name the link **homelink.**
27. Preview the page in the browser. It should look similar to Illustration B.
28. Test the link to the CinciTorial site to make sure you entered the link properly.
29. If necessary, modify the Flash text object to correct the link.
30. Close the browser.
31. Close any open pages.
32. Exit Dreamweaver.

Illustration A

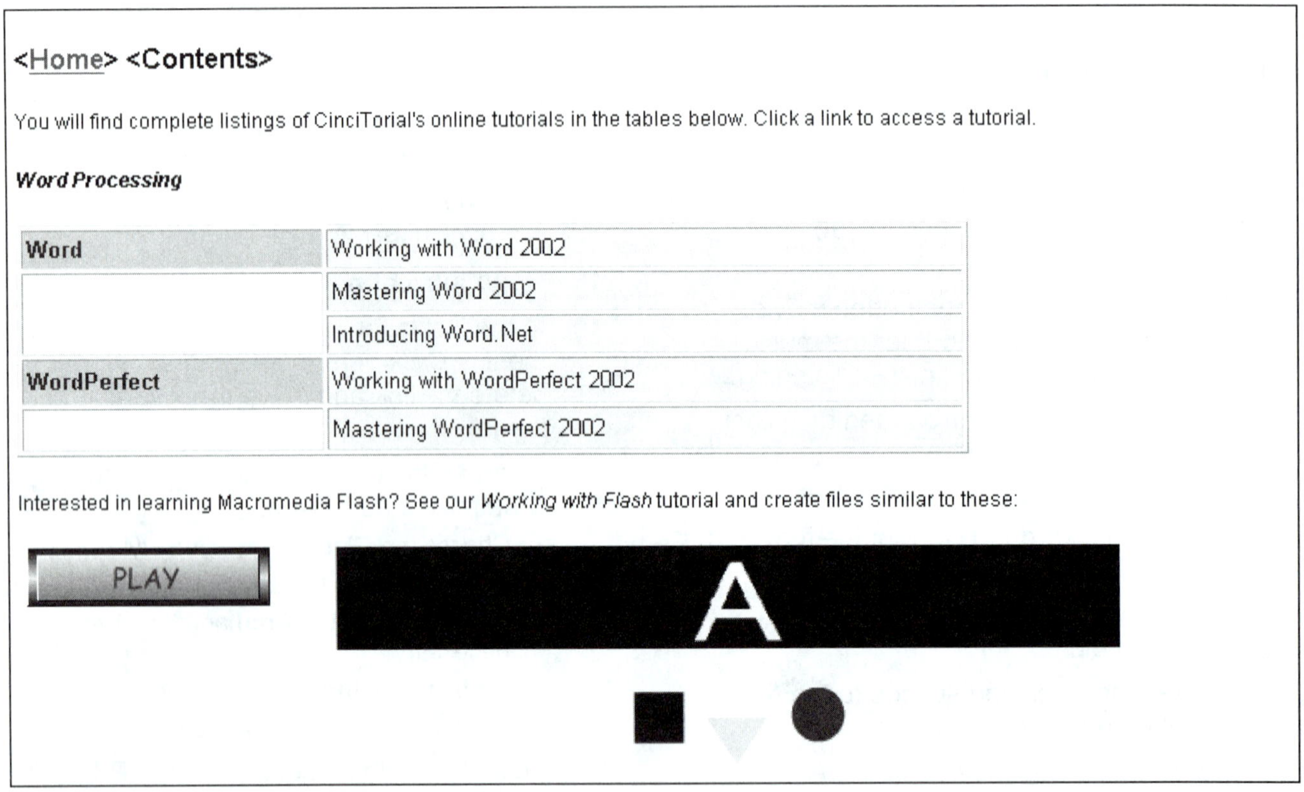

<Home> <Contents>

You will find complete listings of CinciTorial's online tutorials in the tables below. Click a link to access a tutorial.

Word Processing

Word	Working with Word 2002
	Mastering Word 2002
	Introducing Word.Net
WordPerfect	Working with WordPerfect 2002
	Mastering WordPerfect 2002

Interested in learning Macromedia Flash? See our *Working with Flash* tutorial and create files similar to these:

Illustration B

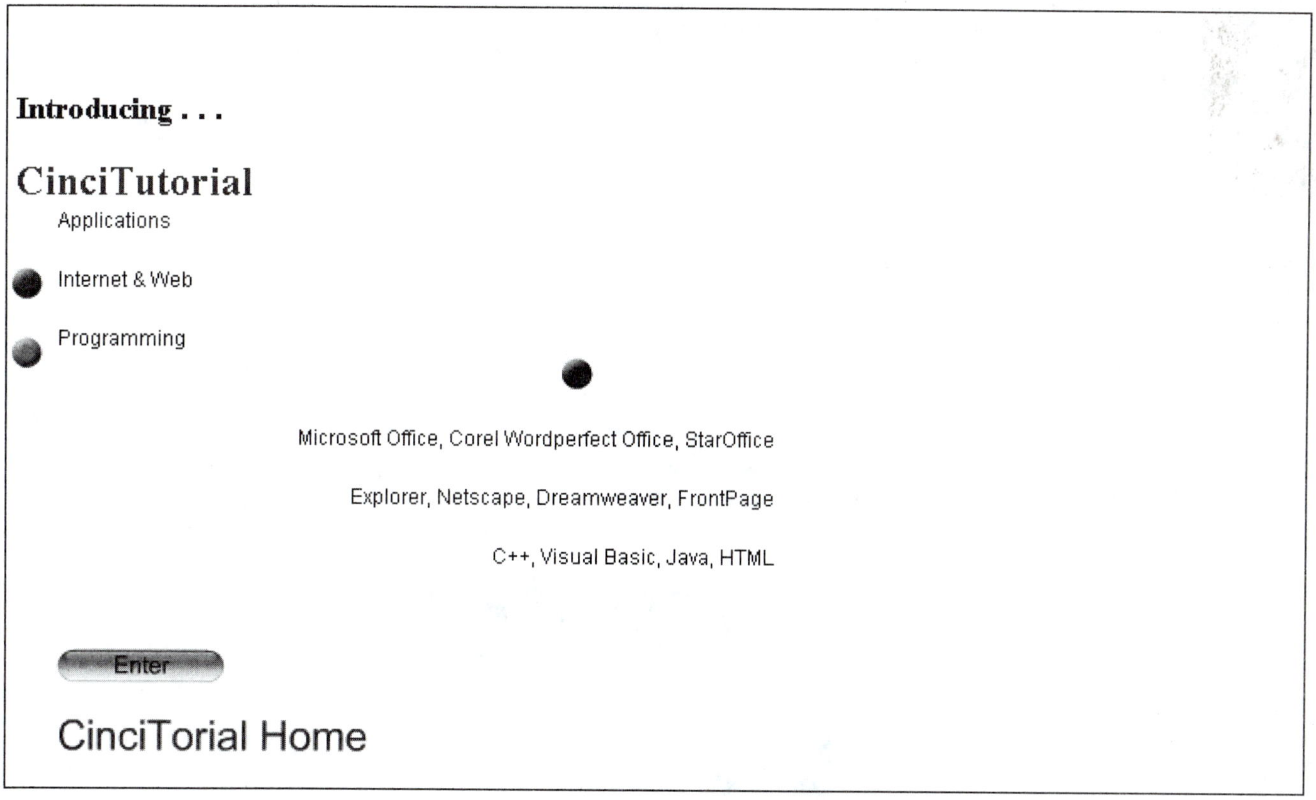

Next Chapter

Chapter

17

Managing and Publishing a Web Site

After creating your Web site, you can use Dreamweaver tools and features to manage the site and publish it to a server. Dreamweaver allows you to target specific browsers, check and modify links, and keep track of files by checking them in and out. You can put files on an FTP or local server to make them available to visitors. You can also manage your assets and view reports.

In this chapter, you'll learn how to:

- Manage assets
- Target specific browsers
- Check and modify links
- Run reports
- Validate Web pages
- Publish a Web site
- Check files in and out
- Copy files from a remote server

Manage Assets

- You have already been introduced to some of the features of the **Assets panel** in Chapters 6 and 7. As you have learned, the assets panel gives you a quick way to review and use a Web site's *assets*, such as images you have saved or colors you have used.
- To display the Assets panel, use the Window>Assets command on the menu bar, or click the Assets [Assets] tab of the Files panel group.
- Click a category button—Images, Colors, and so on—in the categories on the left side of the Assets panel to see assets of that type listed in the bottom pane of the panel. Further information about or a representation of the asset may be displayed in the top pane when you click an asset listed in the bottom pane.
- The Assets panel collects and displays the following items:
    - Images ( ) stored in the site.
    - Colors ( ) used in the site.
    - External URLs ( ) that pages in the site link to.
    - Flash ( ) and Shockwave ( ) movie files present in the site.
    - Other movie files (such as QuickTime or MPEG movies) used in the site ( ).
    - Scripts ( ) used in the site.
    - Templates ( ) present in the site.
    - Library items ( ) stored in the site.
- The Assets panel makes it easy to insert objects and format pages throughout a site. To insert an image, for example, that you have already saved in the site, simply position the insertion point, click the image file in the Assets panel, and click the [Insert] button on the Assets panel.
- By default, the Assets panel displays objects for the current site (the Site option is selected just below the Assets tab at the top of the panel). However, you also can add assets to a Favorites list to make it easy to locate specific assets.

Note: *The Site and Favorites options are not available in Templates and Library categories.*

- Click the asset you want to make a favorite and then click the Add to Favorites button on the Assets panel. To view your favorites, select the Favorites option at the top of the Assets panel. You can right-click any item in the Assets panel to access a shortcut menu with commands that allow you to add the item to the Favorites panel, edit the item, or insert it in a document.
- If desired you can create folders within the Favorites list to store items that you want to group. With Favorites displayed, click the New Favorites Folder button and name the new folder. You can then drag assets into the folder to store them.

Select Target Browsers

- As you create your Web sites in Dreamweaver, you have some options for tailoring content to specific browsers. The Behaviors palette, for example, allows you to select behaviors that will perform correctly in a target browser version.
- At any time during the process of creating a Web site, you can use the File>Check Page>Check Target Browsers command on the menu bar to test your content for compatibility with a specified browser. Checking compatibility both during and at the end of the site-creation process prevents you from designing pages that cannot be viewed in browsers you wish to support.

Caution: *Many dynamic features such as behaviors and movies require browser versions later than 4.0. Keep this in mind when designing pages.*

- To check a page in one of the target browsers, open the page to check, then issue the File>Check Page>Check Target Browsers command on the menu bar.
- Select a target browser in the Check Target Browsers dialog box (see illustration on next page) and click the Check button.

Choose target browser to check

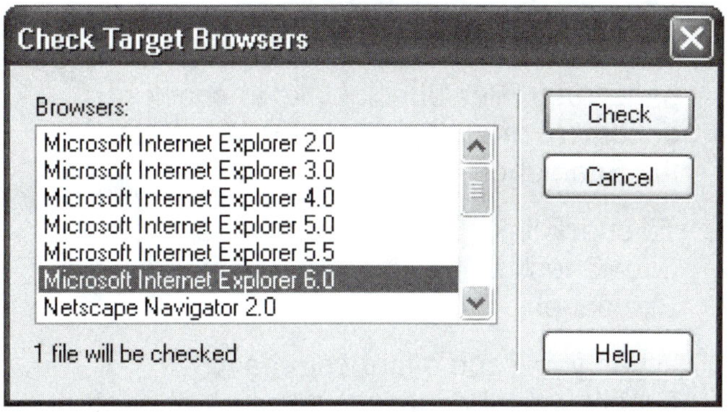

- Dreamweaver checks the page and displays a report in the Target Browser Check panel of the Results panel group. In the example shown in the following illustration, the results for a page containing layers checked against Netscape Navigator 2.0 show that this page cannot be viewed properly in an older browser.

Results of browser check

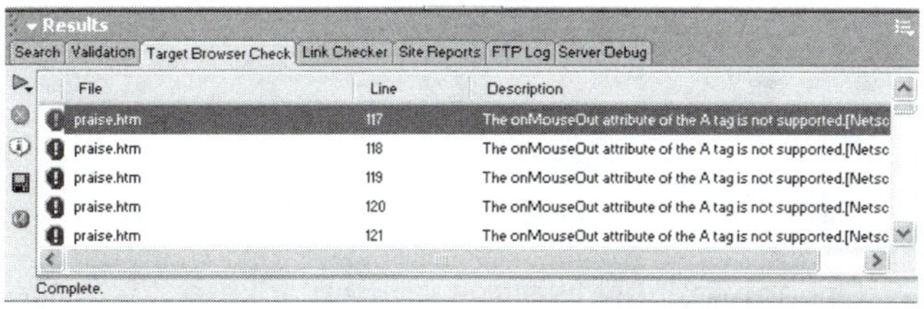

- The report pane in the Target Browser Check panel warns you about the file and the line of code that is not supported by the target browser. There is also a description of the problem. This makes it easy for you to determine if any corrective action is needed.
- To see—and edit—a problem in code view, right-click on the problem listed in report pane of the Target Browser Check panel—or double-click on the problem. The line of code that has caused a problem to be reported will be shown in Code and Design Views with the code selected—and the problem page opened if necessary.
- To check an entire site—or one or more files or folders—have the desired site, file(s), or folders selected in the Site panel. Then open the Target Browser Check panel by using the Window>Results> Target Browser Check command on the menu bar.

Note: *Checking a target browser cannot be performed with the Site panel in its expanded—or window—form.*

- Click the Check Target Browsers button in the Check Target Browser panel toolbar. Then, from drop-down menu, select Check Target Browsers for Entire Site or Check Target Browsers For Selected Files/Folders in Site.

Tip: *Right-click anywhere in the Target Browser Check panel's report pane to select the same menu commands—including checking a single file.*

- As with checking a single file, select a target browser in the Check Target Browsers dialog box, and click the Check button to generate a list of results in the Target Browser Check panel.
- The Target Browser Check panel toolbar also has buttons for you to manage your results report.
- In some cases, you may need to stop browser check before it is completed. To do this, click the Stop Report button.
- If the Description column is too narrow to read information about a problem line of code, select the problem line in the Target Browser Check panel and then click the More Information button to read the description of the problem in a dialog box.
- Because the report you see in the Target Browser Check panel is a temporary file, you may want to save it for you or others to reference in the future. Click the Save Report button to save an .XML text file of the report in your Web site folder.
- An HTML document of the report can be created by clicking the Browse Report button. The report opens in your Web browser (see illustration on next page) and it provides the same information that the Test Target Browser panel provides in an easy to use and read format that you can also print.

Target Browser Check Results report in Web browser document

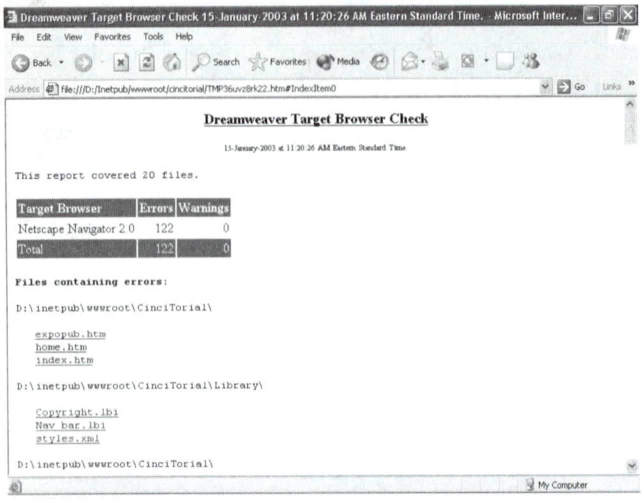

- To clear the report in the Target Browser Check panel, right-click anywhere in its report pane and select Clear Report.
- In the expanded Site panel window, you can also right-click a file in the Site Map and choose Check Target Browsers.
- If you plan to support more than one browser or several browser versions for your Web site, you will need to perform this task multiple times.

Check and Modify Links

- As pages are added to and removed from Web sites, it is all too easy to forget to update or remove links. Maintaining and fine-tuning your Web site's navigation structure are important parts of Web site upkeep.
- Clicking each link on a number of pages to check its source can take a considerable amount of time. Instead, use Dreamweaver commands to speed the process.

Check Links

- Dreamweaver gives you a great deal of flexibility when checking links in a Web site. You can check links from either the Document window or the Site panel—either in its collapsed or expanded form—using commands on either File menu.
- To check links in the current document only, use the File>Check Page>Check Links menu command in the Document window. In the Site panel, use File>Check Links to check a document or multiple documents selected in the Site panel.
- To check links throughout the site, use the Site>Check Links Sitewide command in the Site panel.
- When you issue either command, Dreamweaver examines the current open document or Web site and lists any link problems in the Link Checker panel of the Results panel group, which can be opened to check links on one page or sitewide by using the Window>Results>Link Checker menu command (see illustration below).

Link Checker panel displays link problems

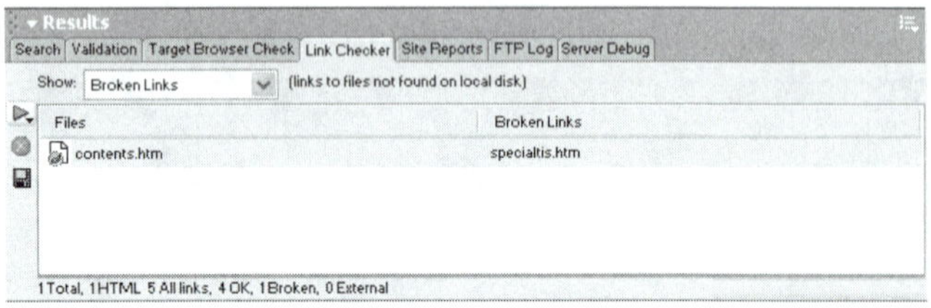

- Dreamweaver displays broken links by default in the Link Checker panel, but you can click the Show list arrow to see lists of external links (links outside the site that Dreamweaver cannot check) and orphaned files (files that are not linked to other files).

  Note: *Don't be alarmed if the Link Checker shows a number of orphaned files. Files such as style sheets and temporary browser files are included in this list.*

- The Link Checker panel features a toolbar from which you can click the Check Link button and from the drop-down menu select Check Links In This Document, Check Links For Entire Site, or Check Target Browsers For Selected Files/Folders in Site.
- In some cases, you may need to stop the Link Checker before it is completed. To do this, click the Stop Report button.

- Because the report you see in the Link Checker panel is a temporary file, you may want to save it for you or others to reference. Click the Save Report button to save a .TXT text file of the report in your Web site folder.
- In the expanded Site panel window, you can also right-click a file in either the Site Map or Local Files pane and choose Check Links. The submenu allows you to check Selected Files/Folders or the Entire Site.

Repair Links

- Identifying link problems is just the first step to maintaining links. After you have identified problems, you have a number of options for fixing links.
- To repair a link identified as a problem in the Link Checker, click the file name to select it and then click on the link in the Broken Link column to select it. Dreamweaver highlights the link and also displays a browse folder icon (see illustration below).

Repair a link in the Link Checker

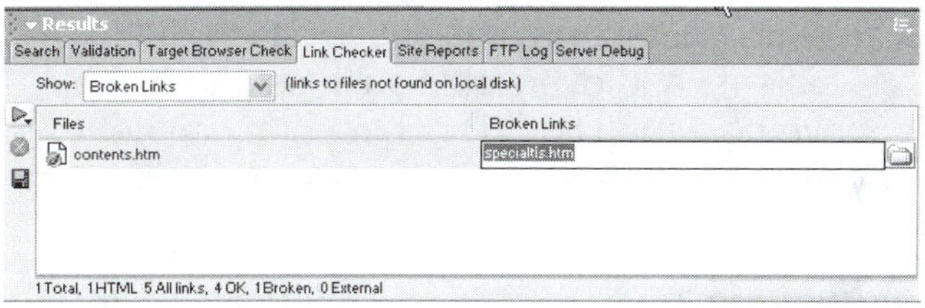

- You can either type the correct file name for the link, or click the folder and navigate to the correct file in the Select File dialog box. When you click OK, you will be prompted to fix any other instances of the same broken link, which Dreamweaver does automatically.
- If your site contains a number of links to a specific file that you want to change to another file, you can use the Change Link Sitewide command in the expanded or collapsed Site panel to substitute one link for another throughout the site.
- Select the file in the Local Files pane and then issue the Site>Change Link Sitewide command in the Site panel's menu bar. Dreamweaver displays the Change Link Sitewide dialog box displaying the selected file name. Simply type a forward slash (/) and the name of the file to link to instead (see illustration below).

Change a link sitewide

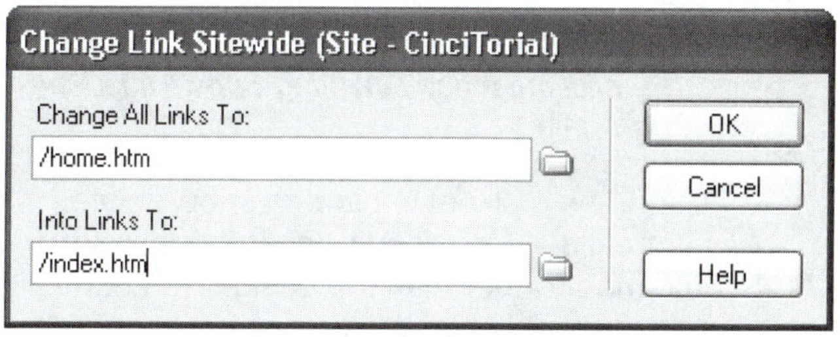

Modify Links in Site Map Pane

- The Site Map in the expanded Site panel window gives you a number of other ways to view and modify links. You can select a page in the Site Map and modify its links using commands on the Site panel menu (or right-click the page and select commands from the shortcut menu).
  - Link to New File allows you to insert a link to a new Web document. This allows you to create the document and the link to it at the same time. You supply a file name and page title along with the text of the link.
  - Link to Existing File launches the Select HTML File dialog box in which an existing file can be linked to the selected Web document.
  - Change Link also launches the Select HTML File dialog box in which a new file can be selected to replace a link. When you change a link, you may be prompted to update other links in the site that are affected by the change.
  - Remove Link removes a link and also launches a dialog box that gives you the option of updating links throughout the site that might be affected by the modification.
  - Open to Source of Link opens the source file of the link in the Document window with the link text selected for editing.

- Two additional commands help you control the display of linked pages in the Site Map:
  - Use Show/Hide Link to view a portion of the Site Map. You can, for example, hide e-mail links or dependent files by choosing this command to hide them. To display a hidden file again, use the View>Show Files Marked as Hidden menu command.

    Tip: *The file name of a hidden file is italicized. Unmark a hidden file by right-clicking it and selecting Show/Hide Link again.*

  - Use View as Root to place a subordinate —or child—Web document at the top of the site map, rather than the designated home page. This allows you to concentrate on links to and from a specific page.

Note: *The Site Navigation field above the site map displays the original path from the home page to the page chosen to view as the root. Click once on the home page in the Site Navigation field to return the site map to the original layout.*

Run Dreamweaver Reports

- Dreamweaver's Site>Reports command in either the Document window or Site panel menu bar displays the Reports dialog box (see illustration below). From this dialog box, you can run a number of workflow and HTML reports to check your site before publishing it.

Reports dialog box

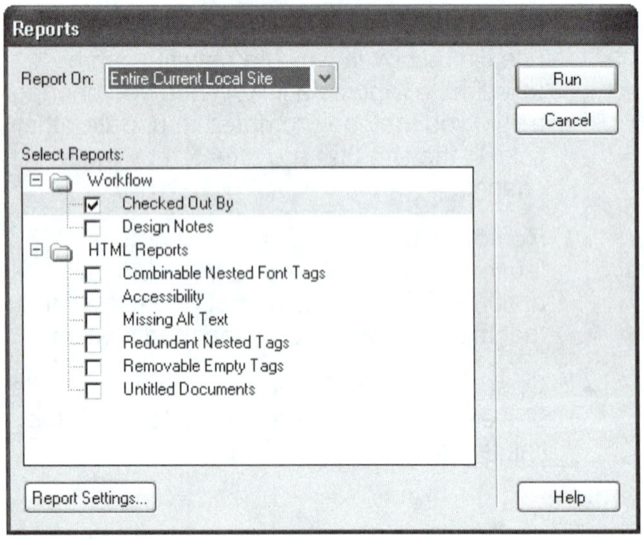

- To run a report, first choose what you want to report on by clicking the Report On drop-down list. You can run a report on the current document, the entire current site, selected files, or a folder. Then select the checkbox of the report you want to run and click the Run button.

Tip: *Click the Reports button in the Site Report panel to open the Reports dialog box. You can then select other reports to run.*

- Use the Workflow reports to show what pages a team member has checked out and to find information stored in Design Notes. These reports allow you to specify further settings by clicking the Report Settings button.
- For example, to find out what files a team member has checked out, click the Report Settings button and type the team member's name in the Checked Out By dialog box. When you run the report, Dreamweaver displays a list of all files checked out by the team member you specified.

Note: *You will learn more about checking files in and out later in this chapter.*

- The HTML reports help you locate HTML code problems and oversights such as pages that have no page titles. These reports can help you to locate errors in code you import from other sources.

Note: *Several of the HTML reports search for the same kinds of code problems identified in the Clean Up HTML dialog box.*

- The Accessibility report is a new feature in Dreamweaver MX that reports on problems that might affect your Web pages when people access them using text-only browsers and browsers designed for the hearing or visually challenged.
- When you run an Accessibility report, it opens the Site Report panel in the Results panel group. One of the primary issues it will alert you to is how images, colors, and sounds and other multimedia files will be interpreted by text-only browsers—including the browsers used in cell phones and PDAs—or browsers that actually "read" the content text to a visually challenged person.

- Running an Accessibility report will also analyze your text and warn you if sentences are not in natural English or have other issues that might be a disservice to the physically—and cognitively—challenged.
- By selecting a file in the report pane and clicking the More Info button, the Reference panel will open with a discussion of the issues that might occur and suggested ways to fix it. For example, if the information you convey depends on an image file, you will want to add a text description in the Alt text box of the Properties panel.
- You can run reports one at a time to isolate results, or you can select all reports and click Run to check all categories. Dreamweaver displays the report results in a Results dialog box (see illustration below).

Results of Accessibility report

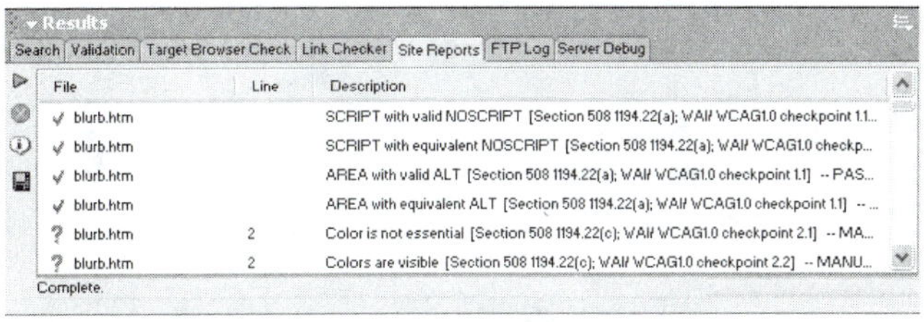

- To open a page identified in a report, right-click its file name in the File column and then click the Open File.
- As in other Results group panels, you can stop running a report by clicking the Stop Report button. Click the Save Report button to save an .XML text file of the report in your Web site folder.

Validating Web Pages

- Use Dreamweaver's Validator feature to locate tag and syntax errors in your code.
- Validator is used much like the other report tools in the Results panel group. You can check one Web page, selected pages or files, or an entire Web site.
- To check the page that is in the Document window, use File>Check Page>Validate Markup on the menu bar.

Note: *If you are validating an .XML page, you use the Validate As XML command.*

- The report that is created appears in the report pane of the Validation panel of the Results panel group. As with checking links and target browsers, the Validation panel has a button on its toolbar that allows you to validate single Web pages, selected pages and folders, and the entire site.
- There are also buttons to stop running a report ( ), to read more information, to save the report ( ), and to open the report in your browser ( ).
- Using Dreamweaver's Validator feature can report errors and warnings that may not require immediate editing or correction. When a problem occurs after you publish your Web site to a remote server, the Validator may provide you with the information that you, your Web server administrator, or your ISP may need to to repair your Web so that it looks and functions as expected.
- Before you use the Validator, you must use Edit>Preferences menu command and click the Validator category in the Preferences dialog box. The default setting for Dreamweaver is to validate against HTML version 4.0 and Internet Explorer 3.0 extensions. You can select and deselect other codes and browsers to validate against.

Tip: *See Appendix A: Dreamweaver Preferences to learn more about setting up preferences.*

- The Options button opens the Validator Option dialog box, in which the different levels of warnings and error messages can be deselected—or selected.
- It is beyond the scope of this book to cover this advanced trouble-shooting feature in length. In many instances, the reports that the Validator creates will alert you more often to possible or potential problems rather than anything that you will notice in your site whether locally or published on a remote Web server and accessed by most version 4 or later browsers.

Publish a Web Site on a Server

- **Publishing** is the process of copying Web site files from a local computer to the server that *hosts* the site and where visitors can access it. The server to which you copy, publish, or "put" files can be an **FTP** (file transfer protocol) server, a **Local/Network** server that can be on your computer, on your network, or a WebDAV **HTTP** server on the Internet.
- Dreamweaver also makes it easy for you to publish your Web site on a remote RDS (Remote Development Services) and SourceSafe servers. It is beyond the scope of this book to discuss how to configure a connection to these specialized servers. Consult Dreamweaver Help and your Web server administrator or ISP for more information.
- When you created your site as described in Chapter 2, you had the option of selecting and configuring your remote server using the Site Definition wizard. In the following section, you will learn how to publish your Web using the Site Definition dialog box on either an FTP, WebDav, or a local network server—three of the most common ways to publish a Web site so that it can be accessed on the Internet or on an intranet.

Associating an FTP Server with a Web Site

- Use the Remote Info category on the Advanced tab of the Site Definition dialog box to enter the appropriate settings to publish on an FTP server. You specify the same settings whether you create a site using the Site Definition Wizard or create the site using the Site Definition dialog box's Advanced tab, so the procedure discussed here can be used when you first set up your site—or if you need to edit an existing site to specify settings.
- Use the Site>Edit Sites menu command to open the Edit Sites dialog box and select the desired Web site. Then click the Edit button.
- Select the Advanced tab's Remote Info category in the Site Definition dialog box and choose FTP on the Access list. You must then supply the following information:
  - Enter the FTP server's address in the FTP Host text box. The illustration below shows the proper syntax. You do not need to enter "ftp://" before the address because it is already incorporated.

Set up FTP connection in Dreamweaver

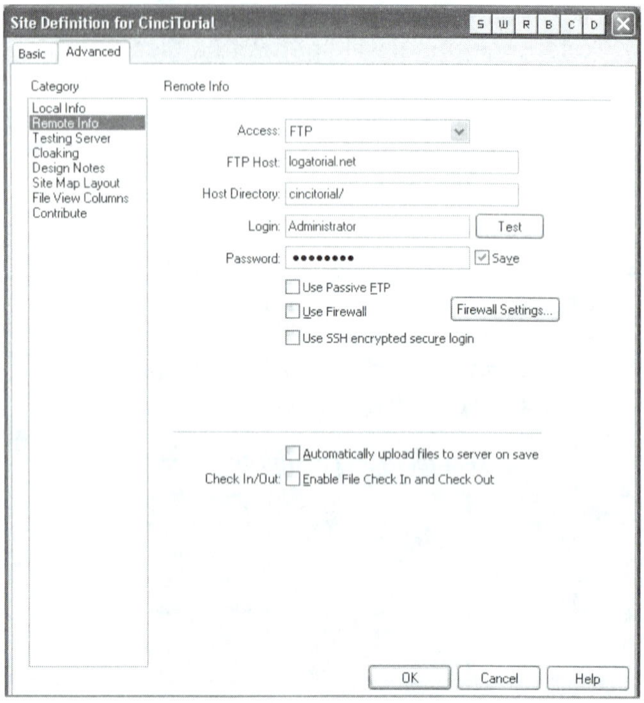

  - In the Host Directory text box, enter the name of the folder on the server that contains the site files.
  - Most servers require a login name to connect to the server. Enter that name in the Login text box. If you do not enter a login name, a dialog box will request it—and the password—when you attempt to connect to the FTP server.
  - Most servers, for security reasons and to prevent "hackers" from tampering with the Web site, also require a password. If you do not supply a password and click the Save option, a dialog box will request it when you attempt to connect to the server.
- The options for Use Passive FTP, Use Firewall, and Use SSH encrypted secure login may need to be selected. Consult with the Web administrator of the FTP server to find out if you need to select these settings.

- To make sure that your FTP settings work, use the Test Test button to test them. Dreamweaver will then attempt to connect to the FTP server and tell you if the test is successful—or unsuccessful (see illustration)

FTP test messages

Note: *File check in and check out is discussed in a later section.*

Putting the Web Site on the FTP Server

- Once the FTP settings have been specified——or the settings for other kinds of server connections discussed in this chapter—the Web site is ready to be copied to the FTP server.
- You can publish your site—or *put* to use Dreamweaver's term—using the Site panel in either its collapsed or expanded form. Using the expanded form, however, gives you the best view of the process because it easily shows both the local and remote site files in one window at the same time.
- In the expanded Site panel window toolbar, click the Site Files button to display the Remote Site pane and then click the Connects to remote host button to establish the connection to the FTP server.
- A message box informs you when you have made a connection with a server. If you cannot connect, you will receive messages explaining why. A live connection will be indicated by a green light inside the button.
- In the Local Files pane, select the desired files to be published on the FTP server and drag them onto the host directory folder in the Remote Site pane. Or, you can select the desired files in the Local Files pane and click the button in the Site panel toolbar.

  Tip: *Typically, you will want to publish all of the contents of the local folder. You can simply select the local Web site's folder at the top of the file tree rather than select files individually. You may need to click Yes to put all of the files.*

- The Site window's status bar records the progress of the files that upload from your local server to the FTP server. You may also need to make decisions about newer versions of files. The process is completed when the files appear in the Remote Site pane as shown in the illustration below.

Files "put" on FTP server

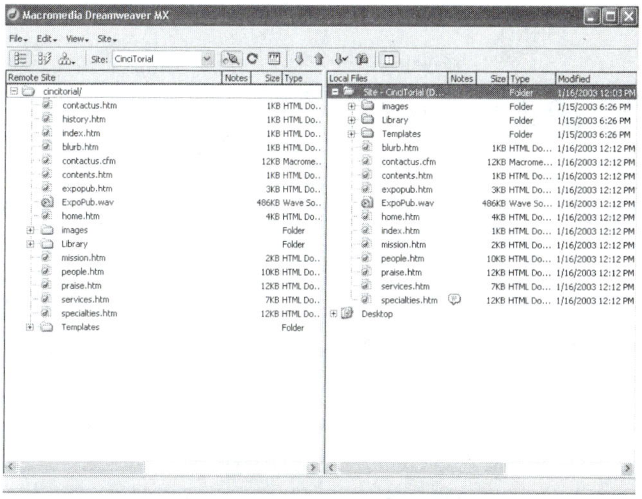

Note: *Dreamweaver may ask during this process if you want to include dependent files. Be sure to click* Yes*, or files such as images will not be transferred to the server.*

- You can put an open document on the server from the Document window. Click the File Management button on the Document toolbar and select Put from the menu. You can also use Site>Put on the menu bar.
- Click the Refresh button to arrange the folders and files in the Remote Site pane in the same order as the Local Files pane. When you have finished the process of copying files, click to disconnect from the server.

Tip: *The View FTP Log button in the expanded Site panel window opens the FTP Log panel in the Results panel group, which displays a log report of all the activity experienced by the FTP server. It can be used for a number of administrative purposes, including security.*

- The FTP server administrator or your instructor can supply you with the URL for the Web so that you can see the published Web in a browser.
- You will need to enter the URL in the HTTP Address box in the Site Definition dialog box's Local Info pane (see illustration below).

Specify URL for published Web site

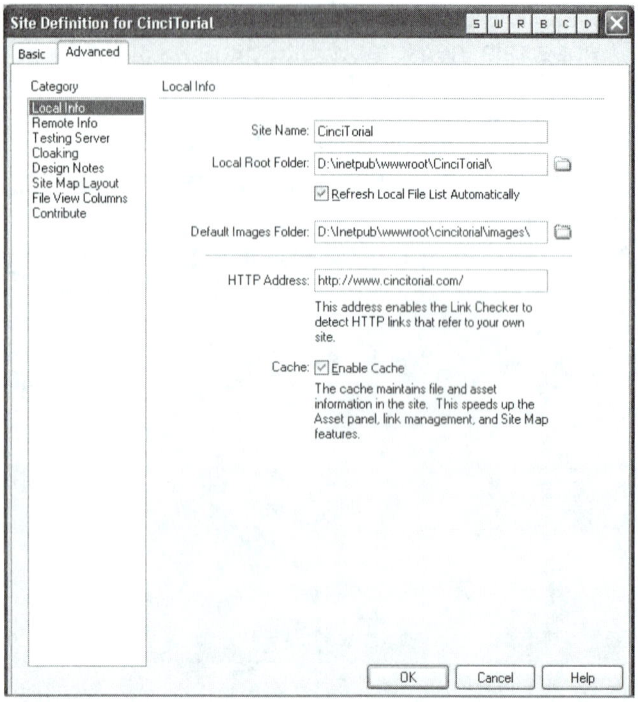

Associating a WebDAV Connection (HTTP server) with a Web Site

- If you are going to publish directly to an HTTP site, you can use the WebDAV standard. WebDAV, or Web-based Distributed Authoring and Versioning, uses the Microsoft Internet Information Server (IIS) 5.0 that comes with Windows 2000, Windows 2000 Server, Windows XP Professional, and the like.
- To configure a WebDAV site, you must have its URL and any login and password information that you will need.
- As with configuring an FTP site, you must set up a remote HTTP server by selecting the Remote Info category in the Site Definition dialog box and choose WebDAV on the Access list and click the Settings button. You must then supply the following information in the appropriate text box: the site URL, Username, Password, Email address (optional) (see illustration).

WebDAV Connection dialog box site

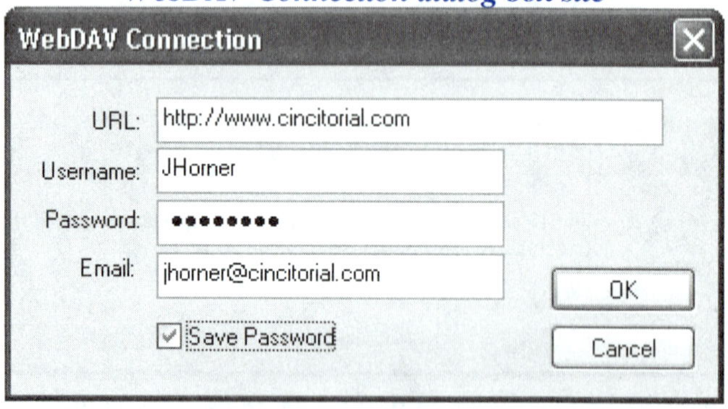

- If you want Dreamweaver to remember your password, select the Save Password checkbox.
- To publish to a WebDAV server connection, use the same procedures for putting files on an FTP site in the Site panel window. (You may encounter different message boxes.)

Associating a Local or Network Server with a Web Site

- You can also publish if your Web server is mounted as a network drive (Windows) or as an AppleTalk or NFS server (Macintosh), or if you are running a personal Web server on your local machine such as Microsoft Personal Web Server (PWS) or Microsoft Internet Information Service IIS.
- Just as when specifying FTP and WebDAV settings, you specify local/network settings in the Site Definition dialog box. In the Remote Info category, select Local/Network from the Access list.
- Type the path to the local network's folder, as shown in the illustration below. You can also use the browse folder icon to navigate directly to the local or network folder where the Web site will be stored.

Set up local network connection

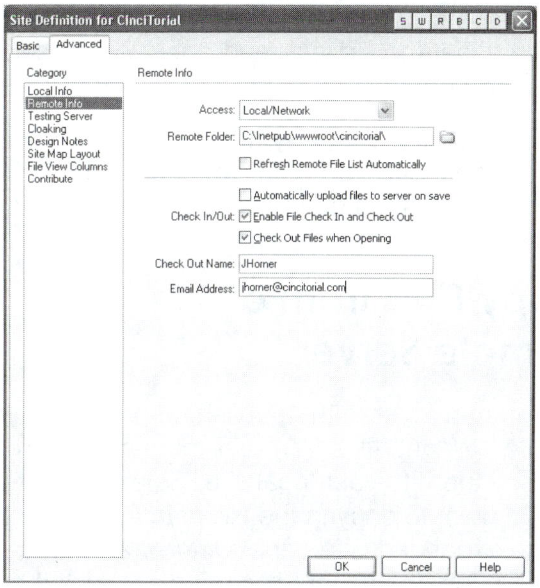

- You can also choose options to refresh files on the server and to upload files to the server when they are saved.

  Note: *File check in and check out is discussed in the next section.*

- To publish to a Local/Network server connection, use the same procedures used to put files on other servers in the Site panel window. (You may encounter different message boxes.)
- Consult with your instructor or Web site administrator for any special instructions and obtaining the correct URL for the Web site after it is published.

Check Files In and Out

- When you define a remote server site in the Site Definition dialog box for an FTP, Local/Network, and RDP connection, you have the options of enabling the file check in and check feature.
- Established Web sites are frequently managed by teams of several members. Team members typically drag files from the remote server in the expanded Site panel window to their local computer to work on the files. Or, they may select files on the server and then use the Get File(s)  button on the Site panel toolbar to copy the selected files from the server to the local computer.
- Obviously, unlimited access to a Web site's files can result in problems, such as more than one team member working on the same file at the same time. Dreamweaver's Check In/Out feature can regulate files to prevent such problems.
- When a file is checked out on the remote server, all team members can see who is working on it and can therefore avoid working on that file.
- You enable check in/out in the Remote Info category of the Site Definition dialog box for the FTP, Local/Network, and RDP server connections. Note that this feature is not active unless a remote server location has been established for the Web site.

Enable Check In/Out options in Remote Info category

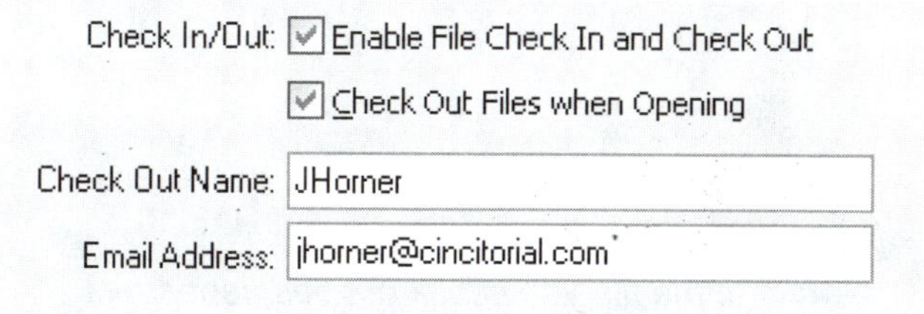

- If you have enabled Check In/Out, files you put on a remote server are automatically checked out to you at the time you publish them.
- Select the Check Out Files when Opening option to automatically check out files when you double-click to open them from the Site panel.
- You can also supply your e-mail address so that team members can send e-mail to you while you are working on checked-out files.
- When you enable Check In/Out, the Check Out File(s)  and Check In  buttons are activated on the Site panel's toolbar in both the collapsed and expanded form.
- To check out a file on your computer, select the file (or select more than one file) in either the Remote Site or Local Files pane and use the Site>Check Out command on the menu bar, or click the Check Out File(s)  button on the Site panel toolbar.

  Note: *You can undo the check-out process using the Site>Undo Check Out command, or right-click the checked-out file and select Undo Check Out on the shortcut menu.*

- Checking out a file tells others that you are working on the file now. If they open the file, it will be a read-only version.
- When a file is checked out, a check mark ✓ displays next to the file's icon in both the Remote Site and Local Files panes (see illustration below).

mission.htm file has been checked out

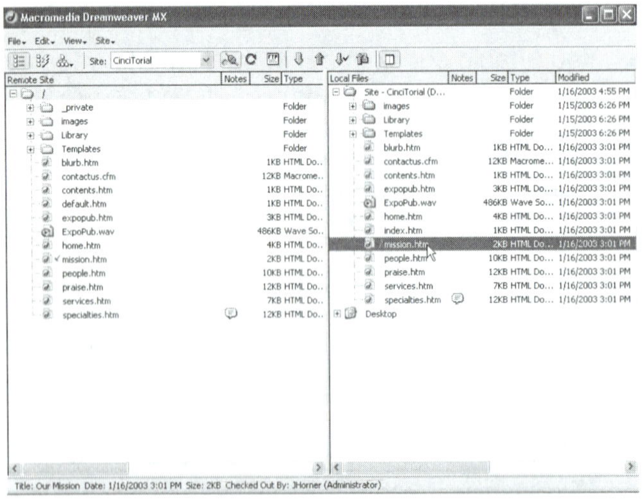

> **Note:** *If the file you check out has dependent files, you will be asked if you want to include them when checking out the file.*

- Check mark colors give you additional information about who has checked out a file. You will see a green check mark when you have checked out a file on your computer. A red check mark means the file is checked out by another person on another computer.
- The name of the person who checked out the file is also displayed in the status bar of the Site window (see above illustration).
- When you have finished working on a file, you check it in by selecting the file in either the Local Files or Remote Site pane and using the Site>Check In command on the menu bar. Or, click the Check In button in the Site panel toolbar.
- Checking in a file makes the file available to other team members to check out and edit. The green check mark in the Remote Site pane is removed and a lock icon displays next to the checked-in file in the Local Files pane.
- While the lock icon displays, other team members will see a message box informing them that the file is a read-only file that can be viewed but not changed.
- To remove the lock symbol so other team members can open the file, right-click the file and select Turn off Read Only in the shortcut menu.

Copy Files from a Remote Server

- You can reverse the publishing process if you need to "get" files from a remote server and copy them to your local site. Select the files you want to copy in the Remote Site pane of the expanded Site panel window and drag them into the Local Files pane. Or click the Get File(s) button in the Site panel toolbar.

> **Note:** *You can get files while working in the Document window by clicking the File Management button on the Document toolbar and selecting Get from the menu.*

- If the Check In/Out feature is active, dragging a file or files—or using the Get File(s)button—results in a read-only local copy of the file. The file remains available on the remote site for others to check out. If Check In/Out is deselected in the Site Definitions dialog box, then copying/getting a file transfers a copy that has read and write privileges.

Procedures

Display Assets Panel

F11

1. Click **Window**............ Alt + W
2. Click **Assets**......... A, A, Enter

OR

- Click the Assets tab on the Files panel group.

Manage Assets

1. Click category button in Assets panel to see assets for that category.
2. Apply or insert an asset on any page by selecting asset and clicking Insert.
3. Add asset to Favorites:
   a. Click asset to select it.
   b. Click in Assets panel.

   OR

- Right-click an asset's name and then choose Add to Favorites from the shortcut menu.

4. Display Favorites by clicking **Favorites** option in Assets panel.
5. Create folder in Favorites:
   a. Display Favorites in Assets panel.
   b. Click in Assets panel.
   c. Type name for new folder.
   d. Drag favorite assets into folder to organize.

Select Target Browsers

On Current page

1. With desired Web page open, click **File** .... Alt + F
2. Click **Check Page** .... H
3. Click **Check Target Browsers** .... B
4. Select browser to check page against in Check Target Browsers dialog box and click Check.
5. View report of errors and warnings in the Target Browser Check panel and perform the desired task:
   - Click to stop report.
   - Double-click a problem in the report pane to open the page in Code and Design views.
   - Select a problem in the report pane and click to read expanded description.
   - Click to save report.
   - Click to view or print report in Web browser.

Entire site, selected files or folders, or single Web page

Ctrl + Shift + F8

1. Click **Window**............ Alt + W
2. Click **Results** .... R
3. Click **Target Browser Check**................. B
4. Click in the Target Browser check panel and select from the menu:
   - Check Target Browsers [for Current Document]
   - Check Target Browsers For Entire Site
   - Check Target Browsers For Selected Files/Folders
5. Select browser to check page against in Check Target Browsers dialog box and click Check.
6. View report of errors and warnings in the Target Browser Check panel and perform the desired task:
   - Click to stop report.
   - Double-click a problem in the report pane to open the page in Code and Design views.
   - Select a problem in the report pane and click to read expanded description.
   - Click to save report.
   - Click to view or print report in Web browser.

Check Links

On current page

Shift + F8

1. With desired Web page open, click **File** .... Alt + F
2. Click **Check Page** .... H
3. Click **Check Links** L
4. View report in Link Checker panel:
   - Click to stop Link Checker.
   - Click to save report.
   - Repair link if desired.

Entire site, selected files or folders, or single Web page

Ctrl + Shift + F9

1. Click **Window**............. Alt + W
2. Click **Results** .... R
3. Click **Link Checker**............. L
4. Click in the Link Checker panel and select from the menu:
   - Check Links For Current Document
   - Check Links For Entire Site
   - Check Links For Selected Files/Folders
5. View report in Link Checker panel:
   - Click to stop Link Checker.
   - Click to save report.
   - Repair link if desired.

Repair Links

In Link Checker panel

1. Select **Broken Links** from the **Show** drop-down list if necessary.
2. Click file name to select it.
3. Click link in **Broken Link** column to select it.
4. Type correct link.

   OR

   Click and select correct file in Select File dialog box.

Change Links Sitewide

In Site panel window

1. Select file in the Local folders pane to which other pages link.
2. Click **Site.**
3. Click **Change Link Sitewide.**
4. Type **/** in **Into Links to** box and then type file name for page to which links should point.

   OR

   Click and select correct file in Select New Link dialog box.

Modify Links in Site panel Map Pane

With site map displayed in expanded or collapsed Site panel

1. Right-click on a page in the site map that displays links.
2. Modify links as follows:
   - Click **Link to New File** to create new document and link at same time.
   - Click **Link to Existing File** to choose file to link to.
   - Click **Change Link** to replace link with link to another page.
   - Click **Remove Link** to remove link from page (or remove page from site map).
   - Click **Open to Source of Link** to open a page with the link itself highlighted.

Run Dreamweaver Reports

In Document window or Site panel menu

1. Click **Site** .... Alt+S
2. Click **Reports** .... T
3. Click **Report On** list and select subject for report.
4. Select checkbox for desired report.
5. Click Report Settings... if necessary (for Workflow reports) and supply additional settings for report.
6. Click Run.
7. View report in Site Report panel:
   - Click to stop site report.
   - Select a problem in the report pane and click to read expanded description in the Reference panel.
   - Double-click a problem in the report pane to open the page in Code and Design views.
   - Click to save report.

Validate a Web page

On current page
Shift + F6

1. Click **Edit** .... E
2. Click **Preferences**. .... S
3. Click Validator in Category list.
4. Choose Validator options and click OK.
5. With desired Web page open, click **File** .... Alt+F
6. Click **Check Page** .... H
7. Click **Validate Markup** V
8. View report in Validation panel:
   - Click to stop Validator.
   - Click to save report.
   - Click to view or print report in Web browser.

Entire site, selected files or folders, or single Web page

1. Click **Window** .... Alt+W
2. Click **Results** .... R
3. Click **Validation** V
4. Click in the Validation panel.
5. Choose Settings.
6. Choose Validator options and click OK.
7. Click in the Validation panel and select from the menu:
   - Validate Current Document
   - Validate Current Document as XML
   - Validate Entire Site
   - Validate Selected Files in Site
8. View report in Validation panel:
   - Click to stop Validator.
   - Click to save report.
   - Click to view or print report in Web browser.

Set Up FTP Connection

In Site Definition dialog box (Advanced tab)

1. Click **Remote Info** category.
2. Click **Access** drop-down list arrow. Click **FTP**.
3. Enter FTP settings:
   a. Type FTP server address in **FTP Host** box.
   b. Type name of folder that holds files in **Host Directory** box.
   c. Type name or code necessary to log in to server in **Login** box.
   d. Type password necessary to log in to server in **Password** box.
   e. Click Test to test the connection.
   f. Select firewall options if desired.

   ✓ *Select Save checkbox to avoid having to enter this information each time you log on.*

Set Up WebDAV HTTP Server

In Site Definition dialog box (Advanced tab)

1. Click **Remote Info** category.
2. Click **Access** drop-down list arrow.
3. Click **WebDAV**.
4. Click Settings... .
5. Enter the following information in the proper text boxes:
   a. Type URL for Web site.
   b. Type username.
   c. Type password
   d. Type e-mail address (optional).
   e. Select save password checkbox if desired. Type name or code necessary to log in to server in **Login** box.
6. Click OK .

Set Up Local/Network Server

In Site Definition dialog box (Advanced tab)

1. Click Remote Info category.
2. Click **Access** drop-down list arrow.
3. Click **Local/Network**.
4. Type path to local/network folder in **Remote Folder** box.

OR

- Click and navigate to folder.

Enable File Check In/Out

In Site Definition dialog box of FTP, Local/Host, and RDP servers

1. Click **Remote Info** category.
2. Click **Enable File Check In and Check Out** checkbox.
3. Click **Check Out Files when Opening** if desired.
4. Type name to be used to identify you in **Check Out Name** box.
5. Type e-mail address in **Email Address** box.

Put Files on Server

In expanded Site panel window

1. Click (**Site Files** button) on Site panel window toolbar to display Remote Site pane.
2. Click on Site panel window toolbar.
3. Select file, files, or entire root folder in Local Files pane.
4. Click on Site panel window toolbar.
5. Click OK if necessary to include dependent files.
6. Click to refresh files in Remote Site pane.
7. Click to disconnect from remote server.

Check File Out

Ctrl + Alt + Shift + D

1. Select file in Remote Site or Local Files pane of Site panel (expanded or collapsed).
2. Click **Site.**
3. Click **Check Out.**

   OR

   Click in Site panel toolbar.

Check File In

Ctrl + Alt + Shift + U

1. Select file in Remote Site or Local Files pane of Site panel (expanded or collapsed).
2. Click **Site.**
3. Click **Check In.**

   OR

   Click in Site panel toolbar.

   ✓ *To remove the Read Only lock icon from the file, right-click the file in the Site panel and click Turn Off Read Only.*

Copy Files from Remote Server

1. Select file or files in Remote Site or Local Files pane of Site panel (expanded or collapsed).
2. Click in Site panel toolbar.

Exercise Directions

1. Start Dreamweaver.
2. Open the **tutorials** site.
3. Check links throughout the site. Note that one page has a link to the **home.htm** page, which does not exist in the site.
4. Change the **home.htm** links to link to **index.htm**.
5. Check the entire site for the Internet Explorer 6.0 browser.
6. You may receive warnings about the Flash movies you inserted and style tags for the **style.xml** file—as well as some JavaScript codings.

   ✓ *If you are using the Internet Explorer 6.0 browser, you will have noticed that Dreamweaver "quibbles" over issues that do not affect the appearance and operation of your Web site.*

7. Close the Results panel without taking further action.
8. Open **index.htm**.
9. Display the Assets panel. Use the Colors category to apply the #000066 dark blue color to the word *Home* in the link bar below the main heading.
10. Open **contents.htm** and apply the same color to the word *Contents* in the link bar below the Heading 2 heading at the top of the page.
11. Run a report on accessibility for the entire site.
12. In the report pane of the Site Reports panel, select the first problem shown with a red X.
13. Read the description of the problem. Repeat step 12 for the next two red X problems that follow. Click More Info to read a suggested solution in the Reference panel for a missing ALT entry.
14. Note that the suggested solution for this problem is to select <empty> in the ALT box of the Properties panel for each of the three color bullets at the top of the contents.htm page. Select each bullet in the Document window and perform the suggested solution in the Properties panel.

    ✓ *The other red X problems in the site do not affect the operation of the Flash objects.*

15. **Optional**. Switch to the **CinciTorial** site and open the **expopub.htm** page. Run an HTML 4.0 Validator check on the page and view the report. (*Hint: Make sure HTML.4.0 is selected in the Validator category of the Preferences dialog box.)* Perform the suggested code corrections for the two warnings you will see for the en and em dash that begin with the following description:

    Windows CP-1252 numeric character reference found. This character not in the HTMLlat1 or HTMLsymbol entity sets. Consider using [. . .].

    In code view, make these suggested corrections by replacing the en dash code – and em dash code — with – and — respectively.

16. Close the Results panel group.

    ✓ *If you performed the optional step, switch back to the* ***tutorial*** *site.*

17. Save and close the pages.
18. Publish your Web site to a server or to a local folder. Put all the files on the remote site.

    ✓ *If you did not select a remote server yet, your instructor will supply information for putting your Web site files on an FTP, WebDAV HTTP server, or a local network server. If no server is available, create a folder on your hard drive. In the Site Definition dialog box, use the Local/Network server access option and make sure the path to the folder you created appears in the Remote Folder box on the Web Server Info or Remote Info category. Then publish your Web site files to this folder.*

19. Use the Site Definition dialog box to make sure the Check In/Out feature is enabled for the current site. (Be sure to insert your name where indicated so it will display when you check files out.)
20. Check out the **index.htm** file, if necessary, and rest the mouse pointer on the file name to see your name in the Site window's status bar.

21. Run the Checked Out By report to see what files you have checked out.
22. Check in the **index.htm** file. Click in the file and then remove the lock symbol from the local version of the file and any dependent files.
23. Disconnect from the server, if necessary.
24. Close any open pages.
25. Exit Dreamweaver.

Next Chapter

▶▶

chapter

18

Challenge Exercises: Web Mastering

You have mastered many important Dreamweaver tools in the past 17 chapters. Use what you have learned to complete the challenge exercises in this chapter.

Exercise 1—Plan a Web Site

In this exercise, you begin work on a new Web site by learning more about Web site design and then applying what you have learned to create a design appropriate for your Web site. You then identify tasks that need to be completed and set up progress evaluation materials.

Choose a Web Site Topic

1. Identify a local community organization that needs a Web presence. For example:
   - A local animal adoption agency.
   - A school supply donation center.
   - A blood bank or clinic.
   - An environmental group.
   - Your town or village council.
   - A community center, senior center, or homeless shelter.
2. If you can't identify a community organization in your area, you can create your own "virtual organization" or come up with another service-oriented Web site topic. For example:
   - An organization that takes pets to children's wards in local hospitals.
   - An organization that collects used eyeglasses for reuse in disadvantaged countries.
   - A Web site that can be used as a tutorial for those new to computing or Web browsing.
   - A Web site that helps students and their parents evaluate local colleges and universities, with attention to housing, financial aid, and career decisions.
3. Do some research on the value of "Web presence" for your organization. Start by searching the Internet for information on the impacts the World Wide Web has had on society. Consider:
   - How has the Internet changed the way people find information?
   - Why have so many organizations established Web sites in the past few years?
   - What can a visitor learn from an organization's Web site?
4. If possible, interview someone from a community organization in your area that has a Web site. Gather information on how the organization's Web site has contributed to the organization's successfulness.
5. Visit the Web sites of several organizations similar to the one you have chosen as your Web site topic. Use personal observation to determine how effectively the sites deliver information and explain the organization's goals to visitors.

Research Design Issues

1. With your Web site topic in mind, explore Web sites and search for Web site design information to develop a plan for the new Web site. Evaluate sites for design (content delivery) and functionality (navigation schemes, interaction features).
   - Determine a method for evaluating the Web sites you visit. For example, you may want to create a checklist that allows you to assign numbers from 1 to 5 to topics such as effectiveness of presenting content, ease of navigating the site, usefulness of interactive features, and so on. Or, look at the sample site evaluation form included later in this chapter for ideas to help you get started with your checklist.
   - Compare your evaluation method with those of several classmates to refine your system.
2. Also evaluate individual page design for effective presentation of content. For example:
   - Does the site use standard pages with text and headings?
   - Does the site use complex layouts that may be controlled by tables or layers?
   - If the site has frames pages, are they effective in controlling navigation and access to information in the site?
3. Next, use the Internet to research established design principles that can improve page layout. For example:
   - Consistency—make sure items such as headings, body text, horizontal rules, and so on have the same formatting.
   - Repetition—elements are repeated on the page and throughout the site to unify the site.
   - Alignment—text and graphics should align in an identifiable "grid" that makes the content of the page easily accessible and easy to absorb.
   - Proximity—related elements are grouped to improve comprehension.
   - Text/white space ratio—pages should allow sufficient white space around text and other elements to avoid a crowded appearance that makes comprehension difficult.

✓ *"White space" doesn't literally mean white. You can still use color and graphic backgrounds. But these, too, should not make your page hard to read.*

4. You may want to create a "digital portfolio" of pages that display these design principles and any other interesting design elements you see during your research.
   - Capture a page on your screen using a screen capture utility or by pressing the Print Scrn key on your keyboard.
   - Insert the captured screen in a word processing document. If you used Print Scrn, all you have to do is click the Paste button. You can then crop or modify the screens as necessary using tools such as those on Word's Picture toolbar.
   - Add captions to the inserted screen captures to point out the design principle illustrated in the picture. You may also want to add notes on how you might modify elements for your own use. Be sure to add a citation that gives the Web site address, using the method for citing Internet resources your instructor requires. You'll find a sample citation on the next page of this chapter.

Finalize the Site and Design

1. Join several other students to form a team to create the Web site. As a team, decide on the final topic for the Web site by weighing the pros and cons of various organizations team members have already identified.

   ✓ *If you decide to create a site for an existing organization, be sure to secure permission to do so from the organization. Make sure that you also have permission to use any copyrighted text, images, logos, and trademarks.*

2. Delineate tasks involved with creating the site. For example:
   - Learn about the organization's mission, structure, staff, services, etc.
   - Research on the Internet to locate other similar sites or parent sites of local organizations.
   - Finalize the design.
   - Create content for the site.
   - Determine how the site will be published.
3. Create a list of tasks required to construct the site and establish a timeline for those tasks. Assign tasks to various team members. Set up a rubric for evaluating progress. The illustration in the next column shows a sample.

Sample rubric

	In Progress	Complete
Define organization mission	____	____
Gather information from similar sites/parent sites	____	____
Finalize design	____	____
Write page text	____	____
Create graphic buttons	____	____

✓ *A rubric lists the small goals that go into making larger goals, such as your Web site. The items here are a starting point. Consider adding more. Your teacher can help you create others.*

4. As a team, evaluate the page properties you reviewed during your research.
   - Separate the page properties into groups, such as color usage (color of text, objects on page, links, background) and text properties (font, font size, and font style).
   - Assign a team member to each group to review and evaluate samples to determine the most effective combinations. Create another rubric for this task.
5. Based on the team's evaluations, choose properties for your Web site. Make sure the formats you choose are appropriate for your proposed Web site.
6. Gather feedback on your design. Provide an evaluation form for peers and professionals to use.
   - Ask several other teams to comment on and evaluate your design plan.
   - Consult a professional Web site designer, if possible, and ask for feedback.
   - If you are creating the Web site for an actual organization, allow a representative from the organization to review the design to make sure it is acceptable.
7. After receiving feedback on your site, resolve any issues by accessing, researching, and comparing your site to others in terms of content and structure. Revise the Web site design as necessary.
8. Create an outline in a word processing program that shows the pages you think you might need and tentative content. E-mail the outline to your instructor.

9. Create a Web page that displays the formatting options you have chosen for your Web site, such as fonts for body text and headings, colors, background color or graphic, and navigation scheme so that team members can use this template as a guide when creating page content. E-mail the page to your instructor and other team members.

Exercise 2—Create Content for the Site

In this exercise, you create content for the Web site. You and your team members create not only the site's text, but create or locate graphic content. You also explore options for adding other multimedia content, such as digital video and sound.

1. Using a word processor or Dreamweaver, create the text content for your Web site pages.
   - If there is a parent organization, gather information and synthesize it for local use. Make sure to plan for a link to the parent organization.
   - Write all other content using notes you developed during your research into the organization. Use vocabulary and writing style appropriate for the site. Make sure you use a spell checking utility to verify spelling of all text. Save all pages as HTML documents.
2. As you create pages, try to vary the content to provide value for your visitors. For example,:
   - Add information about the history of your community and how the organization fits into that history.
   - Discuss the economics of the organization. Locate financial information, for example, and use mathematical formulas to manipulate the data. For instance, average numbers of abandoned pets by month or year, or show maximum and minimum units of blood collected throughout a year.
   - If your community has a significant population of non-English speakers, consider creating one or more pages in a second language, such as Spanish, with a link on the home page to allow visitors to jump to those pages.
3. Create graphics content for your pages:
   - Create graphic objects for the site such as navigation buttons and other symbols in a graphics (draw/paint) program such as Fireworks MX or Adobe Illustrator.
   - Optimize the graphics for use on a Web page and save in GIF format. Make sure to consider the file size when optimizing to create graphics that download quickly when the page opens.
4. Locate additional graphics for the site:
   - Search for appropriate clip art graphics on your computer, LAN, or the Internet, and download the graphics.
   - Locate several photographs for the Web site. You may find useful photos on a parent Web site or in a clip art collection. You may also use a scanner to scan your own photos or take photos using a digital camera and download them locally or across your network.

   ✓ *Like text, images can be copyrighted. And you may need a signed release to use the image of a person publicly.*

   - If necessary, modify the file format of the photos to make them more compatible with Web page requirements. For example, open an image in a graphics program and adjust the quality/size setting, save it in a different format such as JPEG, crop it, apply special effects, etc.
5. Create source citations for text material you may have acquired from other sources and for scanned or downloaded images. Use the citation style requested by your instructor. The MLA style, for example, is shown below.

Sample citation

Creator's name (if given). Web Page Title. Institution or organization. Date of access <URL network address>. For example: Holcomb, Emma. Hummels Galore. 12 Nov 2004 <http://www.hummels-r-cute.org>.

✓ *Bedford/St. Martin's Publisher's has a Web site that explains several different styles of source citation for Web pages, e-mail messages, and the like. Just navigate in your browser to http://www.bedfordstmartins.com/online/citex.html*

6. If possible, locate an audio file appropriate for the site. Or, use a voice/sound recorder to record a message or a sound effect related to the site.
7. If you have access to an animation program such as Flash, create a simple digital video for the site.
   - Use one or more of the symbols you created in the graphics program as the basis for the animation, or create another graphic to use in a graphics program or in the animation program.
   - Test the animation to ensure it streams properly at a variety of browser speeds. Publish it to create a Flash SWF file.
   - Help other classmates who may not be proficient in Flash by writing a list of steps they can follow to create a simple animation. Then give a brief tutorial on the process.
8. If you have access to a digital video camera, shoot some footage that relates to your site. For example, you may want to interview a representative from the organization or a person who has been helped by the organization (or a classmate acting either of these roles).
   - Use a video-editing program to create a short video from your source clip(s).
   - Export the video in a format suitable for use on a Web page, such as AVI.
9. Create a chart in a spreadsheet program such as Excel that deals with your site in some way. For example, make a chart of financial contributions or operating costs by year. Publish the chart as a Web page that you can edit in Dreamweaver.
10. If you are creating a Web site for an actual organization, make sure you allow a representative from the organization to read and comment on your text and view your graphics for accuracy and appropriateness.
11. Review your progress and check off completed items in your progress rubric. E-mail the rubric to your instructor for evaluation.

Exercise 3—Develop the Site

In this exercise, you define the Web site and add to it the content you have already created. You create other materials you need for the site, add special effects as necessary, and do a series of final checks to verify site content. Finally, you publish the site.

1. Define the Web site in Dreamweaver. Make sure you create an images folder to hold the graphics you have created. Insert keywords that identify the site so search engines will find it.
2. Import any text you created in a word processor, or use a file management utility to copy HTML pages into the site. Use Dreamweaver's Clean Up Word HTML utility to clean up unnecessary word processing codes.
3. Lay out the pages of the site with attention to the principles of design you identified in Exercise 1.
   - You may want to create a page template to simplify the process of creating and formatting multiple pages.
   - Use tables as desired to create interesting page layouts, and remember the importance of aligning to an invisible grid.

   ✓ *To see Dreamweaver's Document window grid, use the View>Grid>Show Grid menu command. Use View>Grid>Snap to Grid if desired.*

   - Consider creating a frames page to add variety.
   - Remember that bulleted and numbered lists can help to organize text on a page.
4. Format text and headings according to the styles you finalized in Exercise 1. Consider creating a cascading style sheet to control styles on site pages.
5. Modify colors of text and links according to your design plan.
6. Insert the graphics you have created or downloaded. Make sure to save them in the images folder. Place graphics in appropriate locations and modify image properties as necessary.
7. If you have created graphics you intend to use multiple times throughout the site, make sure to store them in the library for easy access.
8. Insert the animation SWF (Flash) file on the home page. Test the animation in Dreamweaver and in the browser to make sure it works properly.
9. Insert sound objects where appropriate.

10. If you created a digital video file, insert it on an appropriate page. If necessary, download from Macromedia's Web site a utility extension to handle inserting the AVI file on a Web page.

    ✓ *Use the Insert>Get More Objects menu command if you are online to access the Macromedia Exchange for Dreamweaver site. Make sure that the extensions you download are compatible with Dreamweaver MX.*

11. Test to make sure the video works correctly, and pay attention to the download speed for that page.

    ✓ *You may need to return to the video-editing program and shorten the video if it takes too much time to download.*

12. Open the page that contains the published Excel chart and supply explanatory text. You may want to add a table that shows the data used to create the chart.
13. Create any additional pages you need in the site. For example:
    - Create a form to gather information to be stored in a database; for instance, a form for prospective members or requests for further information. Be sure to use behaviors to validate the form fields.
    - Create a page that contains useful links to other online resources related to your site. Make sure you also have an e-mail link on the home page so visitors can contact you. (Use your own e-mail address for the link.)
14. Set up the navigation structure for the site.
    - Create a navigation bar you can use on all pages, using graphic buttons you have already developed for the site.
    - Use a graphic or a thumbnail of a photo at the top of each page to link to the home page.
    - Consider creating image maps from some of your graphics to link pages in the site.
    - View the site in Map view to verify the links.
15. Work cooperatively with your team members, using Dreamweaver's collaborative features: Use Design Notes to help other team members understand your progress, and use check in/check out to make sure no one duplicates work on the site's pages.
16. As you work on the site, pay attention to your timeline and use your progress rubric to review and evaluate your progress.
17. As a team, view your site and note any corrections that need to be made and any improvements you think necessary. For example:
    - Use layers to control the position of text or objects on a page.
    - Define behaviors to create interactivity on some pages. For example, you may want to swap images on the home page or create a pop-up window that gives information about special programs or features.
    - Modify links or add links on pages that can be used by visitors who have touch-screen capability. (Links for touch-screen users may need to be larger to allow for easy touching.)
18. Use Dreamweaver utilities to make final checks.
    - Check links sitewide and repair any problem links.
    - Use the Reports utility to show problems and clean up HTML tags.
    - Use the Validation utility to locate potential problems in the site and correct the problems.
    - Run the Accessibility report to make sure your site can be used by visitors with various disabilities or by visitors viewing on cell phone browsers.
19. When your site is complete, present to the class the information your team has gathered and explain the focus of the organization and its goals.
20. Publish the site and invite classmates and your professional advisor (and a representative from the organization, if you are using a real organization as your Web site topic) to view it and offer constructive comments. Provide a rubric for evaluation. The illustration at the top of the next page will give you some starting ideas for your form.
21. Respond to input by modifying your site. Republish the site. E-mail the link to the site to your instructor for evaluation.

Sample evaluation form

SITE EVALUATION FORM

DREAMWEAVER MX – Challenge Exercise

Site Topic	______			
URL	______			
Reviewed By				
First Impression of Site	☐ Poor	☐ Fair	☐ Good	☐ Excellent
Text				
Is the text easy to read?	☐ Yes	☐ No	Comment: ______	
Are there misspellings or grammar errors?	☐ Yes	☐ No	Comment: ______	
Are fonts appropriate for text and headings?	☐ Yes	☐ No	Comment:	
Graphics				
Do graphics support site content?	☐ Yes	☐ No	Comment: ______	
Are graphics optimized to download quickly?	☐ Yes	☐ No	Comment: ______	
Are graphics positioned attractively?	☐ Yes	☐ No	Comment:	
Navigation				
Are links easy to find and use?	☐ Yes	☐ No	Comment: ______	
Are there any broken links?	☐ Yes	☐ No	Comment:	
Multimedia Features				
Does the site include multimedia features?	☐ Yes	☐ No	Comment: ______	
Do the multimedia objects play correctly in the browser?	☐ Yes	☐ No	Comment: ______	
Do the multimedia objects add value to the site?	☐ Yes	☐ No	Comment:	

Exercise 4—Final Considerations

In this exercise, you explore issues that relate to publishing a Web site to a Web server. You will need to have this information when you propose a final publishing location for the organization.

1. Research characteristics of Web servers. You can explore online or call or visit a local Web hosting service. (If you have a local Web server such as Personal Web Server or IIS, you can also list information about this feature.) Discover the following information about the server:
   - Optimum RAM.
   - Storage capacity.
   - CPU speed.
   - Connection options; HTTP/WebDAV, FTP, etc.
   - Server software, including the servers used by Dreamweaver to develop and test Web sites.

   ✓ *For example, ColdFusion MX test server that can be set up in the Site Definition dialog box and wizard.*

2. Using the same sources, research Web server security. Find out:
   - What kind of firewall the server offers.
   - Options for controlling viruses and spam.
   - Options for controlling access to a particular site on the server, such as password controls and global access/deny controls.
   - How the server ensures secure transactions from server to client.
3. Write a report on what you have learned, citing your sources. Illustrate it if possible with graphics you have located on the Internet (of servers, firewalls, etc.) Choose the system you think will meet your needs. Submit the report to your instructor for evaluation.
4. Now that you have completed the exercise and this text and know Dreamweaver's capabilities, compare Dreamweaver to other Web site design programs to identify the program you would buy to start your career as a Web designer.
   - Create a table or spreadsheet in which you can record your evaluations of *quality*, *appropriateness* of features for your Web page projects, cost, and availability.
   - Research on the Internet or by testing products you have available, such as Dreamweaver, Notepad, FrontPage, or GoLive. Compare *effectiveness* and *efficiency*.
5. Create a report on your findings in which you indicate which program you would buy for your own use, and the reasons for your decision. Submit the report to your instructor for evaluation.

Appendix A: Dreamweaver Preferences

Dreamweaver Preferences

- Dreamweaver allows you to customize the Dreamweaver environment using the Preferences command on the Edit menu. Once you have become proficient at using Dreamweaver, explore the Preferences dialog box for ways to tailor the Dreamweaver environment to your needs.
- Preferences you may find particularly helpful include:
    - Use the floating panels view of previous versions of Dreamweaver
    - Display the Site window only when you start Dreamweaver
    - Customize the Launcher to display only the panels you use most often
    - Use the Accessibility dialog boxes to make your sites "user-friendly" for text-only browsers
    - Set a default font other than Times New Roman for your Web pages
    - Add browsers to the preview list to make it easy to test your site in more than one browser
    - Change the default connection speed used to calculate download time in the status bar.

Use the Preferences Dialog Box

- As you become familiar with Dreamweaver features, you can consider changing default configurations to make the program more responsive to your particular needs.
- You change default settings in the Preferences dialog box. Display this dialog box using the Edit>Preferences command on the menu bar, or use the Ctrl + U keystroke combination as a shortcut.
- The Preferences dialog box (see illustration below) contains a list of categories at the left of the dialog box. Settings for the selected category display in the main portion of the dialog box.

Dreamweaver MX Preferences dialog box

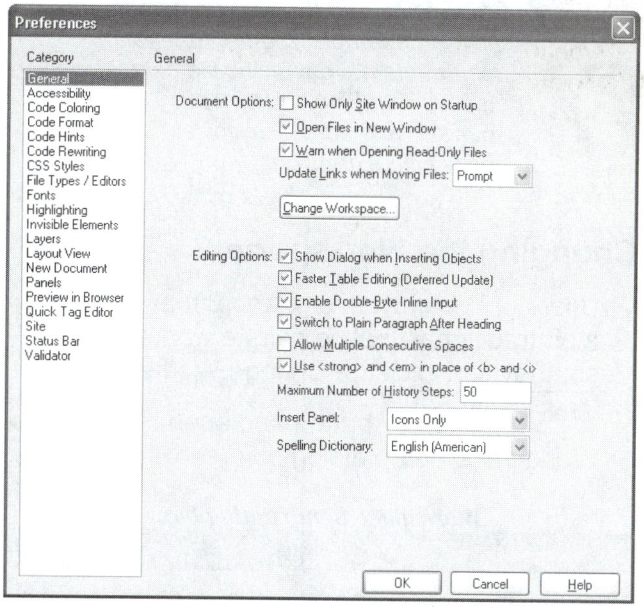

- The Dreamweaver MX Preferences dialog box contains a list of categories that you can select and configure as desired before and during the creation of a Web site and Web pages. Selection of these preference categories is discussed in the following sections.

General Category

- The General category provides settings for startup and general operations. Concentrate on the following items:
    - By default, Dreamweaver opens with the Site window and a new, blank document. To open the program with the Site window only, select the Show Only Site Window on Startup checkbox.
    - By default, Dreamweaver prompts you to update links when you move or rename a page. You can change this setting to Always or Never to automatically update links or never update them.
- If you routinely work with large, complex Web sites, consider increasing the maximum number of History steps. Remember, you can use the History panel to repeat steps on any page, so the more steps you track, the less work you might need to do to copy text and formatting.

Note: *Previous Dreamweaver versions offered an option to "Add Extension when Saving checkbox." This option no longer appears since your site may have pages that end in other file extensions, such as .cfm for ColdFusion and the like. Some servers, may, for example, require that your documents have specific file extensions, such as .html instead of .htm. Consult with your server's administrator or ISP for the correct file extensions.*

Changing the Workspace

- Users of Dreamweaver 4 and 3 may prefer their traditional floating palette workspace. If so, they can click the Change Workspace [Change Workspace...] button and open the Workspace Setup dialog box (see illustration).

Workspace Setup dialog box

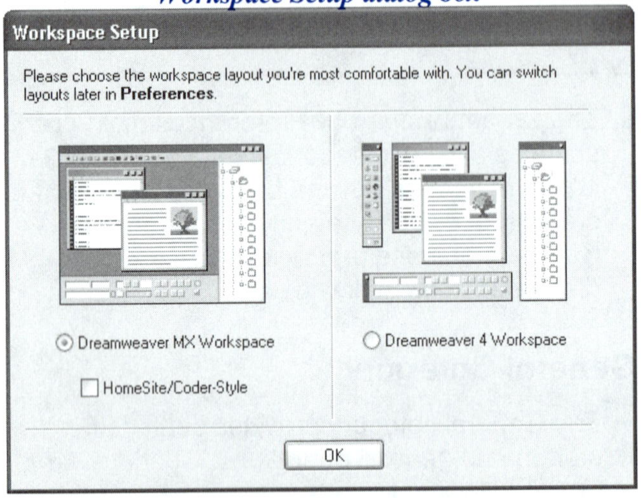

- Select the Dreamweaver 4 Workspace option if desired. The only drawback, however is that Dreamweaver MX's Help is designed for the new "integrated" workspace.
- The Home Site/Coder Style gives you the option of placing the panel group pane on the left side of the Dreamweaver MX screen rather than on the right (see illustration). Code View is also selected, too.
- You must close and restart Dreamweaver to see workspace changes.

Accessibility

- The options for this category are used to activate special dialog boxes that appear when you insert images, movies, and other kinds of nontext objects—and you are making the content of your pages accessible to all users, from people who use cell phone browsers to the visually challenged who use text-reading software to "hear" the content of your pages.
- To do this, you must activate the Accessibility dialog boxes for Form Objects, Frames, Media, Images, and so on so that Dreamweaver prompts you for the information you need to add for accessibility. Such information can mean typing information into the ALT box of a Property panel or entering special coding.
- It is beyond the scope of this book to discuss the Accessibility features in detail. Check Dreamweaver MX help for more information.

Code Coloring

- The Code Coloring category (see illustration at top of next page) allows you to select default colors for various features such as text, tags, and so on in the different types of documents that Dreamweaver creates. For example, you can select HTML as the document type and click the Edit Coloring Scheme [Edit Coloring Scheme] button. In the Edit Coloring Scheme dialog box, you can apply different colors to the various kinds of tags and attributes that appear in HTML pages. Besides changing background, text, and tag colors, you can select colors for script objects such as keywords and strings.
- Setting colors in this category can save you a great deal of labor you might otherwise expend in creating style sheets or formatting text manually on Web pages.

Code Coloring category

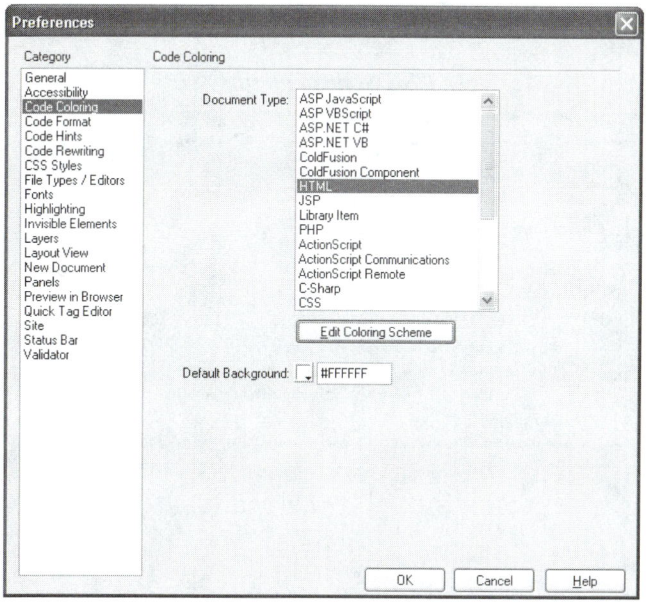

Code Format

- Use the Code Format category (see illustration below) to change default HTML settings such as items to indent in displayed code, what tags to use for specific formatting such as centering, and so on.

Code Format category

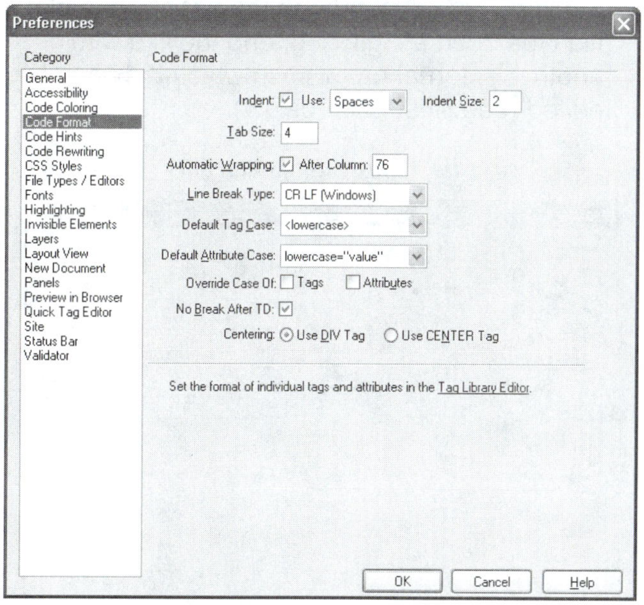

- To control the indention of code, use the Indent Size setting. The default setting is two spaces. You can also specify that the indent use tabs.

- If you prefer to see HTML tags and attributes in all capital letters when viewing a page's code, you can select uppercase in the Default Tag Case and Default Attribute Case lists.

  Tip: *To make it easy to differentiate between tags and attributes, you may find it helpful to use different case options for the two items.*

Code Hints

- The Code Hints category allows you to insert tag names, attributes, and values as you enter code in Code View (see illustration).
- By default, the Enable Auto Tag Completion checkbox is selected and is most useful when you are writing code from scratch. When editing code, you should deselect it, for it will automatically enter the corresponding end tag code as well when you enter a begin tag.

Code Hints category

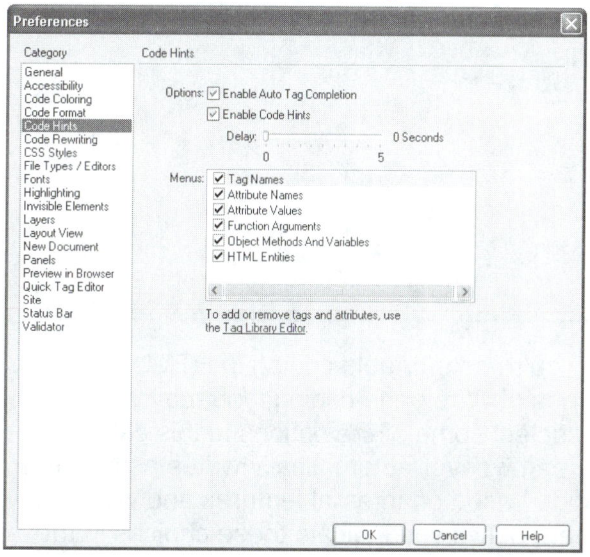

- The Enable Code Hints checkbox is also selected by default. You can adjust the Delay slider control to control when the hint menu appears. You can also select and deselect the kinds of code hint menus you want to see.
- More advanced Web page designers can add or remove tags and attributes by clicking Tag Library Editor to open the Tag Library Editor dialog box.

Code Rewriting

- If you plan to use previously created or imported documents coded in HTML, ColdFusion, and the like in your site, take time to set up the Code Rewriting category (see illustration). Settings in this category will clean up nested or overlapped tags, insert proper quotation marks or closing brackets, and protect the layout.
- The Code Rewriting options are applied when Dreamweaver opens the document. It does not rewrite when you actually create or work with a Web page after it has opened.

Code Rewriting category

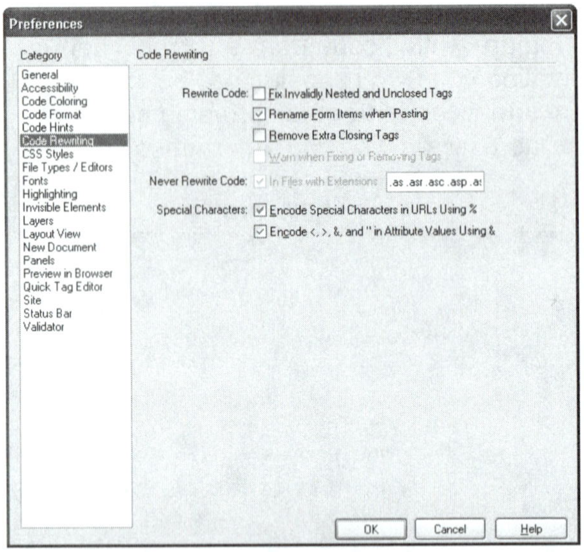

- If you're comfortable coding in HTML or other kinds of Web page coding, you may wish to deselect some of the options in this category. Dreamweaver automatically writes associated code based on internal features and will modify them only if you indicate these choices in the Code Rewriting category.

CSS Styles

- CSS (cascading style sheet) information can be written in a shorthand form that some people prefer. Older browsers, however, cannot interpret CSS shorthand correctly.
- By default, Dreamweaver does not use this shorthand notation to write CSS code. If you wish to use shorthand, you can specify when to use shorthand in the CSS Styles category (see illustration at top of next column).
- You may also need to adjust these settings if you are using code from another source that contains CSS shorthand.

CSS Styles category

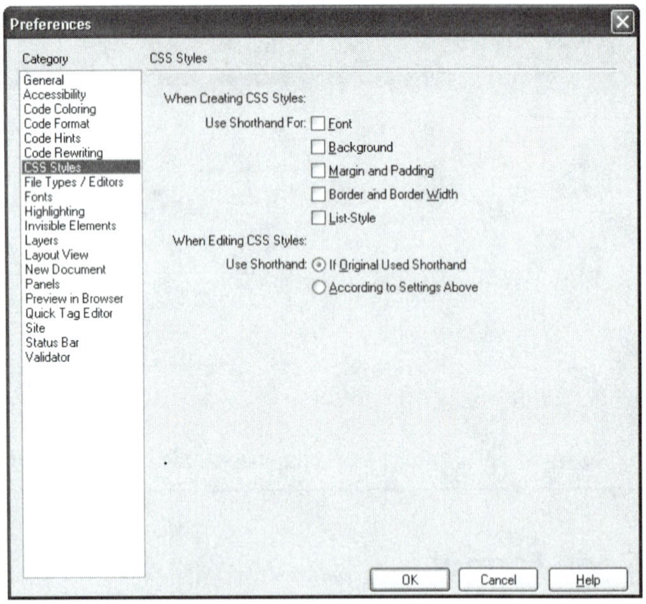

File Types / Editors

- You can specify different kinds of code editors to supplement Dreamweaver by associating a file type with another code editor or program.
- Similarly, you can change the association of a file type such as .gif, .jpg, and the like with another external program in which they can be edited (see illustration below).

File Types/Editors category

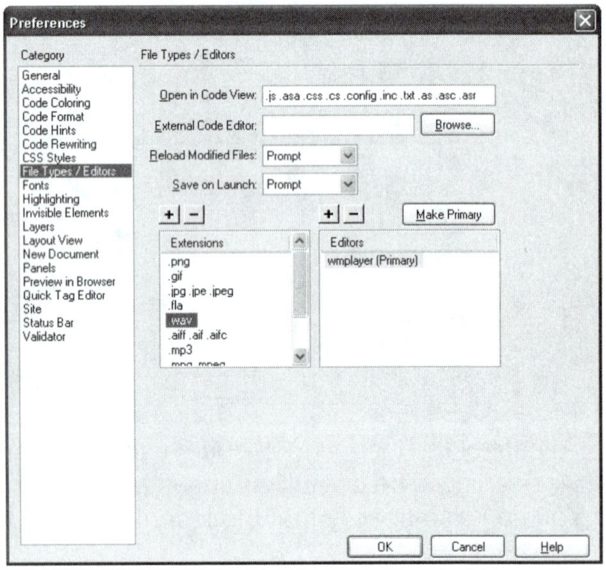

Fonts

- Use the Fonts category (see illustration below) to select default fonts and sizes for Web pages and HTML code. Settings selected in this category will be applied to each new document you create.

Fonts category

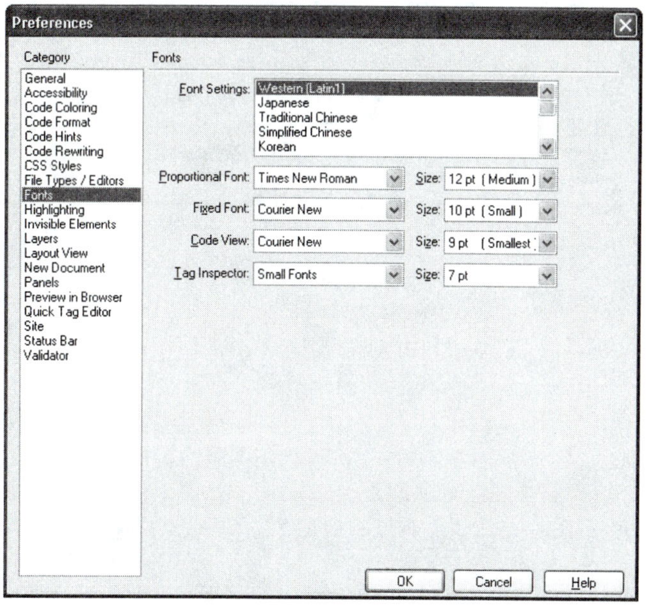

- This category allows you to work in the font and size you prefer while maintaining the default encoding that will display in the browser.

- For example, you can choose a sans serif font such as Arial as the default proportional font and create your Web pages using this font. When the page is displayed in the browser, however, the browser will use Western (Latin1), which is a serif font similar to Times New Roman.

Highlighting

- Use the Highlighting category (see illustration in next column) to select colors used to highlight editable and noneditable regions in templates and library items. You can also select a highlight color for third-party tags supplied by external editors.

Highlighting category

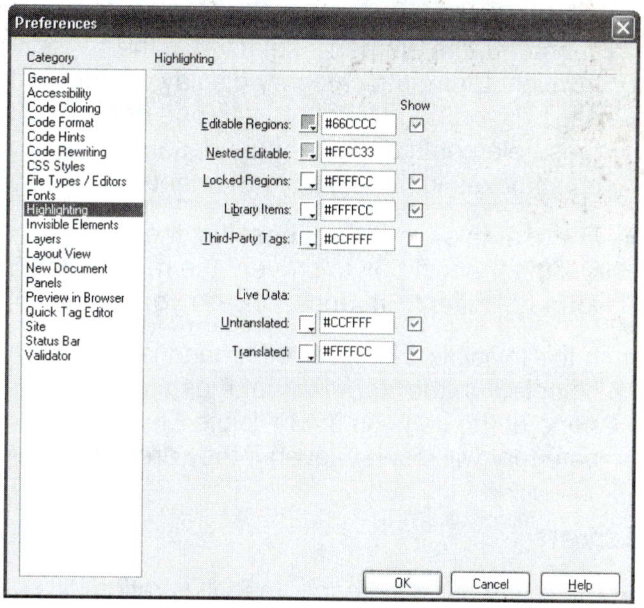

Invisible Elements

- The Invisible Elements category (see illustration below) works in conjunction with the View>Visual Aids>Invisible Elements command on the menu bar to display nontext items on your Web pages. Remember, for example, that a named anchor is designated on a page by an anchor marker.

Invisible Elements category

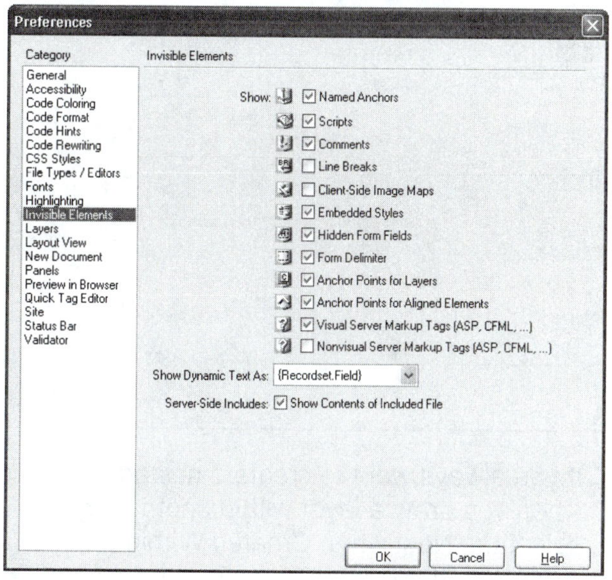

- When the Invisible Elements command is selected (checked) on the View>Visual Aids submenu, the elements selected in the Invisible Elements category display on your page. If you do not want to see one or more of these elements on your page, deselect their checkboxes in the Invisible Elements category.
- For example, you might deselect the Form Delimiter checkbox to prevent the red dashed form delimiter from appearing on your page.
- If the Invisible Elements command is *not* selected on the View>Visual Aids submenu, none of the items in the Invisible Elements category will display, even if they are selected.

Layers

- Use the Layers category (see illustration below) to make a number of changes to default layer properties. You can specify what tag set is used to create layers; default visibility settings; and width, height, background color, and background image settings.

Layers category

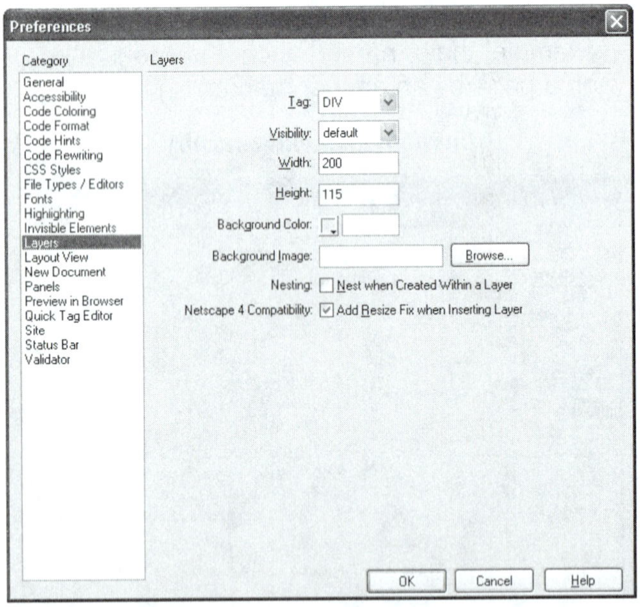

- If you always want to create a nested layer when you draw a layer within another layer, select the Nest when Created Within a Layer checkbox. If you want to leave your options open, clear this checkbox. You can hold down the Ctrl key while drawing a layer to nest it within an existing layer.

Layout View

- The Layout View category (see illustration below) allows you to specify settings for Layout view. You can specify whether a spacer image is used to autostretch tables and if so, the name and location of the spacer image.

Layout View category

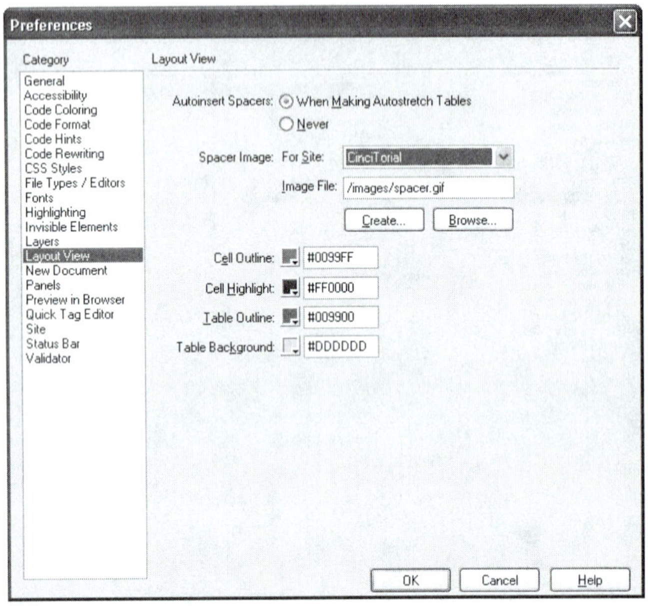

- You can also select the colors used for layout table and layout cell outlines (the outlines that display when a table or cell is selected or highlighted) and the background color of the layout table.

New Document

- By default, Dreamweaver opens with a new, blank Basic Page, HTML document. The New Document category allows you to change which document type Dreamweaver opens as a default document for a site (see illustration on next page).
- For example, if most pages in your site are a different file type such as Cold Fusion or ASP documents, you can reset your document preferences so that your new document preference matches the kind of file type.

New Document category

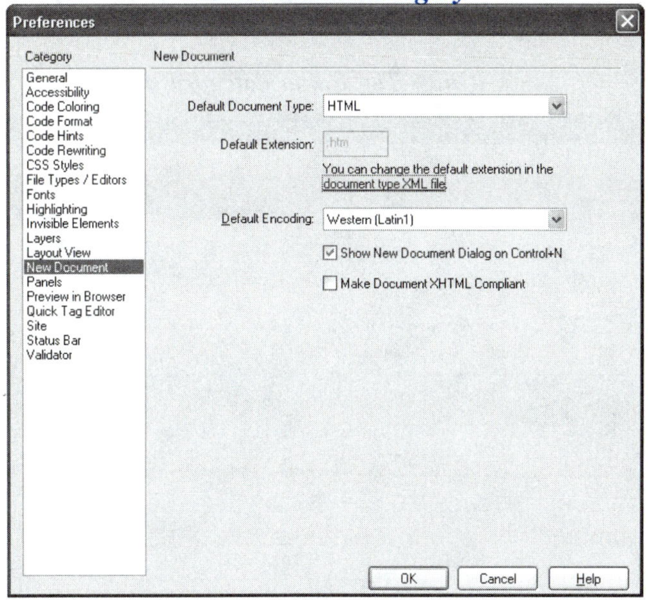

- The New Document category gives you the option of making any new documents that you create the default document type. Clicking the Show New Document Dialog on Control+N checkbox automatically creates a new document of the default document type when you press this keyboard shortcut command.
- When you select the Make Document XHTML Compliant checkbox, you can automatically make your Web pages comply to XML coding, which is a type of Web document code used for working with dynamic databases.

Panels

- By default, panels are configured to display on top of the Document window. This means that when displayed, they are always available for use.
- If you want to allow the Document window to obscure some of these panels, deselect the panel name in the Panels category (see illustration in next column). This can help reduce clutter on your desktop.

Panels category

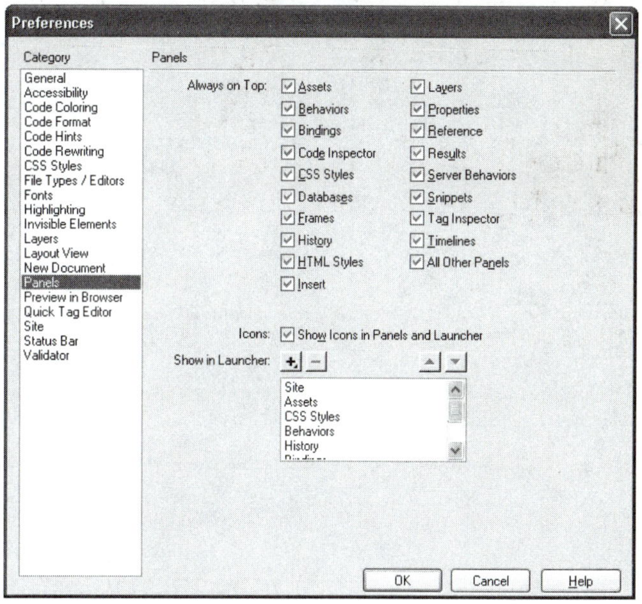

- You can also use this category to select and choose which panels are represented in the Launcher. Use + and − to add or remove panel names and ▲ and ▼ buttons to reorder the list.
- If you are using the Dreamweaver 4 floating panel workspace, this category is listed as Floating Panels.

Preview in Browser Category

- To make it simple to preview your pages in one or more browsers, set up browsers in the Preview in Browser category (see illustration at the top of the next page). Your default browser will be listed first and will have the F12 shortcut key.

Preview in Browser category

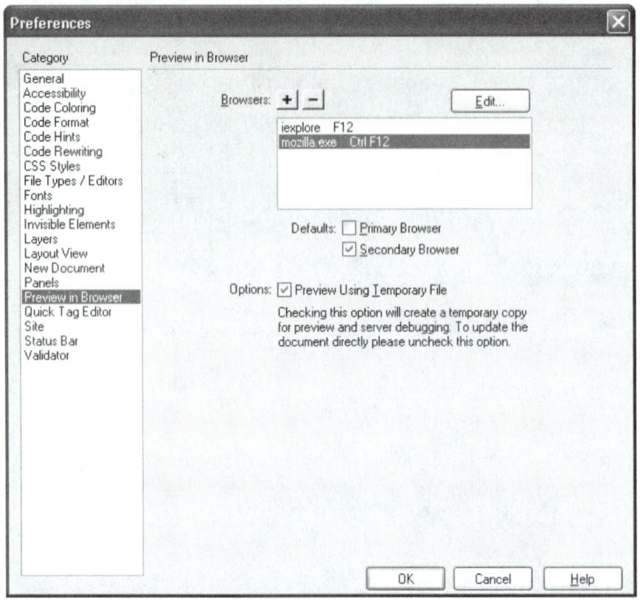

- Use the + button to open the Add Browser dialog box, in which you can specify the name and location of another browser. (You will find the executable files for browsers in the Program Files folder on your hard drive.) You designate this (and subsequent browsers) as secondary browsers that use other keystroke shortcuts to start.

Quick Tag Editor

- Dreamweaver's Quick Tag Editor feature lets you quickly insert, edit a specific HTML tag (see illustration below), or wrap a tag. To display the Quick Tag Editor, press Ctrl + T. Pressing these keys again toggles the Editor from Insert HTML to Edit Tag to Wrap Tag.

Quick Tag Editor

Note: *For more information on how to use the Quick Tag Editor, see Dreamweaver Help.*

- The Quick Tag Editor category (see illustration in next column) allows you to control how the Quick Tag Editor and Document window interact. To see changes immediately in the Document window, make sure the Apply Changes Immediately While Editing checkbox is selected. You can also, if desired, specify a delay before changes display.

Quick Tag Editor category

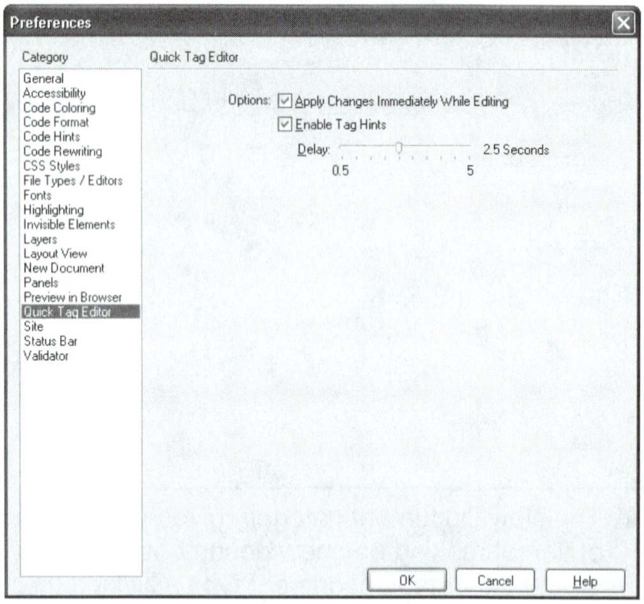

Site Category

- The Site category (see illustration below) lets you manage the Site panel window in its expanded form as well as FTP settings for a Web site. (Some settings will also apply to the Site panel in its collapsed form.) You can choose where to display local files, for example, and activate options to prompt for dependent files.

Site category

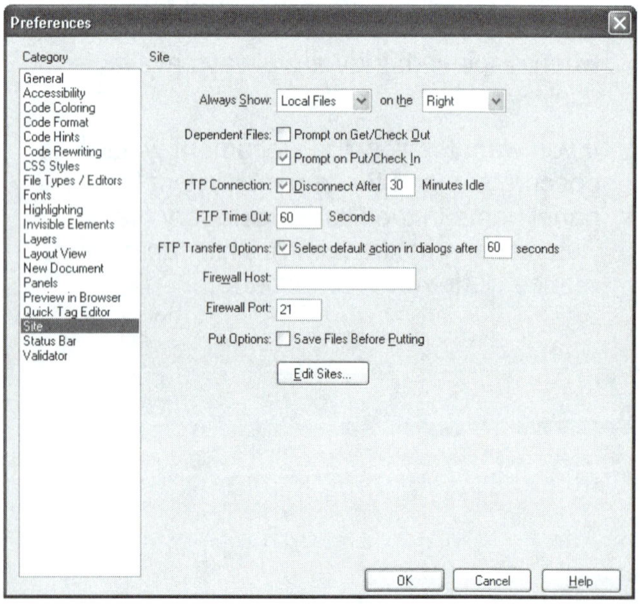

- If you use a firewall to safeguard your server, you can supply the firewall host name and port in this category.
- If you use another kind of remote server setting, such as WebDAV, you can still use the FTP connection settings to control how long a connection is maintained and the like.

Status Bar

- Use the Status Bar category (see illustration below) to customize status bar elements.

Status Bar category

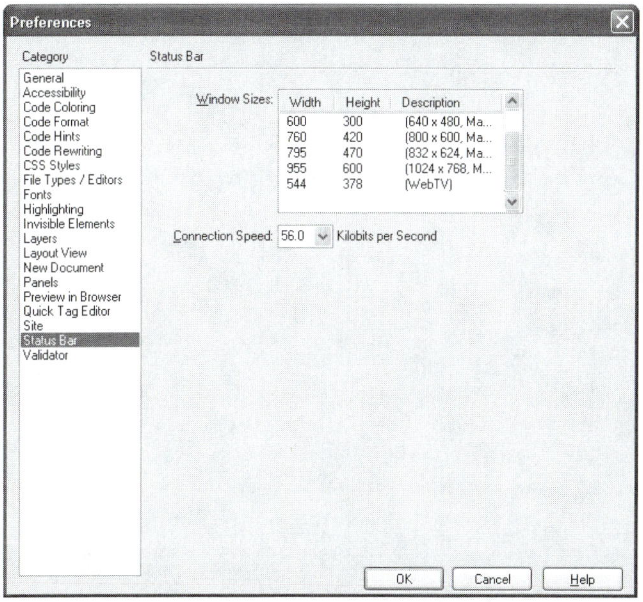

- The Document window status bar contains a pop-up menu (see illustration below) that allows you to choose a specific size at which to display the Document window, such as 592 pixels wide or 600 pixels wide by 300 pixels high.

Status bar window size menu

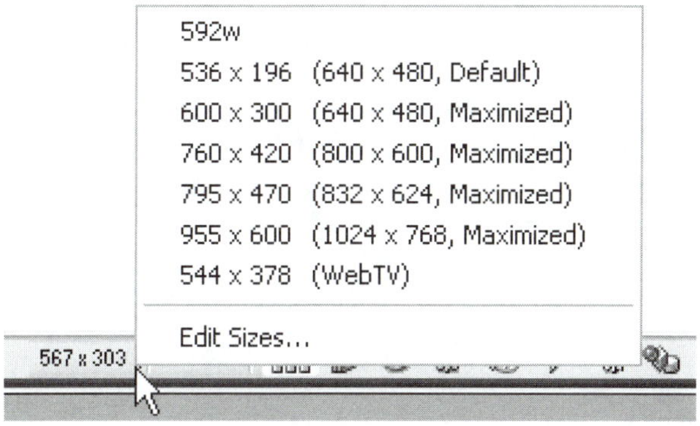

- You can edit the default window sizes or add new sizes of your own that will display on the pop-up menu.
- One setting on the status bar you should always pay attention to is the download time for the current page. The connection speed used to calculate the download time is selected in the Status Bar category (28.8, by default).
- You can choose a new default connection speed that more closely reflects the hardware capabilities of your intended audience. If your Web site will be published on a corporate intranet, for example, you can choose 1500.

Validator

- The Validator category (see illustration below) allows you to control the types of code tags that the Validator reports against in the Validation panel of the Results panel group when running its reports.

Validator category

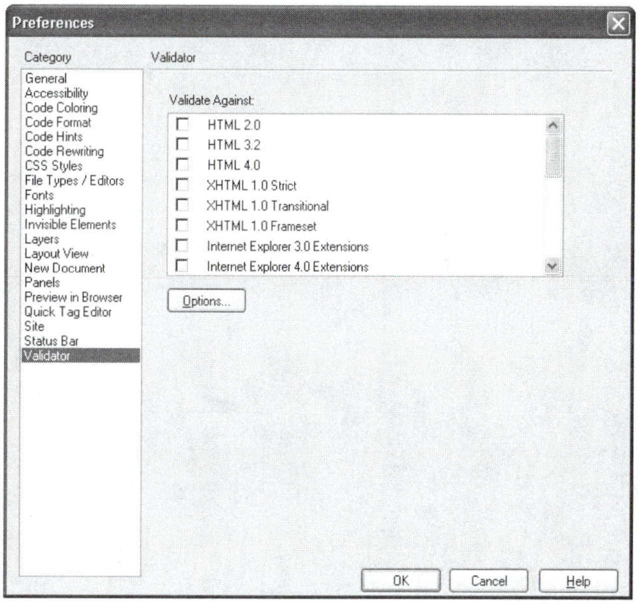

- Click the Options button to choose the kinds of errors that you want reported (see illustration on next page)

Validator Options dialog box

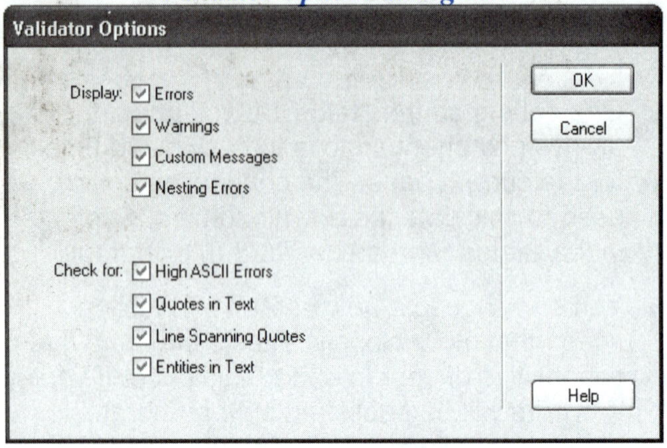

- See the discussion of the Validator in Chapter 17 and Dreamweaver Help for more information about using Validator preferences.

Appendix B: Computer Basics

Introduction to Operating Systems

- An **operating system** is a software program that enables your computer hardware and all other software programs to run. Also referred to as an OS, an operating system, such as Windows, Linux, or the Macintosh OS, is the brain that controls the processes, resources, and memory in your computer.
- Operating systems can consist of a number of types of files. For example, Windows contains small software programs such as games and WordPad, as well as system files that help your hardware to run, and resources such as fonts and Windows desktop icons.
- An operating system controls how you manage files, modify your desktop display, allocate disk space, and even set your computer clock and date.
- New versions of operating systems are released every few years as enhancements in technology become available. That is why you may have heard of or worked with Windows 95, Windows 98, Windows NT, Windows ME, and Windows XP. They are all versions of the Windows operating system.
- Software that runs on your computer, such as word processors and spreadsheet programs, is also released in new versions every few years; these versions are designed to work on the then-current version of an operating system.
- Most operating systems are **backwardly compatible**, meaning that software that worked on an earlier version will probably run adequately on a newer version. However if you have an older version of an operating system you are not likely to be able to use software written for a later version.

Overview of Software

- Software is essentially a set of features you can use to get work done, such as designing company brochures or creating a department budget. Software contains sets of features that you can use through tools such as menus and toolbar buttons.
- Software can fall into several categories. For example, you could use:
  - Financial software that works with numbers and calculations, such as Quicken or spreadsheet programs such as Excel.
  - Word processing software, such as Microsoft Word or Corel WordPerfect, which is used for writing documents such as letters and reports.
  - Desktop publishing and web design software, such as Adobe PageMaker, Microsoft Publisher, Macromedia Dreamweaver, or Microsoft FrontPage, which provides tools for designing documents such as newsletters and brochures or Web pages.
  - **Utilities** that help to maintain your system or manage files, for example, antivirus programs to prevent and clean up computer infections and zip programs to compress large files into smaller files.
  - **Drivers**, which are software applications that run your hardware, such as print drivers for a printer and a display driver to enable your operating system to interact with your computer monitor.
- To use software, you first **install** it on your computer. You can then open the software program by using your operating system; for example, you can start installed software programs on a Windows computer by selecting the program name from the Windows Start menu. You can also start a software program by opening any file originally created in that program.
- When you save a document you have created in a software program, it will be saved in that software format with a name you give it. The file name will include an indication of the file format. For example, a Microsoft Word document might be called "Rent Letter.doc", where Rent Letter is the name you give the file to identify its contents, and the .doc extension indicates that this is a Word document. Some common file extensions are .txt for Text file, .rtf for Rich Text Format files, and .xls for Excel spreadsheets.

Networking and Communications

- All computers communicate. The CPU talks to the hard drive controller; the video card communicates with the monitor and the CPU. The printer and the CPU talk to each other. Each element uses a communications protocol—a set of send and receive signals following rules that have been agreed upon by computer manufacturers or established by governmental or professional organizations.
- For example, when you print a document, the program in the computer that handles printing sends a signal to the printer that asks whether it is ready to receive data. The printer normally signals that it is ready. When its print buffer (a place where the document "lines up" waiting for the printer to be available) is full, the printer signals the computer that it cannot receive more data. The computer waits, periodically asking if the printer is ready for more, until the printer signals its readiness.
- When people talk of computer communications, however, they usually mean the ability of one computer to talk with other computers. When personal computers became common in businesses, users began to look for ways to make it possible for personal computers to share data and programs with one another.
- The first solution was **sneaker net**. Users copied files from one computer and carried them to another on a storage media such as a floppy disk. That method, however useful, had limits. If the receiving computer was across town, it took a while for the communication to be completed. In addition, businesses have large amounts of data residing under the control of their mainframe computers, but the personal computers on desktops at first couldn't make use of that data. Communication was a problem that needed to be solved.
- Today, PC users can share data and programs over **networks**; they can use the facilities of the company's mainframe computers using terminal emulation software and hardware. They can communicate with colleagues in remote locations through networks, electronic mail, and the Internet and World Wide Web.
- If you use a personal computer in a reasonably large organization—school, university, or company—you probably work on a Local Area Network or LAN. Your computer can work locally, using the programs and drives that are installed on it. Your computer, however, is also a workstation; that is, a machine that can use the drives, folders, files, and programs on the computer network.
- LANs generally operate in one of two configurations:
  - **File server**, in which a central computer or group of computers controls access to the network's facilities.
  - **Peer-to-peer**, in which users share the resources of their local machines with one another.

File Server Local Area Networks (LANs)

- On **file server** networks, one or more computers act as the central filing system for the **clients** on the network. Data and programs that are to be shared reside on the disk drives controlled by the network programs.
- File server LANs usually connect users in the same building or group of neighboring buildings that can be connected directly by cables.

File Server Network Components

- File server networks include the following elements:
  - The **server** provides files or services to other computers. The server has hard drives and programs that let it communicate with other computers and provide services to them.
  - **Client workstations** are computers that request files or services from servers. Most modern networks can mix computers of different types and capabilities, including Apple machines running Mac OS, PCs running Windows or DOS, and computers running the Unix or Linux operating systems. In a peer-to-peer network, each computer operates as a client when it requests services from other computers and as a server when it provides services to other computers.

- **Printers** may be shared across the network. Each shared printer is identified by a name. When users want to print, they choose a printer through the application they are using. Other peripherals, such as scanners or plotters, are managed in the same way as printers.
- **Network cards** convert binary data from the computer into signals that can be transmitted over cables to and from other computers. Each workstation requires a network card in one of its bus slots. Network cards are specific to the type of network to which the workstation is connected.
- **Cables** connect computers to one another and to the server.
- When network wiring stretches over long distances, a series of **hubs** may be used to strengthen signals transmitted along the cables. The distance from one hub to another depends on the cable type; fiber optic cables allow the longest runs without a hub to boost the signal.

Network Use

- When you turn on a computer attached to a network, the computer boots up, but before you can start using it, you are requested for a **login name** or **username** and **password**. The login name (also called **user ID**) identifies you to the network and the password ensures that only an authorized person can use the name. If you do not have a valid login name or you don't remember your password, you are not allowed to use the network.
- If you cancel the login process, you can use the machine as a stand-alone computer, but some drives, programs, data files, and printers may be unavailable.

✓ *All the illustrations in this section are drawn from DDC's Novell file server network. The objects on your network will have different names.*

Windows Login Screen for Novell Network

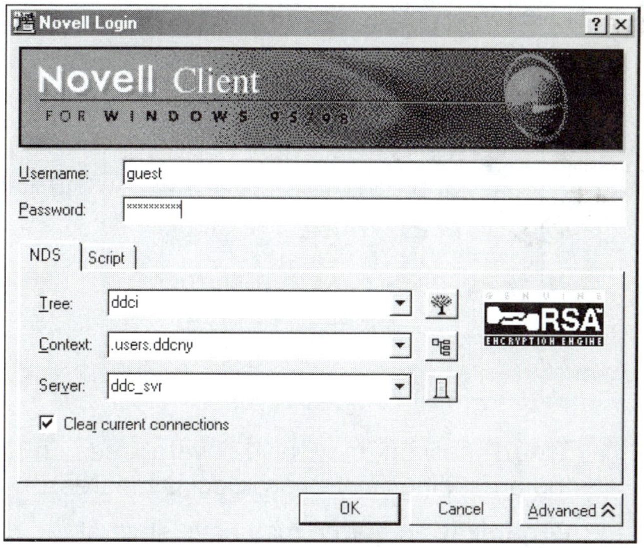

MacOS Login Screen for Novell Network

- The **login name** is a string of characters assigned by network administration that identifies you as a network user. The rights to use network folders and files are associated with the login name.
- On LANs your access is usually restricted to certain drives, folders, and files. On a file server network, maintaining access rights is the job of the **network administrator**. The network administrator assigns login IDs, defines and maintains access rights, ensures that backups are performed regularly, and works to keep the network operating smoothly.

Structure of a File Server Network

- A Novell file server network has a hierarchical structure:

Sample Tree in Windows

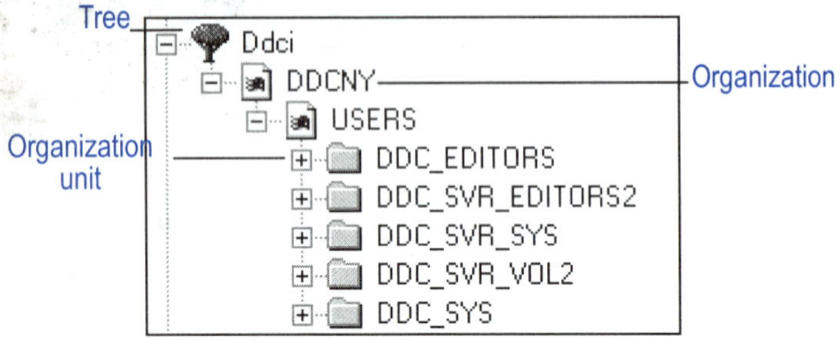

- **Tree.** A network may have several trees. In the preceding illustration, Ddci is the tree.
- **Organization.** A tree may have several organizations. In the sample tree illustration, DDCNY is the organization.
- **Organization unit.** An organization may have several organization units. In the sample tree illustration, USERS is the organization unit.
- **Server.** An organization unit may have several servers. Server names usually represent disk drives under the server's control.
- **Volume.** A volume is a name given to a disk drive or a portion of a disk drive. In Windows, drive identifiers (letters) are **mapped** (assigned) to a volume or portion of a volume. These drive letters appear in Windows Explorer just like local drives. On the Macintosh, a volume to which you have access appears on the desktop.
- **Folder.** A container for files on a volume.

Introduction to Peer-to-Peer Networks

- On **peer-to-peer** networks, each workstation has disk areas that are accessible to other users. In such a network, no machine acts solely as a server. If you want a file from another workstation, you act as a client and the other machine is the server; if someone retrieves files from your machine, your workstation is the server and the other is the client.
- Peer-to-peer networks usually work best when only a few users are involved. Because they require direct cable connection from workstation to workstation, they are usually restricted to a single geographic location.
- Combinations of file server and peer-to-peer networks often exist within a single company. Several users who are working on the same project may work on a peer-to-peer network. They may need, for example, to retain close working-group control of specific files. But when members of the group need to communicate with or use files that belong to the organization as a whole, they may access the file server network that everyone in the company uses.

Explore a Peer-to-Peer Network on Windows

- You can explore a peer-to-peer network on Windows through Windows Explorer. The illustration that follows shows a five-workstation, peer-to-peer network displayed in Windows Explorer.

Five-Workstation, Peer-to-Peer Network on Windows

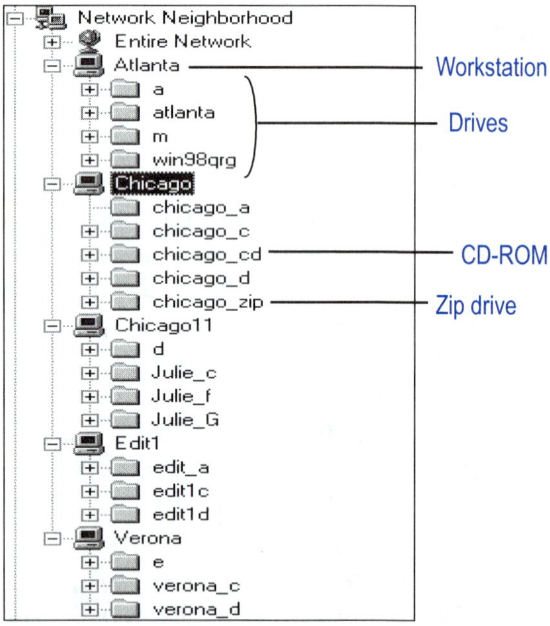

- Any drive on a machine can be shared. Note, for example, the Chicago workstation can give other users access to its CD-ROM and a Zip drive that provides additional storage on 100 Mbyte, removable disks.

- When you right-click on one of the workstations or drives, a shortcut menu appears, as shown in the illustration that follows.

Windows Peer-to-Peer Workstation Shortcut Menu

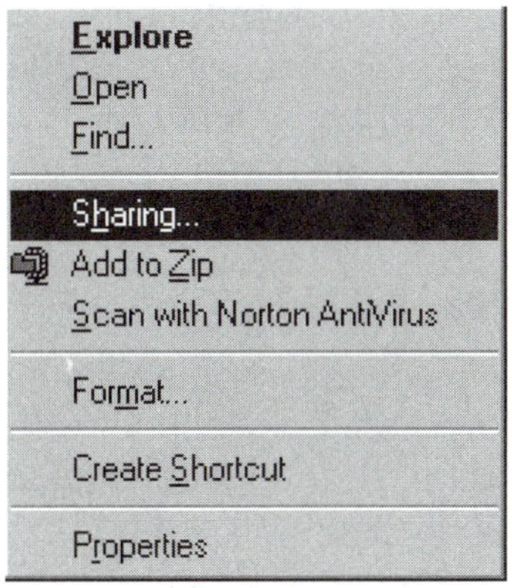

Wide Area Networks

- Another kind of network is called a **Wide Area Network** (**WAN**). In some companies, a WAN is used to connect workers in different geographic locations. In the central location, the network operates like a LAN. Workers outside the central location communicate with the network via modem, satellite, or leased telephone lines through hardware and software facilities called *gateways*. The gateways give distant users access to the services of the central location.
- Some people reserve the term WAN for networks that serve only members of the same company or organization. Others consider AOL, Prodigy, CompuServe, World Wide Web, and even the Internet as WANs.

Intranets

- Many users within an organization may have access to the Internet, using their Internet browsers to find information, send e-mail, and exchange files with co-workers. But when they leave the Internet, many of them have to use other applications to review information and exchange files.
- Increasingly, therefore, companies are creating internal Webs to allow employees to access company information using the same application they use to access the Internet. These internal Webs are known as **intranets**.
- Intranets are created and managed within an organization. Users outside the organization generally cannot gain access to them. This means that information that is inappropriate for an Internet site, such as personnel policies or intra-company news, can be provided on an intranet. Using their Internet browsers, workers can use the intranet in the same way they use the Internet.
- Some companies also provide access to their intranets to authorized outside users. For example, a company may wish a supplier to be able to review specifications for a purchase that is about to be made. The supplier then uses an Internet browser, contacts the intranet (often through the Internet), and gains access to the intranet by using an ID and password. The companies that provide such access call this an **extranet**.
- An intranet may have connections to the Internet, but these connections are constructed to prevent unauthorized access. The term **firewall** is used to describe protecting a network or computer from unauthorized access.

Telecommuting and Networks

- More and more workers are working away from the office. Some of them simply use their PCs as local machines and communicate with the office only when they have files they want to send or receive. Such users may use the Internet or e-mail service as their way to communicate with the office and never actually log in to the office's computers.
- Other workers, however, connect via telephone lines and work directly on the office network. Telecommuting of this type requires hardware and software on both the workstation and the server. Usually the telecommuter starts the communications software on the workstation, dials up the office computer, and logs in as a network user. The full facilities of the company's network are then available to the workstation.

PC-to-Mainframe Communications

- To use a company's mainframe computing capacity, workers require a **terminal**. Terminals are pieces of hardware that have no software of their own. They are connected to the mainframe computer via cables and their communication is managed by a **controller**, another piece of hardware that provides the link between terminals (one controller can handle many terminals) and the mainframe. Terminals are single-use devices; they cannot function apart from the mainframe. If they get disconnected from the computer or the mainframe stops working, their users are no longer able to compute.
- In the first days of the personal computer, users thought it would be good to use computers just like terminals. But terminals operate differently from PCs. PCs do not require controllers and ordinarily do not speak the same language as controllers. Often workers who needed both a personal computer and access to the company's mainframe had both a PC and a terminal on their desks. Soon after the introduction of IBM's PC in the early 1980s, however, both hardware and software solutions were created.
- **Terminal emulation software**, programs that mimicked mainframe terminals, was created as early as 1981 for computers built by Digital Equipment Corporation. DEC mainframes used ASCII (American Standard Code for Information Interchange) for encoding characters. Since PCs also used ASCII, it was possible to create software that let a PC work with a DEC mainframe.
- IBM mainframes, however, were a different matter. Rather than use ASCII codes, they use a coding system called EBCDIC (sometimes pronounced EB-sid-ick, short for Extended Binary Coded Decimal Interchange Code). Differences between the ASCII and EBCDIC coding systems made it necessary to create **terminal emulation hardware** so the PC and the IBM mainframe could communicate.
- In most installations where PCs and mainframes communicate today, a combination of hardware and software does the job. In many companies, users are connected to a local area network and log on (or sign on) to the organization's mainframe without disconnecting from the network. The personal computer then operates not only as an independent machine but also as a network workstation and as a mainframe terminal.

Wireless LANs

- In smaller business or home computing settings, a wireless network solution makes most of the cabling of other networks unnecessary. Using radio frequencies or infrared optical signaling and protocols such as Bluetooth, computers can communicate and share peripheral devices such as printers by use of a network card and wireless access point.
- One problem with wireless networks today is that communication can be interfered with by walls, pillars, or other equipment that can disrupt a radio signal. However in smaller offices and homes where computers can be set up to avoid these obstacles, wireless networks are a handy networking solution.

Appendix C: Peripherals and Storage Devices

Introduction to Computer Peripherals

- The processing of data in your computer takes place in the central processing unit (CPU), a microchip. The speed of this chip helps determine how fast your computer runs. Intel is one example of a company that produces CPUs, for example, its Pentium III chip or Pentium 4 processor. CPU speeds are determined in megahertz or gigahertz. But it's nearly impossible actually take advantage of all that information and computing power without the use of computer peripherals.
- A *peripheral* is a device such as a printer, keyboard, or monitor that is attached to the CPU and managed by the computer's microprocessor. That attachment may be through any of a variety of cable types such as parallel or USB (universal serial bus), or through a wireless infrared connection.
- Peripherals require software called *drivers* to enable them to communicate with the computer and function. A peripheral driver is very specific to the device it works with. By using drivers to control peripherals, the computer operating system is freed from the task of incorporating those controls within its own program and allows the operating system to coordinate with a wide variety of hardware products.
- *Plug and play* refers to the ability of a computer to make automatic settings to configure a peripheral you add through a cable or wireless connection. Plug and Play is also the name of the set of specifications developed by Intel and Microsoft that enables this automatic configuration to occur. The preferred connection for plug and play devices is the USB interface.

Input Devices

- The process of computing is, at its most basic, the process of putting information into a computer, having the computer manipulate that information, and generating output, such as a business letter or budget.
- The process of putting information into your computer, whether in the form of commands or content, is called *input*. Various devices can be used to input data into a computer, including a mouse, keyboard, speech commands, and something called pen technology which allows you write on a computer screen with a special form of pen.
- One of the concerns about most input devices is the area of *ergonomics.* Because these devices are used repetitively and for long periods of time, they can cause damage to the user. For example, using a keyboard for years on end can lead to a condition affecting the nerves in the wrists called Carpal Tunnel Syndrome. For this reason you will see some models of input devices touted as being ergonomically designed.

Mouse

- The mouse is a pointing and selection device. Although the mouse itself isn't the primary way to enter content into your computer, it is considered an input device because it enables you to interact with computer data. A mouse can also be used to select commands through tool buttons or menus to perform various actions such as formatting text or saving a file.
- A mouse can be used to place your computer's insertion point in a document so that you can begin to enter content with a keyboard or other method. A mouse can also be used to select objects by clicking on them, and to select text and move it around a document through a method known as drag and drop. The mouse is also the primary device used by most people to draw objects.
- Early mouse models sported a trackball on their underside that the user rolled around a mat on the desktop. The movement of the mouse around the desktop was mirrored in the movement of the cursor on the computer screen.

- Later mouse models moved the trackball to the top of the device, where, instead of moving the mouse itself around the desktop, the user could roll the trackball with his thumb or finger and that movement was mirrored on screen.
- Today, there are optical mouse models. An optical mouse uses light sensors that detect movement, rather than any moveable part such as a trackball. Many new mouse models are also cordless, helping to get rid of some of the clutter of wires surrounding a computer setup.
- The mouse of today typically offers three parts: a left button, a right button, and a center button called a scroll wheel. The left button is used to select things; the right button displays context-sensitive shortcut menus, and the scroll wheel makes moving through a document—especially lengthy Web pages—easier. You can control how your mouse functions to a large extent by using your operating system controls.

The Windows Mouse dialog box, accessed through the Control Panel.

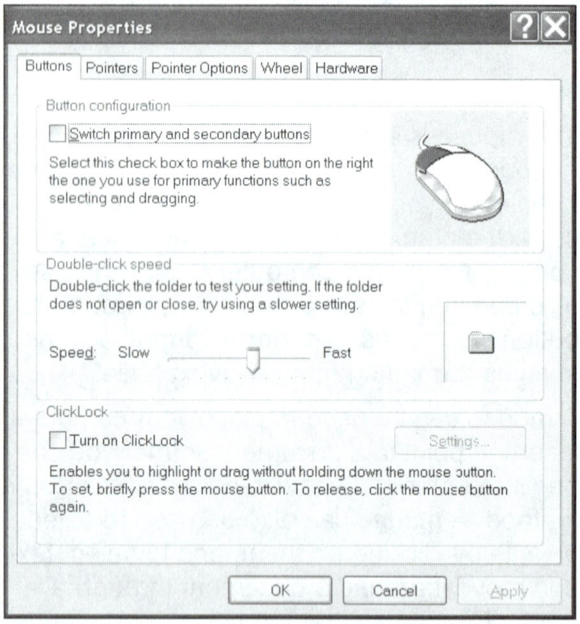

Keyboard

- The keyboard used with your computer has as its ancestor a typewriter keyboard. The arrangement of letters on the keys themselves, called QWERTY after the six letters in the top left corner, has remained largely intact from the old fashioned manual typewriter to the modern day keyboard.
- In addition to the letters, numbers and functional keys such as the Enter or Spacebar that a typewriter included, computer keyboard may contain several other types of keys:
  - A function key is a key numbered from F1 to F12 that may be displayed across the top of the keyboard, or, with certain portable keyboards, embedded within the standard keys. A function key will invoke a function such as displaying a help screen or activating a menu bar. Function keys are sometimes used in conjunction with other keys such as the Alt or Ctrl key to perform secondary functions.
  - Internet-ready keys give you one touch access to online elements such as your email or home page.

  ✓ *Internet-ready keyboards have up to seven programmable Internet-ready keys. You can set these up to access areas of the Internet you visit frequently with a single keystroke.*

  - Directional keys allow you to move your cursor around a document. In addition keys such as Home, End, Page Up, and Page Down allow you to move quickly to another area of a document or screen.
- There are a variety of keyboard designs available, with most designed to ease repetitive stress to the user's hands and wrists. Ergonomic keyboards may have a curvy appearance, or even be split into two sections. Many keyboards provide a wrist rest area at the bottom of the keyboard, or you can buy a wrist rest at any office supply store to work with any keyboard.
- Wireless keyboards provide some freedom for the user. Wireless keyboards can either use infrared technology (just like a television remote control) or radio frequencies to establish a wireless connection. With infrared technology the computer and keyboard have to have their infrared ports facing each other. With radio frequency, the connection can be made with the equipment in any position, and often up to thirty feet apart.

Speech

- Speech recognition (also called voice recognition) is a technology that is still evolving. Essentially voice recognition software can be trained to your own speech patterns by having you read sample text into a microphone attached to your computer. The software then matches your patterns to stored speech patterns and turns your spoken words into text in a document. Speech can also be used to dictate voice commands, such as "Save," or "Open".

  ✓ *Speech recognition is useful for those with visual impairments and provides one viable way for these people to interact with a computer.*

- Because there is such a wide variety of accents and inflections among human beings, speech recognition software is not one hundred percent accurate. Content entered using speech sometimes needs to be corrected using a mouse and keyboard. For that reason few computers make do with only speech recognition as a method to enter content.

Pen

- Pen technology has been around for the last ten years or so. Pen technology uses a combination of handwriting recognition software and a specialized pen device that you can use to write either on an input panel or directly on certain computer screens.
- Pen technology is traditionally used by people who work with graphics, because it provides a much more natural method to enter drawings into a computer document. However, to date, this technology has been slow to be accepted.
- With the release of a new computer format called Tablet PC in the fall of 2002, pen computing is undergoing something of a renaissance. The handwriting recognition software that underlies pen technology in Windows XP for Tablet PC has advanced to the point where approximately ninety-seven percent of what you write can be converted to text automatically with no error.

  ✓ *One big advantage to pen input is that even those who don't know how to type can input content into a computer using it.*

Scanners

- Scanners are another method of getting input into your computer, though they are usually not considered an input device. These peripherals allow you to scan a hard copy document into an electronic format, creating a computer graphics file. Scanners come with their own software to perform the scan and also to manipulate, edit, and save the scanned image in a computer file.

A scanned image displayed in the HP 2210 flatbed scanner software.

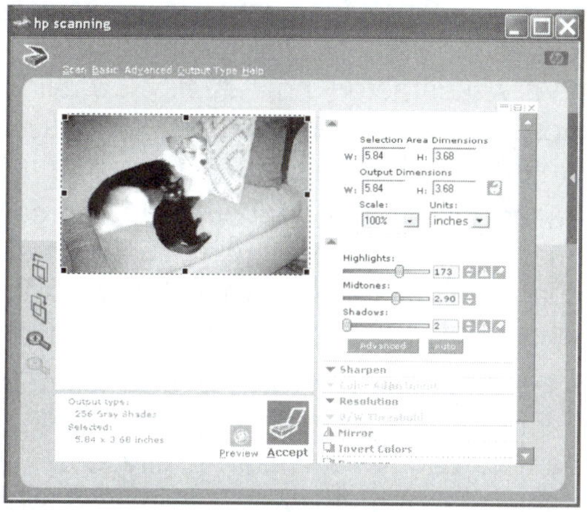

- One important feature of a scanner is the degree of image resolution it can produce. The higher the resolution, the better the image quality. Images are made up of tiny dots called pixels. The higher the resolution of an image, the more pixels per inch. An optical resolution of 1,200 dots per inch (also called dpi), for example, would be very high quality (and more than most consumers need for their purposes). 300 dpi is adequate for most people's needs.
- The speed with which you can transfer data from a scanner to a computer is a consideration. A USB connection allows transfers of 12 megabits per second, compared to only 2 megabits per second through a parallel port.
- Scanners are available in flatbed models, which allow you to place documents or media such as book flat on a panel for scanning. They also come in sheetfed models where you must feed a printed document through the device. This makes scanning bulkier document formats such as books and magazines impossible. In addition some multi-purpose machines may include printing, faxing, copying and scanning capabilities in a single unit.

Output Devices

- Getting content into a computer is only one-half of the process. Peripheral devices are also used to generate output. Output may come in the form of a printed document, or a faxed document.

  ✓ *By networking computers, you can share peripheral devices such as printers or fax machines among several computers.*

Printers

- Printers today provide a lot of technology for a very reasonable cost. Purchasing a color printer with very satisfactory print quality is within the means of most computer users. Printers come in two main types:
  - Laser printers use a laser beam to create an image on a drum that holds an electrostatic charge. The charge attracts toner (ink), then uses heat to apply the toner to a page.
  - Inkjet technology sprays a liquid ink onto paper to form letters or graphic images. Inkjet printers can have similar quality to LaserJet printers, though they are typically slower.
- You can find both black and white and color printers, though the color feature has become so affordable that most newer printers are color printers.
- Printers print with various resolutions, a measure of the quality of the output. A good quality resolution would be 1,200 x 1,200 dots per inch, though both higher and lower quality exists.
- The speed with which a printer can print a document has always been a consideration. Newer printers take advantage of a USB connection to provide faster transfer of data from the computer to the printer. Printers will output a certain number of pages per minute, a gauge of actually printing speed.

Faxes

- Faxing sends a copy (or a facsimile) of a document in digitized form over a phone line. Originally faxing technology was only available through machines connected to a phone line through which you would feed a document. The recipient of the fax also had to have a machine which printed the digitized version of the document (typically a bitmap image) on paper.
- Today many people find it convenient to skip the fax machine altogether and fax digital files directly from one computer to another, or one computer to a fax machine, via a fax modem that uses faxing software. The recipient who receives the fax on his or her computer then prints it out on a standard printer.

  ✓ *If a document isn't available in a digital file format, you can use a scanner to scan it and save it as a computer file, then fax that file from your computer.*

- To fax from a computer you essentially print a document to a fax rather than to a printer. Faxing software walks you through entering recipient information, and even building fax cover sheets.

The Windows fax wizard

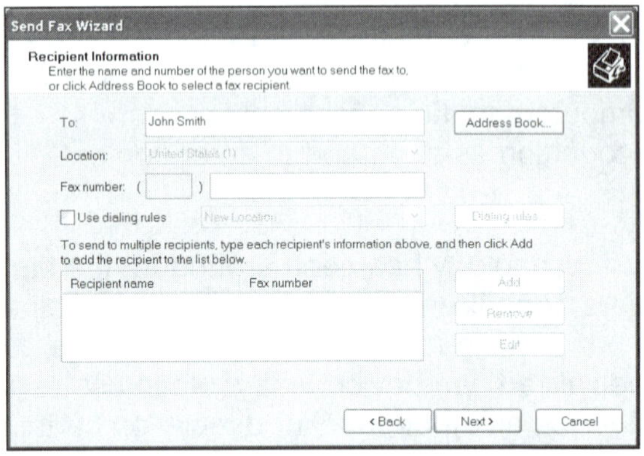

Storage Devices

- Computer files are saved on storage devices using drives. The storage medium itself, called a disk, is placed in the drive and your computer writes data to the disk.
- Your computer's hard drive is one kind of storage device that's built into your computer. Hard drive capacities today are measured in gigabytes. Other kinds of storage media include:
  - Floppy disks; though no longer floppy (they are encased in hard plastic) these contain a film that is coated with particles that can hold a magnetic field. A computer writes data to the disk in binary code using 1s and 0s.
  - Zip or Jaz disks are similar in appearance to a floppy disk, but they can hold up to 100 megabytes of data.
  - CD-ROMs (compact disc read-only memory) are compact discs that contain data, such as software program or even music. CD-ROMs are read only, meaning the user cannot save data to them.
  - CD-RWs are rewriteable CDs, meaning that you can both read information off of them and save information to them.
  - CD-ROMS and CD-RWs can hold around 650 megabytes of data, much more than floppy disks or even zip disks.

    ✓ *Note that a floppy or zip medium is called a disk, but a CD is named a disc.*

Computer Displays (Monitors)

- Not much can be accomplished with your computer without a monitor to show you what you're doing.
- Most monitors today use a CRT display. A CRT is similar to a television screen, but the images on them are even more precise. In the CRT model electron guns send beams of electrons to the end of a tube covered with phosphors. The glowing of these phosphors results in images on your monitor. CRTs are analog devices and though their image quality can be high, their analog nature means they can produce inaccuracies when rendering video images.
- Flat panel monitors are the wave of the future. These display devices use a liquid crystal display technology (LCD) that has been popular in notebook computers for years. LCD displays put liquid crystals between two layers of glass. Voltage is actually applied to the crystals to rearrange them in a way that allows light to come through forming an image. The introduction of thin film transistor (referred to as TFT or active-matrix) technology to the scene provided better quality by giving each pixel in the image its own controlling transistor.
- Improvements that are occurring in flat panel technology will bring their refresh rates (how frequently all the information on the screen has to be redrawn) and color quality in line with the traditional CRT standards. As that happens, flat panels will be preferred for their thin size and more accurate digital image technology.
- You can set your monitor resolution and other display controls using your computer's operating system controls.

The Windows Display Properties dialog box

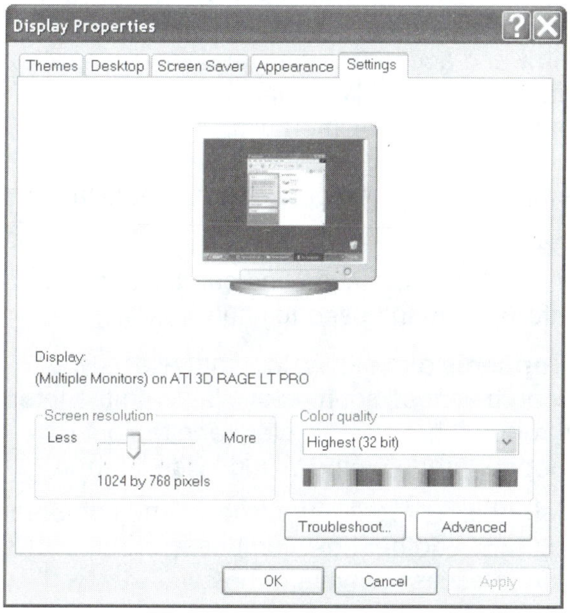

Appendix D: Using the Internet and Intranets

The Internet and Intranets

- The **Internet** is a worldwide network of computers that makes it possible to view and access information of all kinds. The Internet consists of all the computers, telephone lines, satellites, and connection devices and organizations that enable this exchange of information.
- The **World Wide Web** is a component of the Internet created to allow you to use an easy, **graphical interface** to view information organized as pages. Web pages support graphics as well as audio and video files. The coding used to create Web pages also supports **hyperlinks**, used to move quickly from one Web document to another.
- An **intranet** is similar to the Internet, in that it is a network of computers that allows people to view and access information. However, rather than being a publicly available network, an intranet is usually internal to a company or other organization and accessed mainly by the employees or members of that organization.
- Company networks such as LANs and WANs also store information and can be searched for information and used to share resources.
- **Gopher** is a menu system that allows you to search various sources available on the Internet through a browsing system of directories. Gopher predates the World Wide Web.
- **Telnet** is a program that allows one computer to log onto another host computer. Telnet allows you to access servers remotely.
- **WAIS (Wide Area Information Server)** is a system that allows for searches based on contents of files, not just file titles; somewhat outdated.

The Structure of the Internet

- The computers linked on the Internet are linked together using variety of connections—cables, telephone lines, satellites. They pass information back and forth using the communications protocol called **TCP/IP** (Transmission Control Protocol/Internet Protocol). TCP/IP is actually a suite of protocols that work together to make the Internet work.
- TCP/IP performs the following communications functions:
    - Permits login from remote computers.
    - Routes data between Internet servers.
    - Makes sure that data packets are error-free and assembled in the right sequence.
    - Converts text-based domain names into numerical IP (Internet Protocol) addresses.
- The computers that form the Internet or intranets can be divided into the following groups:
- **Clients** are computers that connect to the Internet to do research and send e-mail. Most personal computers that access the Internet fall into this category. Client computers access the Internet in one of three ways:
    - Online service, such as America Online (AOL) or Prodigy.
    - Internet Service Provider.
    - Direct access through a dedicated communications line (telephone or cable, for example) that is continuously connected to the Internet.
- **Online services** provide a variety of shopping, research, and e-mail services and also provide access to the Internet. America Online (AOL), Prodigy, and MSN are popular online services. Such services are not actually part of the Internet, but most users do not distinguish between AOL and the Internet.
- **Internet Service Providers (ISPs)** are computer servers that provide other computers

with access to the Internet. Networks such as Earthlink, NetCom, and AT&T Worldnet are ISPs.

- **Internet servers** (sometimes called hosts) are computers that provide access to information. When an Internet user contacts an Internet site, the computer that contains the site is a server. Internet servers may also act as clients when they request a link to another site. Some servers offer specialized services, such as e-mail and file transfer.
- **Search engines or sites** are Internet computers dedicated to providing information about other Internet sites. Yahoo!, Excite, and Lycos started life as search engines but now have expanded to offer a wide range of services in addition to search capabilities.
- **E-mail servers** are computers that provide electronic mail boxes and e-mail services.
- **File transfer protocol (FTP) servers** are computers dedicated to allowing the transfer of files from one computer to another.

Internet Addresses—URLs (Uniform Resource Locators)

- Because the Internet is not a single network but a collection of networks, a naming system called the **domain name system** is used to identify the exact location of Internet servers and their primary Internet activity. It is something like the telephone numbering system that includes country codes, area codes, and individual phone numbers.
- An Internet address (IP address) is made up of a four-part series of numbers. The domain name system translates the numbers into a user-friendly system of text-based names. So instead of typing in 128.337.392.449 to order a pizza over the Internet, you can type in "www.pizzahut.com." Text is simply easier to remember.
- To locate an Internet site, you enter an address called a **URL (uniform resource locator)**. Usually this address is a group of characters that looks like the following: http://www.amazon.com
- In this address, note the following items:
  - **http** stands for HyperText Transfer Protocol, the communications protocol used by sites on the World Wide Web. (An FTP site's address would be preceded by ftp instead of http.)
  - **www** stands for World Wide Web, the largest part of the Internet.
  - **amazon** is the name used to identify the organization who is responsible for the content of the site. It is usually some form of the name of the company or organization, for example, amazon is the identifier for Amazon.com, an online bookstore.
  - **com** is the **domain** identifier. Different types of organizations have different domain names.
- Common Internet domains include the following:

Domain:	Used By:
.com	commercial/business
.gov	government
.edu	educational
.org	various organizations, usually non-profit
.mil	military
.net	network resources

- In addition, many domain names include an abbreviation of the country where the site is located; for example, *uk* in a URL indicates a site in the United Kingdom (Great Britain and Northern Ireland).
- Companies or personal users can obtain a domain name by purchasing an existing domain name or by registering a new one. To register a domain name, you can go to any number of authorized registry sites (see http://www.icann.org/registrars/accredited-list.html) to confirm that your choice is unregistered and pay for your domain name.

Using a Browser

- To use the Internet or an Intranet you need and **Internet browser**, such as Microsoft Internet Explorer or Netscape Navigator. A browser is an application that:
  - Lets you connect to the Internet either directly or through a modem and a telephone line using an ISP or online service.
  - Lets you enter URLs.
  - Displays information provided by an Internet site.
  - Lets you save or print displayed information so it can be reviewed later.
  - Recognizes and lets you activate connections (called **hyperlinks)** to other addresses.
  - Lets you save addresses that you'd like to visit again using **favorites** (Internet Explorer) or **bookmarks** (Netscape Navigator).

Web Page Basics

- Though Web pages differ widely in design and format, many Web pages share some common features.
- On many Web pages, information is organized using **frames**. Often, a frame at the left side of the Web page holds links that act as a table of contents for the Web site.

Sample Web Page

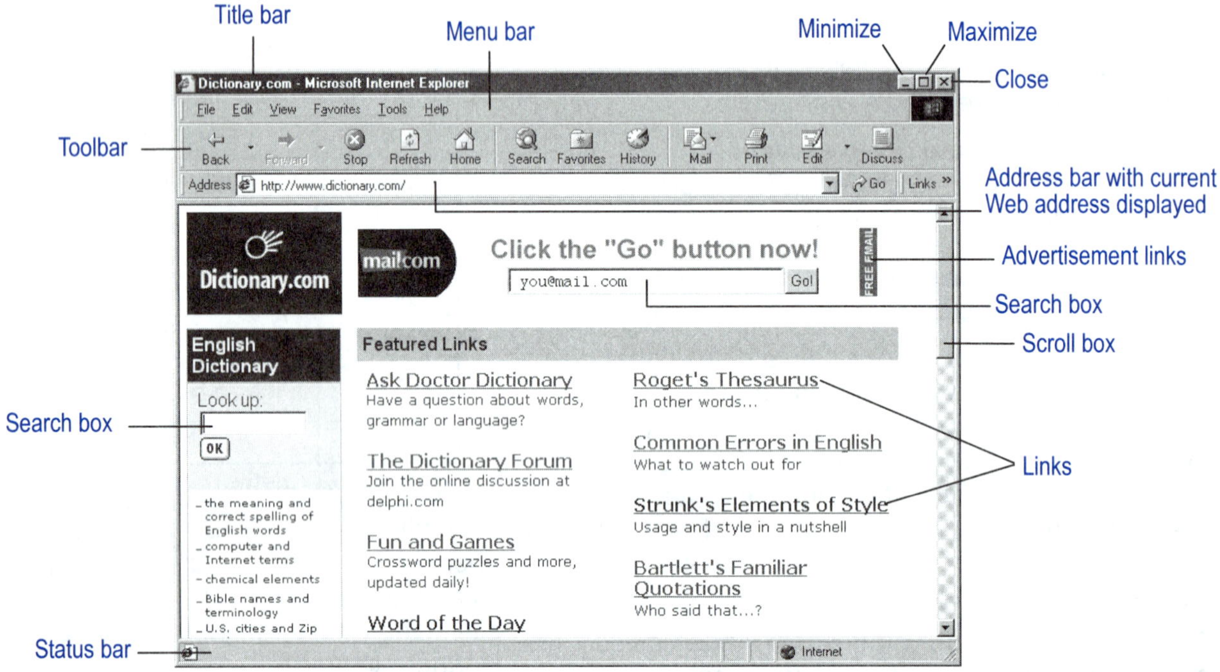

- The browser window that displays the Web page has additional features that will be familiar to you from other applications:
  - The title bar displays the name of the current Web page.
  - A menu bar offers menus of commands for displaying and controlling Web pages.
  - A toolbar contains buttons for executing frequently used commands and functions.
  - If the page has more content than can be displayed in the current window size, scroll bars become active.
  - The address bar displays the Internet address of the current Web page.
  - The standard Windows sizing controls also appear in the Internet Explorer window.
  - The status bar displays the progress of a Web page as it **loads** on your computer screen. It also displays the current Web page address and changes to show the addresses of links as you point to them.

Standards of Online Behavior

- Searching the Net—commonly known as Surfing—is fun and exciting. The Net is a great resource for everything from understanding the do's and don'ts of buying a new car, to paying bills, to researching school term papers. Over the Net you can purchase concert tickets, order steaks for the weekend cookout, and make new friends. The ability to communicate with people and visit places all over the world from the comfort of your home, classroom, or office is amazing.
- It is important, however, to use this great communication tool responsibly. Respectful communication with others and a cooperative attitude are indispensable when taking advantage of the many resources available.

Netiquette

- Generally speaking, there are very few actual "Net Laws" at this writing (excluding Federal laws for prosecuting Internet hackers, virus terrorists, and the other "cybercriminals"). Those that exist are generally devised by the Internet community itself.
- For example, when you sign up with an Internet service provider (ISP), you will probably be asked to agree to adhere to strict usage rules that, if you disobey them, can result in a loss of service—and possible prosecution.
- Netiquette (net + etiquette) has developed over time as a set of behaviors that should be adhered to when you travel down the information super-highway. Various subsets of netiquette apply depending on what activity you're engaged in at the moment.

FTP Etiquette

- FTP, or File Transfer Protocol, allows you to transfer data files and software programs from FTP sites to your computer over the Internet. If you are using a browser program to access an FTP site, you will use anonymous FTP. This means that you won't need a login name or password to gain access to the FTP site server. We are allowed access to these vast storehouses of information through the generosity of the individual FTP host institutions (universities, organizations, etc.), therefore; it is important that we play by their rules.

Some FTP Netiquette Hints and Tips:

- Respect any posted hours at an anonymous FTP host. As a general rule, most sites ask that you not access their databases between the hours of 8 am and 5 pm, as these are the hours when they are busiest. Remember to verify time zones: for example, when it is 5 pm on the East Coast it is only 2 pm on the West Coast.
- If you log on to an anonymous FTP site (without using a browser application) as an anonymous user, it is recommended that you use your full Internet e-mail address as your password.
- Use available site help files before asking for help. Many sites provide README and INDEX files that provide answers to commonly-asked questions.
- Many FTP hosts post rules particular to their site. Be aware of these postings and follow the rules strictly.
- Only download files you know you will need. Don't tie up the network downloading information you don't need.

E-Mail Etiquette

- The written word is a powerful tool for communication, so you should exercise caution in how you use words on the Internet. Remember: an e-mail message will almost always be taken at face value. The reader is not afforded the luxury of perceiving nuance. Since your message will not be accompanied by facial expression or vocal inflection, it is imperative that you write with clarity and courtesy. Keep sarcasm to a minimum, or avoid it altogether.
- This does not mean that mail to friends cannot be funny or mildly satiric, but be aware that your message can be misinterpreted. Know your audience and, above all, minimize the risks or misinterpretation.

Some E-Mail Netiquette Hints and Tips:

- Using all capital letters gives a word very strong emphasis. It can also have the effect of SHOUTING! In general, it is better to use upper- and lowercase letters as you would when writing a letter.
- Enclosing a word with *asterisks* has a different effect. Asterisks indicate a mild emphasis and serve the same purpose as italics.

- Signature "smileys" can help to indicate mood or tone of voice:
  - :-) I'm happy. (Made with a colon, dash, and right parenthesis. Tilt head to the left for full effect.)
  - ;-) Just joking. (Made with semi-colon, dash, and right parenthesis.)
  - :-(I'm unhappy. (Made with colon, dash, and left parenthesis.)
- Be careful when replying to a message. If your reply is to be automatically sent back to the originating address, verify that the address is not connected to a list or group. A personal response intended for a specific person may end up in the hands of many.
- Electronic mail is not protected and not private. Your message can be forwarded or copied to anyone, anywhere. Think of it as an electronic postcard—fully exposed and able to be read by anyone who comes in contact with it. Computer and network hackers can easily access anything sent across the Internet. Assume that anyone with a computer has the potential to read your message.
- Never send chain letters over the Internet. Not only are they annoying, but they are forbidden by many Internet service providers, and if you participate in sending them, your privileges may be revoked.
- Sending angry or heated messages is called "flaming." Everyone seems to agree that "flames" are childish and never necessary. If you are feeling emotional, take the time to calm down before sending responses.
- Use the subject or RE: line to clearly state the topic of your message. This is the first thing the recipients will see in their e-mail directory.
- Keep messages concise. When replying to a message, be sure to include enough information from the original message so that your reply is understood. Delete anything from the original message that is irrelevant.
- Messages should have lines that are no more than 65–70 characters in length and generally no more than 12 lines. Do not assume that the person has the same size screen or that the wrap feature will automatically make the message "fit."
- If you send a long message, it is a good idea to tell the recipients at the beginning of the message so that they have the option of downloading the message to read later.
- There are many other rules and procedures that you will learn as you become an experienced Net user. Typically, your ISP service contract, which you have agreed to, will contain specific rules about sending e-mail through its server. School labs and office environments will have their own procedures that are strictly enforced. Check with your teacher or Network administrator for more information.

Internet Ethics

- Ethics is the study of standards of conduct and moral judgment. Ethical behavior is as important when you use the Internet as it is in any other part of your life.
- Internet ethics is a hot topic on the Internet, as users attempt to define standards of behavior that all can adhere to. Remember that, generally speaking, the Internet is regulated only by those who use it.
- Use the following points as a guideline for ethical behavior when you use the Internet:
  - **Plagiarism:** The Internet is a vast resource of information. If you use material from a source on the Internet, cite the source properly.
  - **Privacy:** Networked systems make it all too easy for determined snoopers to read other people's e-mail or review documents on their computers. Respect the privacy of others, as you expect them to respect yours.
  - **Piracy:** Piracy of copyrighted materials, such as software or music, has always been a serious problem. Do your part to respect copyrights.
  - **Hacking and Viruses:** Hacking and the spreading of destructive viruses are legal issues. No matter how much fun you might find it to access a server illegally or pull a prank with a virus, you can face serious charges if you do so.
  - Avoid "spamming"—sending the same e-mail message to many recipients.

- Respect the privacy of other Internet users.
- Adhere to any guidelines set up for you in the setting in which you will use the Internet such as your business or school.

- Remember that whenever you use the Internet, you are part of an entire community of users who rely on you to behave sensibly and ethically. Keep both ethics and Netiquette in mind as you use the Internet.

Searching Online

- Searching is the systematic approach to finding information on the Web. This differs from surfing, which is simply jumping from link to link.
- With the help of online Internet search tools and a basic knowledge of how to search, you can greatly increase your chances of finding specific information.
- When you use a search tool, you are not searching the Internet live. You are searching a database or **index** maintained by the search site. Because methods for compiling databases differ among search sites, you can expect search results to differ as well from site to site.
- There are two major types of search tools available on the Web: **search engines** and **directories**.

  ✓ *Some Internet guides refer to all search tools as search engines.*

- Both directories and search engines maintain Web sites that you can access just like any other Web site: click a link or type the site's address in your browser's address bar.
- Some search sites provide special features that direct you to certain kinds of results. Google, for example, is a search site that allows you to search for certain types of files (such as PDF or non-HTML), retrieve news stories related to your search term, to restrict your search to their directory (which contains over three million sites), or to a specific Web site.

Evaluating and Validating Online Information

- There are millions of pages of information to be mined on the World Wide Web and on the Internet. Not all of that information can be trusted.
- A healthy skepticism about all information found on the Internet is a good thing. Anyone with a computer, very little technical expertise, and an opinion can post information on the Internet.
- Following are a few suggestions to keep in mind as you explore the Internet:
  - Check to see when the site was last updated. Most sites include this information somewhere on the home page.
  - Be wary of sites that contain many typographical or grammatical errors.
  - Go to sites run by established organizations.
  - Long Internet addresses with many backslashes (/) and tildes (~) often indicate personal Web pages.
  - Check several sources before deciding whether information is accurate.
  - Look at the end of the Internet address to see what type of organization is running the site. For example a .gov at the end of an address indicates a government site, and a .edu indicates an educational organization such as a university.

Searching Basics

- You perform a search in a search engine by entering a keyword or phrase in the search text box, then clicking a button typically labelled "Search" or "Go". The search engine then displays matching sites.

  ✓ *Most search engines display results with a ranking of how relevant each item might be to the keyword you entered.*

- Web sites get listed in search databases with associated keywords that they feel relate to the interests of those searching and to the topic of their site. When you perform a search, the search engine looks for matches between your keyword and the keywords organizations and individuals have associated with their sites.
- You can use as many keywords as you like, dividing them with commas which act like the word "and" to add words to the search string. However, too many words can for a less accurate list of results. Where the keywords **Dogs, Retriever** might get the results you want, **Dogs, Retriever, Golden, Puppies, Canine** will probably provide an odd mix of results.

- Google works a bit differently than some other sites. Google searches only sites that contain all the words you enter. So if you enter **golden retriever,** you won't get sites with the words **golden** but not **retriever** and sites with the word **retriever** but not **golden**, as you may with other search engines. This feature helps narrow down your search quickly.
- If you want a specific phrase to be found, put those words in quotes. For example, if you want to find the World Health Organization, enter the keyword as "**World Health Organization**". Only specific matches to the phrase will be searched for, rather than sites that match either World, or Health, or Organization.

Use the NOT (-) Operator

- You can *exclude* information from your search results using the **NOT operator**. The NOT operator helps you to eliminate certain search results that you know you will not want.
- Suppose you want to explore the Web for pages relating to grandfathers, and you want to eliminate references to grandfather clocks. You would create a search string like this:
  - grandfather NOT clock
- Running the search with this search string displays Web pages relating to many other kinds of grandfathers, but not to grandfather clocks.

Northern Light NOT Search

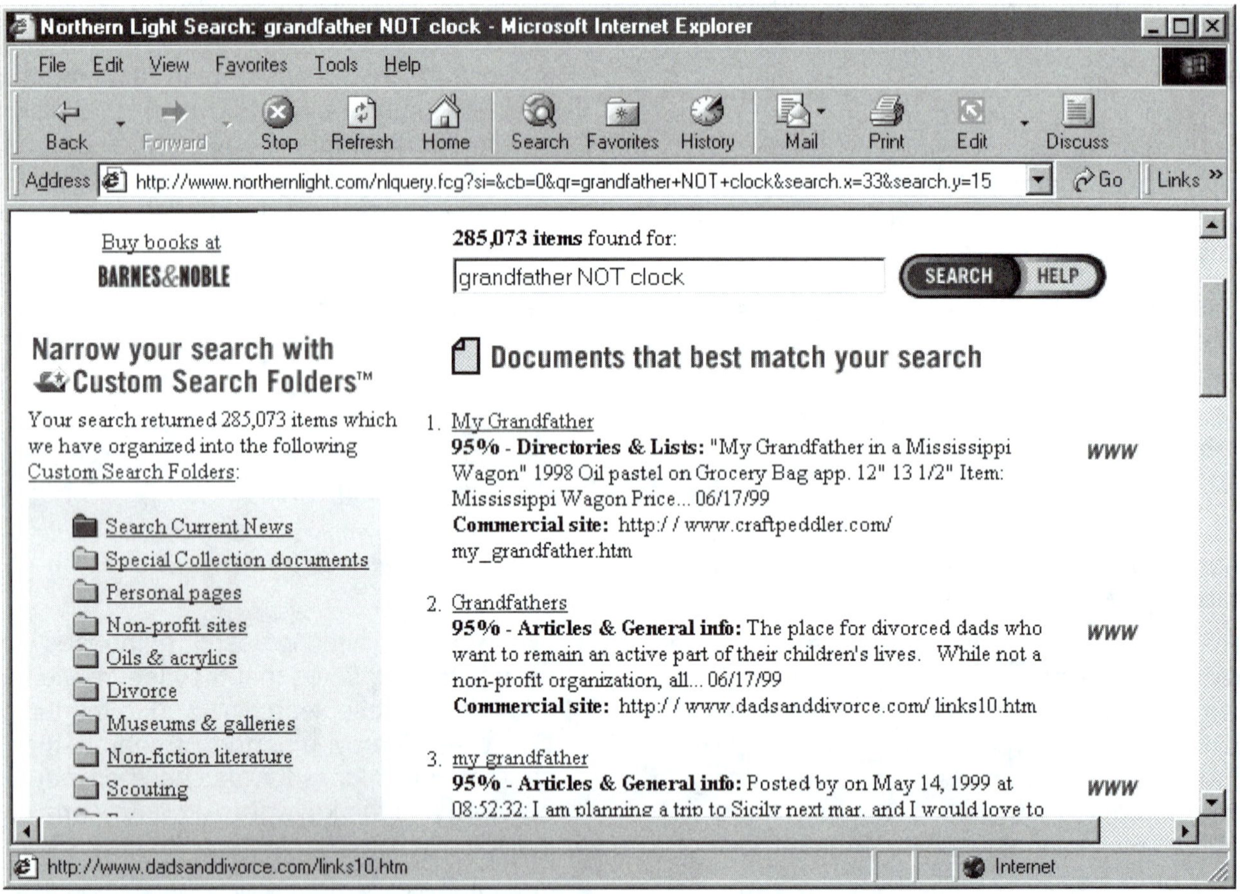

✓ *You might still receive hits for "grandfather clocks" from the previous search string, because the search engine understands that* clock *is different from* clocks*..*

- Generally, you can use the – sign (use the hyphen key or the minus sign on your keyboard's number pad) in place of the NOT operator, in the same way you use the + sign:
  - Grandfather –clock

✓ *Google ignores words such as **how** and **where** in its searches, as well as single characters such as numbers or letters. You can use the + sign ahead of such a common word to have it included in your search.*

Use the OR Operator

- The **OR operator** is used to broaden a search. An OR search string looks like this:
    - El Nino OR La Nina
- This search string will find any pages that contain El Nino or any pages that contain La Nina.
- The OR operator can be very useful when you are not sure how a particular subject might be indexed in a search engine's database.
- For example, if you want to find Web pages relating to pottery, you could create the following search string to make sure you find as many sites as possible:
    - pottery OR ceramics

Use Truncation (Wildcards)

- Some search engines, such as Northern Light, automatically search for plurals of singular words, as well as singulars of plural words.
- Other search engines consider all words created from a common stem to be different in terms of search results, so that the following search strings may yield very different search results:
    - Run
    - Runs
    - Runners
    - Running
- **Truncation** allows you to create a search string using a word stem such as *run* along with the * **wildcard**.
- The * symbol stands for any number of letters at the end of the keyword, so you can find information about a particular subject without having to enter multiple keywords. The search string *run** would find all the variations listed on the left.

  ✓ *Northern Light also offers the % wildcard, which can be used to stand for any single letter in a keyword.*

- Wildcards can also help you find information when you're not sure of the spelling.

  ✓ *You can insert a wildcard anywhere in a keyword, not just at the end of the word.*

- Suppose you want to find sites that contain the phrase compu, such as CompuTek, computing, computers, and so on. You could set up the following search string:
    - compu*
- Running this search in Google gives information about any site containing a word that begins with **compu**.

Google Wildcard Search

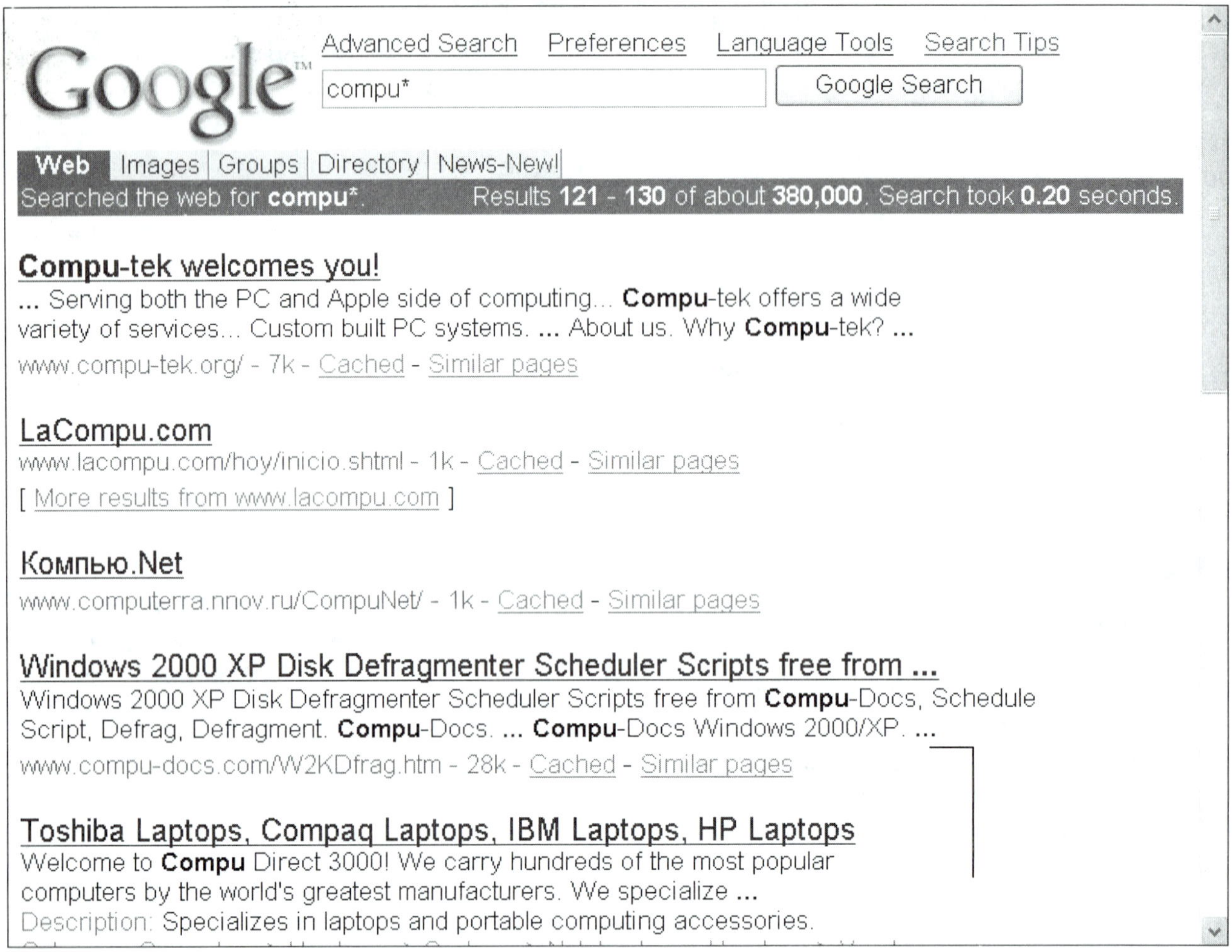

- Not all search engines support the use of truncation and wildcards. You can find out if a search engine does by checking its Help page.

Use Multiple Operators

- You can use more than one operator in a search string along with keywords to further limit your search results.

Using Multiple Operators in HotBot

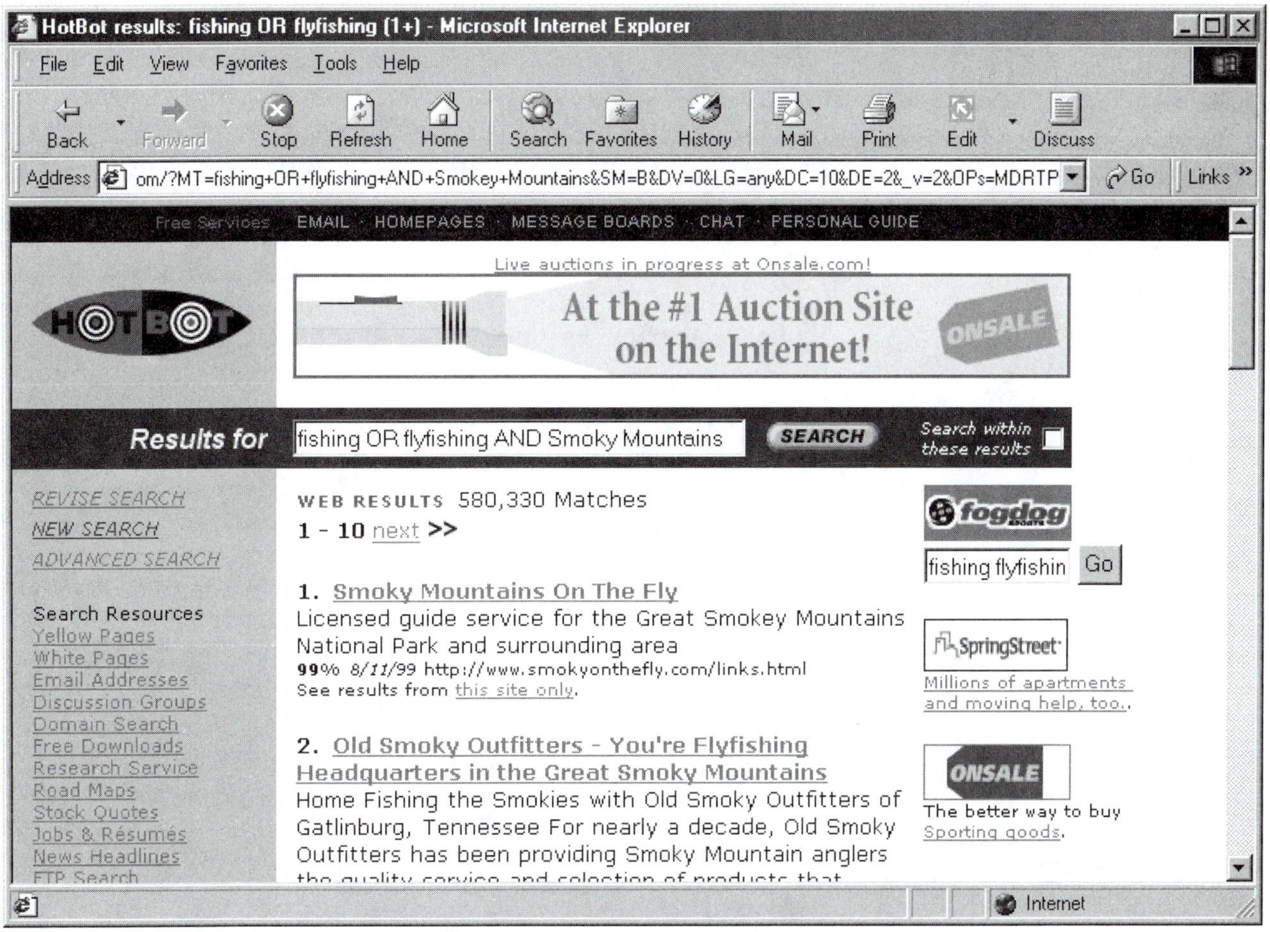

- Suppose you're looking for information on flyfishing in the Great Smoky Mountains. To get the most responses, you should consider using both *fishing* and *flyfishing* as keywords. You could create the following search string:
  - fishing OR flyfishing AND Smoky Mountains

✓ *You can use operators and signs interchangeably in a search string. For example, you can compose a search string using both the (+) and the AND operators.*

Use Parentheses

- You can further control search results when using multiple operators by enclosing some keywords and operators in parentheses.
- As in a mathematical expression, parentheses tell a search engine how to relate the keywords in the search string.
- Suppose you want to find a resort for your vacation. You might want to golf or go sailing at this resort (but not necessarily both). You could create the following search string:
  - resort AND (golf OR sailing)
- The parentheses tell the search engine that it should find Web pages that contain both resort and golf OR resort and sailing.

Northern Light Search Using Parentheses

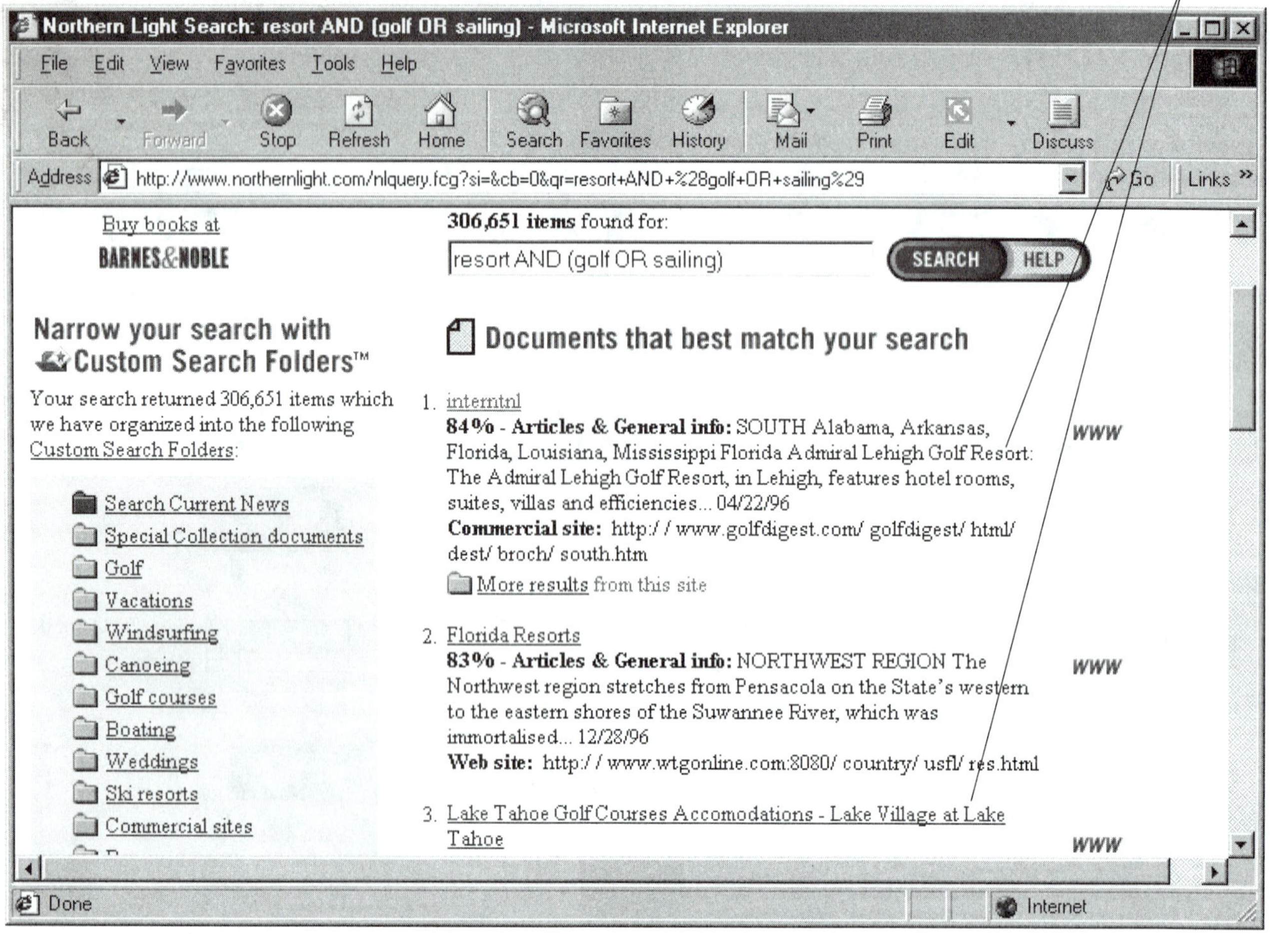

- To further refine a search, it is possible to nest parentheses within parentheses, just as you do in a mathematical equation.
- For example, you might create a search string to find out information on Baroque music, specifically violin compositions by Bach or Handel.
    - Baroque AND ("violin" AND (Bach OR Handel))

    ✓ *Just as in mathematics, you have to have a closing parenthesis for each opening one. Make sure you have all your parentheses in the right places.*
- The more comfortable you become working with a search engine, the easier you will find it to create complex searches that give you just the informaton you need.

About Natural Language

- Many search sites allow you to create search strings in the form of a question. These questions are called **natural language queries**.
- A typical natural language query might be:
    - What is the capital of Assyria?
- Notice that you do not need to use quotes to surround the search string. Nor do you need to use operators. The search engine extracts keywords from your question and bases the search on them.
- AltaVista, Excite, and Northern Light are some of the search engines that allow this type of searching. In addition, the Ask Jeeves(sm) Web site is designed specifically to handle natural language searches.

✓ *To find out if a search engine supports natural language searching, check the search engine's Help pages.*

Perform a Natural Language Search

- Natural language searches are among the easiest searches you can perform. All you need to do is think up a fairly specific question.
- Suppose you want to know who is the richest person in the world. You could create a search string like this:
  - Who is the richest person on earth?

    ✓ *To help the search engine locate proper information, be sure to capitalize terms and proper names as you would see them in a reference book.*
- Running this query in Ask Jeeves results in sites that exactly match your query.

Ask Jeeves Natural Language Search

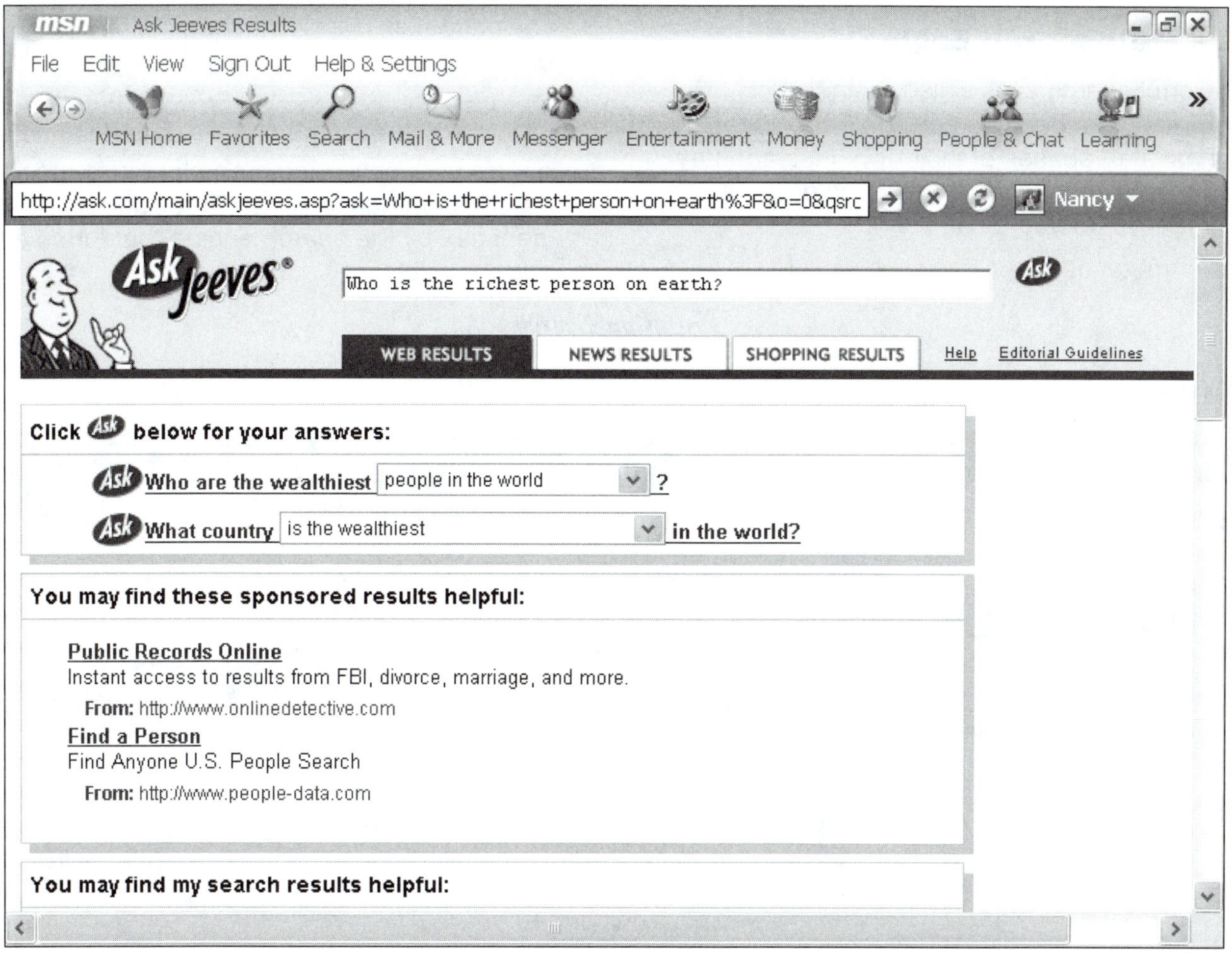

- As with other kinds of keyword searching, it pays to be as specific as possible when creating a natural language search. For example, these queries will yield different results:
  - What are the seven wonders of the world?
  - What are the seven natural wonders of the world?
  - What are the seven wonders of the ancient world?

Use a Metasearch Engine

- Powerful search sites called **metasearch engines** have become popular. These sites do not have databases of their own. Instead, they use the databases of other search engines to find results for your search string.
- Major metasearch engine sites include:
  - ProFusion® (www.profusion.com)
  - MetaCrawler (www.metacrawler.com)
  - Metafind (www.metafind.com)
  - Search℠ (www.search.com)
  - Dogpile (www.dogpile.com)
- Because they submit your search string to a number of different search engines and directories at one time, you get the benefit of seeing results from a variety of different databases.
- Metasearch engines also do you the favor of weeding out duplicate pages so that you see a page's URL only once. Search results are usually summarized under headings and identified by the search engine that found the page.

Profusion Search

Results of search on metasearch site.

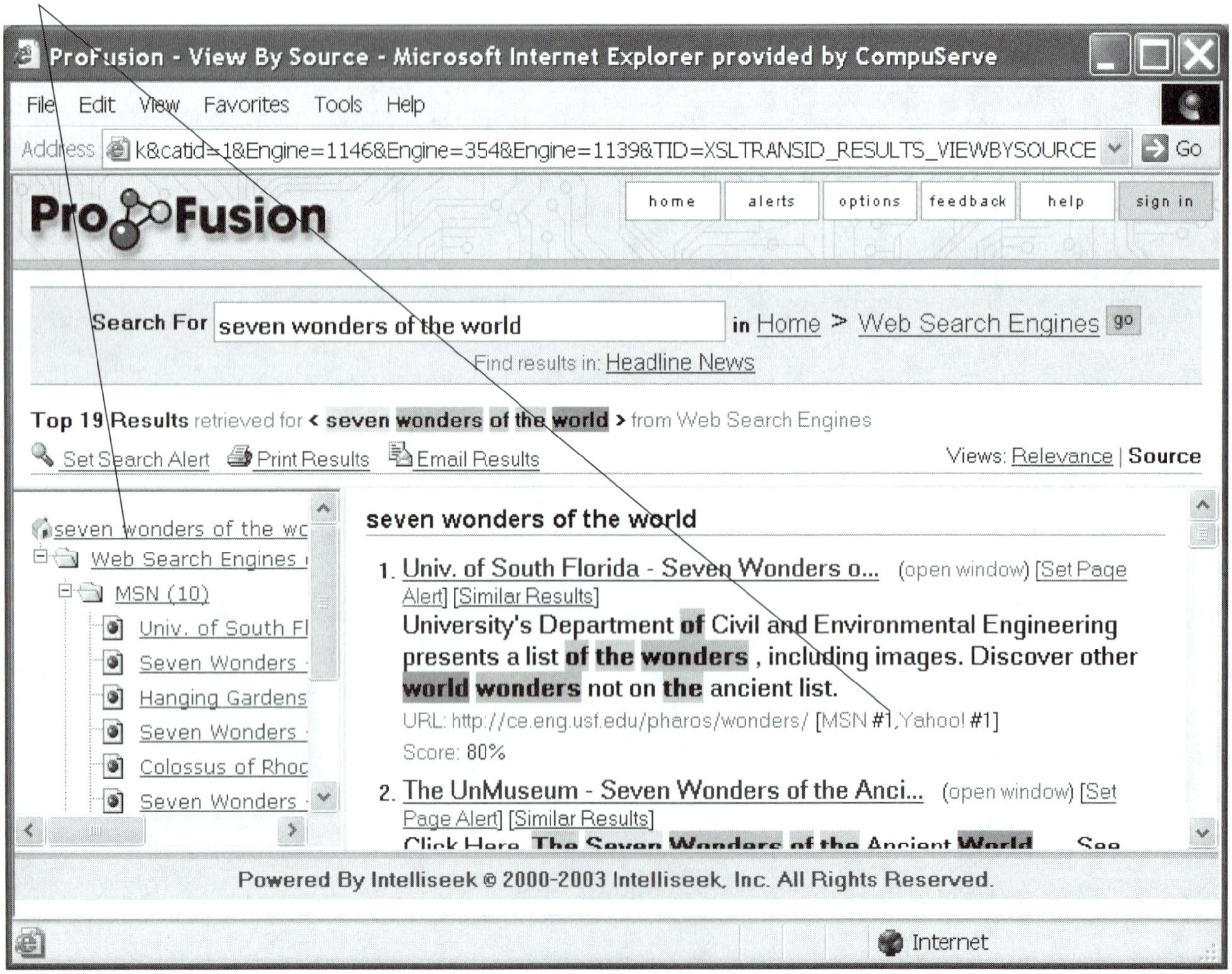

- Most metasearch engines allow you to customize your search options to choose the search engines and directories you want to use for a search.
- You usually also have a number of options you can choose from to control the way the metasearch engine passes your search string to other engines.
- One downside to using a metasearch engine is that one or more of the search engines queried may be "busy" at the time the metasearch engine sends the search string, so you don't get results from as many sources as you expect. The metasearch engine usually tells you which search engines responded to the search string so you know from which search engines you have received results.

  ✓ *If you do not receive results from as many search engines as you want, run the search additional times until all the search engines respond.*

- Metasearch engines support the same search conventions as other search engines. You can use multiple keywords and operators, quotes, and parentheses to create your search strings.

  ✓ *If a particular search engine does not support the operator you use in your search string, the metasearch engine takes care of rephrasing your string so that search engine gets the proper information.*

- The Ask Jeeves Web site deserves additional mention at this point. Designed as a natural language search site, Ask Jeeves is also a metasearch engine of sorts.
- In addition to answering questions from its own database, Ask Jeeves supplies possible answers from other search engines. You can click the link to the other search engines to see their answers to the search string.

Ask Jeeves' Answer to a Question

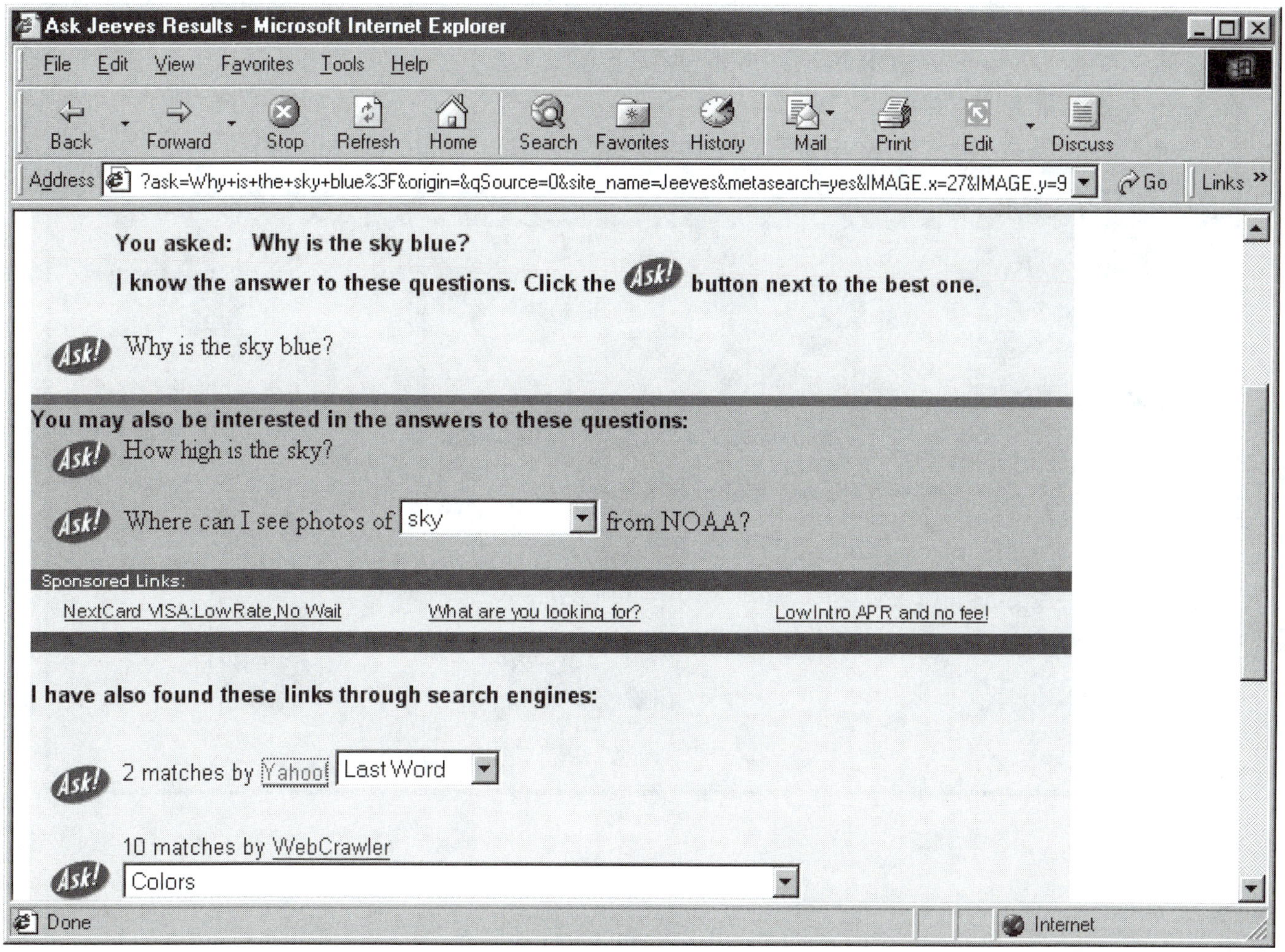

- Using metasearch sites such as Ask Jeeves can save you considerable time in creating search strings and sorting through the search results.

Search for Items other than Web Pages

- Up until now, your searches have concentrated on finding Web sites and Web pages as well as listings in directories.
- You can also, however, search for very specific items on the Internet, such as pictures, sounds, companies, publications, and so on. You can also restrict your searches to parts of Web pages, such as URLs or titles.
- When you open a search engine's Web site, take a moment to look at the options available for searching. Some search engines, such as Google, Lycos, and HotBot, give you options right on the home page to find pictures, sounds, video, or specific types of results such as news stories.
- After you select one of these options, keywords you enter will give you search results specific to the option you selected.
- Suppose you want an interesting bird picture to use as wallpaper on your desktop. In Google, you can click the Images option and then type the keyword *birds* to display search results containing only pictures of birds.

Google Image Search

Images option selected

- If the search engine doesn't offer a specific option such as Images, you can often find pictures, sounds, and video links simply by typing a search string containing the keyword of the medium you want to find.
- For example, the search string *bird pictures* will provide you with many hits containing images of birds.
- If you want to locate information based on only a part of the indexed Web page, you can do so by selecting an option or typing a specific keyword in the search box. For example:
  - Type URL: and a keyword to find URLs with the keyword in them.
  - Type TITLE: and a keyword to find that keyword in Web page titles.

Use Advanced Search Options

- A number of search engines offer you additional help with advanced searches. Clicking a link such as Advanced Search, More Search, or Advanced Text Search opens a page containing a series of fields you fill in to define your search string.
- Advanced search assistants often give you a number of choices for refining a search that you cannot specify any other way, including:
  - Language of search results
  - Category to which the search topic belongs
  - Specific type of item, such as a book, dictionary, home page, or even recipe
  - Date of Web page creation
  - Area of the Web page that should be searched
  - Keywords that must be excluded
  - Media type for search results
  - Number of results to display
- After you have filled in the advanced search form, you can run the search just as you usually do in the search engine.

✓ *Google advanced search even allows you to search all government sites, all university sites, or all mail order catalogs.*

HotBot's Advanced Search Assistant

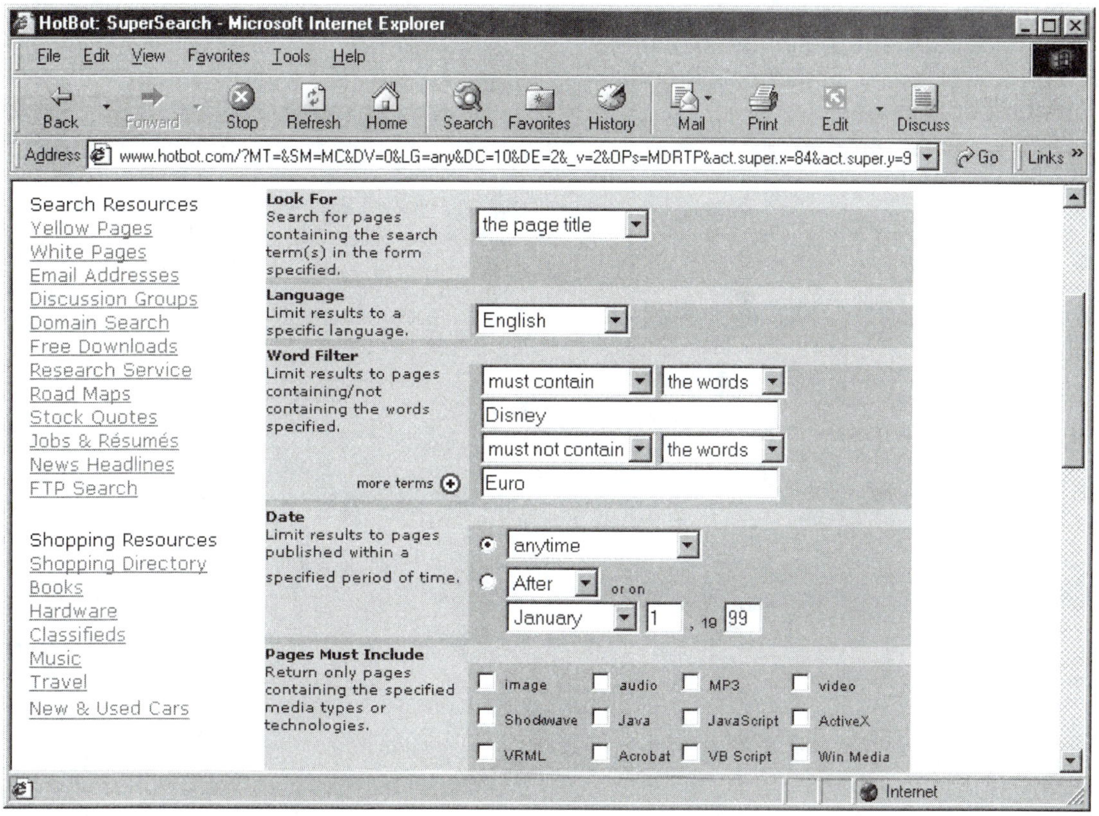

Copyrights and Source Citation

- When you find information that is useful to you on the Internet, you cannot use it as your own because of copyright laws that protect peoples' and organizations' intellectual property. Just because information or other content has been posted online, it is not available for the taking.
- If you use text or images or sound files, you must provide appropriate credit and in some cases obtain written permission. Obtaining written permission is suggested if you are using material in a publication you will sell rather than for personal use, if you take large amounts of information that you do not put in your own words, or you use media such as a photograph or piece of music.
- References to electronic information are similar in format to those for offline articles, in that you must provide the author and title of the content. However, you also need to let your reader know how to find the content, which means you must list the online provider of the content and any medium on which the content is available, if that's relevant.
- If data exists both online and in print its useful to provide information about how to locate both sources. You might also list the length of the publication on a Web page using paragaraphs rather than number of pages.
- Here are some examples of citations for online sources:
- **Internet site**: Schwartz, Delmore, "Survey of Our National Phenomena." The *New York Times Magazine*, April 21, 1996; 17 paragraphs. Available http://www.nytimes.com/specials/magazine/titles .html.
- **E-mail messages**: Smith, John (john@microsoft.com). "New Product Overview." E-mail to Nancy Jones (jones@home.com). August 22, 2002.
- Discussion board: "The Next Threat to Homeland Security." Online newsgroup posting. Discussion of Homeland Security. Available e-mail: listserve@national.edu.Homeland/asp. November, 2001.

GLOSSARY

A

Absolute link Link that uses the complete URL. Used for linking to outside Web sites.

Action Prewritten JavaScripts that perform specific tasks in a Dreamweaver behavior, such as playing a sound when a window opens.

ActiveX Microsoft-developed technology that allows software components to work with other software components regardless of the language used to create them.

Alignment Horizontal placement relative to left and right edges of a page.

Animation Collection of images that, placed on a timeline, create the illusion of movement.

Animation bar In a Dreamweaver timeline, the bar that represents the duration of a layer or image's animation.

Applet Small Java application that can be embedded in a Web page to create interactivity or animations.

Application Program that performs a task for the user (spreadsheet, word processor, database, slideshow software, and so on); also known as a *program*.

Assets panel In Dreamweaver, a panel in the File panel group that displays the "assets" of the site: images, colors, URLs, library items, templates, and other objects used in a Web site.

Attribute HTML specification that modifies tag behavior.

Autostretch Dreamweaver feature that allows you to specify that a table column will adjust automatically to full browser window width.

B

Behavior Interactive feature that takes place in a browser.

Behaviors panel Dreamweaver panel in the Design panel group that allows the user to select actions and specify triggering events for behaviors.

Broken link A link to a page that is not available in the site because it has been deleted, renamed, or not yet created.

Browser Program that works with an Internet connection to display pages located on the World Wide Web. Microsoft Internet Explorer, Netscape Navigator, and Mozilla are examples of popular Web browsers.

Bullet An indicator or simple graphic file used to denote individual points or items in an unordered (bulleted) list.

C

Cache (sounds like *cash*) Extra memory or disk space set aside by the computer to expedite the recovery of frequently accessed information. In Dreamweaver, a cache is maintained to speed the information that the Files panel group displays about a Web site.

Cascading Style Sheets (CSS) HTML 4.0 specifications that permit you to design style properties, save them, and apply them using global formatting at a later time.

Cell Intersecting point of a table row and column.

Cell padding In a table, space between cell content and the cell border.

Cell spacing In a table, space between cells.

CGI (common gateway interface) script HTML form and query syntax that allows data to pass from browsers to servers.

Closing switch The / character used in a closing tag.

Closing tag HTML tag used to indicate the end of a defined section. For example, </body> is the close tag for the Body section.

GLOSSARY

Code inspector Dreamweaver feature that displays HTML code used to create page elements.

Code view In Dreamweaver, view that shows HTML code. Show entire page of code or show both Code view and Design view on a split page.

ColdFusion ColdFusion is server scripting software used for creating robust Internet applications such as interactive Web page forms and databases. Pages scripted with ColdFusion code have a .cfm file extension. Dreamweaver MX is bundled with a standalone copy of ColdFusion MX.

Columns In a table, divisions that run across the table's width.

D

Definition list An HTML list type that includes a term set on one line and its description, indented below.

Delimited format Format for saving application data that separates columns of data with characters such as commas, tabs, or colons.

Design view In Dreamweaver, the default Document window view that shows page content similar to how it will appear in the browser.

E

Editable area In a template, area that an author can change in a page to which the template is applied.

Element (1) Name of an HTML tag. (2) Entry in a Dreamweaver navigation bar.

Event Operation that triggers an action in a Dreamweaver behavior.

Expander arrow Small arrow icon at bottom right of Properties panel that, when clicked, opens enlarged Properties panel to reveal additional properties.

External style sheet A CSS in a separate text file with independent style definitions that can be linked to any HTML file.

External editor Application you can select to edit Web document code outside of Dreamweaver such as Notepad.

F

Flash Macromedia product used to display many types of multimedia files.

Floating panel Dreamweaver MX container for tools and properties that is undocked and can be repositioned anywhere in the workspace or closed if desired.

Font A design of type. Also called a *typeface*.

Font combination Collection of fonts that can be applied to text on a Web page. The browser will display the first face in the collection, or other faces in order if it does not support the first.

Font style Format applied to a font to change its appearance, such as **bold** or *italics*.

Form Interactive area on a Web page that allows a visitor to supply information or answer questions.

Form field Object inserted in a form that gathers a specific type of data, such as a text field or checkbox.

Frame (1) A container for Web page text displayed within a *frameset*. (2) In Timelines panel, a division of time along the timeline.

Frameset A container for HTML frames.

FTP (File Transfer Protocol) A method for copying files to and from servers on a network.

G

GIF (Graphics Interchange Format) A bitmapped image format designed for on-screen viewing of images.

GLOSSARY

H

Head An important section of Web page code that contains information that browsers need to display the document, such as the page title and the character set used to create the page.

History panel A Dreamweaver feature providing visual maps of past work on Web pages.

Home page The first page displayed when a Web site is accessed.

Host Any computer that can connect with other computers on the Internet.

Hotspot Region on an image map that provides a link to another Web page.

HTML (Hypertext Markup Language) The code used to create all Web pages. The current version if HTML 4.0.

HTML style A style defined by one or more HTML tags.

HTML tag Formal name for an HTML markup element. They appear inside angle brackets (<tag>).

HTTP (Hypertext Transfer Protocol) Fixed set of messages and replies between a browser and server on the Web.

Hyperlink See *link*.

I

Image map GIF or JPEG images with a corresponding set of coordinates designed to select specified areas and set hyperlinks to other documents or areas of the Web site.

Initial value In a form field, the text or value that will appear in the form field by default when the form page is opened in a browser.

Insert bar A panel group in the Dreamweaver window divided into tabbed categories from which to insert objects into a Web page including graphics, layers, special characters, tables, multimedia objects, and the like.

Insertion point Blinking vertical line that indicates where text will appear when typed or an object will appear when created.

J

Java Programming language that operates on multiple platforms and operating systems.

JPEG (Joint Photographic Experts Group) File format particularly suited for Web graphics, such as photos.

K

Key In the Design Notes feature, an identifier for a set of information, such as *status*.

Keyframes In a Dreamweaver timeline, a point on the animation bar. Keyframes appear at the beginning and end of the animation bar by default and can be added anywhere on the bar.

Keywords Words or phrases relating to the site that search engines index.

L

Label In a form, text that identifies the function of a form field.

Layer Design feature that allows the user to position text or graphics precisely on a page.

Layer marker Invisible object that marks the location where a layer has been inserted.

Layout view Dreamweaver view that allows you to build layout tables.

Library Dreamweaver feature that stores text, images, or other objects for easy insertion on any page in the Web site.

Library items Items stored in the Library.

Line break A <br> tag that starts a new line but not a new paragraph.

Link (hyperlink) Connection between locations in the same file or different files.

GLOSSARY

M

Macro See *Recorded Command.*

Merge cells In a table, combining several cells to create one larger cell.

Multimedia Information presented by video sequences, animation, illustration, and sound.

N

Named anchor Named location in a Web page used for links on the same page.

Navigation bar Dreamweaver feature that allows the user to set up links to a number of pages using graphic images as links.

Nest Place one object inside another. HTML tags are often nested.

Noneditable area In a template, area that is locked so that the author cannot change its content.

O

Object Element such as a form, image, or multimedia file added to a Web page.

One-sided tag HTML tag that does not require a closing tag. A <br> line break tag is a one-sided tag.

Opening tag Identifier in HTML of the start element. The opening tag for a paragraph is <p>.

Ordered list A list—also called a *numbered list*—whose items must be in a certain order. See also *Unordered list.*

P

Panel Dreamweaver MX container for tools and properties that is integrated into the Dreamweaver window either alone or part of a panel group. Panels can be undocked and repositioned anywhere in the workspace or closed if desired. See also *Insert bar.*

Parameter Settings that control the appearance or actions of an object.

Plugin Utility programs that extend the application capabilities.

Points Measurement used for fonts. There are 72 points in one inch.

Program Application that executes user functions.

Property Object characteristics that define the value, appearance, and state.

Properties panel Dreamweaver panel that displays properties for the currently selected object. Also called a *Property Inspector.*

Publishing Copying Web site files from a local computer to a server.

R

Recorded command An automated command—similar to a macro in Microsoft Word—created by recording steps, mouse clicks, and keyboard commands to perform repeated tasks automatically such as inserting an image.

Reference panel Dreamweaver panel that supplies reference material about HTML tags, CSS, and JavaScript.

Relative link Link set within a specific site that does not include the domain name.

Remote server A server, such as an FTP or WebDAV server, on which you put or publish your Web site that is typically the server from which your Web site's visitors see and interact with your finished Web site.

Rows In a table, divisions that run down the table's length.

S

Script Series of instructions to perform specific steps.

GLOSSARY

Scripting language Computer language that can run inside a Web browser. HTML 4.0, CGI, and JavaScript are widely known scripting languages. The term means the same as *code.*

Search engine Web site containing searchable databases or programs designed to retrieve information from other Web sites.

Server Computer connected to the Internet that sends files to other computers.

Server technology In Dreamweaver MX, this term means the software used for the testing server, such as ASP or ColdFusion.

Shockwave Macromedia product used to display many types of multimedia files.

Snippets Predefined HTML forms, tables, menus, and other Web page scripts that can be inserted from the Snippets panel in the Code panel group.

Split cells In a table, divide a single cell into multiple rows or columns.

Stacking order Order in which layers are added to a page. The lowest number is at the bottom of the stack.

Style A collection of formats that controls the appearance of text on a Web page. In Dreamweaver, styles can be applied with the CSS Styles and HTML Styles panels in the Design panel group.

Style sheet A collection of styles created for a page or Web site. See *Cascading Style Sheets.*

Syntax Rules that govern the use of HTML code and are a connected, orderly system.

T

Tag Tags are the main component in the markup languages used to write Web page code such as HTML 4.0. They are identified in code view by their angle (<>) brackets. See also *HTML tags.*

Tag inspector Dreamweaver panel that maps and shows the properties of the tags used in a Web page code.

Template Collection of formats and page elements that can be used to give pages in a Web site a consistent look.

Timeline Dreamweaver feature that creates an animated effect by displaying a series of layers or behaviors.

Timelines panel Dreamweaver feature that allows the user to create and modify timelines.

U

Unordered list A list that does not have to be in order. Also called a *bulleted list*. See also *Ordered list.*

URL (uniform resource locator) Server and path information used to locate documents on the Internet.

V

Value (1) In HTML code, precise instruction for a particular attribute. (2) In a form field, the actual result that will be returned to a server after a visitor types text or makes a choice.

W

Web page Single file in a collection of files that make up a Web site.

Web site Location on the Internet, made up of one or more pages that are located on a Web server.

Wicket In HTML coding, the brackets (< >) that surround the HTML tag.

Workspace In Dreamweaver, the desktop area in which the Document window and floating panels appear.

Z

Z-index Stacking order of layers on a page.

INDEX

A

B

C

M

N

O

U

V

W

Z